PARADISE
WILD

PARADISE WILD

Reimagining American Nature

David Oates

Oregon State University Press
Corvallis

Dedication

This book is dedicated to my partner and companion
Horatio Hung-Yan Law
thanks for your art, your inspiration, and your love

The paper in this book meets the guidelines for permanence
and durability of the Committee on Production Guidelines for
Book Longevity of the Council on Library Resources and the
minimum requirements of the American National Standard for
Permanence of Paper for Printed Library Materials Z39.48-1984.

Library of Congress Cataloging-in-Publication Data
Oates, David, 1950-
  Paradise wild : reimagining American nature / David Oates.
—1st ed.
     p. cm.
Includes bibliographical references (p.   ) and index.
  ISBN 0-87071-553-4
  1. Human ecology—Philosophy. 2. Human ecology—United
States. 3. Environmentalism—United States. 4. Nature—
Religious aspects. I.Title.
  GF21 .O33 2003
  304.2--dc21

                                    2002012187
                                    Rev.

Oregon State University Press
101 Waldo Hall
Corvallis OR 97331-6407
541-737-3166 • fax 541-737-3170
http://oregonstate.edu/dept/press

OREGON STATE
UNIVERSITY

Contents

Preface & Acknowledgments

A lot has happened since the first step toward this book—the little essay called "The Practice of the Presence of the Wild"—appeared at the beginning of 1990. It has been a long journey.

In the intervening decade, the fundamental distinction I drew there, between "wild" and "wilderness," has grown more and more important. Writers and thinkers whom I admire, and in many respects follow, have carried the idea forward in their various ways: Anthony Weston, Gary Snyder, Will Wright, and above all the late Paul Shepard. In this book, I develop it in my own way, taking it into the lingo-jungles of language and art, inwards into the heart and the dear body, and outwards into the strange and ever stranger living world, that matrix of all wildness.

And when the manuscript was almost finished—when I was writing and rewriting the last chapters—the savage outburst of September 11, 2001 also intervened.

I kept working. But I wondered why such a blow had not deterred me. Was I obsessed? Unfeeling? Then I realized that the outburst had not silenced me because it was so entirely in keeping with my theme. It had illustrated the brevity and unpredictability of our lives in the real world. Just what our too-cozy civilization had taught us to forget. If the intentional deadliness of it had surprised me, our vulnerability had not. It will be my point that this fact of our mortality, and the wildness which keeps it new, require nothing more complicated from us than a kind of consciousness. Not "consciousness" in the fancy and obscure way New-Agers use the word, but in the simple sense of, as Thoreau put it, being *awake*: an alert, wary, enjoying mind. That the wildness around us, deadly and lifegiving by turns, may be greeted by the wildness within.

A book that stretches as far as this one, covering so much ground, must I guess make a fair number of mistakes, large and small. No one's fault but my own. Reader, I've come to believe that some occasional rawness and imperfection—some dust and heat—may be the price of getting somewhere. I've spoken personally, and not concealed my own private stake in these issues; where I stumble, perhaps you will at least see why. Even the questionable trick of taking you verbally, dear Reader, by the crook of the arm in this strangely old-fashioned way, and asking you along; you will forgive it, perhaps, for the sake of the journey.

For the parts of this book that went right, I have many to thank. First of all, I must thank former Acquisition Editor Warren Slesinger at Oregon State University Press, for the awakening suggestion that it was time for this book to be written; and his successor Mary Elizabeth Braun; and my favorite editor and dear friend, Jo Alexander. I am indebted to Clark College for providing a year's sabbatical to finish this work. And to the amazing, industrious librarians at Cannell Library, Clark College: Joan Carey, Thao Ly, Betty Stout, Leonoor Ingraham-Swets—thank you for your friendship, your enthusiasm for helping me and indeed all our students, and your excellence. At the Holt Atherton Library, University of the Pacific, Stockton, many thanks to the librarians who guided me through the Muir collection: Don Walker and especially Janene E. Ford.

Beth Hadas provided helpful advice and cheerful encouragement. Two fine writers who saw merit in some of these ideas in an earlier form—Alison Hawthorne Deming and Walter Pavlich—helped me keep faith and keep working.

I relied on scientists and engineers for the middle stretch of this book. They fielded my many questions gracefully and helpfully. Thanks to Dalles Dam engineers Steven P. Dingman and Kevin Perletti; to Chief of Emergency Management Les Miller; and to Operations Superintendent Jim Williams. Certain scientists in our area grew used to my pestering calls and emails: thanks for your help and most of all for your patient, disciplined dedication to the truth, as we are able to piece it together: Jim O'Connor of the USGS, Portland; Jim Pringle of the Washington State Department of Natural Resources, Division of Geology. And most especially the long-suffering salmon biologists who helped me: John Tyler of the Clark County ESA Program, Anna M. Farrenkopf of the Center for Coastal Land-Margin Research, and Raymond "Skip" Haak of Natural Resource Solutions, Portland.

I am grateful to Dr. Larry Hanson, Chair of Sciences at Marylhurst University, for help with geological terminology and ice-age chronology; and for setting up a class of dedicated students with whom to explore these topics; and thanks, students. Likewise, thanks to Dr. Evan Williams, Chair of Environmental Studies at Lewis and Clark College, for a chance to share some of this work at his program's annual Environmental Symposium.

To friends who were also readers and listeners I say thank you, many times over, for encouragement: Gail Robinson and Rita Carey, talented writers who gave me courage to speak honestly and personally; Alex Hirsch; Vickie Myers; and Steve Karakashian. Legal research came with the help of Ian Simpson, and moral support from many friends including Jim Brown, John Behrens, and Clark College's irreplaceable Shirley Sackman. Thanks all. I thank also Tom Spanbauer, fellow Portlander whose work reminds me to be brave but to speak quietly; and Ken Wilson, whose conversations at 10,000 feet under a wildly cold and starry sky helped me begin.

Parts of this book have previously appeared in books and periodicals: *EarthLight, Friends Journal*, the poetry journal *Nimrod International*, the essay collection *The Soul Unearthed: Celebrating Wildness and Personal Renewal Through Nature* (edited by Cass Adams), *The Bear DeLuxe,* and *Northern Lights*. Thanks to editors who helped these ideas take shape.

David Oates
Portland, Oregon

Introduction

What would it be like to stop mourning for nature? To live in the natural world, to savor it and cherish it, even to use it, as all living beings must, without feeling that everything was terribly wrong?

I wonder what would it be like to live in my own body without shame; to live in my own land, without the sense that nature (aside from some faraway wilderness) is already lost. Don't you wonder, too?

This is a book welcoming nature into the midst of daily life. It's here, I want to say—nature is—and we're it. Fresh wildness working in us and around us all the time, playful, exuberant, surprising.

That sounds like paradise, doesn't it? It is, in a way. But Americans have been telling themselves they are in the Land of Eden, that original paradise, for a long time now, and the story has produced very mixed results. For 150 years, we've had a sinking feeling that the pristine and untouched Eden-land of America has been wasted, polluted, lost. You know the litany: Felled forests. Slaughtered innocents. That's what we keep hearing from all the best environmentalists. And since we really have done such desperate damage, it seems all too plausible. Eden-grief overtakes us. Too late! All over! The End of Nature!

For Eden is where you get kicked out of.

Yet (I want to insist) we cannot be exiled from nature. That story of the North American Eden is a hijacked myth, a myth turned into a lie, and it has locked us into a mourning that's not decent—an unseemly sentimentality, passive and negative. The wilderness over the next ridge may be getting logged—or saved—but *wildness* is a quality you cannot lose. Wildness is your birthright, like God's love or the act of breathing: a wholly different paradise, closer to the bone, inside the bone of bone and the flesh of flesh—infra-paradise.

In this sense, there is no "nature problem." We don't need to save nature (as if we could). We aren't separated from it (and never have been). Many voices have been blamed for convincing us we *are* separate and therefore have a "nature problem"—Descartes, self-consciousness, consumerism, industrial capitalism, Christianity. Take your pick. But if you could get Michel Foucault to talk to Paul Tillich, they might come up with this: our separation from nature (like our separation from God) is a self-deception. The Nature Problem is a crazy buzz in the head. If we stop believing in it, it vanishes.

What it leaves, alas, is a swarm of real, not illusory, problems. Misdeeds, goof-ups, outrages. Threats to ourselves and other living things. Extinctions. Poisonings. Real problems and real losses; and more to come.

But "problems" are not the same, epistemologically or emotionally, as THE NATURE PROBLEM, that vast and terrifying abstraction. Problems can be approached one by one. We can fix some, cope with the others, and do some decent mourning where necessary. That's life.

A vignette: It is the winter of writing this book. I'm exploring these ideas in an environmental studies class at a university in Portland, Oregon.

And my students, at a certain point, look so stricken.

We have been taking stock of our cherished idealizations of nature. That it was "Eden" until the Europeans arrived … except that so many people were already here. That it was "pristine" and "untouched" … except that it was already rather heavily altered and managed. That nature wants to achieve a sort of trans-temporal steady state called "climax" … except that to scientists this state is mostly a useful fiction, not a literal reality.

My students report that their dreams are troubled. They are idealistic, young and old—an artist, several environmental studies and biology majors, a couple of professionals—all with sterling love of nature and steely determination to do some good in the world. And day by day, they bring back from their studies not excitement but disillusionment. What then shall we do—how then shall we live—if Nature is not an Eden in which to invest all our longing? They are brave but brokenhearted.

This book is about what we might have instead of a faraway, mourned-for, always-about-to-be-lost nature. What we have instead of exile: the challenging, intimate wildness which that class, in weeks of searching and talking, began to rediscover. The nature that includes us.

A thousand and one books of nature writing have announced some form of this message: we are one with nature. That's a nice thought, except that, at the same time, we threaten and consume nature, we build up a heedless alternative human reality of ideas and movies and cities. We are also two with nature, in other words.

Getting around that paradox is probably impossible. I learned once to recognize a "big truth" by the fact that its opposite is also true. That's the case here. Though *Homo sapiens* is in and of nature to its very inmost core, we humans also live in an otherworld of thought, where we reflect, mirror, and create. Walt Whitman captured it:

> *Apart from the pulling and hauling stands what I am,*
> *Stands amused, complacent, compassionating, idle, unitary,*
> *Looks down, is erect, or bends an arm on an impalpable*
> *   certain rest,*
> *Looking with side-curved head curious what will come next,*
> *Both in and out of the game and watching and wondering at*
> *   it.*

It may be our species' particular gift to notice this side of the two-sided truth, this inner world. Sometimes it makes us feel lonely. Two with nature.

But this twoness is also natural: we're not the only creatures with minds, with inner patternings that persist against the world's continual counter-pressures. Gregory Bateson has taken us a long ways down this road, and I like what I see there. He says mind is nature, and is at work everywhere in nature.

The picture, then, is this: we're in a mystery, a paradoxical world we belong to yet may feel alienated from. It defies our understanding, yet we understand it well enough to have persisted as living things for a billion years. We must, I guess, know something about it.

There are good ways to think about such unknowables, but they require us to be at once more simple and more subtle, willing to think in analogical terms, to mix metaphors and see likenesses. It seems to me that science alone can't do this thinking for us: for this we need story, parable, koan. We need myth.

The chapters that follow explore how such a myth ought to work, and how a half-dead myth like Eden, snatched from myth-time and pushed into history, has trapped us—but might yet liberate us. Eden re-mythologized as an idea, a force, a mystery. I'm interested in how we "construct" the nature we encounter, myths and sciences alike; but even more interested in how nature manages to speak to us right through, or even despite, our constructions.

I don't kid myself—the paradoxes won't get resolved. We're stuck with mystery. That's good news, surely.

My students remind me that what we know is always personal. My aloof, professorial persona has become (at last) a needless defense. I must admit that I've played out my own little version of the American Eden story (that's why I know it so well). So there are personal stories in this book of how I went to the woods, and why. How God and Eden, gender and nature got all mixed up together; how, as a gay boy, I found myself exiled from my fundamentalist family and faith, and took to the hills for refuge. How, even as I got a Ph.D. in literature, I shaped a side-identity as some kind of nature-outsider, borrowed perhaps from Muir and Thoreau. A construct, that identity—practically a cliché; yet something spoke, high in the Sierras. Something real happened, something from far beyond my imagining and outside my construct. What was it?

In the mountains I go back to year after year, or hiking in forests and deserts, or simply staring, winterbound, through the raindrops on my Portland window, this discovery, this obvious fact, returns to me. *For no reason at all except that this is how the world is, we shall be comforted.* We won't escape sweat and chilling rain, predation and neglect. We won't always know the way. We will sometimes suffer, and we will die in the end. Yet—and how much of a life is paid to reach such a conjunction—yet there is no moment that does not also offer consolation, if we can bear it.

William Ashworth, whose *Left Hand of Eden* is such an essential guide to these topics, tried formulating where we ought to go next. "Protect nothing; venerate everything," he said. That was a brave saying, which I fear must bring him much grief from environmentalists. It stopped me dead in my tracks, for I had been going there for a long time. "Very well, then," I said, heartened by his courage and insight. "But how?"

I think the idea of *wildness* might serve. A wild process that courses through us and all living things. Not an Eden to be fenced, lost, saved; but an Eden to be rediscovered everywhere. Inside the designated wilderness, and out.

I hope that by reforming the language and thought of environmentalism, we can do a better job of treasuring our forests, wildlands, and peoplelands, right down to the last square centimeter of backyard garden, the remotest juniper snag on an unnoticed cliff, the least cell in the body.

I know that challenging the rhetoric of environmentalism will sound like disloyalty. In a cold war, dissent is treason. It's us or them. But this is no war: "them" *is* us, since we're all polluters, all part of the "cancer of civilization" (another phrase we must retire). We can't think about nature clearly until we overleap these Lost Eden dichotomies: Golden Past vs Wretched Present; Nature vs Human: Pristine vs Raped; Us vs Them.

True-believing activists don't particularly want any challenges to their orthodoxies. I can't really blame them: they're out there doing the hard work. Why criticize the environmentalists, since they're the good guys?

Because "they" is me, also. I've pitched my tent on the environmental side for decades (a tent bought from a consumer-capitalist source, alas). It's easy to point fingers and depict the other guy's faults, the developers, the greed-heads. What's hard is to see the self clearly. To choose who and how to be.

So this is for clear thinking. This is for mental and spiritual hygiene. Without this, we ARE the developers, reversed and reflected back in their dirty mirrors. Stuck in the same us-versus-them dichotomies.

But I decline to let them define me. We must define ourselves and deal in truth. Even if truth is complex and makes lousy slogans.

Where we live may not be fresh Eden but it is paradise enough, lived in for a long time yet new every morning. I want to recover the real, life-giving myth of this ruined, unruinable paradise. People have been here—in the Americas—for twenty thousand years or so, goofing it up as well as getting it right. Where we have built our freeways, they had trod their pathways, and animals had already made tracks. Our fellow-creatures have lived it out before us, laying in the patterns we follow and revise. Wherever we look, we ought to see a place we belong to: our nature. Long-lived, told over and over.

In fact, it seems to me, our stories and myths (and even our nature books) are a kind of nature themselves, a reflected-nature; they are patterns that add to the whole thing: nature, human nature, nature unknowable; and I'd like to add my stories to the general richness, and your reading of my stories, dear Reader: layer upon layer, like soil building up, like footsteps making paths.

And so these chapters also explore the words we tell each other about nature: words of John Muir, Henry Thoreau. Words of Terry Tempest Williams, Ed Abbey. The faint murmur left by William Bartram. These men and women are nature too. Their words have become our own, part of the wild patterning of our minds; when we walk, we take their steps and think their thoughts, re-experiencing the natural world for the first and thousandth time.

On old parchments, you can sometimes see past writing erased, written over: the grooves and hints make what is called a *palimpsest.* Or on canvases, shadows of under-art that's been painted over: *pentimento.* We build our experience of nature as a kind of palimpsest, a blurred record of many passings. Personal memories, family histories, myths and dreams and tales, language itself, even the ancient body-knowledge coded into legs and lungs and cells: these make strata uncounted, sweet as baklava, rich as meadows, persistent as bedrock.

All of it makes wildness: that pattern of patterns that we will never fully grasp. It grasps us, though, and gives us a shake, a hug, a death grip, an embrace. That's wild.

Palimpsest:
The Practice of the Presence of the Wild

When I returned to live in Los Angeles after years away, I also began attending a Quaker Meeting. That surprised me—I had not thought to be in any kind of church, ever again. But then, I had not expected to live in LA again, either. In any event, these weren't church Quakers. They welcomed people rejected elsewhere— lapsed Catholics and Baptists, a scattering of self-made Hindus and Buddhists, New-Agers, twelve-stepping ex-addicts. And lots of gay folk, too. I stayed. The Quakers added a dimension to my life that, newly immersed in the sprawling city, I sorely needed.

Their worship was simple, without clergy or obvious creed. Following a meditative tradition dating from the 1600s, they simply sat in silence "in the manner of Friends." Out of this silence someone would occasionally speak. Or sometimes not. But the silence, even when long continued, surprised me. It was full, rich with an unexpected depth and connectedness.

What I heard at Meeting startlingly echoed what I had found, by myself, in the high mountains. By that time I had stopped working as a mountaineering guide, and had taken to making long solos high up beyond trails where the summer peaks edged vast, quiet lands of rock and ice. It had comforted me, somehow, to be alone and silent up there.

Eventually I began to understand that the two experiences, seemingly so unlike, shared something essential. It was wildness: the uncontrolled and uncontrollable. Alone on a mountainside it is an obvious meditation to recognize how big the world is, and how much bigger the cosmos beyond it, and beyond that how encompassingly small the little life is that holds the beholding mind. Small and easily damaged. In a silent meeting there sometimes comes a similar recognition. Out of the dark into which the mind descends, a becoming humility settles. There is much in that dark silence, much that is not understood or understandable. But some of it emerges during a well-gathered meeting, either to stir an individual with unexpected intuitions or to impel someone to stand and speak words just a little truer than ordinary talk.

The silence is wild. No one controls it or measures it. Without this silence, Quaker meetings would be shallow talk-societies. In the silence is the depth and the profundity. In it one encounters the truth: a person is a small bit of intellectualizing jetsam afloat on a mighty and incomprehensible stream.

City folk are prone to believe that if anything goes wrong, it must be someone's fault. They suppose that we humans control all: if someone is hurt, some official must have screwed up. It can never just be the fact that humans are mortal, and life dangerous. Skiers who run into trees blame resort operators rather than the laws of gravity. Earthquakes are followed by lawsuits.

Civilized life fosters this delusion. City lights blot out the starry sky, that insult to mortal pride. Day and night can be ignored. Weather is minimized. Edges are rounded. Health care is good enough, with a little luck, for one to go years without an obviously unsolvable problem.

What losses these comforts are! What a revelation simple hunger can be—how sharpening to the senses, how bracing to the mind. What sleepy, deluded, dull people we turn into under such a regimen of toasty quilts and surfeit. What a silly theory it is to think that all hazards are, or ought to be, marked with red triangles and registered with the appropriate authorities. How badly we need a sharp pinch now and then to bring back to us the reality: though we try to provide for our needs, life is nevertheless both uncertain and painful. Best not to forget it.

The common thread in all these urban delusions is denial of nature as an encompassing reality. We label it "natural resource" and chop it up for raw materials or we think of it as "out there" in a designated wilderness. Certainly not where we live.

But nature is present all the while, undeterred by our silly denial. That's what I discovered in Meeting. Sickness, accident, old age, and death remind us, eventually, if nothing else does. But the systematic loss of awareness of this reality leaves us unable to comprehend. We think there must be some mistake. It is the urban/civilized lie that humans can control all, much, or even an important part of life. Most of what counts is far beyond our reach. By limiting our focus to those few trivial elements that we can manipulate, we shrink our lives to pitiable smallness. And all the rest of the cosmos goes unnoticed. It is a high price to pay for the illusion of safety.

If the reality of nature is as present as all that, then we do not have far to look for deliverance.

Even right now, in the midst of the city, the wild surrounds us. The wild is everywhere, despite the city-lie. Wildness is the medium in which we live, as near as the night sky, a brush with death on the freeway, a deep breath, a dream. By learning to welcome the unplannable, the uncontrollable, and the incomprehensible as nature itself, we can refresh and renew ourselves daily. Thoreau knew what he was saying—that in wildness (not wilderness) is the preservation of the world. Tracts of unexplored or lightly peopled land are wonderful: but the wild is within us, as well.

A few places to look:

Silence

Thoreau again, from his 1841 journal: "I have been breaking silence these twenty-three years and have hardly made a rent in it. Silence has no end: speech is but the beginning of it. My friend thinks I keep silence, who am only choked with letting it out so fast. Does he forget that new mines of secrecy are constantly opening within me?"

The Body

Almost everything about it defies will and intention. Health and ill health, equally, are mysteries. I get spooked when I so much as lay abed for a day with a cold: it makes me think of dying and of the frailty of my daily happiness. These are good thoughts. A little exercise feels as good as a walk in the woods. It is me in my body, this amazing, difficult, recalcitrant, biological marvel. Myself my own zoo.

And sex, too. What a roller-coaster it is, and how far from rational control! It seems a perfect wilderness to me, a place where one goes along for the ride and is grateful for it.

The Mind

Our cultural theory, derived from Descartes, holds that the mind alone is apart from nature. This is baloney: the mind itself ranges far beyond our civilized control. It is a wild place, as every night's dreams prove. Even what we call "reason" is hidden from us. Try to trace how a conclusion arises! A sensible owner of a mind would welcome the whole thing, reason and unreason, waking and dreaming, bound and loose, known and mysterious. To explore it is, I think, to go on a vision quest.

Language

How could this most human of artifices also be wild? Because it is a patterned organic process that operates by its own logic. Because it uses us as much as the other way around. Because our thought and our sense of reality are built as much of language as of our own perceptions. And because it comes to us unbidden and uncontrolled. "Language is simply alive, like an organism," suggests Lewis Thomas, a student of both biology and language.

Poetry

And all the other arts, no doubt. The reason they refresh us is precisely that they go beyond the merely measured and calculated response. To dive into a poem is to go places you cannot predict or control. That is what makes it a poem. Its resonances are wacky, like those in a cavern. It talks back to you from the strangest angles.

No matter how reasoned and clipped and formalized their above-ground manifestations, mind and language possess a deep taproot of wildness. The poet who wishes to explore there must perform an act of courage: abandon the control our waking lives are based on. Loosen the strings that tie together the personality and make the world safe and comprehensible. Allow the carefully made whole to fragment. No one who has even fleetingly experienced the vortex of the unreasoning mind will underestimate the attempt.

The creative journey is perilous because it encounters the unknown and uncontrolled forces of nature residing deep within us. It is for this very reason that the creations of art, literature, and music are renewing and redemptive.

Failure

By my accounting, the little death. The ego comes crashing down. Plans fall apart. Goals recede, unreached and perhaps forever unreachable. Shame and embarrassment crowd out the mellow feelings of social worth and acceptance. Bereft of the social clothing, one is reduced to the basics—a poor, naked, forked animal. A beast that eats, sleeps, and thinks beneath the sun and the seasons. No longer a controller of destiny; now just an inhabitant, wandering among the marvels and dangers. It's an experience we all need, periodically, lest we forget.

There are, no doubt, many more of these potential encounters, many ways to catch sight of the wild. They are the antidote to the accelerating madness of our war-making, money-hoarding culture. The human spirit is refreshed as it looks straight into the realities. In the presence of this wild chaotic orderliness, the fantasy of control and the neurosis of denial fall away. Unclenched from its fist, the open palm may be crossed by what sand dollars and sweet scents—wealth that is wholly temporary, yet wholly sufficient. And utterly unpredictable.

A season in the wilderness is the primal way to learn and relearn this lesson. I guess there are plenty of nature-books to tell us so, with heroes braver than us. But in between sojourns in the high country, the open sea, or the wide clean desert, we can daily restore the vital balance of action and acceptance, planning and improvisation. We can welcome the unknown and the uncontrolled that sweep us into such fearful, beautiful patterns.

That is the practice of the presence of the wild.

Section I: Be/Longing in Eden

Somewhere around 250 B.C., Qoheleth ("The Preacher") gave this admonition: "Don't say to yourself—*Why was everything so much better in the past than nowadays?* When you ask that, you've run out of wisdom!"

There's something comforting in seeing that people of our time have so much in common with the ancients: the destructive fantasy of Golden Age and Good Old Days, the strange pleasure of longing for the impossible. In our case, we have placed a Golden Eden in our "virgin" land of America, and committed ourselves to mourning its passing. No ache ever felt better than that sense of a lost green paradise. But it's not true, it doesn't work, and we need to stop it.

The following chapters explore the workings of this false consciousness, this Paradise-Lost nostalgia, in our dealings with the natural world. I take a personal approach—through walking at first, and through memory, and then through grappling with some exemplary battles over nature here in the Northwest: how to use the forests, and whether it is barbaric to hunt animals and eat them, and how we could possibly look at our world as a holy place and still be permitted to live in it.

Sometimes Walking

Sometimes walking, I think: *I was born for it.* Walking loosens what was bound, lifts barriers; rhythm of motion softens my hard thinking, and the body's mind takes me along.

What would that mean—"Born for it?" If there *were* a human nature, could we know it by experience, simply by paying attention?

Walking, thoughts crowd my head—words, memories, possibilities—and I select one and walk with it as a friend, never letting it go, step by step, until we have arrived somewhere interesting. I may be in my Portland neighborhood, with its artificial savannas of lawns and street-trees, or out on Powell Butte, where downtown sparkles in the distance through old-growth firs and cedars. Or I may be far off in a mountain range, happy on a trail by morning. It almost doesn't matter: suddenly I am able to breathe and think, and I move with that mysterious coasting serenity that carries the world past my eyes as if I were riding on a vessel struck by silence and this was a new continent unfolding. *Born for it*, I think.

I can walk so easily on these spider legs, these long-drawn distance-running legs. I used to hate them for their knobby ugliness. Yet somehow they have gotten the job done. And all the damage they've sustained! Veins zigzag over the knees, bypassing old hurts. Scars ladder up and down the shinbones. There's a notch in the left Achilles tendon and a weird bump among the rightside foot bones....

Sometimes, now, I'm at peace with my ugliness. We've been doing this for four or five decades: Walking. Running. Then at last (and best), hiking. Lifting a backpack, feeling the first-day weight against the hamstrings, stepping off the end of a forest road or the edge of a mountain two-lane, turning away from everyday sins and necessities, one foot after the other into the woods, up the ridges, over the tops and saddles, threading a thin line of confidence into some unknown place, confidence based on what, I wonder. Nothing really. Got food; got rain slick; whatever comes … okay. As long as the legs keep working.

Once I walked high into the mountains, those Sierras I loved so well, lake after lake, day after day, finally over a pass and up a long slant canyon towards the very top where trail ended and, I had imagined, an adventure might begin. I wanted to find a way over the topmost ridge; I was here to go as far as possible. All morning I had been traversing the wet hillside, watching a far-below stream slowly coming up to meet me while ragged clouds drifted up the deep, narrow canyon under a high grey sky. Underfoot was a slick-looking serpentine rock, green-grey, woven into the country shale on my side but not on the other which looked like regular Sierran granite. I ducked along between thinning Jeffrey pine and sprinkles of fir and rain, gaining altitude steadily.

I went alone on that trip, like so many others, and the rain was getting to me. Fatigue had accumulated over several days, and the sleeping bag had got damp and then wet, and my clothes would not dry. I kept looking ahead, trying to see the steeps I had come to find, wondering if they would be passable. Finally the stream came all the way up to meet the trail, we were near the head of the canyon, and in a light misty rainfall I stood where the view finally broke open for good. Whitecaps on a silverdollar lake in its little bowl of talus, edged in willow, mountain ash, and fragment meadows. Despite the weather I felt a sense of warmth. Satisfaction. Trail ending here, canyon ending here; stream beginning here, where the little lake let it out. Raining, raining. The cirque all around, shadowing its snow in steep pocked curves. Broken rock, boulderfields, summity ridgeline—I had seen all this before, so many other places. Too high for big trees or sheltering groves. When I walked over to the lake, I found stubby whitebark pine, or maybe limber pine, hardly taller than I could reach but krumholzed into wide skirts for nine-month winters. Patches of Alpine grass, tender gentian, penstemon, rock and gravel. Territory I loved, but not especially welcoming. Suddenly I was tired.

That was the reality all at once: wet and tired, anxious, wondering if I would find a decent place to set up camp. Wondering what might come of a lone hiker who tried those ridges in wind and wet, not knowing where to go. Wondering at the edge of my mind, not admitting it, whether I could bear to go back without succeeding.

To give myself heart I set down my pack, finished some chocolate, drank water. Then on a whim I fitted myself, half standing, half reclining, into the Y-notch of the largest evergreen thicket, leaning against a gnarled, slanty trunk that brushed out overhead against the rainfall. Rain gear drawn snug and hands tucked away, I rested my head sideways onto the trunk. Pine sap, pine smell, bark finer than lodgepole. The rain-cowl made nylon noises when my beard scraped it and light windy noises when the raingusts blew; it made a tunnel for my eyes and through it I looked at the ascending curves around the lake, the snow and talus walling up on all sides smooth and logarithmic. I closed my eyes for a while, thinking.

I saw how anxiety was with me like a companion. I saw how food, water, a little shelter, would keep it at least a little distance away.

I saw that I would have to go out the way I came in, after all. After all. It was too hard, in all this weather, even after days of getting here and a whole plan in my mind's map to explore up the cliffs and over the ridges and then down into a remote and untrailed little valley, a two-mile fold of the mountains, way high up but with a trout stream and two lakelets, seemingly inaccessible from all sides, suspended, like something held high in two cupped hands. I had found it on maps and dreamt about it. But not this trip. Not this route. Too hard.

Later I would make tea, I thought, and set up a tent for dryness. I gave up my plan without a fight and I surprised myself, falling asleep, at how easy it was. How I didn't feel like a worse person, or weak, or ashamed. I had come in twenty or thirty miles. I was strong enough, my legs could do it. But this wasn't the time. Things lay before me and around me pretty much as they were. I passed among them harmless and unhurt.

Born for it, it seems. I got some lucky genes along with the usable (if unglamorous) legs: mosquito bites have no effect on me. Nor does poison oak (conclusively proven, somewhere in the Coast Range above Santa Barbara, by stumbling into a deep red-green patch while bare assed for swimming). For no reason except that it pleases me, I account these convenient adaptations to my half-Indian grandfather. Or was he quarter? Family lore is sketchy, though his high-cheekboned, hawkish profile was convincing. I don't care, actually. I like knowing that some of my blood and some of my thinking comes that way, at three or four removes. Maybe the immunities and the good legs; why not? Maybe even the love, sometimes, of walking.

Three or four removes. That's what family is, isn't it? What comes to you comes to you. Grandpa's name was American (William) and his mother's Victorian-American (Zirilla) but Grandpa said she was the daughter of a chief of the Cherokee. Maybe full-blood, maybe not. By then the Cherokee had been "removed" to Oklahoma. Zirilla made an escape, I guess, by marrying a white man. He did contract grading for the railroad; their house was in a nowhere called Winnewood, Oklahoma. Being a chief's daughter didn't count for much around there, I think. When the husband died, some fellows from the railroad came by and simply took everything, claiming back debts. Who was to stop them? They took graders, wagons, a score or two of mules to pull them. No one bothered much about a squaw (their word) with twelve kids and no white man to answer for her. Grandpa was ten and he went to work picking cotton, right then.

One more generation back puts Grandpa's grandfathers and grandmothers in the forests of north Georgia and Tennessee, the Cherokee end of the Appalachians. Zirilla's father may have begun there, before the catastrophic trek of 1838. It's far by automobile, deadly far by foot, yet how many worlds away can hardly be calculated.

I walked in those Cherokee mountains a few times when I was a graduate student in Atlanta. I had never seen such lushness in my life. My forests had been Western: dry, rangy pine-lands, brushy foothills. But oak and dogwood and rhododendron, wet earth and rushing streams and water-laden logfalls—all that was new to me. On an autumn day I remember seeing cartoon mushrooms, fat and red with white polka-dots. And yellow mushrooms, and cream and white ones, combed or tuberous or strangely fanned out, and beside them lichens and wet mosses unimaginable to my scrub-desert eyes. I felt something opening in my mind: what those Cherokee had lost.

I had hardly known they didn't really belong in Oklahoma. The trail of tears, the terrible winnowing death-marches, the leave-takings in which mothers and grandmothers were seen touching individual plants, stroking them and saying tearful farewells, these were not part of my awareness. Our family tales were incomplete, to say the least.

Whoever made it to Oklahoma must have been a pretty good walker. There were many (up to half) who never got there.

I have no idea how much Grandpa knew about it. He didn't say. Not a word. But that silence may be the most Indian thing about us. That silence, part of who I am. Part of what I was born for.

In the family Grandpa founded the men follow a kind of stoicism that is difficult to describe from the outside. It's not hardness, exactly. It's more centered than hard; it comes from training and a sense of self-regard. It is, in fact, exactly what Indian men of Zirilla's generation describe—those whose words and lives got into books, like Luther Standing Bear or Black Elk. They were Sioux. And they sounded awfully familiar to me, when I began reading these famous books in my twenties. Still later I found an older key, another confirmation. What I learned from Father, who had it from William who had it from Zirilla and uncountable foremothers before her: that quiet fortitude of Cherokee people described by William Bartram in his account from the 1770s, when he found them "grave and steady; dignified and circumspect in their deportment; rather slow and reserved in conversation."

Standing Bear describes childhood games that challenged boys in various kinds of endurance: running, withstanding cold, riding. Every day, boys strived to live up to the bigger boys and the warrior adults in "tenacity and poise." Though winning must have always been best—and no doubt accompanied by a certain amount of swaggering and envying—there was something else beneath (or above) the winning that was the real point, on which the whole social system was organized. Standing Bear emphasizes the generosity and humility that was to frame masculine strength. The warrior "never forgot pride and dignity, accepting praise and honor and wearing fine regalia without arrogance."

Pride, strength, longsuffering, humility. This is a gender formula that is not quite familiar to modern America. It is precisely what I was taught. What is it for? "To endure pain, to bear the scars of life and battle." The ideal of Indian manhood, sums up Standing Bear, was a courage that was inward as well as outward: "Physical hardihood ... matched with spiritual hardihood."

Until reading Standing Bear and Black Elk, I had assumed it was just our own family strangeness that put such silence into us. It can be maddening, in this talky age that takes disclosure of all things at all costs as the mark of mental health. And I admit there are things I cannot get my kinfolk to unfold to me, privacies and denials and refusals that wound us all. Yet there was always more to it than that. There was also grace and strength, or the possibility of it. My father, whose olive skin and dark hair echoed the prized Indian heritage, trained us gently and persistently into it. We called him "Sir" as often as "Dad," but somehow that was understood as respect and not distance. He played with us, hiked with us, brought us home again safe. If there were slivers to remove, he would tell us "Be a good Indian" before the pinch was felt: that meant, no flinching. The same for the cuts and gashes of my banging-around, falling-out-of-things childhood. He'd pour alcohol or hydrogen peroxide into the wound and it would sting or fizz. And I would be proud of not wiggling, not an inch (well, not more than that surely). Not wailing or blubbering (even if some tears could not be helped).

Year by year he showed us, time after time he reminded us: Be a good Indian. I learned to contain myself before reacting, to consider before speaking. I learned that to react thoughtlessly was to be controlled by outside forces: that to maintain poise was a form of power. I learned that fear and pain can be known as experiences, not masters. Sometimes when bad things have happened this has been useful to me: rather than yielding to emotion, I have been good at doing what needed to be done. People have relied on me because of this, and I have not often let them down.

Our sentimental age may see such teaching as masked brutality, as the imposition of power and patriarchy. But my father was not imposing power, he was *conferring* it: teaching us that power lay within and belonged to us. Even if we were skinny boys whose limbs trembled and whose eyes teared up.

My father's hand is warm upon my forehead. He is about to stop the bleeding where I have opened up my shinbone. "Be a good Indian," he murmurs. The rain blows into my face and I am far from home, tired and alone. Anxiety gnaws at me but it does not overcome. The whitecaps blow and begin to seem both beautiful and alien. "Be a good Indian" he murmurs. Nothing here cares for me but I am okay. Or I will be.

With time I learned that Black Elk and Standing Bear were objects of controversy. I feared that I had become tangled in the cheapest clichés and stereotypes. "Cherokee" of course; it's almost always "Cherokee" and often as not a "princess" that some white person will claim as an ancestor. All around me, as I lived in Santa Monica or Portland, I saw a touching, alarming eagerness for a kind of denatured Indian "spirituality." That long line of worshipful autograph-seekers, for instance, at a New Age bookstore, waiting for some blonde author who had entitled herself "jaguar-woman-shaman" (or some such thing), her west-side-of-LA followers granting her this authority uncritically, eagerly, pathetically. There's a whole meditation waiting for someone to write, about the genuine spiritual hunger of these credulous dupes, and their inability to find actual sustenance.

"Come to a sweat," I was beckoned in Portland. I wouldn't. Read the *Seven Arrows*, I was encouraged. I won't.

I claim no special authority by this meditation on my family and its particular past. Rather the opposite: this is authority every one of us has, coded in the body, near-to-hand in family and forebears, that most intimate chain, loin to loin, breath to breath, word to mind—that connection every one of us has to the old way. Walking with each other, walking after each other, living in bodies that are wild, fabulous records of everything. Everything.

I can't think of anything simpler. I walk, I feel good. Like I was born for it.

It's not fancy. The phenomenal world does not crack open, its spiritual essence is not revealed, I am still limited and obtuse. But whatever I am feels connected to itself. *Born for this*, I say, but I have no idea what master plan that phrase could refer to except the inner one, the one that says "Breathe" or "Sleep now" or "Don't eat that—it smells funny." There are capacities whose use produces a simple satisfaction. We might learn about ourselves empirically— as if from the outside—by noticing these capacities, these pleasures, and seeing what sort of being they add up to.

What we would be noticing is wildness: patterning not planning. The lay of the inward land that is just as contingent and just as lovely as any basin-and-range, any forested folded hillhome, any natural place. An inward place equally beautiful and strange.

I count just three or four generations, at least through one family branch, back to a hunter-gatherer life. That seems interesting to me. We all feel pretty civilized, don't we? Yet none of us is really all that far from the other way of living, the one that goes all the way back. The one I feel when I'm walking.

Now, the Cherokee were not in some sort of primordial state, as if they were nature and not culture: their culture is precisely what enabled them to live so well in their place. Their knowledge was extensive, contained in words and traditions painstakingly transmitted generation by generation; and they were among the quickest to adopt elements of the invading Europeans' ways. They were always adaptive and resourceful. In fact, when Europeans first encountered them, the Cherokee lived a mixed hunter-gatherer and agricultural life, in towns and villages of plastered homes and public buildings, with sporting events and entertainments and all the hubbub of cosmopolitan life. Not at all the "primitives" of American imagination. Beyond the towns were cultivated fields of corn and squash that, travellers remarked, seemed to go on and on. Yet beyond those fields were deep woods, where men and women regularly hunted game and gathered plants for food and medicine as people had always done. This wasn't sport or recreation, but a steady and reliable portion of their existence.

There in the hills of Tennessee, Georgia, Carolina, the Cherokee kept one foot on the old, old way, the trail that goes all the way back, what the classic mid-twentieth-century anthropologist Paul Radin called "a human experience that has now lasted more than

half a million years." A trail most of us reading this book must do
some work to rediscover. That is the hunter-gatherer style of living
most of our kind have followed for at least a hundred thousand
years. At least a million years (as we now know) for various other
two-legged tool-using trying-to-speak people. All along this million-
year way we have been adapting, learning. We have been adding
knowledge to brute force and fleetness as biological strategies for
survival. Learning what sort of temperament, what sort of strength,
must be cultivated. In this perspective it's hard to separate "culture"
from "nature," since all the adaptations and handed-down tricks
have helped us survive, have shaped us into what we are. And not
just humans: other animals do the same. There's a lot to learn to be
a successful lion, say, or elephant, or chimpanzee. Ethologists
(animal behaviorists) like Elizabeth Marshal Thomas or Donald
Griffin won't call all of it instinct—it's only human snobbery that
refuses to call it "culture" too. It is knowledge, tradition even, passed
from parent to child (or cub or foal).

Our city style of living goes back at most some six thousand years.
And we usually overplay its significance, teaching it as "history," as
if it were all that mattered. But the way I count it (thirty years per
generation), six thousand years is just two hundred generations.
That's an evolutionary eyeblink. And in fact most of us connect to
the older way much more recently than that: think of who Caesar
found when he crossed the Alps—wild Teuton tribesmen, fighting
naked and painted blue, living a mixed life like the Cherokee. Think
of peoples hunting up and down the Americas, roaming plains and
pampas and woodlands; and their cousins elsewhere, itinerant on
steppes and savannas, rummaging in canebrakes, waiting patiently
in jungles and forests, on all the continents. Ainu, Inuit, Iroquois;
Yanomamo, Irian Jaya, Papago; Karen, Kurd, !Kung, Hmong—
peoples who are still around, not "vanished," whose cultures, various
mixes of hunting, herding, growing, and gathering, show a clearer
continuity with the long human past than our own does.

What we are, what "human" is, was formed by that old way: living
in groups of twenty to forty adults—that famous anthropologists'
number, so remarkably consistent across times and places—foraging,
telling stories, walking. That's what human was, before cities, before
agriculture, before priests and kings. That's what our bodies still
tell us, what our minds whisper. There's something else close by,

that does not exclude culture but that also is a step closer to the natural conditions that produced us, body and mind. That path we've always been walking.

Grandpa's people had walked for a long, long time before I became their cousin or lost-and-found son. Historians guess the Cherokee had been in their Appalachian home for hundreds of years when De Soto met them in 1540. The famous Walum Olum account of the Delaware people, a set of hieroglyphic sticks recording events before the Delaware's first contact with Europeans in 1609, tells of a prolonged war some twenty-five chiefs back, apparently against Cherokee migrating from the west, who were defeated and forced to continue southward. They had walked, by some route or other, down from the Bering land-bridge some ten, twenty, or thirty thousand years before. They had walked across mountains and plains, walked all the way to the Mississippi, to the eastern forests, to the Delaware, and finally into the hardwood forests and wide-rivered plains they settled in north Georgia, the Carolinas, and eastern Tennessee. Walking for a living the whole way, striding, skipping, strolling, they hid and fled and chased, found food, killed things, dug stuff up or plucked it, or scared away other scavengers and then ran for their lives. They made a home in the mountains for thirty generations. Then they survived the trek to Oklahoma.

And all of that history is deposited in me. By natural selection in the shape of my body; perhaps also in my body's happy trick of ignoring annoying bugs and plants. And by family culture, including what Zirilla gave to William to Father to me.

White culture calculates kinship with mathematics, counting quarters and eighths like splitting up a bank account. That's not how heritage works, though. What comes to you is yours and is not diminished but actually increased by how many others might have received it. It is not a blood fraction but a wholeness that has come to me from Zirilla. And I claim it.

This kind of treasure is not diminished by sharing and not concerned about purity or mongrelism. That's something the Indian community knows that the rest of us need to learn. Our theory of value is an individualist one based on owning, accumulation, and scarcity. Authenticity and purity are *our* hang-ups. Indian cultures emphasize continuity, and define value in a communal gift-economy, whereby sharing one's wealth (not hoarding it) creates the intangible value of connectedness. It does not hurt if someone from another tribe has married in, or is just sitting in; as long as the circuit, the handing-around, goes on. Our zero-sum sensibility just doesn't fit. The Native American scholar Jana Sequoya writes: "Most Native American communities define members on the basis of kinship affiliations and social acuity rather than blood quantum, so that the key to being Native American … does not depend on the degree of Indian blood, but on the degree of incorporation into the social network of that community."

None of us has to deny our kin because our blood is not "pure." If our game is handing-around and not appropriation, then the mysterious flow of living pattern goes on. I don't kid myself—I'm no Indian and I wear no feathers or beads. I have no Indian community to belong to, only a few family members (and I do a pretty bad job of staying connected there, too). But I know who walked with me in the woods the first time, who trained me with fortitude. I see my father's body when I look down at myself. When I look inside, I see fathers, grandfathers, grandmothers all the way back. I hear some of their words. And I wear some of their flesh.

The deep past laps like a silent ocean right up to the very edge of the present. All it takes is a walk to reawaken it. The Old Ones, the forebears, are present with us, whether Indian or wild blue Teuton, fierce Mongol or clever Bushman. They're not that far back, not for any of us. We have their genes and their minds. If we're lucky, we may have some of their thoughts, too. Who knows where that look from your mother came from, that tilt of the head, that shape of your inner self? What delights you and brings you satisfaction may be news a long time in arriving—something to do with who you are. What you were born for.

Sometimes walking, I think: Is this wild? Is this civilized?

Of course it is.

Wilderness

At sixteen years old, in the company of two school friends, with a backpack, a tiny black goatee, and a shapeless green hat, I hiked into my first real mountains—faraway, high-up, Sierra *wilderness* mountains. From a trailhead in Sequoia National Park, we rambled our dusty twelve or fifteen first-day miles through beautiful dry coniferous forests, then rose the next morning to climb past higher and higher lakes until we stood at last in a perfect granite gap and I saw, for the first time, the whole of Nine Lake Basin: its left-bending glacial sweep green with alpine grasses and dotted with hemlocks, a snowy cirque at its back, and a sky-blue chain of tarns and lakes dazzling in the clear light of twelve thousand feet. "Wilderness," we called it. I was enchanted.

For the next several decades of my life, I thought wilderness was what I needed. With each new experience I craved it more. Every trail crossed a dozen others; every pass and peak unfolded further dreams. Between college terms I went to work for a "wilderness education" program, not because of its noble purpose but because—Wow! I'd get paid for spending a whole summer in the Sierras!

After a few summers immersed in it, wilderness meant everything to me. Wilderness meant an alternative to city streets and consumer culture and television. Wilderness meant something "pristine," clean and pure, removed from the smudged world of people. Just twenty when I started mountaineering, a secretly gay Baptist kid, I was working obsessively to cleanse myself of my unforgivable humanity, and the unforgiving granite peaks of wilderness offered me some kind of absolution. The "virgin" in "virgin wilderness" is not an accidental trope. I brought my virginity, obsessively guarded, to the supposedly virgin wilderness, obsessively violated. It seems clear enough that wilderness meant a chance to prove myself as a man, to do something hard and dangerous. "Wilderness" was my watchword and, I hoped, my redemption.

Even a few years later, while I worked on a doctoral degree in Victorian literature at Emory University in Atlanta, I preserved three months of every year for exploring the wilderness. But I kept them completely separate from my academic ordeal. I refused even to take my backpack to graduate school during the other nine months, fearful it would undo my resolve. The wilderness in my life was segregated from the human world, on my personal calendar just as the national parks and designated wildernesses were set off from the rest of our human space. They were other, apart.

My illusions and tangled motives, the projections of gender and sin and power, were not mine only. They belonged—and still belong—to our American culture, which defines itself in such strange relations to "nature": the Hemingway machismo, the division of nature from culture, the projection of purity to a virginal far-off preserve. What wilderness did for me and to me makes a good story, fine for telling over beers or campfires, with plenty of irony. For it seems to me now that what I wanted was not really "wilderness," that illusion of a nature in which humans do not participate as natural themselves. What I needed, and got, was a touch of the wild, of wildness that was indeed powerful, scary, and redemptive.

Was it, after all, wilderness I hiked and climbed in, all those years? It was certified and labelled as such: National Forest Wilderness, National Park, Sequoia, Kings Canyon, Great Western Divide.

But if wilderness means virgin and untouched ("pristine")—nature raw, without civilized packaging or protections—then probably little of this qualified. Trails in the national parks are usually obvious and well-trodden, requiring no more skill to find than a sidewalk. Popular routes like the Muir Trail or the Pacific Crest Trail grind deep ruts into meadows and vulnerable soils; they cross boggy lands or big streams on boardwalks, hewn logs with handropes, even engineered bridges. Many backpacking trails are, in fact, more civilized than the average "road" between the lesser towns of England or Europe of a few centuries ago.

Even when my companions and I went up beyond trails, proud of our daring, to climb peaks, we followed well-mapped routes all the way, augmented by precise descriptions in climbing books that metered the physical challenge to decimal exactitude ("5.0" a tad easier than "5.1"). At the summit, we would usually find a nice little book in a weather-tight aluminum container, for recording one's wilderness experience in spaces provided after the scores, hundreds, or thousands that had signed in before. On my first summit (Brewer Peak, elevation 13,570 on the Great Western Divide of the southern Sierra), I believe I wrote, in the jargoned innocence of twenty, "Praise the Lord." The way we went was a walkup, mostly just thin-air scrambling, "three-point-five" (try not to fall off the boulders).

Were these wildernesses? Not in the heroic sense certainly. Maybe in Alaska, or in grizzly-bear quarters of the far upper northwest, or on the open sea—maybe those are truly untouched, in places. But in another sense, could mine have been "wilderness" adventures simply because I experienced them that way? Perhaps *enough* of civilization was peeled off to allow something else to show through. To let me know I was not in charge; to make me pay attention and take care. Good enough, perhaps. Perhaps.

But of course to say "enough" is to shift from the Romantic absolute—pristine, untouched—into a language of graduated difference. Just what the mythology of "wilderness" tends to prevent.

In fact these questions—the definition of wilderness, even its existence —have pushed the environmental movement into new territory over the last decade. Classic environmental battles have usually focussed on preserving set-asides of "wilderness" lands. The now-familiar phrasing of the 1964 Wilderness Act defines wilderness as an area "untrammeled by man, where man himself is a visitor who does not remain." The operating assumption, a kind of formula, is that *wilderness* equals *no people.*

And the corollary of the formula, felt with equal force, is this: *where people are* equals *no wilderness.* The presence of people changes everything, degrades "pristine" wilderness into … what? Depends on your value system, I guess: profane space (no longer sacred); civilization (not nature); human contamination (not pure and untouched); fallen lands (no longer virgin). As many have noted, the classic environmentalist approach is predicated, quite unconsciously, on a clear division of the world into two incompatible and opposed elements: the natural and the human. Even a trace of the human makes the wild somehow ruined.

In a famous poem of the early twentieth century, Wallace Stevens placed a jar on a hill in Tennessee, and found that the presence of the slightest human element would transform all:

It made the slovenly wilderness
Surround that hill.
The wilderness rose up to it
and sprawled around, no longer wild.

It's like Robinson Crusoe's discovery of a single human footprint on the sand. It's like my finding fire pits in off-trail places I thought were remote and untouched. It changes everything. I remember feeling pretty grumpy, too, on that first backpack trip, when we discovered another hiker already in Nine Lake Basin. *He* was an interloper. *We* wanted our fantasy of untouched land, empty of humans: wilderness.

Our American sense of this continent is framed by this dualism, with its interesting premise that lands "we" pioneer into are fresh and new. On this point environmentalists are in full accord with the dominant culture. They share this premise with the crassest shopping-mall consumerist, a basic division of the world into human and natural. The last decade of discussion in environmental circles has been triggered by the shocked re-discovery of an obvious fact: that most of those pioneered "wildernesses" had been the well-used homeplaces of native peoples for many, many generations when Europeans arrived. Historian William Cronon, who has spearheaded the "wilderness definition" debate, wrote in 1983: "It is tempting to believe that when the Europeans arrived in the New World they confronted Virgin Land, the Forest Primeval, a wilderness which had existed for eons uninfluenced by human hands. Nothing could be further from the truth."

Arturo Gomez-Pompa and Andrea Kaus, environmental scientists studying the South American rain forests, generalize the point further: "Scientific findings indicate that virtually every part of the globe, from the boreal forests to the humid tropics, has been inhabited, modified, or managed throughout our human past. ... Although they may appear untouched, many of the refuges of wilderness our society wishes to protect are inhabited and have been for millennia."

Historical geographer William M. Denevan's influential 1992 article summed up the case against the myth of the Eden continent. The first explorers who followed Columbus probably saw "a humanized landscape almost everywhere" (though they probably did not realize it). Denevan estimates a New World population at the time of contact of between 43 and 65 million, though only 3.8 million in North America (excluding Mexico).

Of course, rapid Indian depopulation from disease followed contact, thus setting up the illusion of emptiness. As far back as the 1580s, Sir Francis Drake's raid on coastal Florida brought plague that may have devastated Indian peoples up-coast as far as Virginia. The Pilgrims themselves arrived at a land already ninety percent depopulated by disease, according to historian Alfred W. Crosby. Yet the fact of this massive die-off only underlines the fact of a powerful, shaping human presence in the New World before Columbus. "A good argument can be made that the human presence was less visible in 1750 than in 1492," says Denevan; paradoxically, there was "undoubtedly much more 'forest primeval' in 1850 than in 1650." Once smallpox and other diseases had removed the indigenous humans, many places had a century or two to revert to a state they had not been in for a very long time—which pioneering Europeans of course mistook as Edenic: original and fresh from the hand of God.

We are finally ready, it seems, to challenge this myth. It falls to us to revise our sense of place: to recognize that these territories settled by our forebears were landscapes already rich with human history and, indeed, with tragedy. The empty lands and towering forests of our myth were grown in a brief, sad interregnum between groups of inhabiting people. The *increase* of pristine forest during the one or two centuries between human dwellers lent plausibility to the myth of Eden. The land was actually ripening toward Edenhood! In fact, the modern concept of really empty wilderness gained its current strength right as the last Indians were being forcibly removed, progressing right along with the nineteenth century from about the 1830s onward. Cronon observes: "The removal of Indians to create an 'uninhabited wilderness' ... reminds us just how invented, just how constructed, the American wilderness really is."

In our time, many Americans have come to identify with the Indian, even appropriating Indian names and Indian religions. The romantic Indian, all nobility and nature, has enough clout to propel a movie like *Dances with Wolves* to its Oscar, or to sell an antipollution campaign (Iron-Eyes Cody's famous tear). But before Indians were safely out of our way, neither they nor the land they lived in were regarded so benignly. Classics of environmental history like Roderick Nash's *Wilderness and the American Mind* have documented an earlier attitude, that old-world *contemptus mundi* that saw this earth—and specifically this continent—as a realm of sin and struggle, that only the ferocious piety of God's people could redeem. Wilderness, for our Puritan parents, was no Eden: it was an unregenerate Canaan, an evil place full of evil people. Invasion and pacification were Godly duties.

Luther Standing Bear recorded his perplexity at such European constructs of North America. In words that have become a familiar part of the wilderness debate, he draws the contrast: "We did not think of the great open plains, the beautiful rolling hills, and winding streams with tangled growths, as 'wild.' Only to the white man was nature a wilderness and only to him was the land 'infested' with 'wild' animals and 'savage' people. To us it was tame. Earth was bountiful."

That Puritan idea of evil-wilderness faded, as settlement made the territory safe and as the Romantic Revolution presented a very different view of nature—as God's home. (I'll return to this revolution in a later chapter.) On our side of that divide, we can shudder at the brutality of those old anti-wilderness, anti-Indian sentiments.

Yet Standing Bear's word "tame" rings very strangely to us. We want to cling to an idea of a rough and inhuman wilderness that stands apart from ourselves—certainly not a "tame" one. How could those herds of stampeding buffalo be tame? How could the windswept prairie, the prowling grizzly, the ravages of hunger be tame? Perhaps the word is ill chosen. Or perhaps the meaning is that both buffalo and Indian, both Indian and natural milieu, knew each other well, and knew what to expect from each other. Maybe each was tamed to the other, shaped to ways that both could live with.

A mixture like this, of tame and wild, is simply unthinkable in the traditional American terms that mark out logically opposite quantities, the human/artificial and the natural/wild. It is worth a longer look, to catch a vision of how people have shaped the living world and been shaped in return.

Elizabeth Marshall Thomas offers a splendid example of this coevolution that surely must have typified most of the long history of people in their environment—those hundred-thousand years before cities and plows, those million years on two legs. Thomas is in a rare position to report. Raised from early childhood by anthropologist parents travelling across the Kalahari with the !Kung people, she saw a modern hunter-gatherer life first hand, with all that it might reveal about our collective past. She herself became an ethologist. In a long and fascinating article, she reports a kind of detente between the peoples of the Kalahari and the local lions—a style of cohabitation that, to an outsider, seemed unbearably threatening. They had developed a "restraint" by which the lions left the people and cattle alone, and the people followed a careful decorum about where they went, and when. Thomas calls it amazing, "almost incomprehensible." But she saw it in action over a period of five years, lions prowling for game just yards away, yet observing some co-evolved set of rules that allowed the humans their space, and the lions theirs. The arrangement called for attentiveness and detailed local knowledge, perhaps wisdom of a very concrete sort. She calls it "the old way," and wonders what it might tell us about how people have lived in the world together with other animals. To us, it is a category-busting mixture of wild and tame.

In the case of Standing Bear's people, those vast prairies that depended on bison also depended on fire. The consensus now is that Indians regularly fired the grasslands in order to generate the new sprouts favored by the bison. In doing so (along with lightning-caused fire) they helped create the prairie's typical patchwork of deep-rooted, quickly regenerating grasses and broadleaf plants. The self-integrated climax grassland that so impressed early-twentieth-century scientists like Frederick Clements (and in fact gave rise to modern ecology) turns out to have an anthropogenic element: it was human-managed, human-sustained.

Wild or tame? Both, of course, if people are not excluded from membership in the natural world. The terms do not really oppose each other, if "wild" means, as I have been using it, a kind of thriving vitality, a process we all share; and if "tame" means, perhaps, accomodating-each-other. Though to Americans of the eighteenth and nineteenth centuries, for whom "wild" connoted dangerous, unrestrained, and uncivilized, the opposition would be complete.

It is traditional to say that America defines itself in its relation to nature, in its confrontation with the big, apparently raw, continent. Raymond Williams reminds us that a version of nature is always a version of human nature. Standing Bear's concept of nature included humans. But our American version of nature, and of ourselves, plays out that old Judeo-Christian plot of separation. Since our life comes from somewhere else (the hand of God), and our fate destines us for somewhere else (heaven or hell), we can see "nature" as simply a stage, a place, a *thing* that is not-us. The really interesting discovery is to see how this sense of separation clings to us, as we change or even reverse our other concepts of nature. Evil-wilderness or Eden-wilderness—either way we are not a part of it. The operant definition of nature has been, for much of the environmental movement as for much of American history, nature "out there," way out west, nature as wilderness where people (meaning ourselves) haven't quite arrived yet.

It is more than a little weird when you think of it: an American pioneer, scout, or mountain-man stands on an Indian trail and labels the land it crosses as "virgin." This is an image of mythic standing—except that now we notice something else, something obvious to us but invisible to many generations. Who made the trail?

In his widely read *Mountains of California* (1894), John Muir provides many examples of this strange angle of vision. A favorite Sierran river basin is, he says, "untrodden, hidden in the glorious wildness like unmined gold." Yet the next sentence mentions that Indians had left signs of hunting and camping there. So ... how could it be "untrodden"?

There are several ways to get an answer. Racism is one; so are plain ignorance, and, in a more general sense, the curiously blinding effect of one's cultural paradigm, the ways we construct what we see. All three are common enough in the histories of Western engagement with native peoples and places. But I'll stick with some examples from John Muir, since he's a defining figure in the story of how America sees nature—yet also a troubling figure for me, one whom I'll have to deal with. Might as well get started. I'll get around to praising him later.

First, racism. An embarrassing discovery for environmentalists who actually read Muir is how dismissive he is of the native peoples who live in or travel across his divine territories. Of course Muir was a man of the nineteenth century (born a British subject in 1838); it's surely unfair to project our late-found racial and cultural inclusiveness backwards upon this Victorian American. And, in his later encounters with Alaskans, some interpreters believe Muir shows a developing sense of respect. But like other Anglo-Europeans of his era, Muir usually considered Indians as something not-quite-human, classing them in the "nature" half of the familiar polarity. In both *The Mountains of California* and the later book *My First Summer in the Sierra*, I find that Muir always frames Sierran Indians as features of the natural landscape or as biota, never as human. They are "specimens," they are "geological"; they are like bears, jays, wolves, or (repeatedly) squirrels. In the conventional race and gender categories of the time, only white men are capable of the adult faculties of forethought or probity. Indians (along with other non-Europeans and women) are childlike or animal-like, not fully human.

The point is not to dwell on Muir's shortcomings. His importance and good work in the world tower above them, as above his critics (including me). But it is important to register that this habit of vision is still with us, fossilized in our concept of wilderness as "pristine" and "untouched." The native inhabitants are still edited out of the picture, and to put them back in is to critically reconsider the term itself.

Sometimes plain lack of knowledge might explain the illusion that these "wildernesses" were in some Edenic, untouched state when the Europeans arrived. Gary Nabhan gives the ironic illustration of Yosemite Valley itself. Of course, Yosemite became Muir's spiritual and literal home; Muir led the classic battle (via the *Century*

magazine) to turn Yosemite into a national park, which cemented probably forever his image as the wild prophet of the woods. He lived there for the last decades his life, sage of the wilderness, welcoming visits from Emerson and Roosevelt and sounding the call of wilderness to an increasingly urbanized America.

Yet we now know that Miwok peoples had been burning the Yosemite Valley floor for a long time—a common Indian practice from coast to coast—to create that open forest that Muir so treasured. Botanical archeology has established, in Sierra foothills a little to the north (and at slightly lower elevation), at least three thousand years of Indian-managed burning to maintain the oak/grassland savannah. Yosemite itself has been occupied for at least two thousand years, researchers having found over five hundred sites of habitation and use there. The picture that emerges is clear and surprising: Muir's divine temple, Yosemite Valley, was at least partly created by humans. Now that we know this, how shall we define the "wilderness" of Yosemite and other treasured places?

Journalist Stephen Powers' 1877 report is especially interesting, in that the "thick" Indian population he saw was itself only a sliver of the original population of California. The disease process begun by eastern contact with Europeans had taken two hundred years to roll all the way to the West Coast, and as recently as 1833, malaria had swept through central California Indian populations with a mortality rate of perhaps 75 percent. The combination of disease, dislocation, and organized genocide (which we will revisit) left only a tiny fraction of the original inhabitants—perhaps seven percent by the time of Muir's campaign. The gold-rush decade of the 1850s alone had cut the remaining Indian population by two-thirds. Alfred Kroeber, the great early-twentieth-century anthropologist of aboriginal California, estimated (perhaps conservatively) that in precontact times some nine thousand Miwok had lived along their portion of the western slope of the Sierras; by 1910 he counted just 610.

So to some extent Muir merely failed to notice what no longer existed. Yet, in 1869 when Muir arrived, Miwok and Paiute still plodded some mountain trails, still encountered the lone foot-traveller. Their campsites and abandonments were still obvious to the keenly observant Scotsman. Muir was able to sleuth out glacial events of geological antiquity, with great imagination and penetrating vision, yet he was blind to the present and recent past of the mountains' human inhabitants. Muir's failure to register Miwok in his mountains can be best understood as a darn good illustration of the way cultural preconceptions shape vision, *including* what is expected and *excluding* what one has no words or concepts for. A striking example of this paradigm-blindness is when Muir notices-without-noticing the way the Indians live on the land without hurting it.

> *How many centuries Indians have roamed these woods*
> *nobody knows, probably a great many, extending far*
> *beyond the time that Columbus touched our shores, and*
> *it seems strange that heavier marks have not been made.*
> *Indians walk softly and hurt the landscape hardly more*
> *than the birds and squirrels, and their brush and bark*
> *huts last hardly longer than those of wood rats, while*
> *their enduring monuments, excepting those wrought on*
> *the forests by the fires they made to improve their hunting*
> *grounds, vanish in a few centuries.*
>
> *How different are most of those of the white man.*

There it is staring him in the face, right down to the forest-burning that produced the floor of Yosemite. He sees but does not see. He can't. In his eyes, they are nature, not culture. They are strange to him, usually unpleasant and degraded, and he can draw no applicable lesson for regular humans to use. The above passage is occasionally quoted admiringly, as if to prove Muir's ahead-of-his-time vision, but in context it shows quite the opposite. Four pages later, Muir describes a "debased" Indian woman, dirty, out of place in his mountains; he concludes that Indians are "not a whit more natural than the glaring tourists we saw that frightened the birds and squirrels." Here's an interesting opposition; the Indians are animal-like compared to (real) humans, yet compared to (real) animals, they're all too human. It's double jeopardy, or perhaps a double bind.

John Muir the gentle nature-prophet is on America's inner Rushmore now, iconic and saint-like. Criticism will awaken astonishment and outrage. So let me quickly acknowledge that in no fewer than six trips to Alaska beginning ten years later, Muir may have come to an appreciation of the native peoples he met there (an optimistic reading not supported by all his scholars). But even if Muir's view did shift, *My First Summer In the Sierras* is a very weighty book: in a sense, it is Muir's first and last book. It presents the journal of Muir's 1869 summer, when his life figuratively began anew. But Muir did not get the journal shaped up for publication until 1911, just three years before his death; it was the last book he personally saw through to publication (though several others came out posthumously). For whatever reason, he edited the manuscript only very lightly. And whatever his Alaskan transformation of attitude, late in life he elected to leave in all the strangely offensive language I analyzed above. Let the worm of doubt wiggle on. I never met a saint I didn't more than half distrust.

Even Muir's casual trope—the "unmined gold" of a so-far "untrodden" wilderness—carries disconcerting back-spin. I suppose Muir's unconscious was speaking more truly than he knew, when it chose gold mining for a simile: an extractive resource that diminishes with use, accruing wealth for the lucky first but leaving a degraded and spent landscape behind. For the more visitors to a wilderness, the less it is a wilderness at all. "Wilderness" as a commodity awakens the vices of capitalism: hoarding, possession, strong walls, and good locks. Think about our parks and wildernesses, the drawing of lines on maps, the battles over who owns, who uses, who gets kept out. Think about the world of humans separated from the world of nature. Think of the immemorial association of paradise with precious gold and jewels—the way Eve's apple morphs into the golden apples of the Hesperides, of Botticelli's *Primavera*, all symbols of imperishable bliss. Paradise, Golden Age, unchanging Eden, out of the reach of time and corruption and biology. There's an odd but compelling subterranean connection.

The gold-mining metaphor isn't far from the sexual metaphor more commonly used: "virgin" and "pristine" express the same sense of the wilderness as scarce commodity. For virginity is surely the most perishable of treasures; and when a wilderness is prized for its untouched quality, it seems that attribute has already been lost. Only one explorer can be the first; only he (*he*) can deflower it in the fullness of that term, only he gets to stake the claim and enjoy— once!—the untouched pleasures. (Recording "first ascents" on mountain peaks surely plays out the same set of unexamined values.)

In a system of opposites, perhaps rape and pillage are the logical metaphors. The *human* side penetrates and violates the *nature* side, but cannot abide there. Nature's essence is already lost when Man (per se) arrives. "Untouched wilderness" converts quickly into spent commodity. The virgin becomes a whore.

On that trip to Nine Lake Basin, the first of so many trips, I could never have guessed that the strenuous effort I put into maintaining my categories of saved and damned, straight and gay, sacred and profane, would guarantee that I would eventually cross every line and become every opposite. The foolish definition of wilderness I unconsciously employed was only one of those categories—that blinkered, obviously untrue social construct of some untouched Eden where a person could leave history and the world of people.

And yet.

There is always something more going on than our (mis)definitions can touch. Beneath my cultural illusions, something more was going on. Beyond the commodification of wilderness, beyond the pillaging spirit of peak-baggers and colonists, beyond Muir's lust for new ranges to ramble over, and beyond my own—something more was going on. Something untouched even by the genocide of native peoples and entire species, something shrugging off the cities-on-a-hill and the manifested destinies—something there was, and always has been, abiding and powerful. "Wilderness" we called it: that something that touched and moved and changed me, and does so still.

What is it? What do we discover, experience, intuit, while in the "wilderness"? Must I discount my own experience as culturally conditioned, mere projection and sleepwalking? Certainly any "wilderness experience" comes in a heavily conditioned and constructed form. Indian youths have Indian experiences on their "vision quests"—totem animals, ancestor spirits. Christians experience the fullness of the Christian God; Buddhists discover forms of emptiness. Whatever it is that's there, it must come to us squeezed through the forms of our senses and assembled according to whatever meaning-making pattern we have available. Yes, our paradigms shape our experiences.

And yet—it's remarkable that "something" is always being experienced. Not merely self-generated fantasies, but responses to a force, a reality, an ebullient liveliness, that is greater and realer than our explanations of it. It's there in Muir, for all his blindnesses and baggage (and he went lighter than most!), shining in passages of pure wonder.

It seems to me that, while granting that the forms are socially conditioned, there's a pretty wide breadth of testimony, from far beyond merely Eurocentric limits, that humans do, habitually and nearly universally, experience a "something" when in the forceful presence of nature. The occasion may be some unusually grand or powerful manifestation, a vista, a brush with death, or, merely, a silence. From Gilgamesh in the cedar forest to Elijah in the whirlwind, from Buddha starving on the mountaintop to Jesus starving in the desert, to us, starving in the cities for a taste of something real. What is it? What is that "something"? It could be God. It could be nature. It could be Pan or Jove or one of the goddesses. It could be Tao, Dharma, Brahma, *Wakan Tanka*. That last phrase, traditionally misinterpreted as "Great Spirit," really means something more like "Great Mystery," as Standing Bear usually renders it from the Lakota Sioux language. That's a lead I can't resist following.

For of course I don't know what that something is. But I do wish to maintain that, empirically, something so widely reported ought to be taken seriously. And I wish to maintain personally that I believe in it. That is, I've experienced it—a powerful, numinous *something*. Whatever I thought it was, was no doubt a socially conditioned thought. So I attach little importance to the details of my interpretation. I'd prefer to call it *Wakan Tanka*, part of the Great Mystery. But since my language is not Lakota I'll pick an English, or if possible an American, way of saying it. I'll call it *the wild*.

The wild is what we don't control. What we cannot fully understand, nor indeed understand at all past infinitesimal glimmerings. All of science (as the greatest scientists constantly affirm) just scratches the surface of that great, throbbing realness beneath our feet, over our heads, and within our minds and bodies. We are afloat in it, that mystery!

And the crazy, amazing, remarkable fact is that it doesn't just kill us, us with our huge unknowing arrogance. No: in fact, wildness nurtures us. That great crushing universal wild gives us birth; creates minds and eyes and brains, and sets us loose within itself, and itself loose within us, all within a nested complexity of other lives. (Of course, late or soon it also kills us—that's part of the picture too.)

Wildness is what I found in the Sierras, when my spirit was stifled, a bound and desperate thing that sought what was boundless and full of spirit. Wildness is the truth behind the confusion of "wilderness." The wild is present in the wilderness of course; but is also present in the wilderness-adventurer. And in the doings, cultural or individual, back home. The wild generates novelty, new art, new melody, directions unforeseen, disconfirmation and discovery; the wild pops up willy nilly to challenge dull certainty and routine with patterns new, lovely, amazing, and unforeseen. The wild is generative, fertile, fecund, bottomless.

If you don't think there's such a Something loose in the universe, then you'll have to offer your own explanation of how all this blooming, buzzing, confused, orderly, messy wonderfulness keeps on coming true all around us. Without knowing what it is, I'll just say—it's wild, The Wild, Wildness.

I know it's a danger to name it, since that name will try to thingify, to turn itself into an object or an essence. My best guess is to see it as a process with no home or face but the sheer doing, the on-going. A process, not a thing: how many thousand miles in the backcountry have I walked, alone and ravenous for ever more wilderness—to come at last to this simple fullness? That wild, self-contented, dangerous blooming within.

Paradise Lost

Most of what I write about in this book is already gone or going under fast. This is not a travel guide but an elegy. I was one of the lucky few. I saw only a part of it but enough to realize that here was an Eden, a portion of the earth's original paradise: a living thing which can never be recovered, something precious and irreplaceable about to be destroyed.

Reader, I'd bet you hardly blinked at the above scenario. In fact, you may have found its thoughts so familiar, and at the same time so upsetting, that you decided to skim or skip the paragraph. We've heard the dismal assessment many times before, and each time we feel terrible because there seems to be so little that can be done. A natural paradise, precious and perfect, is all but lost, and we are left to wander in a degraded world, mourning.

Whose words are these? I'll get back to them in a few pages.

Similar thoughts showed up when Rachel Carson started our modern environmental movement.Her famous 1962 volume *Silent Spring* began with a parable of a town "where all life seemed to live in harmony with its surroundings." But then "everything began to change." The perfect harmony is lost. And of course it turns out to be the people themselves to blame: "They had done it themselves." What an irony. What a loss.Who wouldn't mourn? Carson's literary device encapsulated more than just her data about DDT. It also conveyed a deeper cultural storyline, a master-parable of nature lost through human sin. This sense of loss seems to be at the root of an awful lot of our thinking about nature. A huge chunk of all the nature poems I've ever read (and it must be thousands) take that elegiac tone; and a similar proportion of the nature-writing essays. Some mixture of memory and regret will almost inevitably shape the experience. It's a reflex, a habit of thought we never think to notice.

This sad song has been with us for a long time—centuries at least. Maybe millennia. Of course the story is "Paradise Lost"—as named by the seventeenth-century Puritan poet John Milton, who assembled the greatest of English-language epics around this, our culture's definitive story. It is the function of an epic to sum up the story we tell ourselves, our identity. This *Paradise Lost* does brilliantly. It is a musical, majestic retelling of the Genesis story, framed in grief. Its famous opening lines:

> *Of man's first disobedience, and the fruit*
> *Of that forbidden tree whose mortal taste*
> *Brought death into the world, and all our woe*

Twelve books later, we see the human couple (perhaps crouched in shame as Michelangelo depicted them) driven from the Garden into a world of thistles and bloodshed. If you were raised to believe in human sinfulness, as I was and as most folks in European or American homes were until the last few decades, these words are powerful. They seem to explain everything. That's because, as the great Romanian scholar of religion and myth Mircea Eliade has remarked, this is our "essential" myth: the "drama of Paradise, which instituted the present human condition." This myth is not some cultural museum-piece. It is, I am convinced, an emotional force that is still shaping our experience.

We are quite a distance from Milton, but not from Paradise Lost. Consider this intense lyric by the Victorian Gerard Manley Hopkins, a central figure in the canon of nature poets. Called "Binsey Poplars: felled 1879," it starts (in the quirky condensed language of Hopkins):

> *My aspens dear, whose airy cages quelled,*
> *Quelled or quenched in leaves the leaping sun,*
> *All felled, felled, are all felled*

Hopkins feels the "fells" like axe-strokes, and the rhymes seem ominous in context, like fatal echoes. "O if we but knew what we do/When we delve or hew," he exclaims. For this is not just the temporary loss of a grove which, after all, might re-grow with time. It's a total loss, a miniature fall from a local Eden:

Where we, even where we mean
    To mend her we end her,
When we hew or delve:
After-comers cannot guess the beauty been.
Ten or twelve, only ten or twelve
    Strokes of havoc únselve
            The sweet especial scene,
    Rural scene, a rural scene,
    Sweet especial rural scene.

That "unselving" is in one sense a murder, in another a descent into history from the magic of natural paradise. When death and change come into the charmed circle, all is lost. Time cannot heal; time, in fact, only takes us further away from Eden. The ache of loss, the grief of this piece, is so profound that clearly it must be amplifying the larger ache, as so many of Hopkins' poems do: that we live in the sin-world that comes after Eden. Like us, Hopkins sees nature itself as the Eden we are exiled from. That makes Hopkins a modern nature poet. For that is the bedrock of much—maybe most—modern nature writing.

We hear this formulation so often it escapes our notice: we take it as the structure *of* reality, not as a story-form we place *on* reality. I've seen it in countless student essays in college English classes. Ask them to write about nature, and likely as not Paradise Lost is what will come out. I'm convinced that our public debate (and private struggle) over the environment are locked into an unresolvable cycle of use versus preservation because they are founded on the cultural myth of Paradise Lost, reinforced by an unexamined nostalgia. A remembered perfection; an inevitable decay—this thought pattern has already broken the world into two opposites: nature/wilderness/Eden and human/civilized/fallen. Likewise it has divided time into a Golden Age past and an essentially tragic historical present.

Paradise Lost is the myth that shapes our minds when we encounter nature and especially "the wilderness." Our cultural paradigm packages the experience for us in this ancient and persistent narrative. In seeing nature through this distorting lens, we remain stuck in a story with no possible happy ending, short of the end of the world.

The quote at the head of this chapter is not made up. It is a montage (word-for-word from several passages) from one of the best environmentalist books I know, Edward Abbey's *Desert Solitaire*. When I first read those words, not long after publication in 1968, I cherished them. The fly-leaf of my old paperback records the re-readings, the decades of scribbled notes and underlines. Yet now I feel a strange ambivalence. What a writer! I think, grateful for the pages before me. But what a jerk ... and what a desperate imprisonment in Paradise Lost.

Of course, the guy did all he could to offend. Jerkish exaggeration is part of his pose, a literary hyperbole not so far from Thoreau's. Abbey is the father of monkeywrenching and EarthFirst!ing, after all; he's the beer-drinking knucklehead who advocated resistance to all things civilized. "No Compromise in Defense of Mother Earth," his eco-terrorizing offspring chant. But they, like some critics, make an interesting mistake. They read his hyperbole literally. "I'm a humanist," he quips. "I'd rather kill a man than a snake." Either he's exaggerating for effect—that elbow in your ribs is hyperbole—or he's a sociopath.

But it's not the pose or the overstatement for effect or even the swagger that bother me. What bothers me is this: do I really want to dwell in grief and its suburb, anger? For these are Abbey's official emotions. They are the emotions of Paradise Lost. What bothers me is getting trapped in this old and hopeless pattern. For Abbey sets up his book as an "elegy"—loss is there from the start, as the condition of nature. He makes wilderness quite literally his Paradise. On an extended solitary stay near Havasu, for instance, he's "Adam," wandering naked whenever possible. It's "five weeks in Eden." Eden-language comes easily to him, and though his tongue is never far from his cheek, there's always a sense in which he is deadly earnest about this.

The climactic chapter "Down the River" is a good place to see Abbey's formulation of this modern Paradise Lost. In this chapter, the writer and a pal raft down a section of the Colorado River that will soon be submerged behind the Glen Canyon Dam. It's a perfect setup because it seems to justify Abbey's endemic outrage. Here's a beautiful place that really is about to go under, victim of a stupid blunder by stupid bureaucrats acting on behalf of a stupid tourist/ consumer culture. (No wonder, as a young man, I liked this book so much!). It contains an extended defense of the wilderness concept, which climaxes this way: "love of wilderness is … loyalty to the earth, the earth which bore us and sustains us, the only home we shall ever know, the only paradise we ever need—if only we had the eyes to see. Original sin, the true original sin, is the blind destruction for the sake of greed of this natural paradise which lies all around us—if only we were worthy of it."

There's the stinger. We're not worthy, of course—"we" meaning civilization. Interestingly, however, Abbey himself gets off the hook. In Abbey's formulation of this myth, the solitary individual explorer gets to be Adam. He's that old American archetype, the mountain man, the Marlboro man, the rugged individual. The rest of us are citified, effeminated, fallen—"tourists" in Abbey's contemptuous epithet. So this is the secret function of Abbey's hairy-knuckled, screw-you persona: it positions him against the rest of fallen humanity. As he protests (rather too much to believe), he's no over-educated birdwatching back-east dude. He's working-class. He's crude. He's Adam.

The unexamined hyper-individualism is so obvious it hardly needs analysis. Crude individualism is what Abbey cannot see, the most American thing about him, leading him to blandly assume that somehow he is a "social atom," detached and whirling on a solitary course. Yet as Abbey fulminates against civilization, he himself embodies it in every dimension. Who buys his beans, provides his crumby little trailer and its butane heater and flush toilet? The vast apparatus of the US government, the world's biggest bureaucracy, funded by the world's biggest consumer economy. (He works as a summer ranger in a National Monument.) All those taxpayers, all that infrastructure; all those paved roads, those industries that built his truck and delivered his groceries: all so he can sit contemplatively in the desert.

And his complicity in civilization goes far deeper. What's he *doing* out there, if not something he has learned to value from his reading of Muir, Thoreau, Wordsworth? The hermit nature philosopher is a cultural cliché, not a naked adamic invention. Abbey carries a library of Western attitudes and perceptions in his head, and he can no more escape them than he can avoid thinking in English. Can you be said to be free of civilization, if you are quoting Shelley to yourself before sunsets, thinking of Shakespeare and Bach and Schoenberg, Giacometti and Yeats and Balzac and Sophocles? Abbey's individualism plays out our most unexamined fantasies and pretenses—the same ones I have played out in my own johnmuir explorations, offtrail and high up in the Sierras. It's the "American Adam" so well described by our classic scholars: R. W. B. Lewis, Henry Nash Smith, Leo Marx, Roderick Nash.

On their float down the Colorado described in the crucial chapter "Down the River," Abbey and his friend create for themselves an Edenic fiction, a faux innocence, through the interesting expedient of not consulting with anyone about their route, not bringing any maps, in fact not even bothering with basics like life-jackets or enough food: "Actually our ignorance and carelessness are more deliberate than accidental; we are entering Glen Canyon without having learned much about it beforehand because we wish to see it as Powell and his party had seen it, not knowing what to expect, making anew the discoveries of others. If the first rapids are a surprise to us it is simply because we had never inquired if there were any on this stretch of the river."

Elsewhere in the chapter he alludes, admiringly, to the Jedediah Smiths and Jim Bridgers of way-out-west mythology. But we have to ask: are ignorance and heedlessness really a model for "innocent" interaction with nature? Even the mountain men gleaned what they could from the locals. And real natives provide an even stronger contrast—those who lived in this "Eden" before Abbey, Powell, Smith, or Bridger. Traditional peoples live on the land by a detailed knowledge of it, an awareness of place that goes almost foot-by-foot, a shared knowledge passed along through lifetimes of storytelling. It is at once a deeply local, and a deeply communal, wisdom. It is the opposite of these blundering ignoramuses.

But a communal knowledge of this sort is as hard for Abbey to grasp as a communal identity. The most striking aspect of Abbey is his entrapment in this fiction of total individualism. *Desert Solitaire's* occasional outbreaks of bullshit survivalism smell of it. And I believe this unexamined and extreme individualism is what traps Abbey in hopeless grief, as well. For him the loss of Glen Canyon must be total: only his lifetime has any relevance. At one point he ponders, will the canyon be lost "forever" or merely "for centuries"? The questions are not distinguished; they run together and are functionally identical. No frame of reference beyond the individual is considered. Where the isolated individual is the only measure, then of course every loss is total and permanent. It is in that sense cosmic.

But I don't want to live on so narrow a scale. When I accept the identity I share with my culture and my species, I see very different vistas. Loss of Glen Canyon, or Hetch Hetchy, is a serious loss indeed. Abbey was right to be outraged. But they are not the end of the world. They are not the loss of Eden. In time—in real human time, a hundred or five hundred years, three or ten or thirteen generations—they might well be back in their original shape. Or something just as good. The water continues running. The ecosystems, over long patient time, rebuild.

Because this kind of Eden is strangely renewing. It is fresh, in fact, every single morning.

Curiously, that last sentence echoes strongly with another Abbey book, a work of nature writing that stands quietly behind the posturing, rib-nudging roughneck of the *Desert Solitaire* we've been looking at. Of course it's the same book: the secret version Abbey did not dare, I think, to write out without the protective camouflage of the other one. The first chapter, called "The First Morning," feels like this; passages everywhere along the way feel like it: here is a book of tenderness, here is a verbal consciousness lavishing care upon the singular moments of being alive.

> *Each time I look up one of the secretive little side-canyons I half expect to see not only the cottonwood tree rising over its tiny spring—the leafy god, the desert's liquid eye—but also a rainbow-colored corona of blazing light, pure spirit, pure being, pure disembodied intelligence, about to speak my name.*
>
> *If man's imagination were not so weak, so easily tired, if his capacity for wonder not so limited, he would abandon forever such fantasies of the supurnal. He would learn to perceive in water, leaves and silence more than sufficient of the absolute and marvelous, more than enough to console him for the loss of the ancient dreams.*

This secret *Solitaire* is why Abbey will endure; why he will be read alongside Thoreau, hundreds of years from now. Despite its sophomoric strut. And despite its Paradise Lost mythology, which I fervently hope we will soon come to regard as quaint and irrelevant.

Another example, decades closer, shows that this Paradise Lost pattern is not merely the aberration of cranky old nature-boys. When the Curator for Botany at the National Museum of Natural History writes in a big, glossy Smithsonian Institution book commemorating the five hundred years since Columbus, it has the feeling of something like the Official Version. Though paradise seems to be getting lost almost everywhere I look, this little piece says unmistakably, "This is our myth." The book is called *Seeds of Change*, the article "Three Faces of Eden," by Stanwyn G. Shetler.

It opens with a contrast: the author stands on the Potomac looking at its beauty "much as the first Indians" would have, then looks the other way and sees "human intrusion, the irrevocable infiltration of modern civilization with its culturally refined yet environmentally alien emplacements." "Our intrusions are permanent and ubiquitous. ... We have long since invaded the innermost sanctums of the American wilderness." Shetler's language is saturated with value judgments that are, when you look closely, essentially religious: wilderness is holy (the "inner sanctum" was where the Israelite's God was located within the "holy of holies" of the tabernacle); and human presence is a malign "infiltration" like germs or enemies ... or sin.

The familiar polarity plays out: in the "First Eden, nature primeval, pristine; in the other, the Second Eden, nature modified, disturbed, and despoiled." In time, the past contains an Eden now out of reach. In space, whatever is human is not-nature. For when the first human walked over the Bering landbridge those tens of thousands of years ago, the "unnaturalizing of the American wilderness" began. The mere existence of a human in the hemisphere was already the death of Eden.

The Official Voice recapitulates that familiar paradoxical attitude toward the Indians which we have already seen in Muir. Though his dualist doctrine requires him to believe that the "unnaturalizing of

America" was long ago under way, he nevertheless sees the Indians living here at the time of European contact as "transparent in the landscape, living as natural elements of the ecosphere." He's caught in the same trap as Muir, an oddly inconsistent way of denouncing all human works in nature, yet praising the Indians. This is generic Noble Savage romanticism, with its uncomfortable underside of racism. The Indians are not-us, and so somehow escape the Original Sin which drives "us" from Eden.

Eden is timeless: it doesn't change. But you and I (Shetler's not quite sure about the Indians) are locked in the other kind of time, the kind where change hurtles us forward and all actions bear irrevocable fruit. As with Abbey, the arrow of history speeds us in one direction only; whatever it passes is gone forever. It's built right into the myth: Adam and Eve's transgression creates the ever-after: exile from Eden, and all the unfolding of the sad, flawed human tale. History, in other words. Where we live. Short of the apocalypse—the end of Time—we can't go back or undo our mistakes. The changes people have made "forever transform the First American Eden." By definition, the virginal innocence of Eden is irrecoverable.

So Shetler must insist that, when humans came into the picture, "the primeval ecological balance slowly but surely was irreversibly challenged"—changes are "permanent." The obvious question should be—Why permanent? Why irreversible? His data should surely be challenged. (Did no ecosystem ever get bumped by humans and recover? Was none ever predicated on the very presence of these humans?) But to do so would in fact be talking past his essay: despite its appearance as a statement of history, it is not interested in facts. Facts are not even relevant. Because Shetler is doing mythology. That is where the "irreversible" comes from: original sin, going by the name of civilization.

And mythology is where the apocalypse of his finale comes from too. Listen to the hopeless grieving despair of this picture: "The native wealth—minerals, forests, wild game and fish, furbearers— is extracted without regard for a sustainable future; the fertile soils are exhausted, desertified, blown away, or flushed into the sea, as the priceless mantle of continent itself dissolves away; the air is polluted; and the water is poisoned or squandered."

The end of the world—nature "destroyed, desecrated, privatized." *Desecrated*: the presence of the human is the death of the sacred.

This is the way we tell the story, with our version of Original Sin: industry, commerce, overpopulation, urbanization, and all our other errors. Exactly as we saw in Abbey. The inevitable conclusion must be for Shetler to issue the prophet's cry for repentance. "Will the unnaturalizing of America be the undoing of the earth or the battle cry for its rescue?" The tale could not be more cosmic if it were a Babylonian epic or a Wagnerian opera. Nothing less than the saving or losing of the world is at stake.

If you don't feel up to the task, you're not alone. How could you be, unless you're a God or a Hero? That's one of the downsides to this myth. It locks us into a passive despair, a losing narrative. Paradise is already lost; our sins are inescapable; time has already carried us too far to hope for innocence.

We must consider the real events that have triggered such outcries. There are real losses going on, certain and severe. They need our response. But until we reconsider this old myth, I doubt we'll have much success at reimagining or redesigning our interactions with the rest of nature. I think we'll go on losing it, because that's the pattern. And mourning it, because that's the pattern. All we can see is an unhappy prospect, a world of sin that we're powerless to resist. Because that's the pattern.

Unless we adopt a different story. Or profoundly revise this one.

The all-too-human trait of nostalgia seems to account for some of the persistence of the Paradise Lost pattern. Even in cultures very different from ours, the old folks still remember the good old days, and there's likely to be a vague, pervasive sense that things were once a lot better. Mircea Eliade calls it the "nostalgia for paradise" and notes that "primitives" (his word) are especially addicted to it—an interesting fact for Westerners who make the primitive their Eden. Yet, as we will see, in traditional cultures this nostalgia leads to a different conclusion, a sense that paradise can be recovered and is not forever lost. For Westerners, however, the past is gone, and one's personal memories too often invest it with a phony glamour. Only a sharp-sighted few in any culture seem to recognize that the nostalgic are recalling a time when their bodies and minds were younger; of course the world seemed fresher then! (Shetler falls into this trap too: cosmicizing his reminiscence about how "Even as recently as twenty-five years ago one could still have my wild Potomac headland and its river view all to oneself even on fine days.")

I guess if you're sitting in the rec room in a Florida retirement hall, grousing is as good a way to pass the time as any. But romanticizing the actual, historical past—mislabeling it as a time when "everything" was better—can only slander the present and feed a reactionary politics. Surprising (to me) however, is the pervasiveness of this habit, for young and old alike. People who, as I personally know, were *never* "in shape" will talk (idly) about "getting *back* in shape"; Christian conservatives fulminate about "returning" America to God or "restoring" decency to government. (*Please* look at a history text—*any* history text!) A hood of stupidity lowers over the mind when it succumbs to such thinking. The present is demonized, a fantasy past is idolized, and sensible thought is impossible.

On almost any subject, you can hear discussion predicated on this false construction of the past. Education. Politics. Welfare. Violence. Families. The sexes. Even a cursory look into how people actually lived fifty, a hundred, or a thousand years ago quickly creates a different, more nuanced picture: some things were better, and some were worse. On the whole, things were just as stunningly messed up and moronic as they are today. And just as sweet.

The world wears on. People fall in love, suffer, enjoy, and pass on. Few come to wisdom, folly is everywhere, excellence is rare. Marcus Aurelius saw it clearly two thousand years ago: the pageant of human affairs is the same from age to age.

> All that comes to pass is as familiar and well known as
> the rose in spring and the grape in summer. Of like
> fashion are sickness, death, calumny, intrigue ...

Nothing under the sun is new, not in Qoheleth's time, not in Marcus Aurelius', and not since.

But only people who think about it a little will be able to resist the pleasant lie of the good old days.

When I find the Paradise Lost pattern under much of our thinking and writing, I am saying it shapes our worldview. Typically we define worldviews by a few neat word-pictures and phrases: the Elizabethan worldview (hierarchy, the chain of being); the Age of Enlightenment (reason, science, history). I think further that worldviews are built around narratives that appeal on a deep level: fundamental organizing patterns: myths. A myth of this kind may be far under the surface, shaping consciousness but not consciously known as such—part of the "air we breathe," paradoxically self-evident and transparent at the same time.

I'd say that a myth like Paradise Lost is not even *what* we believe. Most of us don't believe it in any doctrinal sense. Rather, it's the *structure* of our believing, the shape of the mental terrain, the gravities and slopes that make everything dropped there roll in certain directions. Travelling in the West, say, it would be pretty typical to note the natural beauties there and regret what civilized blotches and scars appear, and to think about how and why, and whether there's any use in resisting the general decline; and perhaps even to note our own implication in the problem, motoring along on the Interstate. But we will probably never consider that the shape of these thoughts is already given: the opposition of human and natural, the seemingly inevitable sequence of natural beauty threatened and lost, the vague guilt, the helplessness. The myth is built into us (presumably by our cultural training), structuring how we think.

One great difference between a traditional society and a modern one is the explicitness of its organizing myths. Indeed, one way the traditional society is defined is as a community whose long-standing social structures and belief systems are not experienced as problematic. They are simply "how the world is." In contrast, the West has subjected its social structures and myths to much critical thinking, and many of us have consciously jettisoned religious beliefs. We may think ourselves far beyond any such primitive thing as a myth.

But I don't think so. Kees W. Bolle, in his wonderful book *The Freedom of Man in Myth*, comments on the old-fashioned arrogance that drew a sharp line between so-called "primitives" and us sophisticated "moderns." What Bolle sees instead is a continuity. "We" are not fundamentally different from "them" despite our shiny appliances. There's a "unity of all men in behavior and mind," a "unity in the structure of man." (And women too, we presume.) We share the same minds, the same hundred-thousand-year backdrop of human time. But "in our present day world we lack the distance necessary for such clarity in our views of our own myths."

But just because we cannot see them, does not mean they are not there. Myths must be there: I suspect we can't think far without them, nor could there be such a thing as a "culture" without some deep storyline to give it shape. Malinowski comments that myth is "not an idle rhapsody, not an aimless outpouring of vain imaginings, but a hard-working, extremely important cultural force." What that hard-working cultural force does is nothing less than hold our world together. According to Eliade, myth provides us our "ideas of reality, value, transcendence." In a traditional society in which myth is fully operational, the world may seem to make sense—the human, the natural, and the divine are explained and connected. Obviously, the modern Western world does not share that experience. Our world notoriously feels fragmented, problematical. "Angst" at a profound level may in fact reflect just this absence of effective myth. We're left, as Carl Jung thought, in need of myths that do the work of integrating our experience, psychologically and spiritually. Yet, it seems to me, though our myths have receded from conscious participation, they (or their left-overs) remain underneath our cultural structures. For better or worse, they are the lay of the land.

How could they be, if we don't believe them?

The work of anthropologist Claude Lévi-Strauss provides a useful approach. He distinguishes between the details of the myth story, and the *pattern* or deep structure which the story enacts. A myth is, he says, both a specific sequence of events, and a "timeless pattern." He notices for example how myths repeat their details in twos and threes. The reason for this is not that the plot twists and intricacies are themselves important. On the contrary, bodies of myths are notoriously inconsistent and often offer contradictory versions of the same story. This never seems to bother anyone, though. An example close to home might be the dual creation stories in Genesis, which have coexisted for millennia despite contradictory details. Myth-scholars have come to the recognition that it is pointless to search for some "correct" version of a myth: there isn't one. All versions are the myth, agglomerated together in an inconsistent bundle that, somehow, still works. It still works because belief, in a rational sense, is not what matters.

It is the pattern that matters. The repetitions and the various versions "render the structure of the myth apparent," revealing a narrative sequence, a typical course of events. That is where the shape of the cosmos is felt. Lévi-Strauss compares this shaping repetition in myth to that of a crystal that repeats its structure over and over; we might use the analogy of a fractal that repeats its defining shape at all levels, macro- and micro-. The point of a story, in this view, is not *what* happens, but *how things happen.* It is the pattern that tells you how the world works. Did the Milky Way really spout from Hera's teats? (Greece). Or from some kind of cosmic cow or possibly goat? (Russia). Is the sky really Tiamat's skull "split open like a cockle shell"? (Babylon). Did Coyote really eat the turd-sisters and then hear their voices? (Columbia Gorge). These details are absurd, even funny, and every listener knows it, ancient or modern. But the details are not the point. The point is absorbed on a different level, the meta-level of pattern. The structuralism of Lévi-Strauss made assumptions about the "timeless" nature of these underlying patterns that we ought to question. We may instead see the patterns as historically conditioned. But the analysis is still useful, directing our attention away from the surface and toward the underlying narrative shapes that constitute the world within which the stories—and the storytellers—live.

If it is the pattern and not the details that matter, then it is not surprising that I have been seeing the shapes and shadows of Paradise Lost seemingly at every turn—when I think of my own experience of nature, and compare that to our ongoing national struggle over the environment, and behind that to our history, the ways we, with our European ideas, have confronted this large, rich land. "The story of Adam and Eve in Eden has thus a canonical position ... in our tradition," comments Northrop Frye: the story shapes the thought of culture-creators like poets "whether they believe in its historicity or not." I see it everywhere, too, in our fabulous treasure-house of American nature writing. Over and over we recapitulate our master narrative, the myth of a virginal nature all around us, always in the process of getting lost.

And this myth is above all evident in the way we have invested ourselves in the preservation of sacred nature sanctuaries. Bolle asks, "what have societies … found necessary to point to and preserve as centrally valid for their entire existence?" The sacred site is a kind of mirror of identity: it is where your essence is framed, contained, revealed. What we are preserving in our nature preserves may be more than certain attractive acreages. We are equally, or maybe primarily, enacting our story of the cosmos.

Scholars like Bolle point out that it is *separateness* that defines a ritual site, that keeps it recognizable and preserves its power. Think of traditional Christian painting of the Renaissance and Middle Ages, where the "sacred" was clearly divided from the "profane" by a pillar, a post, some definite edge. Think of Sunday mornings and the "sanctuary" of church: ritual times and spaces set apart from the mundane. We seem to be acting out a similar process in our parks and wildernesses. We struggle to keep them as pristine Edens. Somehow, we feel this is necessary to our well-being. We feel it in our bones. Our identity is bound up with this question of how America relates to its wild spaces, to nature itself.

I'd like to return later to the interesting questions thus raised: if our nature-myth is a moribund one, the husk of a discarded story that nevertheless still shapes our thinking—what killed it? What turned it into a deadening habit instead of a lively relation to the world?

And further: How would an effective myth coexist with the science and history that define our thinking? Is such a thing possible? Since I don't think we are likely to be without myth, it seems we must choose a good one. And far from advocating any more demythologizing, I think we need to discover a way to *re*mythologize our world, to regain effective myths that can place the rest of our scientific and historical existence in a larger and more satisfying context. I'll be looking for a more constructive myth than the one which says, You blew it, and all is lost.

I was at a big book fair up in Seattle. A soft, powdery woman in crisp Eddie Bauer clothing addressed some of us in a "nature lit" section. She had come from New York City via the nature-art-and-crystals stop-off of Taos, thence to the Northwest—that well-beaten path. She announced that she had been pursuing "the last wild edge"—that's what she called it—which was now apparently located somewhere up in the Yukon. And soon it would be gone, she said sadly. She told us, as if it were her fresh discovery, that the frontier of civilization had been traveling westward for centuries, but that it had just about run its course. It was over, this wildness. Frederick Jackson Turner and Otto Spengler and a thousand others had been thinking this thought for a long time, but I did not hear them mentioned.

What this urban adventurer had come to tell us was the Paradise-Lost message in its Wild-West form: this, the West, had been Eden. Now it's being lost, our urban and industrial ways have done it, and we need to repent our wicked and destructive culture. "I need a new myth," she said. But she told us the old one.

This was late in the old millennium. Surrounded by dioxins and die-offs, SUVs and cell phones, she told us the old, old story and everyone in the room nodded. The wildlife biologist with his hoary beard. The wiry kayaker with his book of salt. The academics and the good poets and the bad poets and the essayists—we all nodded as if hypnotized, as if we had heard just what we expected to hear. As if that would help us somehow.

We can't go on like this.

Palimpsest:
The Wildness of Failure

My kinsman Bartram would have known what this little plant is, I think to myself—or not rested until he found out. I'm beached at the mouth of the Wind River, quietly looking at the duckfoot and salal and what-is-it.

My mood is not bright, matching the autumn day. A strange comfort there. How many kinds of failure am I? I count to myself, sensing that "nonetheless" will be supplied somehow by the setting, after the doubt and self-mockery have finished. That there will be a kind of going-on lesson, the one we crave from nature. Better capitalize that: Nature. Where we go for solace.

The big slow Columbia, nearly a mile across, moves exactly as it did in Lewis and Clark's day, for I am below the last of its eleven dams and here the river is pretty much what it has always been: a long lake tilting toward the ocean. Canoe route for the last ten thousand years. Palimpsest of chop and whitecap.

Another publisher has refused me. Into the drawer it goes, a personal letter this time—better than those xeroxed half-sheets. This one, in fact, is what I call a "rave rejection": the editor likes this, likes that … wishes it fit her list …

Hard to know how to feel. Mute, mostly. To collect myself I've come back to the Wind River. Here I sat not so long ago, a stranger staring at a strange river, trying for a new start, my back turned on failures that had cascaded all within a few months: a decade's relationship folded up. University job disappeared. Home, hard won in the LA market, sold out. All the props that tell you you're okay. How long have I been here now? The new years run together. I still don't know all the plants.

But for the first time I notice, suddenly unmistakable, a stand of bigleaf maple, with graceful aspen-barked trunks, yellowy crowns, and leaves big as dinner plates. I knew this tree in the hot hills I roamed in boyhood. Here, in this faraway north, it seems a wonder.

Lewis and Clark beached five wooden boats here on the down-current leg of their journey, October 30, 1805. The maples caught their attention too. In his journal Lewis named the river "New

Timber" after the strange trees, but later he scratched that out and tried the name "Cruzatte's" to honor a fiddle-playing crewman (neither name stuck). At midday they shot game and ate it—three ducks and a deer for the thirty of them—and then took off to make more mileage. They could smell success. After so many delays and hardships, the epic crossing of the Bitterroots, the months of uncertainty, now they were making twenty, thirty, forty miles a day. Indians along the north side of the river, drying fish in front of their lodges, assured them that the big bad-tasting lake at the end of the river was nigh. Their victory.

I'm a writer bookless for too many years. My ocean is dried up, perhaps, or I'm lost somewhere mid-continent. Which metaphor to pick? I've compromised too often, I see now, making a living by teaching, numbing my mind in institutions, husbanding my little checks. I've achieved a kind of comfort. But where is my next book? Where did my voice go?

And what do I know, after all, but this—failure—to write about? I'm coming to trust failure more than almost anything else.

But I'm a writer. If I fail, who will hear me sing the praises of failure? This paradox the autumn does not unravel for me.

There's a wild truth in failure that I crave. When I get to it, I recognize it as something that cannot be taken away from me, a kind of birthright. Always there, always waiting. Like an ancestor you may (or may not) acquaint yourself with.

I remember something from graduate school, I think it was the critic Hans Robert Jauss, who described our explorations of the world as a kind of blind man's groping. Science, literature, maybe everyday life: we reach out a hand asking: Is this the way? The world answers "no" quite often, and the shin-barking and finger-busting has a high, if unpleasant, value: the truth. That painful point of contact is where our constructs are tested against the whatever's-out-there. Old omniscient Jacob Bronowski says that science teaches us the "habit of truth" because, however limited by its own concepts and constructs, it nonetheless requires itself to listen for answers, to grope for yeses and for nos. When an experiment fails, there's no appealing the unwelcome news. You have to embrace it.

Will this work? I ask. Can anybody live like this?

I drive back to Portland, read some more about Lewis and Clark, wind up in one of the thousand little pubs that make this such a civilized place. Sitting there with my pint I begin, unexpectedly, to revisit the failures, the disappointments that have piled up too high to bear looking at. All the reality I can see sits there with me, and I allow it: all my incapacities, my fears and losses, my own collaborations in these debacles, my tears, my mocking aloofness from tears … all of it.

And, of course, I find it's not so bad after all. That's the discovery, isn't it. "Well. So this is the pain I have been avoiding." You feel it, you recognize it as yourself, and … That's all. On you go.

Except that the "you" that goes on is truer and wilder than the stiff-necked pretender that walked in. You feel light; you've let the worst happen and suddenly you're fearless, limber. You're a hunter on the edge of the great wide world, waiting for what comes by. There's room in this space, air to breathe. You see the people around you, loud-talkers, idiot smokers, patched-together failures every one, and you feel something different. Recognition. Good humor. Tenderness. Hardly novel discoveries—just novel to me. Same as they are to each of us, when we're forced, at last, to stumble into that place of still waters, that great silent center. "The zero point," I call it—the name that came to me while staring at the foam ring on the battered table under my glass. A big beery O.

This was at "The Horse Brass" in southeast Portland. I suppose a decent nature writer would cut the tavern and transpose this epiphany back to the riverside. But I didn't feel I had really left it, that river. A kind of wildness slickered through the whole day, smoke in the tavern air, hubbub, pint of stout, driving out and driving back, sitting on the Wind River. Something glimpsed that is crazy and free and dangerous. The wildness of failure.

John Keats found it at the water's edge too. Must be something to that—how we go to stare at lakes and streams and oceans. His poem "When I Have Fears" takes us, in fourteen lines, right to the heart of it. As he wrote, his brother Tom lay dying of the tuberculosis that had already killed their mother. Keats, at twenty-two, knew he wouldn't live long either, and this fearful shadow hung over everything that mattered—his longing to write, his love for poor Fanny. He listed his fears just like I did, an inventory of mortality, foolishness, failure. But when he goes past fear he comes to rest at that zero point:

> *...then on the shore*
> *Of the wide world I stand alone, and think*
> *Till Love and Fame to nothingness do sink.*

This is not despair. Wildness courses through these lines as powerfully as through any wilderness epic I've read. For failure, the little death, is a whiff of the sheer rowdy uncontrollableness of the world. It's the chance to see things clear.

My kinsman Bartram, as you may have guessed, is botanist William Bartram, son of John Bartram—regarded as the first Americans to systematically research the plants of the New World. As the year 1776 revolved to its famous conclusions, William chose instead of politics to go for a long, long walk. (That alone makes me think we're related.) A genteel vagabond, he hiked across Georgia, the Carolinas, and Florida, taking notes and inhaling sweetness wherever offered. His diligent father, possessor of a royal commission and a substantial Philadelphia botanical garden, could never be altogether pleased with this son. William was errant, undisciplined. He napped away the forenoons and made friends with whoever crossed his path. He liked Indians. He wrote a book, now known simply as "Bartram's *Travels*."

The book didn't sell and was savagely reviewed. The public forgot him. He got into debt, failed at business, endured his father's censure, lived on. Gardened, taught, kept a journal of weathers and seasons. Loved a nephew who died.

Bartram never achieved the status of a Thoreau or a Muir. He's no icon of the wild. Yet his book went to England and touched the poets Coleridge and Wordsworth, and through them—infused into their seminal poetry of Romantic nature-love—came back to America to shape the language and thoughts of those famous wilderness guys we are all followers of. So you can read Uncle Bartram as failure or success, or both.

He's kin to me through my great-grandmother Nellie, who at the age of one hundred taught me to read, when I was just six. She was born a Philadelphia Quaker girl in 1856, a generation after the famous uncle's death; her own son was christened Bartram to keep the name going. I call William "Uncle" because, like me, he was unmarried and childless. Maybe I think of that nephew. Maybe I think of Bartram sitting by rivers, wondering what he was doing with his life.

He was the opposite, surely, of those undaunted go-getters, the Lewis and Clarks. Those epic victors. But even they faced failure later. Just three years after the glorious success, Merriwether Lewis—rebuffed by the government, unable to make headway on his journals, lost in opium and alcohol and depression—took his own life.

Whatever sweetness is in failure, it is a hard thing to come to. So hard it can kill.

Everyone has to find his or her own way, surely. Kinsmen, as Hawthorne pointed out, cannot help you. Yet I have always found that others have been there, wherever I ended up. Even— *especially*—in places of utter emptiness.

At the outset of his venture, Lewis wrote his eagerness to set off on the "never trodden" way West—then followed Indian paths and "roads" (his word) nearly all the way there. Muir wrote the same thing—used nearly the same word, seeking the "least trodden way" for his famous thousand-mile walk—but he ended up on roads and trails and farmers' paths. Same for Bartram ("not quite pathless," he quips). Our American fantasy of virgin wilderness strangely overlooks this fact: someone was there before you.

"Always coming home," says Le Guin. Behind her, you can just see Novalis, moving his mouth in just those words. We are always together, always alone in this difficult place, this least-trodden way—this crowded road to nothing. Always coming home, always leaving then returning again as if for the first time in human history.

That's the other paradox. If I don't sing the praises of failure, someone else will. It's not some virgin wilderness, "untrodden" until my heroic footstep. It's the place we've always been coming to.

Wild and familiar.

Ending It All

For thirty years now, the call has gone out: a new way is coming. Eco-prophets and nature saints, green radicals and scientists, New-Agers and politicians have written their books and inspired their followers on the hope of "a new way of thinking" about nature. They aim at nothing less than personal and global transformation—it has a deeply religious feeling and an optimistic ring. The Deep Ecology program continues to roll along in books by Fritjof Capra, Thomas Berry, Theodore Roszak, and too many others to count. Even Al Gore's eco book, summing it up for a political audience, issues the standard call: "The real solution will be found in reinventing and finally healing the relationship between civilization and the earth ... the key changes will involve new ways of thinking about the relationship itself."

And a new way of thinking, I keep hearing, needs a new myth. People need a metaphor, a picture, a story that will carry them into the new day a-comin'. It stands to reason. And so comes the plaintive call to poets and artists: find us a new myth, or make us one. Berry says the old story is "inadequate for meeting the survival demands" of the present, and hopes the "New Story" he offers might do the trick. David Orr calls for a change in "mythical symbols." I heard the call for a new myth at that Seattle book fair, and before that at a nature-writers' conclave in the Sierras, where the celebrated nature reporter Bill McKibben asked us point-blank to provide one. In environmental magazines I see books and workshops designed for ecological true believers determined to create a new myth, from old cloth or from whole cloth. Yet it seems that the change is always coming and never quite here. It's been a familiar refrain for a couple of decades now. We need a new myth, they say. But none has come because there's no opening: the spot is already filled. Paradise Lost is already there.

The quasi-religious call to transformed thinking sounds hopeful, but it casts a dark shadow: a cosmic warning of destruction. For Paradise Lost carries with it a plot-line that ends in earthly destruction. Apocalypse shows up as the last chapter of the Fall from Eden. The nature-as-Eden story, coasting of its own momentum from the Fall to the End of Days, subverts a lot of what the environmental movement wishes to accomplish, producing fear and alienation instead of a sense of belonging. We need a new myth, they say; I couldn't agree more. Yet calling for new myths and new ways of thinking has proven quite futile. One reason is the persistent, unexamined, and literalized myth that continues shaping our discourse.

Lynn White, Jr., was one of the earliest to sound the call for a comprehensive rethinking, in his much-reprinted 1967 article "The Historical Roots of Our Ecologic Crisis." His diagnosis was that Christianity was the culprit—its story of the fall, the culture of science and commerce it spawned, its human-centered system of values, and above all its stories. "We must rethink and refeel our nature and destiny." White understood that the imagination shapes human behavior, both the cultural systems of corporations and governments, and the acts of individuals. Our polluting ways are ultimately a product of worldview. He saw the need for radical change in our religious—that is, mythical—formulation of the world's story. I think he was right about that.

In the uproar of the times, others were quick to declare that this radical change was indeed coming—or had already arrived. Charles Reich's *The Greening of America* (1970) announced "the transformation that is coming" based on "organic principles" and "organic community"—nothing less than "a renewed relationship of man to himself … to nature, and to the land." Reich's depiction of the "coming American Revolution" cast a big net from Woodstock to love-ins and is easy to dismiss. But the book struck a chord that would be heard often in other environmental manifestos: the sense of impending change, of a world transformation in the making.

Over the next two decades countless books echoed this call for new thinking and a new myth. The famous "Club of Rome" report called *The Limits to Growth* (1972). Several books by Fritjof Capra (*The Turning Point* of 1982 and *The Web of Life* of 1996). The quintessential statement of green belief, Bill Devall's and George Sessions' *Deep Ecology* (1985). Each of them analyzes and critiques modern inductrial culture, and then makes the announcement of new thought coming. "This change is perhaps already in the air …" (Club of Rome), the "turning point" is here (Capra and Devall and Sessions), and a whole new way of conceiving the world is about to emerge. Of course this transformation will require not just policies but "new values" that will create "a new balance … between individuals, communities, and all of Nature" (Devall and Sessions). It seems to me that much of this analysis and admonition and advocacy is, well, Right On. Every one of these books sees some form of the same problem: the belief that humankind is separate from nature in all its variations: the "separation of fact from value," the famous split of knowing from feeling; the divorce of science from religion; alienating individualism and destructive consumerism; the ignoring of deeper and wider human connectedness to the living world.

But their alternatives are, one and all, inevitably coopted by the "back to nature" premise. The Paradise Lost narrative just gobbles them up. No new way of feeling, no new way of being in the world, no new myth emerges, despite the breathless announcements that it's almost here, it's happening, here it comes. It never does. We're left like Millerites on hilltops in our Deep Ecology bedsheets. Eden is still lost. And we are still to blame.

Because what's really emerging in these narratives is not "a new myth" but the last act of the old one: the apocalypse. The myth of the Beginning calls forth a symmetrical myth of the End, as the critic Frank Kermode has shown. If we began in union with the divine, we will end there too; and if sin caused our Fall, then our Rise must be preceded by a great fiery cleansing. Apocalypse is somehow needed to make sense of the story, the downward slope of decline answered by an upward movement, the return at last to Paradise. The ambiguity of "Paradise" had been there all along— the word is used for both beginning and end, both Eden and Heaven.

We have been living in between, in history, afflicted by change and loss, but hopeful of the New Day Coming.

Environmentalism has been addicted to apocalyptic predictions for a long time. The details vary. Eco-apocalypse may be overpopulation, pollution, resource depletion, loss of species diversity, deforestation, or global warming—the favored cause has drifted over the decades. The tone is consistently shrill and the intent is sincere as hell: the End is in sight, unless we repent. As the twentieth century waned, however, the preaching darkened; the battle might be already lost, the atmosphere fatally polluted, deforestation too far gone. Some analysts think that environmentalists wink when they use apocalyptic language, knowing that it's not quite true: that environmentalists tacitly believe that if the various ends of the world do not quite come, they are at least good motivators. So what if we really weren't "running out of oil" in the late 1970s? So what if world population didn't quite keep up with the scary projections? They were useful fictions serving a noble purpose.

Temporarily.

And then, of course, the backlash. That's where we're at now. Wolf was cried, attention was paid, and life went on with only the usual calamity. And now that there's definitive evidence of global warming, and a real, growing hole in the ozone layer, people are much more resistant to organized responses. They've heard it before; they are apathetic. Self-interested parties and corporate Republicans are positioned to play the wearied public for chumps with pseudo-scientific niggling. I don't think the environmental community is actually so Machiavellian as to intentionally mislead. I think these eco-apocalyptic voices are in earnest, but mistaken. Paradise-Lost thinking—all-or-nothing, impending loss, repent or else—has distorted their sense of nature.

I think we can do better. We need the same fervor, but a different story. Or an Eden, at the very least, that never turns apocalyptic.

Many of these Calls and announcements reveal their quasi-religious nature in using a funny kind of diction that folds time-future into time-present. It's a prophet's way of saying that the great day is already here, at least in essence, that its seeds are planted and growing no matter how slight or hard to find. When the Jesus of the Gospels told his listeners that the kingdom of God was already here, he used just this kind of elusive time: "Behold the time is coming, and now is ..." The whispers, hopes, and hints in eco-texts use the same device (called the "proleptic"). It's coming, it's here, it will change the world. A popular fable in environmental circles in the 1990s was called "The Hundredth Monkey," which illustrated how a single person's awakening could provide the critical mass for widespread change. The other 99 monkeys were in a state of proleptic readiness: they contained the future but didn't know it. It took the hundredth monkey to precipitate the change. Al Gore's book casts the same idea in terms of a physical metaphor. Our global readiness for change, he says, is like a sandpile at the point of "criticality," when a single dropped sand grain may trigger a reorganization of the entire pile. The point is simply to see the world as pregnant with change, poised proleptically with the future invisibly infused into the present.

This rhetoric of prophecy ought to remind us that beneath all the analysis, politics, and ecology—most of which I agree with deeply—these are statements about "how the world works," what its underlying story is, its myth. Prophecy announces turning points in the accepted myth-story: *Repent or God will* ... In this case, there are two Big Changes announced. One is the end of nature in a destructive inferno. The other is the new way of thinking, which gives the spiritual retort to that destruction, providing the upward direction for a whole new story beyond the End.

Repentance—thinking in that new way—introduces an interesting alternative to the End which Carolyn Merchant labels a "restoration narrative." Could the decline be reversed *before* it's too late? Belief in progress seems to reverse the loss-and-decline plot; progress is optimistic, upward-trending. In fact, Protestants in America and England have fought for well over a century over this question. How much social optimism is justified? Can sinful human nature be reformed, short of the millennium? In general, the pessimists have won out; so-called "liberal" denominations who believe in a present-day amelioration of sin are steeply outnumbered by conservative evangelicals who emphasize ineradicable Original Sin. With a literal belief in the Fall, conservatives hold that transformation can only be personal; apocalypse is the cosmic destiny. As is abundantly clear to anyone who has sat through a fire-and-brimstone sermon, the seeming contradictions of repentance and apocalypse actually coexist quite nicely. The flail of a fiery general punishment is a time-honored device to spur individuals to personal transformation: but the overall plot heads inevitably toward destruction. The world, the world, wails the preacher—, is lost and consigned to its fate. The plot of Eden requires it.

The irony, then, is that in calling for a "new myth" before it's too late, environmentalism may be simply playing out the old myth, ratcheting it up to its climactic phase. The timeline of Paradise Lost is downhill all the way to the fiery end. After the end, there's a New Heaven and a New Earth, which prophets announce. But we don't get to live there, except proleptically. Meanwhile, all around us, the world prepares for the flame.

There's a book on my shelf—I just fetched it down again— that took me years to read. Or more accurately, to *begin* to read. I bought it, I avoided it. I winced every time I read the title, and I put it off for another day. It's Bill McKibben's much-noticed *The End of Nature.* It afflicted me with more than mere procrastination: I dreaded that it would take me someplace I simply did not have the strength to go.

Let's call that "someplace" the Nature Problem, humanity's comprehensive cosmic failing. I felt unequal to its challenge, same as other citizens who routinely avoid thinking about global warming or loss of species. I wasn't sure exactly how nature could be ending, but it sounded bad, it sounded hopeless. I went for a hike instead.

What I found in hiking, in walking around the block—or even, as I said in the first chapter, looking at the palm of my hand or closing my eyes to dream—was that nature wasn't over yet. Wildness abounded, and in fact could hardly be constrained. That same poet Hopkins who eulogized his fallen poplars with such lost-Eden eloquence in another mood expressed this contrariwise inexhaustibility of the created world:

And for all that, nature is never spent
There lives the dearest freshness deep down things

Thus strengthened, I faced the end of nature. And found that the end is not yet, not by a country mile.

McKibben's thesis is a little slippery. Most of the time it goes this way: we have crossed a threshold and lost our old sense of "nature" forever. Because we have comprehensively meddled in nature, warming the global temperature and manipulating the gene codes of animals and plants, we have shifted from being one of many creatures to being the masters of the world.

"This new rupture with nature is different not only in scope but also in kind." Until now "nature" was a superior reality; henceforth, our new-found powers have placed us above it. Now our every breath draws in an atmosphere that has been industrially altered. Now every wilderness is a set-aside, defined by people. Now there's no corner of the globe, no natural process, not even any cell that might not be touched by human actions.

> *Nature, independent nature, is already ending.*
> *[W]e have ended the thing that has, at least in modern times, defined nature for us—its separation from human society.*

In various metaphors throughout the book, the author presents formerly independent nature as a reduced thing, managed and tainted: a park, a zoo, a ride, a greenhouse, a shopping mall. Human actions are now "altering every inch and every hour of the globe."

Occasionally McKibben refines this thesis: he recognizes (in passing) a difference between altering nature and controlling it. "Simply because it bears our mark doesn't mean we can control it." But this insight, which significantly undercuts his thesis, soon disappears. On the whole he depicts a nature thoroughly controlled by humans.

But if control is really not ours, then to what extent has anything essential changed? Haven't humans, like other animals, been altering, changing, influencing the environment since … well, virtually since forever? Isn't "nature" in fact a coevolved system? Don't we circle nature in that paradox of oneness and twoness, that figure-ground relation Alan Watts playfully describes, wherein your skin is equally *your outer edge* and the *inner edge of everything else*—simultaneously? The very atmosphere we breathe was created by generations of aerobic bacteria followed by generations of larger oxygen-breathers. Wherever life has existed, its push-pull with the environment has shaped *both* the environment and itself, and does so still. Animals that eat seeds find the seeds using their guts as transport systems. It's not a question of control. It's a question of interaction.

So the old lost-Eden lament—that nature wears our mark and bears our smudge—is deeply mistaken. We are all, from the inception, marked and mingled. This coevolution is another of the many names for the paradox of life: deep patterning that produces complexity. Another name for wildness.

McKibben's thesis has a second stage in which the question of human control intensifies: genetic engineering, the "second end of nature." "It is the simple act of creating new forms of life that changes the world, that puts us forever in the deity business. We will never again be a created being; instead we will be creators." The language is telling. We become godlike, just as the Genesis deity feared—and from the same cause: knowledge. In the Biblical story, God sets two trees in the garden and forbids both. One is the Tree of the Knowledge of Good and Evil. The other is the Tree of Life. Adam and Eve gain godlike knowledge ("ye shall be as gods, knowing good and evil"), but at the price of mortality ("in the day that thou eatest thereof, thou shalt surely die"). They are cast out of Eden not merely for punishment but for fear they should gain the other half of divinity, everlasting life—from that other tree—and thus become rivals to Yahweh. It's a rollicking good tale, with self-serving deities (curiously plural) fearfully protecting their turf against upstart humans. And it ends with a good story's ironic twist: the origin story leaves us godlike in mind but trapped in mortal bodies. "Behold the man is become as one of us"—and thus must die, says Yahweh. Knowledge proves paradoxical: powerful yet fatal.

So McKibben's fear of human knowledge is not novel, though genetic engineering seems pretty new. New knowledge is almost always, from a conservative religious and cultural perspective, impious, scary, and disruptive to order; we think of old battles, the Church silencing Galileo and Copernicus, Fundamentalists driving evolution from Tennessee schoolrooms in the 1920s and Kansas schoolrooms in the 1990s. Traditional societies usually view change as heresy; in our guts, so do we. But we've been manipulating genes indirectly for millennia, through selective breeding. Darwin's famous first book took considerable pains to illustrate that selective breeding had been altering species for a long, long time. He saw that human-managed breeding was really just slow-motion creation, exactly like evolution through natural selection.

What McKibben banners as a terrible shift, a change in kind, is really another step in a very long chain of human cultural adaptation. Perhaps it is a step too far; that would be worth discussing. But we won't discuss it at all goaded by fearful language like this: the villagers with torches and pitchforks are mobbing up the mental courtyard.

Such scientific overreaching as gene-splicing really sounds more like Faust than Adam. The Faust story is, in a sense, the Fall written into modern form. (And Frankenstein is, in its turn, the pop-culture rewrite.) How shall knowledge tempt and corrupt us? What pact shall we make with the devil to get it? Or how shall we resist it? As our powers have grown, so have our misgivings. As I researched some deep background in the sciences, I came across a college biology textbook of the 1930s. It struggled with the forward edge of knowledge about physiology at that time, fearing that as the brain and nervous system were understood, something like the soul was being approached—too closely. How, exactly, does "a nerve impulse" deliver information and feeling? "Here is a veil which can never be rent by mortal man," the textbook solemnly chants, as if led by high priests. In retrospect, such pious veil-drawing seems quaint. Neurology has long since passed this limit, and many more; the world has not ended; there is still an infinite complexity of mystery before us, undiminished. Though our knowledge increases, mystery never diminishes. There is no less to know about the body and the world now than when we started. Ask any medical researcher, any scientist: the depth of living complexity is literally unfathomable, the breadth of the physical world still inconceivable. Yet we still carry the old fears that knowledge is about to catapult us into a dire transgression of some divinely ordained limit.

Faust is often regarded as the defining myth of our industrial/ scientific times, the model of our pell-mell pursuit of power and knowledge. If the Genesis god(s) feared that humans, in possession of knowledge, would become gods too, Faust achieves that godlike power: in Goethe's version, his first act is to separate dry land from the sea through an engineering feat of pumps and dikes. Is this a noble imitation, or a demonic parody, of the Genesis act of creation? Is it good or evil? Goethe keeps it interesting in its ambiguity. Faust does good with his powers. Mostly.

Goethe shows that we do not necessarily have to buy in to these old story lines. What are we, without knowlege, culture, ways of surviving? Can we even be human without them? There is no teasing these elements apart. As I have pointed out, Indians and other non-Europeans who were once seen as simple children of nature really have complex, deeply developed cultural knowledges about the world. And as far back as we can see, our forebears must have been accumulating this culture, this knowledge, this nature. There is no simple, blank, happy savage that constitutes the "Adam" of essential humanity in our nature. We and our genes and our social webs and our knowledge of how to live are all, together, what have survived over the ages. That's what natural selection has recognized as human; that's the unit of survival.

Though there's a useful truth in seeing that a stinger usually follows each of our bright new powers, the Faust story as it is usually remembered perpetuates a dangerous and deep-seated belief that we and our civilization are projections of sin, dragging down the world. As an expression of fear, it may hinder as much as it helps. Few of our eco-writers explore the question as Goethe did. Mostly, they just repeat the old story in its Frankenstein boots.

When McKibben wishes we could "choose to remain God's creatures instead of making ourselves gods," he's locating us in the Eden story with surprising naiveté. Every part of the Genesis story is present in his account: Our knowledge and power exceed proper limits. We become godlike. This is sin. The result is exile from Eden. "We have built a greenhouse, *a human creation*, where there bloomed a sweet and wild garden."

From McKibben's garden we're exiled forever: "its ending prevent[s] us from returning to the world we previously knew..." An irremediable sin pushes us into the one-way decline of ordinary human time. Meanwhile McKibben's unfallen nature-as-Eden is unchanging and outside of ordinary time. Since humanity is defined as unnatural and sinful, our presence ruins paradise. Now "a walk in the woods will be changed—tainted" because it bears a hint or reminder of humanity.

This is my own oddly un-self-aware attitude I reported early in this book: how in the high mountains, somehow I always resented coming across another hiker. It was as if I were trying hard to sustain an illusion, and it had been burst by an unwelcome reality. What that reality was I would not consider; I just headed higher and tried to relocate my Eden. I wondered, in some remote valley, if my foot could have been the first to touch it (a foolish unlikelihood). Sinless Adams in imaginary paradises.

McKibben repeats all this first-footsteps virgin-wilderness business—it's a good way to illustrate what we've "lost." So he imagines William Bartram in the 1770s "discovering" new plants in an "untouched world" along the Broad River, though Cherokee by the tens of thousands had been fingering the place for centuries, and they surely knew many of the plants Bartram "discovered." Strange, isn't it? Even a smart guy like McKibben—or a bearded smarty-pants like me at twenty-five—cannot bear to give up the Eden of our imagining. Bartram merely hiked a few miles up the Broad River from the settlement called Fort Charlotte, "on the opposite side of the river Savanna, and about a mile from fort James." Twenty miles downstream he would later stay in a prosperous farmer's "mansion house." Indian traders were passing regularly through the forts. The Cherokee lived in populous towns and tended their extensive fields of squash and corn. The place was bustling! And though Bartram found lovely, unmarred, exquisite places, his "little botanical excursions" up the Broad were not so different, in form, from our hikes today: he must search out his Edens, and they are bordered by webs of human settlement and communication, paths, roads, and navigated rivers. He leaves a populated place and wanders into unused or little-used nooks, and enjoys them. Same as we do. Though they are probably not "untouched," they look it.

Bartram in the Garden of Eden of America—now long lost to us in the great backward of nostalgia: history transforming into myth. The American Eden is a potent fantasy which we are loathe to give up. I don't know if shining the spotlight on it, as I wish to do, will dispel the illusion. Perhaps.

McKibben seems to sense that the Eden story is somewhere in all this, for he quotes *Paradise Lost* on the last pages. But without Milton's faith in the redemption at the center of the story, all McKibben can end with is fear: that we've arrived at the point (in the story) where "original sin" finally becomes "terminal sin."

So there we are at the end of the Eden narrative: apocalypse. The end of everything. The beginning of something new and frankly terrifying. "The change from five billion years of nature to year one of artifice." "The Year One," as used by French revolutionaries to describe their new beginning: apocalypse, millennium, tribulation, who knows. The old world rolled up like a scroll, a new heaven and a new earth, or else the rampages of the Beast. McKibben transliterates the old story line from Genesis to Revelation with surprising exactness, taking us from the Garden to the End of Nature, with a fearful look into the dark unimaginable that comes after that.

What McKibben's book calls the "end of nature" is (as he admits) really just the end of *an idea of nature*. McKibben means to mourn something cosmic: that we have changed our existential relation to nature. But what he's really mourning is a good deal less, and in fact something to which I say good riddance: that old Western formulation of the human as separate from nature. McKibben writes, "When I say 'nature,' I mean a certain set of human ideas about the world and our place in it ... finally, our sense of nature as eternal and separate is washed away." Yes, we've lost our separation. We can no longer think of ourselves *sui generis*, our actions impervious and nature immune. That's gone, baby. That "feeling"—*that's* the nature that's ending. Not nature out there, but a fable of nature that we've cultivated and enjoyed. A rather shopworn fable, you'd think, by now. Its elements are: no people + no change = Eden/Nature. That's just not a good picture of nature. Its corollary is: humans are therefore other-than-nature. And that's just not a good picture of humanity, either.

Loss of a myth is, in fact, a serious thing. But it should not be overplayed. Nature is not ending. It's going on as always.

What McKibben mourns is not even an idea of who's in control of nature, though as I've said much of his language suggests it. But that idea collapses: we have altered stuff but can't really control it, not in any comprehensive way. So what does that leave?

That we have sullied Eden. That nature bears our mark and our smell, and we can no longer pretend otherwise. That humans are part of the entire world, and it part of us; that our separation is (in his terms) "ended." But that, my dear and faithful Reader, is the nub of the illusion. To sully is to soil with that which is dirty and alien. And we are not dirty and alien on this planet. We belong here. My footprint on the shore is not less behovely than a sandpiper's. My patterns are not less interesting. Though they are problematical: but McKibben mistakes the problem. Or problems.

"Instead of being a category like God—something beyond our control—it [the nature problem] is now a category like the defense budget or the minimum wage, a problem we must work out." Then let us work out the problems, as we always have! How to find food. How to kill things and eat them. How to keep from being eaten. What to do when it doesn't rain. How to keep the rats out, the warmth in, the fields and forests and children healthy. Problems. Nature problems.

But not THE NATURE PROBLEM. As I've been saying, the hypostatized, existential Big Problem is a wrong turn.

Last night was a clear one in Portland. In the middle of March that's a treat in these beclouded lands, and I took a moony walk to enjoy it all. There were three big planets up, and the whole thing worked its reliable magic on me. In the dark, beside houses I couldn't afford, I peered up at the sky through American elms we've managed to save: peeping glimpses of the sempiternal with faint door slams and city echoes in the mix. Who are we? I wondered. Do we make our lives beautiful enough for such an overarch of beauty? The works of our hands, our mistakes and necessary evils and glorious deeds—they are small in this perspective. And this, interestingly, is where McKibben takes his readers, at last, on the very last page. He looks up into the night sky, he sees the extent, the incomprehensibility, the mystery. The way he does it, it's very thin solace: we're gods now and have taken over nature, so these midnight moments don't really help that much.

But I'd suggest that's where we should start (not end), and work from there to where we live. Because we don't need the false emotion of loss that McKibben's title generates. That elegaic tone—can we dump it please? Of course McKibben feels it too, that depression, that angst that kept me from picking up his book for so long. He records his pessimism, his fading hope. The end of nature, he admits, "depresses me more deeply than I can say." But let me repeat: what he's lost is the story. Not nature, but a deeply-ingrained narrative pattern of sin and loss and exile.

It is wrenching to face the end of your myth. But we can do it: we can live without Lost Eden.

When environmental rhetoricians see nature as an Eden that we're ruining, and use apocalypse to depict where it is all leading, they are diverting attention from the present moment and the real task: they are sleepwalking through a narrative that's built in to the culture. As Thoreau's famous book has it, it's time to wake up.

Walt Whitman had heard his share of this talk, good-old-days and end-of-days, even a century and a half ago. He turned his back on it, and walked into a world that was fresh as Eden every single day, even in the clamorous midst of New York City. That's the trick.

> *I have heard what the talkers were talking, the talk of the*
> *   beginning and the end.*
> *But I do not talk of the beginning or the end.*
> *. . . .*
> *There was never any more inception than there is now,*
> *Nor any more youth or age than there is now,*
> *And will never be any more perfection than there is now,*
> *Nor any more heaven or hell than there is now.*

Whitman is not usually regarded as a nature poet—such a city boy—but there it is, as pure and unsullied as on a mountain peak. Thoreau made the same point, if you'd like it from the unimpeachable: "Men esteem truth remote, in the outskirts of the system, behind the farthest star, before Adam and after the last man. ... But all these times and places and occasions are now and here. God himself culminates in the present moment, and will never be more divine in the lapse of all the ages."

What I want is a better quality of stillness. Not an imagined surcease somewhere past the margins of time; but a stillness that answers the change that boils around us daily, hourly. Paradox: to become still, we must relinquish ourselves to the coursing changeableness of life. Do you know what I mean? I'm not making this up. It's the testimony of the ages, always whispering and always ignored, Lau Tzu, Epictetus, Blake: *In the dangerous element immerse.* Stop trying to hold what cannot be held, stop fearing suffering, stop longing for what's past. We yield to the inevitabilities, and suddenly are at peace with them, at rest within the wild and unimaginable moment.

The right quality of stillness is not available until we exit the lost world and enter instead this real one, so shot through with mystery, divinity, completeness. It is quite true we do not stay for long in that stillness, that completeness. We are shuttles, migrants, we hunt along the edges of things restlessly ... and then rest for a little.

We need the rest; we have work to do (and undo). A lot of hard bargains to drive with ourselves, figuring out what to keep and what to change, when to cut, when to dam, when to leave well enough alone. Good work for ordinary people who belong here and nowhere else—people who are not exiles, not fallen, not pure, not cursed, not mourning for a place that never was.

Dealing with Paradise

My friend the Famous Environmentalist likes to call civilization "syphilization." He got that phrase from Ed Abbey, and I used to like it, a long time ago. My friend was a damn good climber; I was a so-so mountaineer part of the year, a graduate student the rest. And young enough to believe that somehow IT—civilization—was not ME. I should have known better.

And so should Ed Abbey, and so should the rest of them. The ideas in our heads, as we tramped the woods, were civilized ideas. We were expressions of our culture. Middle-class America had not only sent us there but swaddled us in Gore-tex and poly-fleece, assured us of freeze-dried food and nylon shelter, zippered and pocketed and mosquito-netted us to the point of luxury. And of course gave us those maps and trails. We were about as far from "syphilization" as from thinking in English.

So … we must have been little flecks of contaminant, right? Little syphil-hikers, bringing the disease of humanity where it did not belong?

Well, we never thought so. Clearly, the fun of snotty anti-civilization language is *not* to go to that level of analysis, but to hold on to the pretense of separation from culture. Of course it appealed to us in our twenties because it made us other, different, superior. That's a pretty common bit of vanity.

And there's some value in the delusion, I think, because by offering a separate standpoint it does open up a critique of culture. Famous Environmentalist went on to do some real good in the world, standing there. But: we need to learn how to stand there in truth. That would mean dropping a lot of rhetoric, a lot of pose. That would mean changing the critique.

Because hating civilization amounts to self-hatred, suppressed and directed outward at a scapegoat: two kinds of lying I cannot live with. "Myself am Hell," intones the Satan of *Paradise Lost.*

"Myself am civilization," I want to say back, devilishly. We all go home from enviro-meetings in our cars, pickups, or somewhat post-neolithic bicycles. We eat food that has cost the planet its toll of erosion, petrochemicals, pollution. We write our protests on paper, God help us. This very page you're reading—there's a clearcut somewhere, and one particular point within it, where the wood fibers between your fingers originated. That's a gap in the world now.

But that's an idea in your head now, too.

So is this a one-way trip to clearcut hell, or a nice eco-cycle passing the natural world through your fingers, your mind, and then back into the world again? And if so, is that a deal you're willing to make?

What would it be like to live in the world, in my skin, in my species, without pretense and without fictive separations? To know how to make or not make deals like that? Nature writers of the hundred years since Muir have explored the question repeatedly, beautifully, deeply. They have understood that we and the trees share a common fate, a common flesh. That's a lot.

But they have too often veered into the dead-end language of Paradise Lost. When the rhetoric of Lost Eden shows up, as it does in classics like Muir and Abbey and lots of recent environmentalist writing and politicking, it pretty much squelches the possibilities for grounded choices, for practical spirituality. For knowing when to keep the tree and when to make it into something else. That's the real work (in Gary Snyder's phrase): smutting along in the world, glorying along in it, growing roses from our dungheaps and dungheaps from our roses. This work takes passion, energy, humility, and perhaps humor. Willingness to try, to get soiled; to compromise, learn, improve.

But these traits we cannot find when we are loaded down with post-Edenic guilt and pessimism. These leave us either in a state of environmental denial, too exhausted from crisis-overload to pay attention; or whipped up into Puritan absolutism, searching for purity in the form of fantasy wildernesses and defeatist politics. "Apathy and dogmatism," in the terms of James D. Proctor's searching analysis of the forest debate. Neither response works very well in the world we actually live in, which generally isn't about purity but is ready to reward attentiveness bountifully.

◎

Here on my desk is the latest publication from the Native Forest Council, a Eugene, Oregon, outfit that fights for wilderness. Its front cover asks the Paradise-Lost question in a typeface of scary dimension:

> *Forever Lost?*
> *or Forever Wild?*

Reader, if you're seeing things with my eyes by now, it's pretty clear to you that framing the question this way places it in a mistaken cosmic context. Questions about how to live with and in the forest become battles of moral warfare on a par with eating that original apple. One false move screws it up "forever."

Nature is curiously precarious, in this view. The reason for that is not anything about nature, which of course is very far from delicate and which is renewing itself constantly, in turn with tearing itself up constantly. But when Eden is relocated into a real-time place—the woods—then it is invested with a falsely heightened emotion, this white-knuckled preparation for grieving. The many in-between possibilities of slightly imperfect, grimy, self-healing natural places do not exist. It's either-or. Pure or ruined. Virgin or whore.

Inside the publication is a familiar graphic: three maps of the US, showing the supposed state of the forests in 1620, 1850, and the present. On the first, everything east of the Mississippi, and most of the Pacific coast as well, is depicted in flawless inky black, meaning primeval forest. On the present-day map almost nothing is left, a pathetic spritzing of dots and commas. The recycled version I'm looking at was published in spring of 2000, but the graphic is the identical one used by the Forest Council ten years earlier, where the inky lands were labelled "the original, untouched forests that existed when the first settlers arrived in North America." In the present-day map, almost no "virgin forests" (their original words) are left—just those forlorn specks. "Only five percent is left," by their analysis.

In fact, this graphic has an interesting history. It debuted some sixty-five years before the Forest Council picked it up, appearing in

1925 in the lead article of the very first issue of the journal *Economic Geography*. There, the Chief of the U.S. Forest Service, W. B. Greeley, documents the decline of the primeval American forest, calling it "a vast virgin forest" which had "scarcely been touched by man." But as we have seen, this description falls somewhere between fallacy and fantasy. So it is interesting that these depictions have remained so completely immune to change. The deep analysis and critique of the last decade have hardly registered. The Native Forest Council has had the sense to remove labels like "virgin forest," but the underlying mythology is, as they might say, *untouched*.

Why?

One answer is that a good, clear contrast is seen as essential to the public-relations campaign. Maybe academic hair-splitting about nuances of language misses the point. These guys are out there getting something done, making places where people like me can go for hikes and see forests instead clearcuts. Perhaps this good work requires, well, very clearcut language.

We've been hearing for some time now about "compassion fatigue." The public is held to be worn out with good causes, including environmentalism: our good intentions aren't equal to the massive bad news, the ravaged Amazonian forests, the species that wink out like stars we've never even looked at, the feverish planet-sickness of warming. What can mere mortals do? We respond with shrugs, fatigue, apathy—"overwhelmed by the magnitude of the issues" as one educator put it, describing her students. Problems that are too big, too abstract, and too complex seldom come to the point of urgency; we're likely to give them mostly lip service. That roughly sums up environmental public opinion and feeling as described in the 1995 study *Unpassionate Environmentalism: Attitudes Toward the Environment*. "Today Americans remain committed to the goal of protecting and improving the environment, but they no longer see an urgent problem. ... They are not inclined to take many additional steps—certainly not costly ones—to improve the environment." No mandate, no energy, no mobilization. We've been working on the public for thirty or forty years now. Why have we moved this rock such a short distance?

The seeming abstractness of global problems, their scale and remoteness, may be one cause of such apathy. Susan D. Moeller, author of the 1998 book *Compassion Fatigue,* has chronicled the public's continuing inability to respond to images of suffering on a mass scale. It seems that without effective context, reports of disaster and suffering generally do not move people. Swollen-bellied children on the other side of the globe come to us not as real people but as elements in an emotionally incomprehensible morass—what Susan Sontag labels "excessive or organic ill." We need some way to measure the dimensions of disaster against a human scale we recognize.

It's not hard to extend the point to environmental problems. What, exactly, is the meaning of an insect species that disappears, when we've never seen it and couldn't find its former home on a map? What is ozone, anyway; and what's the difference between a *huge* ozone hole, and a *colossally huge* one? Or how should we respond to that very symbol of incomprehensibility, the jungle (renamed "the rain forest"), when it's imagined, in our part of the world, as either a steaming labyrinth or a hellish red-earth rape zone of hemispheric proportions? On an emotional level, it's overwhelming; intellectually, it's an abstraction. A huge weird catastrophe happening somewhere that's nothing like here. Denial or apathy (both tinged with guilty feelings) are the likeliest human responses.

Along with the abstractness of global problems, their complexity can defy our attempts to find an understandable political or moral response.

Even the smallest natural system displays an astonishing complexity, a kind of fractal infinity from the smallest details of the cell outwards to the global level, each level of magnitude carrying interconnectedness and subtlety that defy simple analysis. A close friend of mine has worked in hematological (blood) research for about twenty years. When I ask him about complexity, he shakes his head. "Everything you look at, each protein or enzyme, can have multiple functions, behaving differently in different cells and systems, responding and stimulating in ways we haven't begun to trace. We just spent a couple years studying the enzymes involved in a cell's self-destruct instruction. Just to understand this one fairly basic function, you have to look at a mind-boggling array of variables. Tease them out, one by one." He shakes his head again. And this is just one interaction, of the thousands or—who knows?—

hundreds of thousands a single cell performs. Each of them linked in a web of sending and receiving with other cells and systems, each pulse nudging, influencing, shaping the outcome.

And it appears that most of the living world is organized this way. Cells. Bodies. Species. Ecosystems. Maybe even biospheres.

In such a situation, what is crucial and what is trivial are very hard to distinguish. Which interaction is the indispensible one? We have trouble modeling tomorrow's weather; it's a mighty guess to say what the climate might be doing as a whole. Or which species loss might be the critical mistake. We just don't know, in any conventional sense of certainty. Yet we do come to understand certain crucial, even mortally crucial, facts: the planet is warming. Greenhouse gasses are contributing. But even then, the complexity from which this knowledge arises stymies our ability to mobilize social concern. As William Cronon points out, the science in this case is necessarily a complex guess or reconstruction, a kind of virtual reality, that deprives it of simple empirical authority.

This real complexity, and the sophistication of thought it requires, make for distressingly easy targets for those of ill will to muddle and obfuscate. Throughout the decade, the impact of scientific consensus on issues like global warming has been blunted by minority opinions that made them seem open to question, even as the issues, in a practical sense, became clear. National and local news and commentary colluded with the muddlers by giving equal weight to both sides of every issue, even where one side is an insignificant or discredited view. It's a freshman's idea of objectivity, as if judgement and perception were not part of the journalist's job. One crank scientist or paid lackey is thus empowered to counterbalance an entire scientific consensus. And of course, interested parties also conduct PR campaigns outside of journalistic channels, employing mixtures of lies, half-truths, and obscurantism. For example: "The Competitive Enterprise Institute, which is heavily funded by oil companies, states in one radio ad that 'Thousands of scientists agree there's no solid evidence of a global warming problem.'" Meanwhile the "Global Climate Information Project," funded by the U.S. Chamber of Commerce and the National Association of Manufacturers, pursues a $13-million ad campaign against a global-warming treaty.

The desired result: more shrugs from the public. Complexity, phony or real, blunts the moral clarity that makes political response possible. Jedediah Purdy, author of a popular analysis of "Irony, Trust and Commitment," has commented that the environmental movement does best when it is presented as "an uncompromised position, the kind the culture dimly remembers from the civil rights era." But as Proctor points out, moral judgements in the environmental field are seldom so easy or onesided. The "pure stance" Purdy says is most effective simply is not an option in many aspects of, for instance, the ancient forests debate. And where there is a clear call of action indicated, as in global warming, the white noise of complexity makes it very hard to hear. The situation leads to two kinds of response: apathy for most, as we have seen, and a stubborn dogmatism for an activist few.

The Native Forest Council's answer to questions of forest policy is called "Zero Cut: No More Compromises." That illustrates quite nicely the moral absolutism that has come to plague parts of the environmental movement. My fellow Oregonian James D. Proctor observes that while the public at large seems mired in that state of apathy, the two sides in the timber/old-growth campaigns are locked into "moral dogmatism." "[M]any environmentalists assert ... that our duties to nature are nonnegotiable." "No compromise in defense of Mother Earth!" says Earth First!, in a telling multiplication of exclamation points.

I'd say that both attitudes are structured into the debate by its Paradise Lost framework. On the one side, moral dogmatism flourishes in its either-or world. And on the other, apathy is a predictable response to the moral exhaustion of a losing battle. Paradise is, after all, bound to be lost: let's go to a movie.

Meanwhile, the Weyerhaeusers of the world are concerned exclusively to turn out timber profits. Their rapaciousness is innate—as Thoreau pointed out, "A joint-stock company has no soul." For a corporation with salaries to pay, debts to service, and stockholders to satisfy, profit is existence; all else is PR. It's not a new reality, though. A truculent sawmill owner of 1876, probably responding to rising criticism generated by George Perkins Marsh's classic indictment *Man and Nature* revealed his true motivations with refreshing (if scary) bluntness: "You have scolded the lumber-men for cutting so much timber ... now quit scolding us for trying to live ... When we are out of timber, then we will curtail, but until that day, never so help us, Moses!" He was only being a little more honest than our corporate contemporaries.

Our timber guys have had almost a century and a half to learn the same lessons of overcutting, with all the busted, abandoned timber towns, eroded hillsides, and silted-up streams that follow. But experience and knowledge have made no difference at all. The graph of timber harvesting after the Second World War rises on a fighter-jet trajectory, peaking out (according to figures from the USDA) in 1972 at levels twelve times—1200 percent——those of the first half of the century. A dip in this astonishing increase occurs in the 1970s, corresponding to environmentalism's first big heyday and a few years of economic stagnation. But then the Reagan years arrive, official hindrances are removed, and the timber cut of the 1980s soars past even the previous unprecedented levels, to heights unsustainable by any possible measure. "America did not *conserve* its way to greatness," Candidate Reagan had growled. "It *produced* its way to greatness!" A timber orgy ensued, delivering trees on public lands to private corporations at prices so far below cost that the public treasury lost hundreds of millions per year—in 1992 amounting to about a quarter-billion dollars, according to a comprehensive study undertaken by the Wilderness Society and delivered in testimony to Congress. We should have seen it coming.

Not surprisingly, logging on such a scale of greed and rapacity inevitably feeds its own backlash: environmental absolutism. Let's stop the bastards wherever we can. Which then magnifies its own opposite, in an infernal cycle. Virgin-forest finds Plundered-whore in the mirror, world apparently without end. Or until the last stump is danced upon.

The back-and-forth opposition of no-cut, go-cut seems a weary battle of people talking past each other, people whose sense of the world is so different that they don't make sense to each other. Proctor points out that the environmentalist "Ancient forest campaign" relies on a view of forests as refuges from change: resilient and stable *if untouched*. This view supports the notion that the human role is, "simply leave them be ... people should not intervene in nature." Obviously, "nature" here means nature-as-wilderness. There's that dualism again. Nature is in the preserve; whatever's outside it is impure, fallen, human, syphilized. William Ashworth's recent book explores this duality with wonderful perceptiveness: "Preservation and utility are opposite sides of the same coin, distinct but inseparable ... Utility is now linked with destruction, as if to use something you had to despoil it. Preservation is linked with purity, as if to preserve something you had to hermetically seal it. To follow that model is to create a world split equally between toxic waste dumps and museums. And there is not a whole lot of life in either place."

Michael Pollan was an early critic of this "peculiarly narrow" vision that has lots to say about "pure wilderness" but little or nothing to say about the rest of the planet. "[W]e have divided our country in two, between the kingdom of wilderness, which rules about eight percent of America's land, and the kingdom of the market, which rules the rest."

Though the "no compromise" absolutism of some environmentalists draws its emotional life from the mythic narrative of Eden (the melodrama of threatened purity), the resulting black-and-white reading of the political battle leads, in the day-to-day sense, to a polarized politics in which gaming and one-upping seem to take over. Winning at any cost seems enough, when you define your opponent as Evil and yourself as the emissary of uncompromised Good. And of course, this attitude too calls forth the same from the opponents.

If the business of logging believes that its opponents wish to prevent harvesting timber anywhere, ever, for any reason, then perhaps it is not surprising if the questionable genie of environmental absolutism calls forth its mirror twin. Not trusting that a compromise is ever coming, logging operatives like Senator Slade Gorton of Washington slip outrages like the Salvage Rider into public policy. The polarized politics of good and evil produce terrible public policy.

The famous Salvage Rider (with its weirdly apocalyptic name) was a measure tacked onto another bill, apparently without the Clinton administration's negotiators realizing it, that permitted harvesting of six hundred million board feet of timber in the

Northwest alone, mostly old-growth, and specifically insulating the timber sales from any environmental oversight or legal challenge. But, once its mistake was realized, the Clinton White House declined to veto it. Congressional Republicans then insisted on a increasing the eighteen-month harvest from the Forest Service's recommended 1.5 billion board feet, to a colossal 4.5 billion board feet overall. Gorton was heard to mock the bamboozled negotiators as having "just fallen off the turnip truck," as if the fun was in outgaming your opponents. One wonders how far the question of whether the right thing had been done concerned him. Maybe—on a hopeful note—that sour extremism contributed to his narrow defeat in the year the environmentalist candidate for president was also defeated. Or outgamed.

When I look at the politics of the environment, perhaps with Weyerhaeuser in mind, and the Salvage Rider, and the utter rejection of presidential candidate Al Gore by small-town America, I see the missed opportunity of the last ten years: our failure—I include myself—our failure, in the environmental movement, to make common cause with working men and women. Or even to try. In our default, corporate Republicans have worked that old Reagan-era lie, convincing loggers and truck-drivers and mill-workers and all their families and neighbors that the corporations and big-money Republicans were on their side, against the environmentalists.

How in the world did they make this absurd proposition stick? It's been a slick campaign that has kept workers thinking that a slowdown in cutting to sustainable levels represents the long-term threat to their livelihoods, rather than the real threat of overcutting followed by inevitable lay-offs. Logging families have been losing their jobs to the boom-and-bust pattern of overcutting for a long time. W. B. Greeley sketched the familiar story in 1925: "The idleness of cutover land, following the migration of the sawmills, has already been a widespread cause of depopulation, decline in taxable values, and general rural bankruptcy. In the busiest timber manufacturing regions of a few decades ago, there remain today over 80 million acres of practically unproductive and unused land. No country can afford such wastage."

But there's not much counter-pressure from environmentalists to remind workers about this side of the story. Greenpeace and others have occasionally made jobs an issue, but there's often a feeling that the "jobs card" is being played for ulterior motives. And the no-cut, no-compromise crowd often steals the headlines. Few timber-community families, at least, see their fate as any kind of concern to environmentalists. Social-justice environmentalists have utterly failed to convince workers, or the rest of the Sierra-Club-Magazine-reading public, that this is a significant part of Saving Nature.

It should not be such a hard case to make. Loggers aren't the only ones whose jobs the corporate executives find expendable. Weyerhaeuser is the biggest exporter of raw logs in the US. What happens to mill jobs when logs go overseas? Visit Coos Bay, Oregon, or a hundred other communities to find out. But if you do, don't go to a local tavern in your Sierra Club t-shirt. The laid-off workers there are likely to blame the environmentalists, not the corporate owners. Yet according to George Draffan of the Public Information Network, Weyerhaeuser laid off eight thousand employees between 1995 and 1999 as part of a "corporate restructuring." Weyerhaeuser chief financial officer Bill Stivers, in response to criticisms, simply said: "We're not a philanthropic enterprise. We're in business to make a profit." Profit meant sending logs overseas as fast as possible.

The environmental movement has failed in the forests because it has had almost nothing to say to people who work there. Too little to say about how to live in and on the world. How to work out the compromises, the deals, the uses: what to cut and what to keep. As Richard White has pointed out, the environmental movement has abandoned the whole terrain of living and working "in nature" to the other side—loggers, corporations, and the so-called "wise use" movement, with its ignorant individualism and its attempt to turn "place into property." In contrast, far too much of the environmental movement has been founded on *recreational* uses of nature. (There I am, grad student on holiday, backpacking and climbing. Sneering at guys in pickup trucks.) White's analysis points out that most environmentalists "equate productive work in nature with destruction." That's crazy, isn't it? Even crazier, since environmentalists obsessively repeat how humans are "one with nature" or (hideous phrasing) "dependent on the ecology."

But it's an endemic craziness, an urban, suburban, shopping-mall, Bambified craziness that has pretty much captured the environmental half of the culture. Ask one of your eco-friends, living in a wood-frame house, under what circumstances he or she might be willing to cut down a tree. Catch the uncomprehending look. Or try to get one of those eco-friends to actually kill anything for the two of you to eat. You'll have to go hunting, or else go to Chinatown where you can pick a living beast from the tank. "Oh no!" your friend will protest. "I couldn't *kill* anything." I'm not talking about vegetarians here, who are at least (somewhat) consistent. I'm talking about the rest of us, the fish-frying, chicken-chewing, burger-buying millions. What manner of bizarre denial is operating here? What is wrong with these folks? Answer: they hate the actual process of nature—or at the least are wholly disconnected from it. The hurlyburly, the change, the incessant eating and dying, the mess of life. But Nature as a large, prettified abstraction they love. It makes nice calendars, and excellent footage on well-edited, odorless TV nature shows. And impregnably absolutist politics.

But who will help discover the good way of living, if environmentalists don't? Not just good ways of backpacking or enjoying a view. But good ways of cutting trees in just the right places and proportions, good ways of using soils and streams. Good ways of loving, growing, and killing things.

In a neat little essay that is just as right as it is wrong, my unrelated namesake Joyce Carol Oates has famously criticized these same enviro-types, or more exactly their nature-writings, for their predictable proclamations about oneness with nature. But "nature is a mouth!" she exclaims. And she'd rather not "become one" with nature on those terms, thank you. Her unwillingness to go softly into that devouring night is understandable. That's exactly the reality I wish to engage.

Of course, what the famous personage, mouthing her *mots*, refuses to notice is that she herself is a mouth, downing her own daily poundage of assorted other fellow-beings, animal or vegetable. This convenient oversight is the key to her comfortable dismissiveness, her brittle, urban, wiseacre scorn, so primly contained within that provincial fence of city, education, detachment from bloody hands and dirty fingernails. That I'm-too-important-to-know-such-things fence. That I-can't-kill-things fence.

An oversight as comprehensive as this deprives even the brilliant writer of an essential recognition about our lives here on the home planet. It prevents her seeing something like tragedy at the heart of things here. Not the nature-lover's bogus wish-I-lived-in-Eden tragedy … but the real, inescapable fact of eating and being eaten, *the* fact of life. That there is no living without killing. That whatever innocence and freshness are, they must somehow be built from this.

Is it possible to write at all, in any meaningful sense, without finding your way to this? And once there, what will you do with it? Who will stand here with the actual holy tragedy and say: This is life as it is, and any goodness must be somehow consistent with this delicious, horrifying kaleidoscope, this nibbling and gorging and losing and finding?

Pushed by this meditation on my literary betters, I return to something I learned first from my militant, muscular older brother, so far from literature of any sort—he who became a hunter and did not mind bringing me along. That same something which I learned again from Paul Shepard and then from Ortega y Gassett, and then from non-Western peoples around the globe whose lives I read about: the discovery, surprising for a city boy, that those who hunted to live thought it not a terrible thing; that they thanked their meal-to-be, and blessed it, and thought themselves blessed back. They did not think of escaping the conditions of actual life, its brutal involvement in death, but found a deep and heart-breaking beauty there—something that required humility, that saw a spiritual mystery and the type of all inwardness in the connection of dying to living. They were moved to awe in the pathos of their own participation, the round ritual of bloody hands, clean hands; of accepting and giving back.

Humility, awe, participation; not withdrawal into the pretence of purity. That's not a bad place for wiseacre readers and writers and cosmopolites to go to—and we're all such, now. Black Elk prayed to *Wakan Tanka*, the "Great Mystery." So should we. That is the mystery of killing and loving at the same time; of accepting one's place in the round of life, with all its hard decisions of cherishing and use.

Why can't those brainy, bearded, braided, idealistic and energetic green types pour some passion into that? Probably because such deals and seem less drenched with emotion, less stirring than the Eden reflex of grief and tears (balanced by oceanic abstract Oneness).Those habitual emotions are a powerful force; it will take some doing to steer ourselves and our kids around them toward a calmer way of being present to nature.That would be a job for grownups, I suppose. Folks who are at peace with dirty hands. The ache of purity is an adolescent drama; we must respect that by nurturing it towards its adult forms, not by emulating it in Paradise Lost emotionalism.

It will take an army of environmentalists with chain saws to drive the Weyerhaeusers from the hills—environmentalists prepared to kill trees in the most delicate, tender, loving fashion imaginable. Prepared to leave forests whole as they go: that natural magic, which only the deepest of cultured knowledge might win us. If we work hard enough at it.

If we don't do it, who will?

Down in Curry County, Oregon, just south of Coos Bay, someone is trying to rig up a tourist attraction that would string cables and walkways high in the dense rainy forest canopy. People could walk and climb, peer and sit quietly, hundreds of feet up in a part of the woods seldom visited. Part of the motivation has been to find a way to make a living in Coos Bay without cutting down the forest. Maybe treasuring, displaying, and learning about those trees and their whole fabulous system of life would be a good alternative. But (did you see this coming?) such a thing may never come to be. The pure-green environmentalists have been fighting it. Why on earth? Perhaps they have learned from Ed Abbey to despise tourists (and to consider themselves Not Tourists). Perhaps they feel, on some unexamined level, that any human contact with nature is besmirching. That any deal is a deal with the devil. They mention parking lots and roads, throngs of people. An outfit called Wild Wilderness opposes it on principle: they are against "commodifying" nature. They want it left alone.

To me, it looks like a lost opportunity to enjoy the permeable membrane that both connects and separates humans and nature. A good, sober, practical way to coexist in and with this little bit of the natural world. Will there be some losses in this deal? Well, of course. Something is given, something is taken. But is it a good deal? If you count the trees downed for road widening and parking-lot constructing, and count the inconvenienced animals who may not like the stringing-up process, and those (fewer) who won't return when construction is over and the trees are full of featherless bipeds, then is this a fair trade, if it brings knowledge and delight to the people in the trees, and a living to the people in the community? That's a question the pure ones cannot answer. In fact, they cannot even ask it; it is from a different language. As Michael Pollan observed, the pure-wilderness concept prevents such discriminating, choosing, balancing. In the all-or-nothing framework of the Wilderness Ethic (Don't Touch), you're either saved or damned. "Even where we mend her, we end her," says broken-hearted Hopkins. If you think it's Eden, then any touch at all is a sin that makes it noplace. And dogmatic opposition is the reflex that absolves you of making choices, trades, or deals.

Between apathy and dogmatism is something only grownups care about achieving: the darned hard work of hammering out imperfectly crafted solutions to imperfectly understood situations. That's politics, I guess. Politics as it ought to be, anyway—politics freed of the burden of exaggerating Eden mythology. Making deals in the best sense.

One politician who qualifies as a grownup by this measure might be Al Gore. That is: one who has found practical ways to channel idealism; who has been willing to fight for causes and accept partial solutions. One who is not afraid of a good deal. Of course, Gore could also be seen as the one who has lost his ideals and is all compromise, for whom too many deals have become backroom deals, deals with the devil. The Paradise Lost perspective offers some insight on how environmental apathy and dogmatism played out in the presidential choice of 2000.

Philip Clapp of the National Environmental Trust said of Gore, "He is more knowledgable and has done more on the environment than any politician in America." So, how could Al Gore have failed to corral the environmental vote— and faced instead such a major insurrection from green voters? Gore, I believe, found himself politically marooned between the dogmatic and the apathetic on this issue. An impure activist, he did not satisfy the purists. And for the environmentally apathetic, the issue just did not matter. George W. Bush's half of the electorate simply ignored the environment and denied the need for any systematic response to big problems like global warming or species loss. Bush locked up the apathy vote. Strongly motivated green voters, on the other hand, refused apathy but brought a moral fervor to the election, demanding more purity than Gore (or perhaps any working political leader) could deliver. His green manifesto of 1992, *Earth in the Balance,* set Gore apart as a political champion of the environment; eight years of the compromises and betrayals of governing necessarily tarnished his armor.

The pure-green vote, going mostly to Green Party candidate Ralph Nader, turned out to be pretty small—under five percent—but it was enough to defeat Gore in the electoral college. That little activist cadre sharply illustrates Proctor's "moral dogmatism." The real-world consequences of a Bush White House were not enough to sway voters who had purity in mind. Voters who wanted clean hands.

I'm pretty sure that dirty hands, working hands, are the hands that make life happen. We'll have to refocus our emotional commitment from the Nature Problem, that overwhelming abstraction, and get busy on the details. The either-or ethics of Pure Wilderness, that secret Eden plot of too much environmental thinking, cannot help us. It's going to take a lot of dirty little compromises, arrangements, and *ménages,* to fix up what we've done. We will have to go hillside by hillside, community by community, to do it.

I hope we don't lose too much along the way. I hope our idealists arm themselves *soon* with excellent ecology degrees—and excellent chainsaws.

Eco-fundamentalism
and the Forests of Oregon

The environmental movement has been engaging in a rethinking of its most basic beliefs over the last decade. That process has been wrenching, sometimes pitting against each other those who had shared battles against despoilers and polluters, indeed those who still share a love of the natural world and a determination to do better. There's a lot to be worked out, in discovering how to think more clearly about ourselves and our nature. And the literalized Eden, that one-dimensional myth of the past, is a prime object of reconsideration. But no such reconsideration is likely for the hardcore wing, the eco-fundamentalists. These are the true believers in being One with Nature, a kind of undifferentiated merging that does not do justice to the paradox of simultaneous belonging and separateness. Fixed on this unrealizable goal, they are committed to the pain of losing Eden and the pleasure of longing for it. As we have seen, the Paradise-Lost narrative traps us in a one-way slide, ever further from the longed-for state. Mourning—that old elegiac mood of so much nature-writing—is one consolation. Longing is the other.

Eden-grief generates Eden-longing, with its oddly addictive tang. Because for every negative habit, no matter how painful, there's a secret sweetness, a subtle payoff. Many people in my acquaintance are hooked on their sense of a "pristine" nature *somewhere*. They attach tremendous longing to it—they may (surprisingly commonly) declare some faraway patch of "wilderness" their "true home." The emotional formation is precise: to get the full kick of longing, there must be formidable separation, celebrated with mournful resignation. Needless to say, this idea of nature tends to become abstract, despite enthusiastic visits from time to time: its primary existence is in the memory. And equally obviously, this idea of nature structurally excludes whatever place one might be actually living in. The "nature" there does not count: it's not wilderness, it's not far away, it's not pristine, it cannot be mourned or longed for.

Permitting feelings of mourning and longing to seem "natural" is an unclean habit. That these feelings come unbidden is a sign of the depth of the distress. We may be misled to think them "natural," inevitable, part of the terrain. But they are only bad emotional hygiene. We bring the odor with us.

The Sierras were the romantic terrain that awakened these feelings of longing and exile in me, as a young man. Why? Because I hiked there sometimes? Because I had learned the names of things and engaged the place forcefully, in detail? Because the mountains permitted me to develop a critique of my sometimes slovenly and crass culture? Those were good things. But they do not, alone, explain why I claimed citizenship *there* and not "here," in the various heres where I dwelt.

I claimed a solitary, faraway identity because I had not accommodated my mind to the adult realities of sex, belonging to people, finding a productive relation to humankind. In the face of these (for me, at the time) insoluble difficulties, I simply declared for the mountains. The John Muir moment. Problem solved! Except, of course, that Muir could not solve what he agonized over as "the bread question" (not just making a living but, in fact, his implication in the human condition), and neither could I. I did not live there in the mountains, I lived elsewhere. My powers of denial could not sustain the illusion for nine or ten months of the year, year after year, and like most grownups I eventually gave it up. Or rather: I replaced it with a webwork of far more immediate loyalties, accommodations, commitments, and compromises. I did not give up loving and visiting the Sierra. But I learned this difference: it was not I, and I was not it.

The much-criticized yearning for union with nature lurks behind much of the environmental movement's politics and literature. According to this belief (loosely borrowed from the Romantics), though we may be fatally separated from nature, we may also know privileged moments not just of contact or enjoyment, but of total immersion: loss of separate identity: merging. That's the Cosmic

Oneness so justly spoofed by Joyce Carol Oates, and so savagely reviewed by ecofeminists.

The work of the late Paul Shepard has challenged the environmental movement to look more deeply into these feelings. Shepard asked the question that would instigate the environmental reconsideration of the 1990s: Why is our culture locked into the strange dichotomy of preserving and destroying nature? "The contradiction within American Protestant culture—which continues today—is its emotional enthusiasm for the beauty of virgin scenery set against the materialist 'ethic' expressed collectively as corporate arrogance in the destruction of soil, grass, water, and forests. But examination shows the contradiction to be superficial."

Shepard examines this contradiction through a sustained anthropological and psychological comparison of our modern and pre-modern selves. His thesis is that our minds, like our bodies, are products of hundreds of thousands of years of living in small groups of other humans—that often-encountered anthropologist's norm of eight to fifteen adults, plus dependents—engaged in making a settled or semi-nomadic living off of the natural world. Hunting and gathering, in other words. Childhood within this age-old pattern of living constitutes an eight- to ten-year apprenticeship in intimate contact with nature, during which the dynamics and tensions of self and world can be worked out. This developmental norm produces a penetrating critique of the way we live now, with our addiction to consuming nature and our yearning for oneness with it.

The longing to *merge with nature* which forms one half of this dichotomized mentality is, Shepard says, a feature of infantilized or possibly neurotic minds—an arrested psychology that is, alas, "normal" in industrial Western society, as is the unslaked appetite to *consume nature.* "The two opposite sides are merely sides of the puritan passion, aspects of a double vision derived from early-life experiences and psychology."

Shepard emphasizes America's Puritan foundation as an extreme form of this mentality. Puritans, with their rage for purity, express a developmentally immature distaste for dirtiness: a fastidious and morally scrupulous psychology that is repelled not just by sin but by the body's wet biology—the swampy smelliness of it all: "The puritanical fear of pollution as seen in the messiness of the body and nature." Specifically (and Shepard follows Mircea Eliade here), this fear of bodily pollution is an adolescent psychology—normal for young teens just facing their eruptive bodies, but something to work through toward more adult values and responses.

Cleanliness, messiness; clarity, mystery; self, others; one with nature, two with nature—these paradoxes cannot be "solved," but in Shepard's depiction of the hunter-gatherer childhood, nature models to the youngster a complex and delicate intermingling of interests and identities which provides the pattern for psychological resolution. Nature has a "magical capacity to reveal that an ultimate symbiosis holds the universe together."

The experienced reality of this living complexity is the psychological ground of adulthood. Nature provides the means and the model for the young mind to pass from an infantile longing for a merged oneness to an adult appreciation of the webbed connectedness of real social and natural life—what Shepard calls, in a phrase I wish to engrave upon the sky of the mind, the "negotiated affiliations" of self and world. Not the stark either-or of oneness or alienation, but a hard-won, nuanced membership in a community, where "local" knowledge is the only kind that works—person by person, place by place—emotionally close in some cases, distant in others; the kind of knowledge that includes persistence and tact. The natural world which the child explores teaches these lessons both as reality and as symbol: for in its essential mysteriousness, its insistence that there is a life, an otherness, on the other side of each transaction, it demands both.

But lacking this apprenticeship in nature, the mind is thrown back upon its own devices, struggling for emotionally and spiritually satisfying resolutions. It is all too likely to fail in this all-important struggle, to fail to figure out that the infant's vaguely remembered bodily bliss, or the child's idealized natural world of memory, are not recoverable. "What the adolescent should know is that these are aspects of experience, not places, and he is prepared to comprehend them as elements in the amazing myth of creation."

Shepard's analysis uncovers the pathology of longing for paradise as if it were a real alternative to actual life. Such longing is a child's category mistake, confusing the literal with the figurative; a mistake that has become part of the adult Western mentality. Sadly, this mistake has played out in the destruction of North America: "The orgies of spoiling, the messianic and apocalyptic atmosphere, the hatred of history and tradition are all too familiar themes in American genesis, all typical of antinomian behavior, giving literal rather than ritual enactment of adolescence's end of childhood."

The themes of this chapter (and indeed this book) come together in Shepard's and Eliade's analyses. The fundamentalism of our culture, its difficulty in "reading" the world as more than a flat and literal place, result in a psychology of ravening hunger. That hunger for completeness may result in addictive consuming. And it may result in a vague infantile yearning for oneness with nature, which ought to be seen as a mere expansion of self—a dissolving of differences into a vast ego soup. In contrast, Shepard advocates a truly analogical relationship that maintains and explores the webwork of affiliation (not oneness) that is life; a relation that honors the differences and details that form the very substance of life's exacting mutual arrangements.

The historic basis of the modern divided and destructive mentality, according to Eliade, is visible right at the foundation of the New World, and can be seen in the earliest Anglo-American colonists and settlers—in"the literalizing impulse of the sixteenth century ... that show[s] us the shared underpinnings of modern science and Christian fundamentalism, both riveted to a juvenile insistence on positivistic, utilitarian thought."

Literalizing: the simplification of the complex; the externalization of an inner demand: the physicalization of myth. Eden not as a part of a ritually repeatable cycle, but as the embodiment of a psychic wound, projected outward onto nature and society. Paradise Lost in the forests of Oregon.

The melodrama of lost Eden, of purity and paradise, is playing out as I write, not far from Portland—as it probably is just up the road from you, dear Reader. In whatever forest or plain is still designated as "nature," people will be trying to save it, own it, consume it, and become one with it. And will probably be wondering why it all makes so little sense.

I'll look at three examples in detail, to see what can be learned. Right now, on the upper reaches of Eagle Creek, a stream I have often walked, about fifty miles from Portland on the slopes of the Cascades, protesters are stopping a National Forest timber sale that apparently is a model of good forestry (they're stopping it anyway).Further north, the people of an ancient village are preparing to go out and hunt whales against the semi-violent opposition of dogmatic environmentalists. And again, hidden in local forests and university towns, various green/anarchist Talibans are preparing to destroy research and torch equipment that violates their personal standards of natural purity. Three examples of Eden-longing and dogmatism: eco-fundamentalism at work.

Up on Eagle Creek, I don't know if the protesters are right or wrong. They're right enough to have enlisted most of the Oregon congressional delegation in a request to suspend the sale for further review. They're wrong enough to have begun arson bombing (someone blew up a logging truck overnight); and they're committed enough, some twenty to forty of them, to do civil disobedience: linking arms, singing and hugging, and setting up rope-and-nylon bivouacs way high up, to prevent cutting.

I don't know. I'm reading the news reports, like everyone else: no special knowledge to guide me. Because what compels me, here, are the issues under the surface; not just the facts of this case, but the attitudes that bring such abrupt conflict. That's a weird admission because I've been arguing for local knowledge, for a place-by-place responsiveness to the living world, for Michael Pollan's "local ethic." But the protesters themselves have framed the issue in this global way. They admit that the sale is, by ordinary standards, ecologically well designed. Some of them, at least, want to stop it for other reasons. A member of the protesting Cascadia Forest Alliance admitted as much: "It probably is the best [the Forest Service] can do. ... And guess what? That's not good enough. It's not good enough to protect the forests. Nothing short of ending logging on public lands is good enough."

That's the Zero-Cut option. To me, Reader, it looks like something besides reason. It looks like taking a forest and making it a symbol of something. It looks like a blind passion for protecting Eden.

To be fair, the protesters also make a case on the facts. They voice concern that, despite assurances to the contrary, old-growth will be taken. Their website mentions degradation of water quality in Portland's watershed, and violation of the Northwest Forest Plan:

"This sale could never proceed without the blanket legal protections of the Salvage Logging Rider." That point gives me pause. Maybe these kids are right and I ought to be out there myself.

But whenever there's a deductive argument at the head—an argument from principle—then the facts are really superfluous. It wouldn't matter if the facts they list were true or not. The principle would still guide them. Is the principle here really that old fantasy of the Eden Forest, with its Untouched/Don't Touch imperative?

The Forest Supervisor, Gary Larsen, agrees that this is the highest-quality timber cut. That means no clear-cuts; no taking of old-growth; using helicopters to airlift the cut wherever possible; and closing and restoring about five miles of older logging roads. Most of the cut will be thinning of stands, which reduces fire danger while diversifying and opening up the forest, encouraging it toward an old-growth condition. The net result, it seems to me, would be remarkably similar to forestry practiced by Native Americans, who used regular firing to clear the groves of underbrush and smaller growth (an option now closed to us because we have prevented fires for so long). Their practices, of course, may or may not have been good ones. But they suggest the possibility of forest management somewhere *between* the extremes of industrial clear-cutting and don't-touch wilderness. That's the territory I'm most interested in.

So, dear Reader, what to do? Should I listen to the voice of the regional forester Harv Forsgren, who pointed out that if we don't get wood from our own forests, we'll just be letting someone else do it—probably somewhere "where environmental protections may not be so rigorous"? From this wider perspective we face a different kind of choice: not "Cut or don't cut," but "Cut well here or cut badly somewhere else." That's more complicated, isn't it? Or should I just drive up there and put my body on the line for once? I'm very tempted. Despite that absurdly polarizing Zero-Cut statement, it might be the right thing to do. The Salvage Rider was a travesty of ecological law and democratic process. If this thing can only sneak in under that cover, how good could it be?

My questions were answered several ways. In July 2001, the Eagle Creek timber sale entered yet another of its endless moves and counter-moves. An "Independent Review Team" released its assessment, which vindicated the environmental quality of the original plan. While calling for some modifications, its overall conclusion was a strong affirmation: "no adverse environmental effects are expected, such as on water quality, aquatic ecosystems, or wildlife."

Opponents, of course, remain unmovable. I guess that's my point: to the doctrinaire, no possible use of the forest is acceptable. That was increasingly evident to me, as I listened to a radio interview with a member of the Cascadia Forest Alliance. She characterized the four-member Review commission as, in effect, tools of the timber industry. "They spoke timber industry language from the start. We could see that immediately," she said. But the Independent Review includes scientists with decades-long records as champions of the environment: lead scientist Jerry Franklin, often called the "Dean of forestry science," a major force behind the Northwest Forest Plan and a forest advocate of unquestionable credentials; Gordon Reeves, Fisheries Biologist from the U.S. Forest Service's Pacific Northwest Research Station, whose long, heroic, and sometimes lonely fight for salmon is detailed in Joseph Cone's book *A Common Fate*. Reader, these are not timber-cutting stooges. Their records shield them from pot-shot dismissals. They know more about Northwest forests and salmon—and care more about them— than almost anyone else on the planet. For months I was agnostic about this sale, fearful that some kind of creeping conservatism had blinded me to the tree-sitters' moral crusade. But Franklin and Reeves convinced me: this is a place we could cut, a place we could get it right.

But we won't. The other answer to my questions came with the simple clarity of "no, no, no." My own favorite politicians, whom I vote for religiously (the Mayor of Portland, Vera Katz, and the Democratic Senator from Oregon, Ron Wyden) lined up against the Eagle Creek sale and finally won its cancellation. I think, perhaps, they bowed to the symbolism of Eagle Creek, and the fervor of its opponents, rather than taking the more hazardous course of asking how, then, we shall live with nature.

I see people around me—I see myself—loading these issues with personal baggage in a way that really obstructs clear decision making. It is easy to project one's personal griefs outward onto well-defined bad guys, to keen lustily in righteous opposition. It happens all the time in political movements, guaranteeing a dependable source of highly motivated troops. It's a good deal for organizers. But ordinary observers may come away with an uneasy sense that, however "right" the cause, there's something smarmy, the whiff of decay, about the loudest protesters: that sense of cult, of true believing, of unbalanced people barnacled onto causes in lieu of taking care of their own business.

But criticizing the protesters in these cases can seem like collaboration, collusion. Cold-war style, the debate is thoroughly polarized. Writers like William Cronon and William Ashworth, whose work has been so central to clarifying and questioning environmental thinking (including my own), have been targeted by this kind of complaint. In an either-or framework, some readers have seen their work as "a hostile attack on the environmental movement." Their implicit question is, Why are you giving aid and comfort to the enemy? As if the "enemy" is not us—all of us who live on nature's products and leave our imprint on the world. And as if we dare not think clearly about our own commitments, our own assumptions and vocabularies.

Eco-fundamentalism (like all fundamentalisms) is a powerful force against the work of thinking *and feeling* more clearly, in order to create a better way of living in and on our planet. The real work.

But there is so very much nuttiness on the environmental side. That gal who sat in a tree and gave it a pet name: Luna. It danced, it talked to her, it heard her questions. What is so profoundly icky about all this, Reader? Don't you feel it too? It is the sense that sentimentalizing nature like this is nearly as disrespectful as clear-cutting it. That tree, given a name like a pet poodle and anthropomorphized, is hardly even *noticed* as a separate reality. It is absorbed into an infantile ownership, made to carry a projected burden of excessive and wounded tenderness. Treehood, in all its otherness, is extinguished. What's left is weepy, cloying, pathological. (Her name, self-given, is "Butterfly"; her book treats us to photo-images of her schoolgirl "poems," their unrevised gush presented to the world with childish self-approbation.) To literalize the tree's creatureliness into a human-personhood; and to attempt an emotional merging with it; these are not the acts of someone who has a sane method of living in the natural world.

That she's a hero to at least a wing of the environmental movement tells you we're in trouble. On the up side, she helped save the tree. But the price is perpetuating a sentimentalized "one with nature" perspective which is as useless to us in making our way through this world as its bulldozing, clear-cutting opposite.

The same weekend in which that logging truck got torched at Eagle Creek, an Oregon eco-terrorist group quaintly known as ELF (Environmental Liberation Front) took credit for firebombings against a surprising pair of targets: a tree farm and a horticultural research center. The "Jefferson Poplars" tree farm cultivated the fast-growing tree for pulp. And at the University of Washington research center, Professor Toby Bradshaw was studying the genetics of poplars. ELF believes that "Our forests are being liquidated and replaced with monocultured tree farms so greedy, earth-raping corporations can make more money." According to its statements to reporters, ELF thinks these poplars will release "mutant genes into the environment."

Forestry scientist Steven H. Strauss of Oregon State University points out some of the flaws in the ELF thinking. Bradshaw's work, he says, "never created a genetically engineered tree nor released one into the environment." Bradshaw does use DNA techniques to study the trees. Apparently this is enough for ELF; perhaps its members have read their McKibben, and picked up his shrill terror. Certainly they've read their Ed Abbey, and learnt the thrill of monkeywrenching for Eden.

And that poplar tree farm? Far from pushing wild places aside, "tree farms that the company manages have been planted on former agricultural lands; they did not replace wild forests." The question of gene pollution, Strauss says, has been the subject of "intensive" research that concludes "the plantations have extremely little influence on the genetic constitution of wild populations." Why? Their seeds are not viable. They have to be reproduced through cuttings. They are all clones and are lousy competitors in the real world, according to WSU researcher Jon D. Johnson. On the other hand, the environmental value of hybrid poplars is manyfold. Poplars sequester atmospheric carbon dioxide very efficiently, so environmentalists have been keenly interested in their value for mitigating global warming. They are good at taking up leftover farm fertilizers from the soil too, resulting in cleaner water. But Strauss points out the main advantage: hybrid poplars produce wood fiber at a prodigious rate (five to ten times that of a conventional forest), and "can therefore relieve pressure on wild forests for exploitation."

The more Jefferson Poplars, the fewer Eagle Creeks; less CO_2, and cleaner water. Grown on crop land, of course. It's a trade-off, a nicely circular set of bargains and transactions. But such transactions represent a form of logic that is apparently unavailable to elves in Eden. Eco-fundamentalism relies on extreme simplification of the world, reducing it to black and white, good and evil, sentimentalized emotional categories. Mitch Friedman, a former tree-sitter with EarthFirst!, bluntly calls the elves "morons" for their inability to follow the logic of these tradeoffs. He now heads Northwest Ecosystem Alliance, and concludes that "poplar farming makes fantastic sense. Just like hemp, it's a good fast source of pulp. It's probably an improvement over cows and other crops, much better for streams." The prefab emotions of eco-fundamentalism—nature-love and civilization-hate—are no substitute for engagement with the real complexity of the world.

I drove up to Neah Bay, on the northwestern tip of Washington State, during the big confrontation over the Makah Indians' going after a whale for the second year in a row. From five hours away, it seemed like eco-fundamentalism getting in the way of a good thing. Aggression, polarized thinking, sentimentalization—all the elements. I wanted to see it close up.

What I had seen the night before on the TV news was a jet-ski protester who repeatedly buzzed the Indians in their wooden whaling canoe (coming extremely close) and then flipped herself over right in front of an onrushing Coast Guard inflatable. She went to the hospital; the Makah got no whale and returned to shore, while the news media repeated this excellent action footage whenever possible. What I thought was: I wish these guys were attacking the Japanese or the Norwegians, who take hundreds of whales every year. That would make sense to me. But one canoe, trying to take one whale?

I wandered around Neah Bay on the afternoon I arrived, finding it a quiet, not-prosperous-looking village. Junky auto-repair neither closed nor open, as far as I could tell, right across from a patch of stores spiffed-up for the tourist trade. Vacant land and cheesy motels side by side. I walked into one of the nicely remodeled stores, "The Smoke Shop," and found a raven-haired woman in her thirties just closing up. She volunteered her commentary quite readily—a relief to my questionable interviewing skills.

> *I don't know why those people can't just leave us alone. But it's always been like this—they can't leave us alone because they want everyone to be exactly like them, to believe and live exactly like they do. The same as it's been from the beginning for native people.*
>
> *We gave up a lot so that we could keep the right to hunt whale. Our land went all the way to Port Angeles— we gave it up to keep the right. Those protesters don't know that.*
>
> *I agree with them on a lot of issues, like animal rights, logging. I wish they'd protest the clear-cuts all the way along the coast here. And leave us alone. I am very strong on animal rights, but this is not an animal-rights issue. They think it is, though, why? Because the whale has a big brain? EVERY animal has a brain, some kind of consciousness.*
>
> *Every bit of that whale [the previous year] was used. I watched to see how they would handle it—I was skeptical—but they did the prayer, they prayed for that animal's pod, because now that pod was going to have to mourn the loss of the one whale. But we used every bit of it. And that whale tasted good. This isn't an animal-rights issue—it wasn't being left and just the skin or just the baleen taken. It was food. That's the way we believe: everything goes in a circle. We prayed for the whale because it gave its life to us. [Sarcastically:] It's called "the food chain"!*

I can recall right now what emphasis she laid on "That whale tasted good." It was satisfaction. It meant: *That was ours.*

An hour later I went looking for dinner and ended up at a diner a little further down the strip. One old couple sat at the other table. The husband was wizened and silent under rural-standard too-big baseball cap and plaids, while the wife was vigorous and thick-bodied, her face brown and deeply wrinkled. It was a Central Casting vignette. But she was just as willing to talk as the Smoke Shop woman—no stereotyped Injun reticence—and her manner was direct and practiced, with no wasted words. "Are you a journalist?" she demanded when I had barely sat down. I heard an earful.

I spent the next day driving and walking along the Neah Bay coastline. It's one of the most beautiful I've ever seen, and I'll bet you know all the adjectives. Rugged. Wild. Steep. But a lot of it has been clear-cut right down to the water, even on the steepest slopes. I wondered how they did that; more, I wondered *why* the Makah would let them. And who was "them," anyway? I thought about the Smoke Shop woman's reiteration of her support for "animal rights," which somehow coexisted with her people's "right" to kill things and eat them. Whatever she meant by rights must have been different from what their opponents meant.

That night, I tracked down the protesters' spokesman in the village of Sekiu about twenty miles down the coast (Neah Bay doesn't make itself hospitable to protesters, so they stay off-reservation). The spokesman and I stood on the step of a rental cottage at the end of a fair spring dusk. Clear-cut hills above the little bay and its marina were gold-green in the waning light. The protesters had formed their action group from other groups with names like "Ocean Defense International" and "Safe Passing."

I'm not naming the spokesman or any of these people because, well, I'm *not* a journalist, am I? And because I wish to speak personally about them; I think everything about this is personal and I don't want to leave that out.

The spokesman's main line, repeated and I think as well refined for media as the Indians' positions were: the Makah do not have a valid International Whaling Commission license to whale. He says the Japanese have cut a deal with them; the Japanese want cover for more whaling, under the "cultural whaling" category, which (he claims) was invented for the Makah. There are already "subsistence" and "aboriginal" categories, applying for example to one native group in Siberia and another in Alaska. And sure enough, right after last year's Makah hunt, Japan accused the US of hypocrisy and demanded permission for "cultural whaling" themselves. He says Japan was shopping around the world for an aboriginal group to use this way.

The fellow declares that if the Makah had a valid IWC license, his outfit would pack up and go home. But that the Makah will not answer this charge about the license, nor will the media print it. He insisted that the protesters had no problem with other aboriginal whaling, no other reasons to oppose it.

No other reasons? I asked if they were militant vegetarians, for instance. He said they were "mostly *vegans*" (correcting my terminology) but that was "not the point." I wondered if I should believe him about that—though I'm sure he believed he was telling the truth.

When I characterized the Makah as relatively poor and powerless, he pooh-poohed the notion, calling them one of the most heavily subsidized Indian tribes in America—"very powerful" locally and "throwing around a lot of weight."

I asked about the seeming aggressiveness and hostility of the previous day's jet-ski incident. He dismissed it, saying "she sprayed them with water" and that the Coast Guard ran over her "on purpose." I pressed him about violence in demonstrating. He refused to see the jet-skier's action as provocative, hostile, or aggressive. He claimed the canoers had actually "sharpened their paddles with the harpoon and tried to use them against her!" To him, their reaction was obviously outrageous, while her buzzing them repeatedly at high speed was not. His tone was scornful and dismissive in all things relating to the Makah.

Driving back to my motel in the dark on the curvy forest-and-shore road, it struck me how this issue had made enemies of friends. A group of save-the-whale eco-vegans would normally be very supportive of indigenous peoples' rights, and highly sensitive to their plight. But this guy sounded for all the world like an outraged redneck, sick of humoring the Indians (as President Reagan once put it), dismissing their moral and historic claims. He said he regarded the treaty's whaling clause as "defunct" but did not say why. He was hostile to the idea of enforcing "this 1855 treaty." None of these attitudes fit the eco/liberal.

That was striking because, otherwise, the whole trip seemed to be mired in stereotypes. Those old Indians in the coffee shop. I myself, a Portland academic, slender, uncomfortable in the journalist role, not really a people-person; looking and sounding pretty fey, probably, compared with the lumbering outdoorsy types in the village. And the protester guy—he most of all conformed to some kind of B-movie type-casting: a frail bookish-looking man, with tiny sloping shoulders and almost no chin—the comic stereotype of a physically weak man trying to project force through words. Perhaps through righteousness.

I'm positioned pretty well to notice the play of gender stereotypes and roles here. I can see their force-lines drawn through this spokesman. He looks not-masculine-enough but he's playing a purely macho game: the game of "I'm right and you must yield to me." What has that got to do with the whaling question? What do personalities matter? I'm not sure. I'm reading eco-fundamentalism here, and that is a character disorder as much as it is anything else. According to Shepard and Eliade, it's a disorder that is played out right across our culture: psychologically incomplete people, desperate for contact with nature, finding surrogates in militancy, nature-sentimentality, or self-indulgent consumerism. From such mentalities, it is hard indeed to find the way to those "negotiated affiliations" by which we live in the world—those imperfect, hard-won arrangements of love and need.

Nine months after the jet-ski incident and a disappointing failure to get a whale, the Makah faced a National Marine Fisheries Service hearing in Seattle, to determine if the NMFS should re-issue a whaling license. Anti-whaling protesters were at the February 2001 hearing with signs, including one declaring "Killing is not culture." The placard-holder said to a reporter, "I think it's wrong. I really don't think we should kill animals for food any more."

Reader, it may be that vegetarian activists have excellent reasons for their beliefs. There are, after all, ways in which meat-eating gobbles up too many of the world's resources (though in the case of grey whales, it's hard to see how such concerns can apply). And it may be that a redwood-saving tree-sitter, lepidopterously named or not, is hardly a fair target for our scorn ("why break a butterfly upon a wheel?"). And that genetic engineering really is ripe for more careful scrutiny. My analysis is limited, perhaps; incomplete. I'm focussed on the thought-world, the myth, behind the actions. And there we find something troubling which, to be effective environmentalists, we absolutely must address: the fantasy that we can live somehow free of entanglement in the messy, tragic/holy ecological cycles of food-chain and trophic pyramid.

This entanglement is what Wendell Berry calls simply "Getting along with nature." A way of living on our world that respects the whole thing—that treats nature not as a fragile object in a glass menagerie, but as a beautiful complex community which includes us, as we include it, our worlds one and many somehow enfolding each other simultaneously, strangely, like a Klein bottle or a figure in *n* dimensions that you can't quite picture. When the Makah now try to take their five grey whales annually—as the NMFS decision of the following July permitted—they will face this paradox directly, dangerously, in the prows of their boats and the privacy of their thoughts. Sounds right to me.

In every leaf of grass there is a green door. For a long time we have been urged to go in that door. But somehow, we can't. We take our walks, we read our Muirs and our Thoreaus, but we never get there. Come in, come in, they say, dreamlike, and we try so hard … then wake to city streets and disappointment.

It seems to me we never will get in that green door. Because *we are already there.* We are already inside of nature, we ourselves *are* the inside, the inwardness of nature, if anyone is. What we had better do instead is turn around and look out the green door. Then we will see ourselves, looking down at ourselves in wonder; then we will see clearly, it is ourselves we must kill, and ourselves we must save, all at the same time. And that there's no opting out; for this is how the world works, the physical as much as the spiritual. Dying to be reborn. Dying daily, resurrecting daily.

It is up to us, simply, to do it well. Tool up, brothers and sisters. This is real work.

Palimpsest:
The Flower Hunter

"Puc-Puggy" was the name the Seminoles gave him. Flower Hunter.

William Bartram got the name in Florida on his first trip to the south. Like Muir who followed after, Bartram suffered tropical fever when he got to the hot and swampy southern coast. But by March of 1774 he had recovered enough to leave Savannah and begin his explorations among the Seminole.

And they called him Flower Hunter. I wonder if that name didn't have a good deal of irony in it. "Hunter" is next to "warrior" in a traditional culture. Flower Hunter indeed. Was there a gender question there, submerged (again like Muir, who faced the same question)—as if to hunt flowers were not fitting for a man?

Yet Bartram seemed quite proud of the name. Clueless, perhaps. Or better yet, simply not willing to be concerned. I can see both qualities in the Bartram of the *Travels*. A largeness of soul. And a kind of spacy disconnection, the lostness of a man who would never, ever fit in.

The wanderer Bartram came to the Indians with questions, not with answers. That's a Quaker trait, like so much in him. The Society of Friends, as you may know, doesn't really aim to have doctrines, certainly no ministers or liturgy. Friends have "queries" instead, questions that are read to the faithful, who gather in silence to hear them. And then continue in silence to hear answers, if any come. To hear for themselves.

Puc-Puggy came to learn about plants—questioning, you might say, the land. What's this? What's it good for? He's famous for that. Yet he also he came to learn firsthand (very much the Quaker) the truth of the native peoples, "that I might judge for myself, whether they were deserving of the severe censure which prevailed against them among the white people, that they were incapable of civilization."

That much-revered Friend John Woolman had done the same, a story I love to tell. In 1762, at a time when Methodists and Baptists were attempting to convert the heathen, and while his fellow Pennsylvanians were arming against them, Woolman traveled two hundred miles from Philadelphia to meet with Indians, in order, he said, *to listen*: "that I might learn something from them." He felt they might have as much access to the "pure Spirit" as any of us.

Off he went, ignoring the signs of war on the Indians' side and on ours, and had a fine sit-down with them, and returned to his Quaker Meeting untouched. Quakers, of course, do not bear arms against other men or women; they hold to a theory (O courage, to believe such a thing!) that there is "that of God in each person." Their method is simply to speak to this goodness, ignoring all else, and to listen for its answer. Sometimes it works.

Is it idle to wonder what our history might be—what sort of past we might have made for ourselves—if more Americans had approached Indians this way? If we had listened to them occasionally, on the chance they had something to tell us that we ought to hear?

Of course no one can answer such a question.

But I take some pleasure, not knowing exactly why, in finding that our past is not *all* preaching and thieving and philistine self-justification. That there are some threads as fine as silk in this weaving. Maybe they are lasting, too.

Puc-Puggy met an angry young man in the forest one day, and he bore a rifle. "I never before this was afraid at the sight of an Indian," Bartram declares; but this time he read peril. "I saw at once, that, being unarmed, I was in his power. ... I resigned myself entirely to the will of the Almighty ...; my mind then became tranquil, and I resolved to meet the dreaded foe with resolution and chearful confidence. The intrepid Siminole stopped suddenly, three or four yards before me, and silently viewed me, his countenance angry and fierce, shifting his rifle from shoulder to shoulder, and looking about instantly on all sides."

It was a moment, as we say, of truth. Think of the books unwritten that spool forward from this point: Coleridge and Wordsworth left to their own imaginings; the new world left thinner, coarser, by this one slender thread; my great-grandmother Nellie disuncled, her son named something else; the Quaker meeting poorer by one story, one lone soul gone missing long ago and forgotten. And me, in my little part of the whole, sitting by rivers Bartramless and unexcused.

But something else happened. Bartram walked forward, offering his hand to the Indian: "at this he hastily jerked back his arm, with a look of malice, rage, and disdain, seeming every way discontented; when again looking at me more attentively, he instantly spurred up to me, and with dignity in his look and action, gave me his hand."

The Great Spirit spoke, Bartram tells his reader, and the angry fellow listened.

Later Bartram heard that the Seminole had been horribly treated just the day before. At the trading company, the story came out: "Last evening he was here," admitted the head trader; "we took his gun from him, broke it in pieces, and gave him a severe drubbing; he, however, made his escape, carrying off a new rifle gun, with which, he said, going off, he would kill the first white man he met."

But he met Flower Hunter instead.

Our Nature to Read

I'm on the Hawthorne bus, heading down the slope to cross the Willamette River to the university library downtown, and I'm book-voyeuring again. It's a guilty pleasure; but I love the surprises. The roughly dressed guy standing in front of me is a Tom Clancy, no surprise there. Beside him a college-age girl clutches Camus, and in French: *La Peste.* For a class no doubt. Yet who required that heavyset lady in the next row to lug a hefty *Beet Queen*? Who thought Rumi would get on at Grand Street? Surprises like this are strangely reassuring: more going on around me than I think.

In the next row of seats a lined and haggard face, fiercely excluding all else, leans over a Bible, a fundamentalist edition (I can spot this with morbid skill): someone "in recovery," from the look of her. Looking for certainty. Once I scandalized my college chum Roger, who would became a Presbyterian minister, by telling him "the best thing we know about God is that we know nothing about him." Filled with a gospel that explained everything, Roger practically spit his outrage at me. But I was onto something (though I wasn't smart enough to think about my pronouns at that stage): there's more going on than any one reading could exhaust. Even for believers.

I take a deep breath and focus on the river-crossing. River grey, sky grey. Such cold springs here! But it will warm up in the afternoon if we get some sunbreaks. Billboards flash by, lettering on buildings, awnings, trucks. I read them all. Then I've come to Sixth Street and stepped off, reading and negotiating the city streets, the people, the weather, snowcapped volcanoes and forested slopes when I look back over the Hawthorne Bridge, chickadees that surprise in downtown trees: the living world figures itself to me. And the rest of the day disappears into the library.

One way or another, it's all reading. Our nature to read.

What could we learn about our world, and ourselves, by paying attention to this reading? For I've come to see that I'm living in a figurative world just as certainly as a physical one. Figurative: requiring interpretation; not simple; complex; layered. That when I see the world, I am seeing-myself-seeing-the-world, my own face half-mirrored on the bus window. This is not a bad thing, though it is troubling for the naive and the romantic, who want a purer nature to merge with.

That we read the world—in the sense of interpret it—in every waking moment is an acknowledged fact we never quite get used to. We keep having to remind ourselves that the witness of the senses isn't quite as self-evidently *real* as it feels. Seminal thinkers have long since deduced this—Kant is the obvious example. But in the last half of the twentieth century, experimental evidence finally began to come in. Humberto Maturana's famous 1959 paper on the neurobiology of cognition entitled "What the Frog's Eye Tells the Frog's Brain" described an intense circuitry of coding that carried information from receptors to brain. There was a lot of translating, sifting, and shaping to get the world around into the world within. And that was simply about perception; nothing about how the brain then assembled this supposedly "raw" data. Gregory Bateson's career, in its second half, focused a good deal on the implications of this kind of research, because it showed that there really are no "raw data" in a living system. Data get cooked immediately: the impulse that travels up a frog's neural net is froggy data, already processed, damped, amped, according to froggy ways of seeing. Maturana says that is because outside events do not directly enter a cognitive system. They "trigger" it: "living systems … must be treated as … systems in which whatever happens to them is determined in them by their structure. The interactions they undergo will only trigger changes in them; they will not specify what happens to them."

As Maturana's later co-author Francisco Varela phrased it: "we turn to the nature of the chimes, and not to the wind that hits them." When the wind of the world hits a person or a frog, the experience is a surprisingly internal affair. Maturana acknowledges that this fact of life demolishes naive certainty about the world out there: an "absolutely existing external world" is not demonstrable from the experience of us or other critters who live in neural networks. (But, as I'll want to say later, who needs absolute?)

Perception is thus a transforming of physical event into information, a change in kind, as Bateson always insists, from the thing to *the news of the thing*. And this re-presented world, already transformed, requires further interpretation and arranging, as perception cycles into higher levels of cognition. Bateson is fond of referring to the work of Adelbert Ames, who studied the psychology of perception a generation before Maturana; but any freshman psych text goes on at some length, reminding us of what we know but can't quite remember to remember: the complex intellection that co-creates a perceived world. The world figures itself to us: it is present in an act of transformation. Re-presented, indirect, always at this interesting remove.

Without "the release of fact into imagination," as Northrop Frye puts it, there is no transformation of self, no transformation of world from the literal to the represented. To read it all flat is to miss most of it. This world—this nature we live in, write about, abuse, and are—is a figurative reality. The art of reading applies.

In an earlier chapter I made the case that we read a myth not through its details but by perceiving a sense of "how things happen," a pattern. Gregory Bateson might have pointed out that the difference between detail and pattern is one of "logical type": the pattern is different in kind from its details, in the way a drinking glass is different from the water it contains, or as our news of the world differs from the world itself. As we have seen, systems of meaning, like all systems, organize themselves by circuits of these higher and lower levels, nested so that larger brackets enclose or in a sense control the lower. We operate this way without thinking about it, every day: discriminating among levels of meaning, placing details in contexts (Bateson's "meta-levels") that explain and shape them.

When my grandfather, fresh to the big city, went to his first play (a melodrama), he jumped to his feet at the action's climax and shouted threats at the villain. He was serious. What was effortlessly evident to the rest of the audience—the controlling bracket of fictionalness—had escaped him: he was a "bad reader" for a moment, making a classic category mistake. In one sense he was no reader at all. Mired in rural poverty for his entire childhood, he had never so much as entered a classroom. In his twenties (after the melodramatic episode) he taught himself to read. He learned some crucial—you might say crucially human—distinctions, and was not ashamed, many years later, to tell the tale of his category mistake in the theater.

Literature in general exploits the play of possibility among higher and lower, literal and figurative—the layering of levels of meaning. Comedy plays the differences in levels for laughs: deflating a prig or bringing the starry-eyed down to earth. Tragedy explores complexities among the many human levels of loyalties, beliefs, and needs—an Antigone or a Hamlet agonizing over which bracket is the controlling one, the laws of the state or the laws of personal/familial duty. The laugh, or the bite, comes from the mental act of apprehending the difference in logical type, what is higher and what is lower, a big deal or a little deal. Our minds find these discriminations endlessly interesting for very good reason: that is not only how minds work, but in a sense is what they are—layerings of differences, recursive circuitry that creates frameworks of logical type.

The art of reading consists in understanding what to pay attention to and what kind of attention to pay: that is, not mistaking the figurative for the literal. Not failing to get the joke; not mistaking hyperbole for sincerity; not investing belief in what is fictional; not troubling over details when they are not the point. Mistaking the obvious, we're likely to say—except that it's not obvious until it's obvious (a telling circularity).

These distinctions of kind, these categories of meaning, are regularly mistaken by the uneducated or the obtuse, and a flattening-out of the imaginative world is the result. (And what other world do we live in?) Cromwell's fundamentalist shock troops destroyed statues that *represented* certain aspects of the spiritual life, just as Taliban fundamentalists more recently detonated ancient Buddha statues in Afghanistan. In both cases, bad readers literalized the metaphors of religious imagery, stupidly (there is no other word) doing what fundamentalists do: hating everything that is not plotted on their grid, fearing the three-dimensional suggestiveness that frees the heart. These are not trivial mistakes, and in fact they form a central battleground for humankind. Common human failings. Or failings to be fully human.

For not just the art of reading, but the art of being human, inheres in this skill: the subtle art of reading cues, picking up on context, rising or descending gracefully to the right level for the moment. This flexy responsiveness is just what can be so hard, when we find ourselves rigid with self-importance, or fear, or smallness of heart: we become unconsciously comical (or tragically self-defeating), not getting the jokes, not able to choose, trapped in two-dimensional codes of behavior that disable our native ability to respond to the multi-leveled flow of human intercourse.

Literalism is thus the enemy of what is most human. Flatness of affect, dull plodding insistence on details or rules, black-and-white thinking, humorlessness: these are not just sins of the fundamentalists. They are the abiding sins of Western culture as a whole, to the extent that we unconsciously believe that science is fact and fact is all; that "history" is what actually happened; that the map is the territory, and that's the end of it.

Reading nature—being in nature, being nature—requires the same kind of imaginative and interpretive skill. If, as I believe, our problems living in the natural world originate in confused thinking about ourselves-living-in-the-natural-world, then the problem is with what philosopher Robert P. Harrison calls "bad readers ... who either literalize the text or find allegories in it where there are none, which itself is a form of literalization." The "text" here is nature. That is: how we think about nature must be to *read* it.

Notice that this is a way to say our encounter with nature is never all construct. Obviously, there's an interface there. Reality, on the other side of our interpreting, goes on going on. Nature literature is full of words to try to grasp that border where world and self meet; it's a plaguey thing, cursed with the Cartesian dichotomy that all good nature writers are sworn to overcome. So there is no end of terms for this point of connection/separation (my computery "interface" is among the least charming): the oft-encountered "permeable membrane" and "interactivity," Maturana's "structural coupling," Norman Holland's "transactive," Joanna Macy's Buddhistical "dependent co-arising," and my favorite, Varela's "mutual interdefinition." Bateson points out, interestingly, that there's always a "gap" where the real world meets the trigger-activated receptors that translate it into information: receptors are discontinuous (digital) where reality is continuous (analog). Squaring the circle: there's always more going on than the "reading" can capture. Nevertheless, across the gap, whatever we think or do brings results we either like or don't like. Presumably we take note of the results, make adjustments, and on the cycle goes.

Except that the rigidity of literalist thinking tends to prevent response or adjustment. If you believe your map is, in fact, the territory—that your version of "nature" is gapless, simply and self-evidently true—why would you expect surprises? Surprises are what maps are supposed to prevent. And a substantial portion of our culture maintains a naive belief that science is nailing down the mysteries, "conquering" nature, reducing it to a single known reading.

I'm aware of the paradox here. Perhaps the best model of a self-correcting system of thinking is that of Western science. By definition it tests its facts, holding them provisionally, working always on revision. At the same time, however, the impressive success of science and technology has fostered the opposite of this openness and empiricism. It has created an impression that truth is simple, factual, and (when found) absolute. And that delusion is the literalist creed. (Of course, this "naive realism" thoroughly misunderstands science—as Thomas S. Kuhn famously demonstrated; but that has not weakened its grip on the culture).

The glaring instance of this literalizing mentality, the one that exercises all the chapters of this book (and much of my thought life, waking and sleeping, for the last several years) has been locating Eden in nature, in the literal, historical West—or as that writer in Seattle did, moving ever westward, with wild Eden currently "somewhere in the Yukon" and about to drown in the north Pacific. This is a category mistake: investing a mythic pattern with the authority of history and science. The result undermines all three: science is shanghaied (ecosystems as timeless Edens); history is falsified (conditions of life on the Eden-continent before Europeans came are overlooked, ignored, unseeable); and myth, that richly contexted system of meaning, is flattened into a simple, and simply wrong, two-dimensional story. Environmentalists habitually do this when they invest wild places with Eden longing or Eden grief. The consequence is obtuseness, of two kinds (corresponding to the two levels that are being collapsed): failure to understand detail and failure to understand context. And in place of responsiveness to reality, there is blind loyalty to a simple code.

In their commonly black-and-white system of thinking, such environmentalists typically have a hard time discriminating among solutions that are messy, mixed, and imperfect. They cannot read them, in other words. There is no spectrum; there are no middle terms, no differences in kind or scale; nature is either untouched wilderness, or (as Michael Pollan repeats) "you might as well build condos on it." Nothing in between. Pollan, ethnobotanist Gary Nabhan, and others have argued instead for a "local ethic" rediscovered in each place, a hard-won, detailed knowledge that includes human histories and natural histories invested in place and complexly layered there. No rulebook can guide this kind of reading—certainly no one-line recipe that says "nature should be untouched," and leaves the rest of the world undecipherable.

Close to home, I said; so here's a near example. Upstream from Portland's Hawthorne Bridge about a mile, or fifteen minutes' kayaking against the mild Willamette current, is a heart-shaped island. From its sandy margin you can see the damp skyscrapers of the city, the cars streaming over the arches and curves of our bridges, the rich folks' houses tucked into the West Hills behind them. Herons will stir around you if you stay for long. You might see some damaged salmon drudging by, or hear birdsong through the alders and black cottonwoods, carried on the wind from the broad sanctuary of Oaks Bottom just ashore. There may be river otters, nutria, beaver. Right in the middle of Portland. (I really love this place!)

Or you might hear heavy equipment from behind you, just over the tree-choked berm. For Ross Island is, as I write this, a sand-and-gravel operation. For seventy-five years shovelers and dredgers have been digging out the middle of the island: Ross Island is a hollow heart, a thin rim of scoopage and dumped dirt around a watery excavation, with a broad downstream tail and a hard-to-see opening into the huge "lagoon" where, once, someone stored some toxic sludge. But the law has required a certain amount of island reconstruction; I note that trees and shrubs have thickly overgrown the remodeled contours. When I look at the legal documents, I learn that islands once called Hardtack, East, and Toe are now merged into an imperial Ross, but from the west where the tourist stern-wheelers pass it all looks pretty good. One island, four islands—life goes on, alder and bigleaf maple, snowberry I saw holding on, blackberry invading and delicious.

In four years, the Ross Island Sand and Gravel Company will pull out its hoppers and dredgers and haulers. It will finish whatever remediation it is legally obligated for; and the public, some way, will reacquire this island. It will come to the city, or county, or the oddball three-county agency called Metro.

What on earth will we do with it? I've been wondering.

Once I was a wilderness guy; such a question would not have engaged my imagination. So near to folks. So sullied. No kind of theater for my wilderness persona, concocted of Muir, Thoreau, and Byron, with bits of Milton's Satan and Jesus in the Wilderness. I could read, like Muir, glacier tracks in high valleys; I could read, like Thoreau, glimmerings of insight in my soul, communing by wind-ruffled lakes. But a half-destroyed, half-reconstructed island, act of God and artifice of greed, I could not have read. The wilderness ethic would have offered me no guidance; it would not have understood the language. I've been going on walks, thinking about Ross Island. I've been looking at it, beaching my kayak, noticing how nature ignores our meddling. I've been going to committee meetings; I'm aware that some Superfund dredging is scheduled for the lower Willamette, and someone will have to prevent its poisonous muck from ending up in Ross's heart. And most of all, I'm convinced that someone will have to perform an act of deep imagination, reading that heart faintly beating in the body of the city all around it, to see how to bring a new thing into the world, a good thing of nature and human nature combined. I've been burning up a lot of hours in this reading. Something can be done here. Salmon can find clean gravel or refuge in passing. Herons can build up their numbers. Eagles or osprey can nest. It could be a good place to visit. Maybe there will be tiny caretaker's hut, awarded to poets and naturalists on six-month rotations. A path, careful and observant. A place—a compact bowl on one sloping-westward shore—where art could be visible from the river and from the downtown shore: a totem grove, place of aspiration and memory. And preeminently, good nesting, good living for birds, fish, creatures. Maybe there will be an arrangement of pleasures and meanings, an accomodation, a wildness paradoxically nurtured close to home, which may nurture us back if we let it.

The layers here are as interesting to me now as any glacial moraine or solitary soul-plunging introspection. Portland's present is here, a palimpsest of past acts; as with any person or place, acts of nature and acts of culture mingle indiscriminately, rudely. Lewis and Clark paddled by here; Clackamas and Willamette Indians lived here, digging camas in the poopy-smelling wetlands just ashore, thinking their thoughts about eagles or weather or strangers with rifles. I heard that a black bear swam here and rested, on its way to southeast Portland from the coast for its own undisclosed reasons. Lovers had a tryst here, it looks like—here where I've pulled my kayak up on shore. Maybe this was their fire-ring. I think randomly of my beloved, of this beautiful/ruined place, and then have dire thoughts about capitalists, and then realize I am one; and then think fondly of our city government with its astonishing complexity of bureaus and earnest planners, the conversations I've been having with them. I think of restoring salmon runs, and of birdsongs and how I get them mixed up. The sound-world brings it all to my ears in one crystalline interpenetration, my heartbeat at the base of it all, carsound and birdsound, rivercurrent lapping on this tiny shore: no end of chords, counterpoints, melodies.

We need to learn the layering. We need to value the multivalenced places we find ourselves in, all along the spectrum from "untouched" to "mildly peopled" to "densely cultured." Indeed, simply to see it as a spectrum would be a fine first step. The next step would be to understand our relation to place (any place, every place) as complex, not simple: as requiring a canny responsiveness that moves from detail to pattern and back again, reading out the meanings and possibilities. This kind of reading asks us to reacquire our native skills as trackers in the many-layered jungles of culture and wildness. The posture of humility comes naturally, you might say, in this act. We bend to look. We read, sniff, listen, respond. An interpretation is provisional—maybe it will rain. Maybe the animal comes this way tonight. Maybe this is the right thing to do. We give up the idiotic witch-doctoring of the West, with its one-size-fits-all pronouncements, whether wilderness ethics or plans to bulldoze and commodify everything in sight. If we read better, we will discover many sentences in between, many surprises.

Complex and many-layered reading is not alien to our culture, though we have become estranged from it, in thrall to simpleminded versions of science and history. Indeed, complex reading is so endemic in the human mind that examples are everywhere. Lately our critics have made major strut over "polysemy," the fresh discovery that things mean more than one thing. We may vaguely connect the idea to multiculturalism, maybe to feminism; many in our conservative land regard it as a crackpot invention of left-wing professors. Yet I recall that a generation ago, the key word in literary studies was "ambiguity," a less-sweeping way of exploring the same thing. The reason, perhaps, that our thinkers must continue to insist upon the obvious is this resistant cultural layer, the fundamentalist/literalist stratum that wants a flat, one-reading world.

So let us observe that the new is the very old: the fashionably up-to-date word "polysemous" appears in, for instance, a famous letter from Dante Aleghieri in 1319, to the victorious general of the Ghibillenes, Can Grande della Scala (whose name I love to say out loud). Dante was presenting the noble Can with the last book of the *Divine Comedy*, in hopes of patronage of course. The letter details what we now call the medieval "fourfold interpretation," a system of thinking originally applied to the Christian scriptures, but which also formed a more general habit of mind. We might learn from it.

The four levels of this system bear the names literal, allegorical, moral, and mystical or anagogic. Here's how Dante applied them to a Bible story, the Israelites' journey from bondage to Promised Land: "For if we consider the *letter* alone, the thing signified to us is the going out of the children of Israel from Egypt in the time of Moses; if the *allegory*, our redemption through Christ is signified; if the *moral* sense, the conversion of the soul from the sorrow and misery of sin to a state of grace is signified; if the *anagogical*, the passing of the sanctified soul from the bondage of the corruption of this world to the liberty of everlasting glory" (emphasis added). The intricacy of this fourfold system must have been as off-putting to Dante's pupil as to a modern reader (the Can was, after all, a man of action). So Dante immediately simplifies the four terms to two: the literal and the figurative. That contrast is the important one, and moving from one to the other is the basic mental gesture that pops the flat world into dimensions of depth.

While the literal truth of a Bible story was not really doubted by Dante or his contemporaries, it was the least interesting aspect. The obsession with "fact" was unknown to them. What is important—what is human—is the process of connecting fact to meaning. Exactly what Pollan insists on: that we cannot escape the burden of deciding, judging, weighing importances and meanings, sometimes of wildly different sorts.

Dante assembles the four levels into a hierarchy: the mystical presents the highest and most encompassing truth, and other truths are ranged below it. Shall we similarly pyramid our sense of truth? Or shall we, today, arrange it more democratically, more flexibly, perhaps in an ecosystem-like web? I wonder.

But I see that I have all along been using the allegorical level—my sense of *myth* as underlying story that shapes thinking. It's obvious to me that when a Merriwether Lewis or a John Muir steps onto a trail which he names "untouched wilderness," he is reenacting a mythos, an essential pattern for human action. Maybe it would have helped them—or us—to see other overlays of personal motive, cultural baggage, and spiritual meaning that coexist with that myth, shading and shaping it. And, above all, to recognize their fatal mistake of trying to find Eden in an actual place: both overlooking the allegory, and literalizing it.

I'll return to Muir and his struggle to validate some of the higher (or deeper) levels of meaning in the natural world. I wonder at the simultaneous flatness of his literalized world, and his aching need to spiritualize it; how the absence of a publicly validated mystical level was felt as a wound, a void, which all his energy could not fill. I've felt that myself. That would be worth exploring.

What we learn from Dante's way of thinking is to recognize that interpretation is essential, not optional. We have no privileged, unmediated view of the world; we know that our senses themselves are energetic interpreters, and that the real world lives in our minds only in versions and constructs. So we had better think about them. Our pluralistic moment teaches us one thing better than Dante knew: polysemy is a lingo-jungle we cannot expect to tame. The relation of meanings is wild, and not static.

I said that nature is a text we read, but that reading it is consequential: it brings results which we ought to heed—news about the real world out there. That implies the other side of the transaction is a simple reality, a thing, to which we need to bring a lot of interpretive pizzazz. But interpretive complexity isn't just a human skill. It is in nature too. In fact, it *is* nature. I repeat: nature itself is an interpretive complexity.

That sentence will bring me endless hostility, I fear, from the best folks in the world, the nature-lovers, my fellow-travellers. They will think me literarily infected (with a French disease named Derrida or Foucault), will think I believe in a social construct of nature with no tether to trees-'n'-dirt reality. So let me lead into this jungle gently. Quietly.

I bring my students through the steps, talking about our many ways of seeing nature, the cultural constructs we have learned to see and to see through. We list the metaphors, history-of-ideas style: at various times, nature has been a hierarchy. A well-made watch. A ruthless jungle. An ecosystem. Nature is wilderness, is Eden. Nature could be garden, commodity, benevolent mother, vengeful backlash. So many metaphors. How are we to choose?

And it comes to me: the point is not to choose a better metaphor. A category jump: nature *is* metaphor.

What would this mean? The weakest, most limited form would be to recognize that when we use the word "nature" this way we are creating a high-level abstraction. One word to stand for everything, every atom, every being, every process. ... "Singular, abstract, and personified," as Raymond Williams puts it. Do we, in fact, believe that the totality can be summed up so easily? No human word (or encyclopedia!) could possibly contain so much. No matter how full the description, reality is fuller: so the word "nature" and all it includes can only *stand for* nature—that is, represent it, as a metaphor (part for whole or synecdoche, in technical terms). William Cronon points out that such an abstraction is functionally indistinguishable from other vast abstractions like "God." "Nature is metaphor" could be a merely semantic discovery, meaning "The word 'nature' is a metaphor." That's the least it might mean.

But the process by which we create metaphors is more than just semantic. I can see metaphoring itself as natural process, a way nature natures through us. Grammatical, layered, systematic: nature in our minds. That's good, that's true enough. I can use that. I call it wildness.

But "nature is metaphor" goes further than that. The strongest form of this claim beckons me to strangely compelling places. Nature is metaphor not just as we process it in our heads. In itself, on its own side of the great gulf, nature is metaphor. How could it be? Certainly I don't mean that nature is not "there," not independently existing regardless of my presence or absence. It's not a phantasm, it's quite real (though quite mysterious). But it is, nonetheless, metaphor.

First, even in inanimate nature, no thing is just a thing. Everything is also something else and on its way to being something else again. Our nouns try to freeze-frame what is in fact a seamless moving flux; to that extent language itself deceives us. "That is a cloud," we say: but it is not. It is an eye's illusion, a light trick of gaseous water. But each "it" we try to resolve the cloud into dissolves in its turn: it's a haze of water—but water is a *ménage* of molecules, which are alliances of atoms, which are spins of particles, which don't quite exist at all as matter but seem to peep into the thing-world from the energy-world, of which we can only say: it flows.

If we turn the microscope around we see ever-larger brackets of belonging, and the same blurring of identities: cloud, weather-front, season, climate, evaporation, condensation. The cloud *is* all of these things, and *represents* them too.

Nothing is merely presented. Everything is re-presented: represented: thus a kind of metaphor—metaphor being a way of saying two things at the same time, of representing one reality by another: "x is like y" and "x is y." It's the bothness of that saying that is its truth. And it's a figurative truth, because this is a figurative world: a world of mixed realnesses, at many levels. (And I like the way the word "figurative" equivocates about those two kinds of meaning. In the art world, figurative means literal depiction of things, figures; in the literature world, it means the opposite, metaphor and symbol.)

We've already glimpsed this paradox about ourselves: one with nature, two with nature. Always both things going on; and ourselves somehow between them, or shuttling back and forth across the differences. So if that first example was too easy—clouds are after all gauzy, vague things—any other thing or being will do. We know ourselves too well to pretend to be One Thing only. On any level—cellular, physical, social, spiritual, linguistic—we experience ourselves simultaneously as unique solitaire and as embedded part of a larger entity: always point and circumference simultaneously. All we are is given to us and flows through us to someone else. Yet we do not disappear into the flow, we know ourselves to be here.

Okay. Complexity, re-presentation, a figurative world. So far so good.

The same could be said, with varying degrees of intensity, for any living being. Bateson's wonderful treatment of metaphor and life—which is the genesis for this chapter—works through just how life itself, living process, works on a system not of clean, clear noun-like quantities (as our logic and our science imply), but by *likeness*: what he calls the "syllogism in grass" for its way of affirming what classical logic disallows:

> *Grass dies*
> *Men die*
> *Men are grass.*

That's supposed to be a logical blunder, based on misusing the syllogism to connect things through the predicate instead of divvying them up into neat piles of nouns (All men die; Socrates is a man; Socrates must die).

"Men are grass"—*humans* are grass, we would say—is a metaphor. Nature runs on this kind of metaphor, life linking to life through chains of likeness. Science and logic fight it, wanting nouns to deal with because they stay still in their categories and are easier to think about.

"But to try to fight all syllogism in grass would be silly because these syllogisms are the very stuff of which natural history is made. When we look for regularities in the biological world, we meet them all the time." As usual Bateson is concerned with pattern and relation. The trick we learned in studying myth will help us here: the truth is not in the details of "things" but in how they connect, what pattern they are part of. The pattern contains a kind of truth that goes further than the individual part. The relationship here, the pattern, is *likeness*. That is Bateson's key to understanding the living world: "The whole of animal behavior, the whole of repetitive anatomy, and the whole of biological evolution—each of these vast realms is within itself linked together by syllogisms in grass, whether the logicians like it or not."

Likeness. Homology. Adaptive evolution. Descent with modification. The hand, the hoof, the paw, the bat's wing, the whale's five-fingered flipper: likenesses—metaphors—that tell us how nature comes to be, what the pattern of relationship "is." They are "things" (to our eyes) whose identity simultaneously inheres in themselves and in the long chain of likeness whose latest link— whose re-presentation—they are.

That long chain tells us something else. Nature seen through Bateson's lens is motion: is transformation.

In using metaphor, we assert a logical and semantic transformation: *Men are grass.* Ambiguity abounds, various levels of meaning and possible meaning writhe in the mind, seeking the most pleasing arrangement (for it seems to me that thinking thinks us; though we usually pretend we are doing it). Over the boundaries of differences, likeness connects things, and an effusion of energy and perhaps mild euphoria is released into the mind, as one thing "becomes" another. Bateson is insistent that mere simile is not the same thing; a prosaic *Men are like grass* robs it of its vitality.

No: Fluidity and transformation are the power of metaphor. And not just in the mind, as a semantic epiphenomenon. Bateson insists this process, the *metaphoring,* is the nature of nature. A child (or colt or bud or seed) stands not merely in an "as if" relation to its progeniters ("as if it were they"): it is in a metaphoric relation that asserts *both* identity and interpenetration. Itself, not itself; past, present.

Bio-logic, we might say, is not classical logic. Biologic is circular and self-referential. It self-organizes in layers of recursive circuits and uses that organization—that ability to use information—to withstand entropy's constant dismantling, and in fact to swim upstream against it. To that picture we now add that living nature is metaphoric: its way of accumulating change while conserving pattern is through constant ramification of likeness. "Metaphor is not just pretty poetry, it is not either good or bad logic, but is in fact the logic upon which the biological world has been built, the main characteristic and organizing glue of this world."

At the end of his journey through Purgatory, Dante's traveler catches a glimpse of heaven (described in the *Paradiso* which would be offered to the puissant Can Grande; and just in time—the Can would suffer a terrible defeat just one year later). But the heaven that "Dante" sees is dressed in the garb of Eden. It *is* Eden. The poet has felt his way to the circularity of truth, its longing to form circuits that deliver it from the barrenness of one-way linearity. The downward and infernal path turns upward; the long exile from Paradise returns to Paradise. Our poetry is full of this discovery: T. S. Eliot was palming very well-worn coin with his often-quoted

> *And the end of all our exploring*
> *Will be to arrive where we started*
> *And know the place for the first time*

William Blake diagrammed it as a kind of spiral progress, from Innocence through Experience and around again to Higher Innocence: the same place on the circle, but up a level.

That's a Bateson level, a "meta-level," and it represents the nature of epiphany or insight: transformation. The same old world is seen, but as if from a height: a new pattern transforms the meaning of the details. The journey there is not laid out on any map because the new insight is of a different logical type, it jumps off the flat map into another dimension. No rulebook can get there; the path lies through hell, apparently—Dante's Inferno, Blakes' disillusioned Experience, Eliot's cindery dispirited England. It's a pattern that must be experienced, lived through, to get to that unteachable moment, that koan-breakthrough, that gestalt shift that reconfigures the world. No recipe for epiphany. No substitute for the agonizing labor of living, deciding, making mistakes. And then breakthroughs.

That's the way we need to see Eden: not as a tale of a dead quantity lost in the backward of time, but as a living metaphor, a reality in a pattern with our present. Our relation to it is in our daily acts, not just in moments of holiday communion. Paradise lost is no use to us. But the paradise that can be refound is: that's where we might go, ourselves, for transformation. As Dante did, understanding that wherever Eden might have been literally, its transformative meaning was ever-present. But its finding would require an act of interpretation, a reading of his life that opened it out like a book, that translated it into imaginative worlds.

We will have to approach our world, with its fallen forests, purgatorial oceans, and poisoned heavens, with a similar heart. How they mean is metaphor; and our metaphor of Eden should be at home there. As a myth, it can coexist with the other meanings and realities. We layer them, knowing that they are all metaphors, all transformations of that curious unseen world, that wildness, that gives us life and thought. The Eden that inheres in every atom is not less present than the Eden seen in a still-uncut forest; or the Eden remembered in one we are too late to save. Or the Eden we will find, or grow, tomorrow.

In reading these representations, these figurations, we add yet another layer to the wildness of life itself.

Good Indian, Bad Indian

or, The Opposite of Queer is Still Queer

One early-winter afternoon my older brother drove me out into the rolling edges of the northern Sierra, where the not-very-high mountains, long ago smoothed out by deep falls of volcanic ash, were receiving a fresh softening of light snow. Those woods go on and on, round summits and mild valleys and long rhythms of ridges, endless like a forest ocean. I remember looking out the window of my brother's rattling little Datsun truck. I had been staying with him and his wife and newborn while I finished my dissertation; now it was done. This was his territory—my mountains were far to the south—but he said this was a nice place with an easy-to-see trail, and I was happy to think of walking off into the woods, watching my boots print through the inching snow into the cold pineneedle duff, building up a barrier of quiet and solitude that no one could breach until I chose to come out. My reward for finishing. I was twenty-seven. This is the brother I used to describe to my friends as, well, a little scary. After a frailish childhood he turned himself big and athletic, and though he went to a sort of college (a fundamentalist enclave deep in Arkansas) while there he mostly fished and hunted. When he graduated he moved to a remote California village between the high desert and the mountains, joined the smallest and most backward church he could find, and began raising his family. He was unfailingly kind and generous to me. But with his bitter little church and martial-arts masculinity, I never had any place to stand with him. I returned little of his kindness, keeping most of my life to myself, a silent, studious, lonely, monkish brother.

When I eventually came out to him (and to the rest of my family—a dubious decision, leaving disruption and bad feelings all around), my brother and I had just a few conversations before the big silence descended between us. In one, I asked what he had thought of me all those years. I thought I knew what he would say. I never dated; I was always rail-thin, vaguely aesthetic, sensitive to slights, shaky and useless in a fight—surely never living up to the family standards of maleness.

But: "Too masculine, if anything," he said. My amazement could not have been more complete. "Lone wolf," he continued. "I thought you were just too tough and stubborn for anything as soft as settling down."

Things have a funny way of turning into their opposites.

Though at the time I believed I was escaping it, sex was what drove me to the mountains. In this story—my story—gender and nature are twisted together in all sorts of interesting ways. It's not surprising. Sex is nature naturing in us, a motion of biology and body we cannot quite ignore. Sex is always on the verge of overmastering the controls we invent for it. Sex is weedy and rank, sidewalk-splitting, strong-smelling, crawling into beds where it's not wanted.

Avoiding sex, I carried my virginity over granite miles and altitudes. Here the life of the body came back to me in a kind of ecstacy. The bands of forest; the meadows and microclimates, indomitable weathers, ancient geologies, and the slender human weaving that threaded among them. I felt paradoxically safe there, safe amidst dangers, safe amidst cool indifference.

Sex drove me to it, I said. But really it was gender, which like most folks I mistook as the same thing. Gender mingled with obstreperous desire and surrounded me with a nimbus of hostile social definition, penetrated me with self-loathing. Gender made a mess of it; while sex of course was just there—sleeping or waking, placid or desirous.

Nature in its "pure" form of wilderness became for me a place where maleness could be expressed. In the wilderness, sex was transmuted into definitions of self, proofs and warrants of virility: into gender, in other words. If in our culture (as in my family) value is defined by maleness, then facing the wilderness is an essential act, an archetype of the masculine. Accordingly, when I worked with other young men at wilderness guiding, I made sure to best them whenever possible. And the intensity of my determination, the little satanic fires of self-hate that burned within me, powered me past many a better lad. Young Tim B., I recall, an Adonis at twenty-one, possessing all the outward attributes of handsome muscularity that I lacked, and a cocky swagger: I made mincemeat of him, over and over as the weeks at altitude progressed—on-trail, off-trail, running, rock climbing; even carrying a heavy pack, at a dead run, with a difficult climb at the end (we set ourselves these ridiculous tests almost daily)—the muscle-bound pretty-boy could not begin to match my manic scrawnyness. And so I passed, though the others wondered why I was such an asshole. Almost all of them managed their masculinity with less hurt to others.

I used "wilderness" as a place to simultaneously enact and deny my sexuality. I took my queerness to its opposite pole, yet never stopped being queer. Indeed, the queerness of my wildernessing is now obvious to me. And it was more than just overcompensation. I genuinely loved doing it. Still do. What is striking is how easily the queer and the male-male, the fey and the macho, coexisted in me, or even reinforced each other. It's a gender muddle: two sides of a (very clichéd) coin.

Where things are defined in oppositions, in dualities and either-ors, then both elements are needed to define the system. The polar opposites are secret collaborators, though from within the system joining them like this seems perverse.

In some ways this is pretty well-worn insight. It's not uncommon to notice that it takes Puritans to produce good libertines, the prim fifties to produce Hugh Hefner and *Playboy*. Without the priggish regime, lewdness loses its edge. Then it's just sex or normal human randiness or whatever. Not remarkable. Not naughty. (And, probably, not nearly as much fun.)

The general point about opposites needing each other must be a particularly French insight. I encountered it in a Jean Genet play, *The Balcony,* about criminals and judges locked in a fatal two-step of mutual self-definition. Jacques Derrida tortures the point too, under the name of "supplementarity." Michel Foucault pursues a similar analysis in his three-volume *History of Sexuality*, which (so far) I haven't finished reading. Normally I steer clear of academic fads that seem like airless boxes, clogged with self-important jargon and hairsplitting, and especially the scholastic religions of post-modernism, deconstructionism, and the like. Perhaps I'm too shallow for them. Yet despite my misgivings I found Foucault's first volume a merry book, brisk and readable and full of wise-guy insight in overturning the obvious. The nub of it is that things sexual in our Western culture are really not what they seem. We've all bought into what he names the "Repressive Hypothesis": the widespread belief that sex since the seventeenth century has been horribly suppressed, hounded from sight and made an unmentionable secret. All the while, though, the opposite has been true: all this hounding "incites" huge amounts of sexual talk and awareness. Yet we continue to believe in the hypothesis of repression, talking and acting as if sexual liberation were a recent discovery. Foucault outs the plain fact we've failed to notice: we've been obsessively mentioning this unmentionable for quite some time now. The cycle is self-perpetuating.

Wouldn't it be fun to use Foucault's "repressive hypothesis" for nature, especially given the fact that sex is, on some level, nature? Think of all the energy of identifying, blaming, shaming, exhorting we expend upon "the nature problem": we must stop littering, must begin recycling; must drive less, consume less, reduce, reuse, recycle … And at the end of it all, impossibly, we must someway up-end and reconstitute the whole of our global culture of industry and consumption. (Oh, is that all? one is tempted to ask.)

Could this obsessive discourse about "our separation from nature" operate in a similiar dynamic to Foucault's sex-discourse? At the root they are similar indeed: the raising of *a given* (physical existence in a living world) to the status of *a problem*, a single hypostatized abstraction bundling together diverse physical and social strands. The "repressive hypothesis" of nature-discourse is the obsessively repeated claim that "nature" is outside of us and we must get "back" to it. This is the formulation which drives the system. Paradise is Lost. Nature is Lost. We are Alienated. We must Save the Planet.

A typical subtype of the nature problem declares that that our belonging to nature has been masked or ruined by bad thinking (Christianity, Cartesian dualism, consumerism); we must challenge and root out these bad systems of thinking, to rediscover our actual naturalness. Then, our own minds renovated, we can go about saving the planet. There's that saving transformation, divided into two stages: conversion, followed by missionary work.

Foucault's method suggests exploding the whole thing: belonging and not-belonging are elements in a classic dyadic system, a polarity.

So there is never any escaping the badness by going over to its opposite. Real progress or discovery are impossible within this kind of system; all you can achieve is toggling back and forth, addict-fashion (on the wagon, off the wagon; "one with nature" briefly, during your vacation trip, then "alienated" again in your real life).

From this perspective one might notice quite heretically that, in some ways, we are far "closer" to nature now than in 1650 or 1750, when the continent was still in its supposed Edenic state. Consider Americans' blurred perceptions of nature, as described by the French traveller Chastellux in the 1780s: "Anything that had no English name has here been given only a simple designation: the jay is the blue bird, the cardinal the red bird; every water bird is simply a duck. ... It is the same with respect to their trees: the pine, the cypresses, the firs, are all included under the general name of 'pine trees.'" My kinsman William Bartram stands out against this backdrop because his botanical precision was so rare.

The precision of our naming and knowing today could hardly contrast more sharply. The sciences of biology and environment existed only embryonically at the time Chastellux wrote. Nature, like sex, has become "a thing to be administered"; we entrust it to degreed professional competencies of governing, planning, remediation, and management. Business operations know not only what the profitable bits of nature are, but also (equally) how to cozen the other constituencies to get what they want. And for the rest of us there are nature programs and recreations to amuse ourselves; and political factions and nature clubs to define ourselves.

It would not do to overplay this hand. Obviously, some colonial Americans knew a bit about their place. And obviously most of the continent was in incomparably better condition then than now. But in terms of institutionalized and detailed awareness of nature, we presently live in an almost unimaginably more exacting thought-world: what Foucault calls a "multiplicity of discourses" about nature-knowing, nature-saving and nature-governing.

For Foucault insists that discourse, power, and knowledge are inseparable. The elaborate knowledges we have built up, with their precise languages, both reflect and call forth social structures. As Eric Darier points out, for Foucault power is not merely an external imposition of force. The inward structuring of thought by language is itself a form of power. In what Foucault calls the "Rule of

Immanence," "discourse can be both an instrument and an effect of power." Thus, it would seem that a potent concept like "environment" or "ecosystem" must arrange one's experience and understanding, and then support (or demand!) social and political institutions. Foucault's description of power contrasts with the traditional view of power as an external coercive force (with its corollary, the repressive hypothesis). Without the inward dimension, the political forms are dead. Thus, we govern ourselves in expression and suppression as much as any government agency or outward force does—and usually without awareness we are doing so. In Terry Eagleton's memorable phrase, "Ideology seeks to convert culture into Nature." The tendency is to regard our own experience as untouched, authentic, inevitable. That is, as "nature." Without a ruthless, sharp-eyed Foucault, we can rarely see how language, culture, or power are shaping it.

The great example of this ideological shaping of experience is the Romantic immersion in nature, which is still such a force in the culture as a whole and especially in environmental and nature-writing circles. Think of Wordsworth, Thoreau, Muir, or Abbey: a solitary individual communing with nature and achieving epiphanies large or humble, unmediated by social realities, which are supposed to have been left behind. Foucault's approach notices that the language and thought-life of the solitary communer bring society along; and that the communing takes place within well-developed external networks as well. Even standing quite alone, as I have done, on grand granite peaks, staring out over seemingly endless mountain vistas, raw and glorious, the human is webbed in from within and without. Climbing knowledge and social encouragement; spiritual and literary traditions; privileges of leisure, money, and class; governmental permissions, trails, parks. Simply inventorying the many ways I was supported and defined in this solitary activity could fill an encyclopedic work. You, dear Reader, have had your moments too. You thought yourself gloriously stranded beneath the unblinking eye of the cosmos, didn't you? So did I. But we weren't.

We were enmeshed in discourses; inward and outward, official and tacit, they created the elaborate world of "nature" we experienced. There's no unmediated Eden for us, either of nature or of sex.

Which is not to say there's no nature-out-there: it is (of course!) powerful, deadly, ever-stirring. I break with Foucault on this—I'll have more to say presently: I'm convinced a lot more reality is available to us than he admits. We shape it and construct it—but it is still IT. We must reckon with Foucault's analysis and learn to recognize our constructs, and ride them lightly. Provisionally. Humbly. But the point of this humility is to remember the presence of a greater power than we think; indeed, a greater power than we *can* think.

Things have a funny way of turning into their opposites, I said. So it is worth noticing again that the historic American valuation of nature-as-wilderness shows exactly this flip-flop. I take such sudden reversals of valuation as evidence of dyadic (polar) thinking. Classic analyses such as Roderick Nash's or William Cronon's take us right through the mysterious transformation of wilderness (and the peoples that lived there) into their own opposites.

Puritans and other early colonists defined wilderness with what strikes us as a perversely backward valuation: it was the realm of the devil. As many have commented, the natural world they confronted was unknown to them, and hence must have been terribly frightening and indeed often deadly. Later pioneers carried similar attitudes far into our outback. If they searched, it was usually not for wilderness to enjoy: it was for wilderness to transform and get rid of as fast as possible.

It would take a lot of killing and a lot of clearing to accomplish. Indians, of course, fit into the scheme neatly: unredeemed. If God's (or America's) will was to be extended into this strangely populated/deserted wasteland, those who stood in the way would have to be removed. The logic was that of the familiar dualism: human vs. nature. Indians were simply classed as, essentially, not-human. In this sense, the wilderness was empty, waiting for the chosen people to occupy (and redeem) it. I'm interested in this thought process because we today stand on the far side of it: we have flipped the valuation into its opposite. It's a curious process: bad wilderness, good wilderness; bad Indian, good Indian.

Pedro Font, visiting the Colorado Yumans in 1775, wrote with disarming bluntness of the sub-humans he perceived—how they "live like beasts, without making use of reason or discourse, and being distinguished from beasts only by possessing the bodily or human form, but not by their deeds." Nor was this commentary merely the ranting of an unusually bigoted traveler. One hundred years later, George H. H. Redding rode a-fishing from his Sacramento Valley home up into the mountains, where he encountered some of the remaining Wintu Indians near Mt. Shasta. He found them "filled ... with the densest ignorance and the most weird and mythical superstitions," and reflected that, however long their people had been there, they had not taken even the first steps toward agriculture or any other improvement. He employed an evolutionary re-tooling of the previous century's prejudice: "The Wintoons have not yet arrived at any of these stages of civilization." According to the German observer Carl Meyer, who traveled in California in the early 1850s, Americans pretty generally believed that Indians were "not human."

So it is no surprise to learn that Redding's fellow-ranchers in the Shasta area, from the gold rush days through the middle 1860s, regularly hunted and exterminated whatever Indians they could find, in vigilante groups sometimes as large as two hundred, sometimes aided by U.S. Cavalry or led by officials such as R. A. Anderson, Sheriff of Butte County. It amounted to what Meyer had seen as "a systematic war of extermination." After one raid on a sleeping Yana Indian camp, Sheriff Anderson reflected in his memoirs, "There was not a bad Indian to be found, but about forty good ones lay scattered about." Nearly all of the last three thousand Yana were finished off by about 1864.

Good Indians, bad Indians. In a few years—just one generation— the valuation of those Indians would reverse, and Indian spirituality and nobility would become the nearly universal currency of popular thought for most of the following century. The last unkilled, un-Westernized California Indian, Ishi, who walked out of the hills near Mt. Shasta in 1911, would end his days at the Museum of Natural History in San Franciso, admired and extolled by the same Californians who, one generation earlier, had hunted his people to the brink of extinction.

Good Indian, bad Indian. At the beginning of this chapter, I found myself caught in an either-or valuation of maleness that led me into a kind of apotheosis of queerness: the macho man. I found my machismo in the mountains. I struggled with the Sex Problem, and the Gender Problem, until I could submerge both of them into the Nature Problem. My father would remind me, as the summary of all good manly things, to "Be a good Indian." But no matter how stoic I was, no matter how many victories I could achieve, no matter how many wilderness miles I counted, I could never feel fully a man. The worm of queerness ate away at the center of it all. God, I understood, did not like people like me. Nor would the other men in my life: fathers, brothers, teammates.

Not man enough. Be a good Indian. I worried these together with the most severe Bible verses I could find, making them into a kind of poison mantra, a vigilant moral overseer reminding me minute by minute of my deceit and sinfulness, an internal IV-drip of self-hatred and increasingly rigid self-control. No one made me do this; it was my own almost unbelievable stubbornness and pride. I made myself more Christian than anyone in sight, and indentured myself to an evangelical college, as if to prolong the agony. Lord, how I struggled, body and mind, until I teetered on the edge of breakdown and self-destruction and considered whether it was not time, finally, to reconsider. Sometimes hallucinatory in my ragged state, I heard audible voices: Not man enough. I heard voices: Be a good Indian.

And in the end, I shrugged. In the end, I did what everyone does (usually years earlier). I said: I guess I'll be a bad Indian. And then I began my life for real.

The irony of this came to me much later. It makes me laugh even now. Picture, for instance, that slender twenty-year-old in college agonies: walking night by heaven-storming night, tearfully praying to Jesus for deliverance, railing at impossibilities, resisting the love and affection and lust I felt for the trim young believers all around me. The fog comes in, the night passes. The sun comes up on chaparral mountains and sandy coastline. I am staring, all cried out, all prayed out, from a bluff of oak and pine over a rocky beach. This is on the California coast, south of Santa Barbara, which had been Chumash country up until about a hundred years before. Of course, absorbed in my own little melodrama, I didn't think of them, the Chumash, or the magnitude of their true agonies. I was wallowing in being a bad Indian. I was on their beaches, walking (unawares) on the site of their village at Carpinteria, wondering how to become an acceptable man.

I did not know, then, how in common with most of the original peoples of California the Chumash had held a conception of a man—a good Indian—that included a clear and indeed much-honored category of queerness. Their appreciation for *berdache* (a European word for cross-gender sex-roles) absolutely scandalized, for instance, the Spaniards who came to subdue and Christianize them. Poor Pedro Fages, "Soldier of Spain," visited Carpinteria and other Chumash villages in 1775 and wrote: "They are addicted to the unspeakable vice of sinning against nature, and maintain village *joyas* for common use."

"Two or three in each village!" he exclaims. And it seemed that "all these Indians," not just a few, were thus addicted—visiting the *joyas*, marrying them, holding them "in great esteem." If it were not for the deadly consequences about to obliterate not just the fey *berdache* but their entire peoples, this would be a comic narrative: the oblivious, sexually relaxed *Indios*, the steel-helmeted *Españoles*, the amazement, the miscommunication. We could almost laugh at Fages' fellow Spaniard Pedro Font, writing in his diary at the same time and with the same prim ignorance, who denounces "sodomites, dedicated to nefarious practices" among those desert Yumas: "They are so shameless and excessive that I do not believe that in all the world there is another tribe that is worse." But then he adds, ominously, "In this matter of incontinence there will be much to do when the Holy Faith and the Christian religion are established among them."

It was the same nearly everywhere in California, by accounts of the scholars and eyewitnesses. Anthropologists reporting in the 1930s on nearby Mohaves, just over the mountains from where I grew up, cannot quite believe it—how these people enjoy sex in all its variations, and love to talk about it, and have not thought of vilifying anyone over it. In fact Indian cultures continent-wide typically saw sexual orientation in what seems very modern terms: as a basic nature, something that cannot and should not be altered.

And, to bring it home to my story, it was the same in the Los Angeles basin, where I and my parents were born and grew up, in the inland foothill valleys. There, Gabrielino Indians had rivaled the Chumash in cultural sophistication and sway, and in embracing and celebrating their sissy sons. These Gabrielino had had a thriving village in the canyon called Tujunga just a mile or two from to my boyhood home, where in fact I ran cross-country workouts with my high school teammates, where I worked on constructing a foolproof mask of masculinity through athletic victories and Baptist religiosity, to conceal the impossibility of being a good Indian.

This was their land. I was, indirectly, their son. And I had no idea. Surely, some dark kind of comedy is here.

I can't say I knew anything of these departed and to-me invisible people. But what of the Cherokee whose echoes seemed so distant and yet so strong in our family? Again I knew nothing. But the case is there to be made. Europeanized very early, the Cherokee quickly lost their tradition of *berdache*. It's a common phenomenon among subjugated peoples: whatever is disrespected by conquerors quickly becomes a matter of shame and concealment. Yet Walter L. Williams reports a document from 1825, in which a Cherokee told a white traveler, "There were among them formerly, men who assumed the dress and performed all the duties of women and who lived their whole life in this manner." But this was lost in historic times. The broken traditions, the half-remembered stories, the silences. They bless, they curse.

O my father, I want to tell you: I was a good Indian after all.

I wish to live in my nature without fear. To live in nature without false consciousness either of Saving or Losing. I don't need to mourn the world, or fear that God has abandoned me. Wildness in my bones, in my bed; nature in me; God in me; queer or straight, masculine or sissy. Why should any of them be outside the delicate, exotic exuberance of the world?

Perhaps "wild" is after all just another word for "God." Though what I really think is: "God" and all his religions are just languages trying to deal with the wildness of the world. Once the wild world was thought to belong to Pan, that horny goat-god: irresistible force, half animal, half man, wild and civilized, god of music and unceasing sex. Pan seems to have something to do with the power of both sex and nature to burst categories.

"Gender" has been linked to "wilderness" in my private journey, and this has allowed me to reflect on the ways we have constructed nature in these two realms. Both wilderness and gender are taken as givens, as reality, instead of being seen as the overlapping constructs they are. Lots of analysis in the last two decades has explored the "gendering" of nature, often making the point that, for Western culture, nature is a feminine force that must be controlled by the masculine. Carolyn Merchant's *The Death of Nature* is the best-known of many such feminist analyses that see manifest destiny and the pioneering push to "conquer" the virgin West as expressions of an aggressive hypermasculinized culture. In this formulation, civilization is masculine and nature feminine.

Yet the reverse is also observable: the late-nineteenth-century Wild West, where civilization had not quite arrived, was perceived as a specifically masculine zone, and its opposite was "culture," perceived as feminine. Stephen Crane's 1898 story "The Bride Comes to Yellow Sky" is a classic embodiment of feminizing school-marm civilization coming to tame the wild-boy West. Teddy Roosevelt's personal story of going West as a sickly back-east rich boy, and becoming masculinized in the Western rough-and-tumble, helped define a mythic storyline. So the feminist analysis actually reverses the story that would have been told by many of the participants at the time. It makes a pair of opposite readings.

I'd like to offer a perspective that jumps out of the dyadic system altogether. For there's a sense in many of the old mythologies that nature transcends gender: it is both masculine and feminine, a force that escapes safe channeling. Zeus, on the throne of Olympus—the quintessence of masculinity, with his thunderbolts—is married to the august mother-queen Hera: but there at his side is Gannymede, the boy he fell in love with. Hercules, paragon of maleness, in bed with beloved Hylas and a long list of other male love-conquests that somehow never dented his masculinity. And of course Pan, who surely symbolizes the reality that nature exceeds the simple grids and definitions people bring to it. Pan swamps the little two-paddle canoes we come in, immersing us in powers and possibilities that overwhelm easy categorization.

Here is where I come to the limits of Foucault and the entire school of "social construct" thinking. As useful as their analysis is, they oversell it. Just because the constructs we impose are powerful, doesn't necessarily mean they are all-powerful. And the testimony of human experience over many cultures and thousands of years loudly proclaims that the voice of something beyond ourselves is regularly heard, over the nearly deafening noise of our own humanity. God does speak from the whirlwind. We do test, and learn, bumping into the Real and being bumped by it. *It.* Not just by our constructs of It.

The natural-science argument for this obvious point is compelling: regardless of our conceptual limitations, natural selection guarantees us a certain degree of functional truthfulness. Our senses and mental maps cannot be pure fantasy; they have to work well enough for us to survive, at least. The burden of proof is surely on the radical skeptics and social constructivists, to explain away this part of our birthright: that we live in a real world and know it well, if imperfectly. What we have been adapting to, these last million years, is not just our idea of nature.

Foucault is a good (even notorious) example of the oversold "construct" idea. He is almost too easy a target—the snarky Frenchman, urban and fey, smarter-than-thou, dismissive and cocksure. The very image environmental writers love to hate, a person trapped in the urban delusion, divorced from life-giving nature. Foucault's biographer tells how the great man drove through the Italian Alps with a colleague, Jacqueline Verdeaux: "Whenever she showed him some magnificent landscape—a lake sparkling in the sunlight—he made a great show of walking off toward the road, saying, 'My back is turned to it.' "

"*Moi, je lui tourne le dos.*" It's an over-reaction, isn't it? A self-maiming: making oneself blind to the very world, simply to make a philosophic point.

At the end of the first volume of his *History of Sexuality*, it becomes quite clear that Foucault regards gender constructs, like nature itself, as unnecessarily limiting, and that he wishes sexual possibilities to be not just expanded but *unlimited* by biology or evolutionary history. For it is not just gender but sex itself that is constructed: "Sexuality must not be described as a stubborn drive … It appears rather as an especially dense transfer point for relations of power." So sex is not biology or nature, but politics. It's the *not/ but* construction that stops me. Surely the existence of a construct does not have to imply that it is constructed of nothing? For I am convinced that the real action is in playing the dynamic *between* construct and underlying reality. Foucault, it appears, turns his back on nature in any form. He absolutizes his insight about cultural constructs, launching himself in a little capsule of certainty off the planet and out of his body: limitless, unrestrained, "free." It looks like nothing less than an exaggerated "radical" freedom declared against oppressors, repression-hypothesis style. As if to be free must mean to be *absolutely* free. As if grace and beauty were not found in the very act of struggling with the edges, the rules, the materials— not in some formless blurt of "freedom."

That limitless ideal of freedom is an adolescent mistake, a sad fantasy, isn't it? One thinks of Foucault's biography, somewhere between pathetic and disturbing: how the pale academic strapped his not-so-young body into its store-bought leathers and sallied forth into San Franciso to be bad. Despite all Foucault's sophistication, he responded to the San Francisco scene with a sort of bumpkin excess. Leo Barsani, who participated with him, remarked that for Foucault the leather and S/M scene were "explosive," in a way that seemed a little off. "I mean, the scene was fun—but it wasn't *that* much fun." More disturbingly, some of Foucault's biographers have (on evidence from Foucault's own partner) concurred with the rumors that surrounded his death from AIDS in 1984: that Foucault had turned his back on biology again, intentionally engaging in unprotected sex as part of an assertion of radical freedom. James Miller concludes that the philosopher felt caught between a classic opposition of "anxious restraint" or "fatalistic abandon." The looping, cagy complexity of Foucault's intellectual work did not deliver him to a new place at all, but rather dead-ended into a gay-eighties version of the same old puritan-vs-libertine dyad.

Freedom from biology, freedom from limits: they amount to the old error of the West, the fantasy of human exceptionalism. As if bodies, microbes, and mortality were not the conditions of our lives, within which we must make our way. This fetishized "freedom" is another way of placing humankind on a unique little throne, outside of evolution, ecology, biology, the biosphere. Whatever "free" means, it cannot be located in a self-involved turning-away from the natural world. When Pan overcomes us, it is not with the message "I am not here." It is with the opposite: "I, Pan, am here, and full of power which you ignore at deadly peril."

In fact, attempting to turn one's back on the wildness of the natural world—Foucault's response—is such a common reaction that it bears Pan's name: panic. "Panic flight" is a reality that wilderness guides learn to recognize. I have seen it take a grown man, an athlete in full strength, and drive him to headlong, heedless running, until exhausted sleep overtook him miles from the campsite where we waited all night with bonfires to guide him back. He had been caught out at dusk, walking up a stream. As darkness came on, he panicked.

There's a fearful power of life and death around us; we don't know all its names. When Thoreau met it, on the top of Ktaadn, he recorded his near-panicked response, throwing questions at it. I have learned to sit still when this unreasoning fear meets me; I have tried to open my ears; even with the pounding blood-pulse, something can be heard.

Nature speaks through, past, and around our constructs. We are not completely imprisoned; even Paris has roads that lead out of it, winds and rains and rivers that enter from the surrounding largeness, cleansing and refreshing. And lights, as Thoreau says, that arrive nightly from unthinkably far away: how could we make ourselves so provincial as not to see them?

So nature could be queer as me, queer as Thoreau. That's no worse a formulation than nature-as-feminine or nature-as-masculine. The essential gesture, I'd like to suggest, is away from either-or, toward a flexible spectrum—nature's "multiple but finite truths." Many possibilities, within the envelope of nature and body. Queer nature: full of tricks: hard to categorize: consistently outrageous. Pan. Nature. Sex.

So many names for the wild.

Palimpsest:
Queer Pants

I've got these hiking pants I just love, though actually I hate them. The most perfect backpacking pants I've ever owned. Over at Andy and Bax's surplus here in Portland, I found blousy, big-pocketed, can't-bust-'em trousers. Cheap. And my size. But, Lord, all camouflage: olive and tan and black doodles. Pure Gomer Pyle. But otherwise perfect. "I'm not concerned about fashion," I reasoned; "I'm a mountain guy. I should transcend."

But I couldn't. I felt like a creep at every encounter. And I hated driving to the trailhead. After just one hike, I tried to figure how to undercut the militaristic bloomers. "A pink triangle!" I thought.

Jump-cut to the Goat Rocks Wilderness, near Mt. Rainier. I'm several days into a backpack trip, hiking solo. There's a completely scary man, armed with hunting bow, razor-tipped arrows, a gigantic knife, and who knows what-all else. His face is pinched, and he talks hillbilly, like what I've heard in the Appalachians. He's just come out of the brush, off-trail, and I'm standing there feeling like the skinny sissy I truly am, despite being a foot taller.

He's wearing camos, head to toe. He's looking me over. I'm thinking about the pink triangle I attempted to place on the right thigh of my camo trousers, using plastic "garment decoration" goop. I'm thinking about how a label is also a target. A bull's-eye.

But I'm saved by my ineptness as a sissy. I really can't dance, dress, or decorate, and my pink triangle has come out more like a ketchup-blotch. Or maybe a bullet wound. Bowhunter is clueless. He nods, says something so full of arcane diphthongs I can't understand it, crashes off into the canebrake. And I'm left quaking in my queer pants.

Bowhunter certainly was playing out a very familiar social story: *I'm a tough lone-ranger male, out hunting. Me, Hemingway, and the Real Men.* This use of nature became problematic around Teddy Roosevelt's time, right when "the frontier" was observed to be over with, closed, kaput. "Then where will we go to become

Real Men?" wondered the heroic sportsman president. Answer:
let's be sure to preserve some places where we can be toughened
up. And let's join the Boy Scouts too, founded just then for the
same reasons. Shed that weak, morally suspect, faintly effeminate
city-boy stuff. Wilderness manly. Nature virgin. You connect the
dots.

Nevertheless (and let's enjoy the element of contradiction here), I
also think of wilderness as a realm of alternative values, and of the
environmental movement as trying to get these somehow into our
culture. Nature answers (or at least questions) civilization: if you
spend a few days or weeks in the woods, the mall-and-TV world
seem less absolute. We recall there's something else alive,
something else bigger than the human. Life, death, weather, the
body are remembered as having the last word.

Even if we do project our mores and madnesses onto nature
(something that is surely true for environmentalists as well as
developers), nature still has the potential to surprise, challenge, and
overcome our preconceptions. It remains an alt.realm, where a
reality outside the culture-system is glimpsed (or at least
glimpsable).

It's a little game we play, familiar to most of us who go out and
struggle with raw(er) nature: you start off full of yourself and your
plans. Climb this. Hike that. Then reality happens: storms, pratfalls,
incapacities. Then you feel small. That's a good story, though not
the one you thought you were telling.

So what story was I playing out myself? Before I came out, I simply
wanted to claim masculinity for myself in terms that could not be
challenged. That meant being stronger, tougher, better. I seethed
with sexual energy. Boy, did I motor over them hills. But even after I
got laid and came out as gay, I kept up this engagement with the
wild, this flirtation with a kind of machismo I wanted to puncture
and to enjoy possession of … simultaneously. Confusing, really.
Kind of like my queer pants.

A little gay-bashing up in the woods in Washington State
recently helped clear it up, though. Don't fret, this isn't a victim
story, since I more or less came out on top (as the saying goes). A

simple tale: My lover and I walked to a waterfall, just a little two-mile trail. We held hands now and then. Four teenagers happened to be at the falls. It was big place, and we sat far away, comfortably leaning against each other and talking. We gave the teenagers no second thought.

But one was hyper, and he was trouble. When he came over to us, we were bending over a tiny Ladyslipper Orchid, a lovely surprise in the north woods. He looked interested, so I explained. He bent over and bit it off, looking at us mockingly, glancing at his friends for approval.

On the return trail, he ramped it up. Our two groups left at the same time, so whenever one slowed or rested, the other passed. I was a few paces ahead, and did not receive or even notice any of the thrown pebbles or mocking side-comments. Eventually a two-liter bottle (empty) came hurtling over and hit my companion's feet and I looked up. What gives? I wondered.

I had never had such a thing happen to me in my life. I'm a tall white guy who can easily "pass." My lover, however, is Asian. He's short. He made an easy target. Seems the youngster was making cartoon-chinaman ching-chong noises whenever we passed. Playground-bully-style, he kept escalating his harassment as we went along. Until the thrown bottle, I was oblivious. Then I was mad.

Reader, I shoved him. We had a tense standoff, a few feet off trail where he landed (shocked, I think, that a queer would respond this way). As I sized him up, I thought: What is a fey fifty-year-old doing in a fistfight with this little thug? He was smaller than me but muscled over in a fatless, tightly strung way. A Real Man, I thought, would just flatten this punk. But would I?

Didn't have to. We talked, shouted, argued. Young Punk's friends offered sophisticated theological repartee ("Adam and Eve, not Adam and Steve"). He informed us we were damned. Blah blah, but finally we all walked away.

I see now that it's a pretty good illustration of who gets messed with and who doesn't. I was used to passing: well camouflaged by class, race, temperament. But my companion was already labeled in various ways, and he didn't get to pass. So we were targeted as out of line, dangerous, heretic. We upset the boys who simply wanted to own the place and eat it up at their leisure. Their logger-daddies (I saw their pickup in the lot) would not object. Queers, environmentalists, what's the difference?

In fact, there's a sly but unmistakable connection between queerness and wilderness, buggers and tree-huggers.

Did you know Thoreau was as queer as could be? Probably pretty near virgin, sadly. But something queer contributed to his ability to stand aside from the norm, go off into the woods, and confront whatever was beyond the social construct. (Despite doing so in a highly constructed way.)

Think of it: men in the woods, unaccompanied by women. That romantic tale— Hawkeye/Leatherstocking and his injun pal, Lone Ranger and Tonto, Huck and Jim … isn't that the myth? And isn't that the formula that has brought us our most powerful nature writing? Even John Muir, alone in the woods despite (at forty, grudgingly) having a wife and kids somewhere. The story he believed placed him alone in the presence of nature. But he had to fend off questions about the "masculinity" of his raptures over forests and flowers. He was suspect, too.

Buggers—queers—are, in our culture, automatic heretics. And so, by the logic of the system, heretics must be automatic buggers. "Bugger" comes to us from eleventh-century Europe, where some religious dissenters had to be rooted out of Bulgaria. It seemed obvious to Inquisitors that queer in doctrine meant queer in the pants, and so, as the *Oxford English Dictionary* delicately puts it, the name bugger (originally "bulgar") was applied "afterwards to other 'heretics' (to whom abominable practices were ascribed), also usurers."

Jews, queers, nonconformists. There's your package, fresh from right-wing hate mail. In cold-war days, pinko was never far from pink. Queers and commies were nearly indistinguishable. Why not environmentalists too.

Though we project our socially constructed meanings onto nature, and play them out as if they were "real," and confuse our projections with nature itself, Nature Itself is always capable of bursting our bubble, breaking through (usually with a whack or worse), and insisting that Real Reality is bigger and stranger than we've ever imagined.

And when gay people go around bursting gender categories and goofing up the neat either-or schema, we're sort of speaking for nature—doing the Lord's work, you might say. Isn't that a hoot? Insisting that real people and real sexuality are strange, multiform, exciting, unprogrammed, and capable of infinite surprise. Just like nature. Just unlike the staid, safe, stultifying confines of rigid gender categories.

Well, no big surprise. Sex is wild. Literally. A little wilderness right in your pajamas!Sex keeps on escaping the cage, running wild in the streets, eating the suburban poodles, messing up the smoothly running and too-scripted system of Girl, Boy, Marriage, Death. And the numb consumerism that sometimes goes with it.

To oppose these orthodoxies is buggery. Queerness.

I say: let's claim the badge gladly. Let's be queer for the woods. Because this kind of queerness is not limited to gay boys. Over here on Hawthorne Boulevard, I keep meeting guys who sleep only with girls (darn it), but who are clearly not straight. They're so not-worried by the categories, so happy with their gay friends, so full of touch and affection, so relaxed and alternative and willing to push past the social-construct gender limits. They're queer, in other words. Though not gay.

Reader, you revere nature, don't you—else why this book?—and so you probably get it. Those who go *outside* in any sense are likely to discover the queerness of the world. It don't stay put. It keeps surprising. It won't fall into our neat constructs. That's the meaning of a climb, a hike, a close look at an ecosystem or even a square-foot of living soil: reality is absolutely beyond us, and we'd better learn to ride our constructs lightly, provisionally. Maybe a little humorously, ready to be surprised.

Outside the pale, outside the mall. Outside the preconceptions and categories. Outside. Where things are dangerous and amazing and never, never quite what you expected. Get on your queer pants, everybody. Nature's taking us for a ride.

A Mutability Canto

When a tree falls in the forest, it sends out ripples. The news travels in sound, smell, dust, flying bark, broken limbs—killing some, disturbing others, yet hardly troubling the massive calm. There's a rain of needles, a swaying of neighbors. After a few minutes, you have to look carefully to find it.

Deadly change in the midst of stillness. Which is real? A double reality, perhaps.

What I remember most is the smell. I was eating my lunch in a clearing at the far end of a long, thin lake in the Sierra Nevada Mountains. It ran longways into the mountain, and I had made my way around on paths that got lost among logs and deadfall, petered out in talus below cliffs, then reappeared to push through grovelets of new trees and one old, hushed stand. From somewhere over here, the night before, I had heard coyotes baying. Their songs or challenges had drifted over the full-of-stars lake, piercing and echoing and dying away, and I had been perched at the outlet end where the lake poured itself over a rib of granite. In the morning I thought I'd go take a look; by noon I was hungry. I may have had a little peanut butter left in a tube, to squeeze over crackers.

The tree that fell on that clear blue day, about thirty paces from my lunch, sent out a creaking groan, then several sharp retorts, then a tremendous thumping crash and a momentary foot-felt vibration; then, after an uncanny pause, a billow of dust that carried over me the unmistakable moist tang of fresh wood, the life-smell.

The forest closes quickly around such events. I dropped my crackers and aimed my unlaced boots toward the sound but it was over, past, and within a few steps it seemed I had nothing to go on but recollection. Over here somewhere. One downed tree looks like another, and suddenly I noticed how many, big and little, criss-crossed the forest floor.

What gave it away was that smell. I followed it to find a huge layed-out trunk revealing a wetness of exposed skin and the tail-ends of bugs trying to get out of sight along the worm-trailed surface that had been, until a minute or two ago, a safe dark place. Impact had split the bark along the whole length and peeled the tree neatly, dark-red rinds stacked and scattered along both sides. To my hand the fresh wood was cool, damp, faintly gritty. Needles on unbroken branches were closely curved, four-sided: Red fir (*Abies magnifica*), known for size and brittleness. Waist-high near the base, the tree sprawled down a mild slope, across a swale, and down another slope, broken in two places where the contours changed. The head-downwards deposition disturbed me a little, as if it weren't quite right. But it was. In a few minutes the bugs disappeared. I sniffed the cambium layer, picked up some bark, tallied the other trees crushed or knocked around.

I felt like I had chanced upon something private. Of course logs in every state of decomposition lay everywhere. But the woods give us the impression of stasis, don't they?—a kind of eternity we walk into. That's an illusion very hard to shake. The smell of the fresh wood, the death of that long, slow excellent life, stayed on my hands, reminding me. That helped. A year or two later, on another trip, the top of an even larger red fir simply split off before my eyes and crashed onto the trail ahead of me. The smell was the same. So was the feeling: a sense of seeing into the private process of forest, which somehow we usually miss.

I suppose we must be quick, sharp things, from tree perspective. It is hard for us to appreciate their pace, their calendar. We mistake much of nature, actually, as a kind of eternal rest, when clearly it is a boiling of materials, a continual sloughing and shedding and borrowing and remaking. Or rather: we know this as a fact but we don't feel it. A jolt now and then helps, a strong whiff. Environmentalists are pretty good at reminding us to see the swirl of process behind the moments of calm beauty we experience in nature. But only "pretty good," for as you read environmentalist literature a certain countercurrent also emerges. There's something in us that yearns to see a beautiful stillness in nature, a vast bosom rising and falling in calm respiration. That's half true—and half nonsense. The true half has been pretty valuable. The false half keeps getting in the way.

Our human problem with the changingness of things—
"mutability" in an older lingo—plays out in our picture of nature.
Mortality is a hard calling. It's a restless and shifting world we live
in, that threatens our safe harbors and eventually claims every one
of them. We are all too likely to invent a "nature" that's a refuge
from change. You can see it in all kinds of nature writing. You can
hear it on almost any excursion of nature-lovers. The natural world
can seem to us like a safe haven from time. We take our troubles
there and are answered. But as with all oracles, the answers are
clouded. Just below the comfort is something else. That calm,
predictable self-organized ecosystem perches, like the rest of us, on
the brink of ceaseless change.

If we are to find a refuge in nature, it will have to be a bold one.
For every calm beauty is, of course, on its way to becoming
something else. As are we.

The environmentalist worldview that emerged in the twenty years
following Earth Day 1970 rested on that emotionally satisfying
picture of nature as a complex stasis. The science of ecology had
created an idea of nature—a construct, we would say—that
contrasted with the stereotypically Darwinist "red in tooth and claw"
version. By emphasizing the effective functioning of the whole,
ecology provided a means for seeing nature in a more optimistic
light. It was, as a whole, beautiful. Suffering and predation and
competition did not desist; but they were counterbalanced by
symbiosis and cooperation, a present-tense stasis of beautiful,
systematic integration. The great early-twentieth-century American
ecologist Frederic Clements set the course for this emphasis. Though,
as Donald Worster points out, Clements was deeply interested in
change—championing the idea of ecological "succession" of plant
communities—he was also, paradoxically, committed to the idea
that succession would culminate in a final and in a sense permanent
stage: the "climax community." A normal sequence of plant
communities would build in complexity toward this climax, which
would maintain itself in a state of dynamic equilibrium.

Textbooks have since institutionalized the example of "pond
succession." I remember it vividly from my eleventh-grade biology

class: a pond gradually filling in from the edges and becoming a meadow; which then, similarly, is encroached and overtaken by forest; which itself continues changing until it achieves the Clementsian climax. This narrative, ending in a noble forest cathedral, has been canonical for the environmental movement, the emotional and symbolic basis of its version of nature and of the values derived from it. Interestingly, however, Clements and his students preferred to focus on a humbler (yet quintessentially American) formation: the prairie. Prairie followed its own narrative to its own self-healing, endlessly renewing conclusion.

Clements emphasized that this final state of stable climax, whether of forest or of prairie, was not just a convenient word-picture or heuristic device: it was a real thing, a "complex organism" or "superorganism." And all the leading-up stages were its "stages of growth." "The unit of vegetation, the climax formation, is an organic entity. As an organism, the formation arises, grows, matures, and dies. ... The climax formation is the adult organism." Clements detailed the predictable stages ("seres") that would culminate in a particular climax formation, which would be a mixture of plants and animals that was in some way ideal for its place. The whole process could be seen as unified, like an animal's development from embryo to adult. Once achieved, the climax formation would balance its deaths with births and recycle its important materials and nutrients. If disturbed, the system would revert to an earlier stage and rebuild through the seres until the climax phase was again achieved. Barring disaster, it should persist indefinitely.

For the environmental movement, Clements' idealistic concept of climax has become the touchstone of value. It illustrates how nature works, what nature is. This nature is aesthetically beautiful, spiritually resonant, physically stable. It does not waste. It recycles. It is dynamic, but unchanging. It is complex and self-integrated. Within it, many different organisms may compete, but their competitions are constrained and indeed minimized by systemic tendencies—species will gravitate toward separate niches, and each niche will both draw from and contribute to the whole.

In environmentalist writings, the values implied in this picture of nature are held up for human emulation. A decade ago, I analyzed elements of that picture as *balance, cooperation, holism,* and *the cybernetic supermind.* My point then was to notice how the natural-science data allowed us to find a natural world that was friendly to humans and their search for meaning. Each of the four elements was laden with values. And because those values were seen to be drawn from nature, they had authority.

I now see that what all the aspects of this environmentalist version of nature have in common is that they are reactions against change. They set forth a picture of nature in which death and loss are contained within a meaningful whole. And time itself is bent around into a circle, a cycle.

If the human world is a pell-mell rush of destruction, technological innovation, and up-for-grabs values, the natural world, in this view, is found to be practically unchanging and integrated around meaning. This would be, surely, paradisal, the Edenic form of nature. "Ecologism"—the environmentalist worldview—uses science for its proofs, but the underlying drive is to portray a kind of natural perfection. That perfection is, when you peel it, a static, unchanging nature, an Edenic steady-state bubble. Clements pictured the stable climax formation in a state of "dynamic equilibrium." That's a powerful concept—change captured, change systematized and tamed. It is connected to important insights about how systems homeostatically regulate themselves, on all levels from the cell to the organism, the ecosystem, and beyond. And this concept of self-regulation has formed an interesting bridge to more recent developments in cybernetics, system science, and information science. Dynamic equilibrium has been a productive insight into how life works.

But as I read typical environmentalist thinking, the adjective "dynamic" becomes subtly subordinated to the noun "equilibrium," and the term comes to mean something very close to "unchanging." Clements' powerfully appealing concept of an entire biome as a single organism calls forth this sense that, like an individual body, the ecosystem achieves a set and settled form. This, however, would be a static notion of balance. The creative dimension of living process, its ad-hoc sloppiness, is not much included in this version of nature.

Modern ecology sees an ecosystem much more loosely; the word "ecosystem" itself is regarded as little more than a heuristic device, a convenient way to visualize a much more random reality. "Climax," that centerpiece of Clementsian nature, has all but disappeared. My favorite naturalist, the Pacific-Northwesterner Daniel Mathews, observes: "Today, many ecologists avoid the term 'climax' (or marry it to disturbances in oxymorons like 'fire climax,' 'avalanche climax,' and 'disease climax') because they see disturbance as omnipresent, turning the successional ladder into a maze of feedback loops and eddies, with elements of chaos."

Any sense that the "climax ecosystem" is a real, definable object has been abandoned by working ecologists and biologists. But it retains an honored place in much environmentalist writing. Clements' idealist vision of nature casts this shadow into our present, in the environmental movement's gut-feeling that nature is just right as it is, settled into ideal forms, and that any tampering can only harm it.

There's always been an interesting battle, in environmentalist literature, between delicate nature and robust nature. With all the "saving" that we do, all the "endangered" and "threatened" species, it is easy to form the impression that the whole thing is very teetery and frail. So any intrusion into "nature"—any tree cutting or timber harvest, even the best-planned; any hunting, even for the most over-populated species; any building or road project, even the most useful—will be experienced at a deep level as a mortal threat, a shattering of the divine but glass-fragile world. The delicate-nature picture is founded on a static idea of nature, that do-not-touch notion Proctor finds at the heart of the Zero Cut crowd.

When the Native Forest Council, for instance, depicts an aboriginal forest not to be touched or disturbed, the picture is of a museum-piece, something under glass: beautiful, intricate, delicate: "Our Precarious Habitat," as one environmentalist title has it. Given the amount of destruction humans have done, this reaction is probably understandable. But it gives rise to an odd result: a kind of conservatism, a frozen opposition to change. Anna Bramwell, looking at environmentalism as a political movement, has observed the way "ecology" has moved from a scientific meaning, to an "intensely conservative" moral and social meaning: "The normative sense of the word has come to mean the belief that severe or drastic change within [a natural] system, or indeed any change which can damage any species within it, or that disturbs the system, is seen as wrong." Bramwell is profoundly critical of, even hostile to, the environmental movement. But I think she's onto something. Environmentalism looks like a politically leftist movement, with hippy trappings and an anticonsumerist ethos. But it often appears (and is) simply opposed to change, and committed (like politically distant rightists) to an imaginary picture of past perfection that never was. The unchanging climax of Eden-forest or Eden-prairie is as much a fantasy picture as the *Volk*-village or good-ol'-days small town of political reactionaries: they are all mythical reference points, inserted into a pseudohistoric past, and used to oppose change in the present.

It would be wrong to visit all this upon Frederic Clements or blame it on ecologists. Scientists know full well how provisional their picture of nature is; they study the changes. It is the popular version I'm talking about here, the hushed-reverence idea applied to a nature that is typically physically remote from where its worshippers actually live.

But here is an irony too rich to pass up. We have come to learn that Clements' grassland, that paradigm of the untouched Eden continent, probably depended to a surprising extent upon humans to keep it going. Clements himself minimized the role of anthropogenic fire in the grasslands, but more recent science has found that, as Richard Manning comments, the prairie "evolved under fire and grazing," and that a widespread and persistent practice of prairie-burning, to enhance buffalo-grazing and hunting, played a significant role in maintaining it.

Whatever the meaning of perfection in nature, it includes us. And a ceaseless, ad-hoc adaptation to change.

Now, there's a lot to be said about our culture's rate of change. I think it's too fast: it's an inhuman pace and thus unnatural. The rapid change makes us unhappy and insecure, and I think we'd do quite well to slow it down by several magnitudes. Figuring out how to do so might be what the century-after-next is all about. If this book finds any readers in the 2100s, I hope they are stroking their chins at this point and nodding. I hope they are working on choosing how much social and technological innovation to introduce into the human/natural world, recognizing that we will all do better if there's a chance for mutual adaptation. By then, it will have become obvious that some ivy should have time to grow over the railroad ties and transit embankments, some pondwater accumulate in the low spots, some human customs develop around new arrangements, before it's all ripped up again for the next thing.

We, in our time, don't seem to be ready to consider that question. We have more immediate needs and problems (mostly of our own making): species to avoid making extinct, habitats to restore or protect, population to control.

What won't work, though, and what we must avoid in this interim, is constructing a nature that is merely the opposite of our rowdy, too-fast-moving culture—another round of polarity-thinking in which "we" and "nature" are opposites. We must resist the temptation to project our difficulties onto nature, saying that if culture is too fast, nature must be motionless; if change has madly accelerated in our human world, then it must be absent from nature.

Nature is not the opposite of culture. It is at least as full of change as of stasis, as full of danger as of solace. We need to embrace both. If we can learn to experience the changefulness of nature as a version (the master-version) of our own changy ways, perhaps we will find some new solutions. Some way out of the clear-cut/no-cut dichotomy.

Those are some large abstractions: what nature "is," what culture ought to be. But this chapter began on the narrowest scale, that of immediate experience. Let me revisit that with some questions and challenges.

Why was I sitting on that rock, blessing my solitude, in the faraway mountains, on that fir-toppling day? The customary way to tell such nature-writing stories is to keep the point of view but eliminate the truly personal. Charming details (boots, lunch, bewilderment, bugs) add a kind of authenticity, but they also mask an intended objectivity. The observing eye might be human but it is no particular human. It has an Emersonian universality to it.

Would it change anything to admit that I was there in the wake of terrors and losses in my personal life? That far from being a hearty Thoreauvian—disembodied, chaste, and cheerfully spiritual—I was a wreckage of grief, fleeing my insoluble humanity? How would that change the picture? It would reveal that I too sought refuge in nature, solace in the "eternal" mountains. And that I found it. When I dwelt quietly in that montane forest for those few days, I was seeking a sense of how things connect, and how I might connect: a framework. The framework I entered with the crashing of the tree was a framework not only of time, but of place and especially of complexity. A sense—which ecology is exquisitely good at conveying—of the richness of the living world, the multiplicity of interlocking lives. That richness, that complexity, is a context. A context is a layering and linking together of data, of details, of individuals. And that linking yields meaning.

"Meaning," with a capital M, is a kind of cartoon topic ("What is the Meaning of Life?"), so I guess it's a fool's errand to bring it up. But there it is. And there it was—what I wanted. I came to the woods believing myself abandoned, unloved, unlovable. Still disentangling myself from my fundamentalist religion, I was a bad person whom God officially hated. So stumbling into the life of the forest—seeing its process, smelling its deaths and lives in the same breath—gave me a sense of a totality: the stirring, reassuring, beautiful webwork of life. It was a help against the ugliness of my self-loathing, the narrow doctrines and taboos that had split me off from my human contexts.

In this blessed layering I burrowed on that day and for the best parts of my young adulthood, chewing like a bark beetle to ingest as much as ever I could, hiking for weeks and months at a time, or sitting motionless for hours staring through my hand lens at rock crystals or counting tiny stamens and pistils, learning every name I could, inserting myself thoroughly into a realm of pure meaning that had no word of condemnation for me. Only the same words it had for everything else: pay attention. Provide for your needs. Endure if you can.

The death of that big tree reminded me not to get snookered by the surfaces. Here was no safe harbor. It was harbor and voyage all at once, every detail a slaughter of innocents and a rebirth of hope. Here was an Eden that had no ending and that I could never be cast out of, though I would leave and return again and again for the rest of my life. In time I learned to re-enter it from many other places, small and humble ones. My breath. My body. That tree in the yard. I learned to think of the pains I felt as the pains of anything living. Part of the game.

I tell this story because pain is where the topic of time and change must at last take us. "Change" can be another too-large abstraction. What bothers us about change is not abstract, though. The pain of death and loss, and the fear of them, drive us to make fortresses of belief and construct imaginary Edens where time stops. Replacing our fantasy Edens, our imaginary getaways of motionless nature, requires confronting pain, loss, and death.

This is one of the jobs of nature writing, I think: spelling out how we, with our fears and frailties, fit in to the larger picture. How nature confronts us with the vanity of human wishes and that ever-surprising swirl of beauty and terror. That confrontation is what gives Terry Tempest Williams' book *Refuge* its power, a book worth looking at in some detail.

It's a wonderful, direct, personal exploration of nature, death, and fear of death. And most centrally: our desire to use nature as a refuge from reality. It's "nature writing" in the most traditional sense to be sure, and worse yet a kind of birdwatching, khaki-shorts-and-binoculars affair. But the precision and beauty and, finally, the courage, of Williams' writing redeems all that. Where it takes us is, I think, exactly where we need to go. But there's some hard sledding to be endured first.

The "refuge" of Williams' title is explicitly a retreat from change, the toll of cancer and mortality that claims her mother. Birding is her solace. But her place of retreat, Bear River Migratory Bird Refuge, is also threatened. Williams resists, simultaneously, the impending death of her mother, from cancer, and the death of her refuge, from unprecedented rising water levels on the Great Salt Lake.

What the book does not, at first, permit is the observation that, excuse me, aren't deaths natural phenomena? Even the deaths of mothers? What, exactly, does it mean to see nature as a "refuge" from such things?

One thing it means is that when mortality comes to your refuge, you will greet it with shocked outrage. And the core of this reaction seems to be the psychologizing bent that so characterizes our age.

Early in the book, Williams tells a definitive tale. She goes with a close woman-friend to revisit some favorite burrowing owls, and finds they have been removed or even killed. Some good-ol'-boys are the likely perpetrators, and they roll onto the scene with a sort of B-movie inevitability: the pick-up truck. The drawling obtuseness. The beer-guts hanging over belt buckles.

Significantly, on the way to this encounter, Williams and her friend have been having a little automotive heart-to-heart in the language of pop feminist psychology. Are you in touch with your rage? Yes I am. No, not yet. Are you ready yet? No, but I will be. Heartfelt looks are exchanged.

So when the men are discovered to have butchered the owls, the two experiences are brought together. Women and nature: victims of our patriarchal, controlling, death-dealing Western culture. When Williams marches over to the pickup truck and gives 'em the finger, it's a moment of bittersweet triumph: the pyrrhic victory of the underdog, expressing "rage" (her word) even in defeat. "This is for you—from the owls and me," she hisses.

Now, this may seem like good feminist insight. After all, Carolyn Merchant and other historian/critics have established the historic connection, that the masculinized culture of the West has seen nature as a supine female to be raped, impregnated, and controlled. The mistreatment of individual women in our still-unregenerate society mirrors this larger process. To connect the two has been important, energizing, empowering for many women. In Williams' story the intellectual insight of Merchant's analysis is concretized, brought home, given flesh. To that extent, Williams has done her job. She lives out the theories, she brings the rest of us there to feel and experience the reality behind the words.

But what, exactly, does it all mean? As moving as the tale is, and as sympathetic as I am with it (I too am scared of mean guys in pickups, and have been victimized by them; and I too like birds 'n' nature quite well), some analysis is unavoidable. For one thing, there's a strong and not very pleasant sense of "us versus them." The class difference is obvious—pickup/beergut versus classy birdwatcher. They're men in ball caps, members of a cinderblock gun club. Doesn't this all seem a bit too much of a set-up? Do we well-educated environmentalists really want to sit so high on our high horse? Are the avocations of the rich really so much higher than those of the laborers? The mere fact of these guys' look, gender, and social status is played like proof of guilt. This feels wrong.

There's a further problem. Williams reveals that the highway maintainance crew *may* have done the dirty deed. The burrowing-owl nests have been graveled over, after all. Gun guys, highway guys, what's the difference? She eventually dismisses the possibility, but it's not disproven. Rhetorically, this possibility is a lot less useful to her—in fact it introduces some uncomfortable paradoxes. She has ridden there in a car, hasn't she? Someone (one thinks) must have been doing a lot of grading and blacktopping and graveling to get her to her bird refuge. Strange that these useful people are now such villains.

This projection of guilt is an endemic problem with us environmentalists. Destruction is something someone *else* does. I am entitled to unspoiled nature; if loggers or highway crews mess things up, I can blame them. Though I use the paper and wood, and though I drive to the bird refuge on the highways these men (and women) have made, I myself am untouched by guilt. Presumably everything Williams' big Mormon family has done in Utah has supported her comfortable, nature-watching life there—the big house, the garage, the car, the stretching superstructure of roads, jobs, industry. Her family business is laying major gas pipelines, for God's sake! She's a part of it.

So how, exactly, does she get to blame others?

The blaming is largely made possible by Williams' reliance on the language of popular psychologizing. Oprah-world. In this thought- and language-world, when we "get in touch" with our feelings we discover various kinds of abuse, which we exorcise by emotive venting and by naming of perpetrators. When it's all over, we are cleansed, reborn, ready to be strong adults, scarred but ennobled by victimhood.Williams herself frames the tale in these terms: the girl-talk on the way about rage; the explicit fingering of bulldozing gun-toting blue-collar assholes.

We ought to be able to recognize both injustice to women and pointless destruction of nature, without having to fall into the language and mentality of talk-show victimhood. Williams' little story uses a language of psychological analysis to understand our environmental situation. It tells one truth, but conceals others. I wish to use a wider framework, a larger language, to get more of the picture. Because we are both sides of every tale.

Our species is sexually dimorphic: male and female. The two together make humankind. Women have to shoulder their part of the blame for humans' messed-up choices. Similarly, "we" are not the victims of industrial culture. We *are* industrial culture. And "we" are not the victims of nature. We *are* nature. Until we can bring these polarities closer together, we'll be stuck making pointless gestures of rage at each other (and occasionally at nature too). Remember the odd not-going-along-with-this outrage of Joyce Carol Oates, the disconnect from the mouthy and unpleasant processes of nature? Here we are again.

What's missing from these critiques of culture and nature is self-criticism. The critic stands outside the circle. Yet we see plainly: this is impossible. We are implicated in culture. We are implicated in humanity. And we are part of nature. We bite and are bitten. Complaining about it gets us nowhere, on either end of the question. Saying *No* to the use of nature is flatly silly. We'll be using it, eating and harvesting and processing, as long as we live. Saying *No* to nature's use of us is equally silly. That's going on simultaneously, and in the end of course it wins out. Instead of saying *No* to the use of nature, I want to learn to say *How?* How shall we eat, harvest, use? Where? In what quantities? How much of ourselves, our harvest and substance, shall we allow to slip back before we can use it? How relaxed, or how efficient, ought we to be?

Because pretending to be the victim of these processes is just nuts.

Williams gets out of this trap, in the end, by classic means that (for me) more than redeem the misguided girl-talk of the book's early pages. Gradually she allows herself to release her fear of her mother's dying. Gradually she accepts the salty death of her bird sanctuary. As she experiences the excruciatingly prolonged deaths of mother and refuge, she confronts with clear-eyed courage her hatred of change. She lets it go. As she does, the kind of nature she experiences deepens. When she gets there, I find myself deeply grateful for her journey.

She arrives at two kinds of resolution.

One is the classic resolution of all such questionings. Where is God? How can I go on, in the face of death? The answer comes in placing death within a wider perspective, a context. Context is meaning, as I've tried to show. Having moved through grief, she returns to her refuge and sees that the natural world, though no bulwark against change, still offers a swirl of living meaning, a restless seethe of beauty that is simply too compelling to resist—even with a broken heart. "I turn. All at once, a thousand avocets take flight. More. Tens of thousands. A white and black flurry of birds circles me. The soft whistling of wings fills both time and space. I can no longer see the sky—above me, before me and behind me, avocets and stilts flock.//Oh, blessed wings."

Her imagined refuge is now "an ocean" on which she floats. The insecurity of real life is inseparable from its beauty. She accepts them both, and the bright hot point of her grief is suddenly contained in a larger pattern, a totality of mysterious beauty. This is the pattern of theodicy. Where is Adonais? laments Shelley. Hallam, begs Tennyson. Their answers are the same: look to nature: the loved one is everywhere. Nature, in its complexity, its layering, its linkage of each to all, creates grammars of reference and self-reference, a master-language of genuine and inexhaustible meaning. What more could we ask? This is the traditional way to resolve the seemingly unanswerable questions of death and life: Look (as God says to Job) at this created world, and be humble; look (as it says to me) and be connected.

Answers arrived at by this means are *felt* answers. So they probably lack philosophical certainty. They are answers, plural; not the Answer. Those who demand an airtight system building to an absolute conclusion are of course not satisfied. Such demands are insatiable, in fact: the world does not offer certainty. The trick, one supposes, is to accept the answers that are given. Gilgamesh, storming the gates of Hell on this very quest, receives this other-handed answer instead. "The hand of a child in yours, the touch of a lover," murmurs Siduri the beautiful, whom he has met eternally on the shores of death. The chest-thumping Hero has a hard time; it's not the cosmic victory he had come for.

Yet it is enough.

The other resolution in Williams' book is an achievement of special importance at the whining end of the twentieth century: an answer to victimhood. Or better than that, its transformation. Williams faces her own acquiescence in the misdeeds of civilization that have brought disaster to her family. She reckons with the Mormons, the men, and her own family of strong yet obedient women, and says, "We are far too conciliatory."

For it is probably the decade of nuclear bomb testing in the Utah desert that has brought cancers and mutilations to her mother, to so many other women in Williams' family, and quite possibly to Williams herself (she has had her own lumps and warnings). But as good Mormons, good women, good Republicans, they have said nothing. Done nothing.

No more. In a single spiritually compelling motion, Williams gives up her rage for safety, and takes up her responsibility for action. "Question everything," she demands—even to the un-Mormon, un-Tempest-ladylike extremes of rebellion and civil disobedience. And this is the wisdom I gained from this wonderful, tearful book: that the *giving up* and the *taking up* are connected. When she accepts the drifting, swirling dangerousness of natural life, its refusal to provide stationary refuges, then she is able to take the next step of action and adult responsibility. You could say that the misplaced heroism—the Gilgamesh-heroism—of insisting on an Answer has been discarded. Unstrapped from armored belligerence, immersed in the transitory, dying beauty of life, Williams can redirect her courage and outrage at its real targets. It's a softer heroism, clothed in flesh and feeling (yet curiously far from the trembling-victim kind of feeling).

It's a funny sort of peace that comes in that dangerous place. A better kind of stillness. It's the answer that Keats came to—I cannot help returning to this poem—in "When I have fears," where he confronts a predicament strikingly like Williams', knowing that he may soon follow his mother and brother down the path of turberculosis and lingering, painful death. In the brief, epic span of fourteen lines, he faces his fears: that he will die too soon, that he will never write what is in him to write, never fulfill the love that aches in him. But even these compelling fears subside to "nothingness" (such a modern word!) when at last he brings himself to stand "on the shore of the wide world," to be caught up in the sheer inhuman gorgeousness of reality. Reader, that's the Gilgamesh shore; that's Williams' shore, beside the Great Salt Lake, shot through with beauty and pain. This moment connects the viewer to the ultimate framework, the widest context: night sky, shining expanse of water, recognition that the whole can only be accepted, not mastered. That it offers no safety, but experience of indescribable ecstasies. And terrors.

"I have been liberated from my optimism," writes Williams—and the world begins its opening to her, until the sky fills with "clouds like roses," the spirits of the dead and the responsibilities of the living.

This nature that Keats and Williams come to accept looks beautiful but won't hold still. That's the distinction I've been working on, these many pages. These many years. We want a nature we can possess or be possessed by, a beautiful, perhaps divine arrangement: an object. An Eden. Instead it comes at us in a whirl of knives and delights we can never comprehend or keep up with. A process.

What Williams and Keats feel is the surging forwardness of nature, that thing in motion that has been formally called *natura naturans*: "nature naturing." Not a thing at all, but a dynamism. A wild nourishing and killing and creating.

This discovery is the same one made a few centuries ago by the poet whose title I have borrowed for this chapter, and whose poem will give us our last and strangest example. Edmund Spenser's Elizabethan allegory *The Faerie Queene* ends in a odd pair of misfit cantos that abruptly drop the story line of knights and ladies to confront the master-question of change. Spenser embodies the question in a character named Mutability, a mysterious and powerful force neither male nor female (though addressed as Goddess). She challenges everything, demanding whether she, Mutability, is not truly the monarch of all creation, the last word, the ultimate truth. As any bereaved lover or parent asks: What is love, if it ends thus? What is any of it, but vanity and a chasing after the wind?

The pattern of theodicy is to find a wider framework, within which individual pain and loss can be seen as meaningful, connected.

Spenser's "Mutability Cantos" literally move through progressively wider frames, seeking such an answer. The goddess Mutability surges with tidal force past the story-layers of mythology that wrap the faerie-land of Spenser's tale, challenging each framework, just as mutability challenges every human structure. First Mutability confronts the Moon-goddess Cynthia. Everything on earth, everything mortal, is traditionally regarded as sublunary, mundane: inside the orbit of the moon. So Cynthia's is the earthly frame of reference. But it holds no answer; Cynthia is no match. Mutability brushes her aside and blitzkriegs on to the next level, the palace of Jove himself. Now, Spenser's allegory is always winking at its readers: no one took such mythological flummery literally. The habit of reading on multiple levels was well established; Spenser's readers easily understood that the Jovian deity would stand for something else, a larger frame of reference Spenser might not feel had to be precisely defined. (It's a poem, after all, not a theological treatise.)

What I see is that even the Jovian courts and powers cannot contain Mutability. Even the Olympian frame of reference is too small. Mutability points out that the gods too had origins—births, parentage, a war to overthrow the Titans (her own parents) and assume rulership of the world. And therefore they too are subject to change: they are Mutability's subjects. Jove cannot answer. Change is the ruling principle not merely of earth, but of the cosmos.

All that is left is for Mutability to take her case to the highest court, the ultimate framework. She appears before the arch-goddess of all: Nature. She demands to know whether change, endless shifting change—the undoing of all that is done or loved—is not the only rule of creation.

Nature pauses. That's a good moment, all worlds suspended. Then Nature smiles. That's even better. Here is her answer, the very one we've been searching for:

> *"I well consider all that ye have sayd,*
> *And find that all things steadfastnes doe hate*
> *And changéd be: yet being rightly wayd*
> *They are not changéd from their first estate;*
> *But by their change their being do dilate:*
> *And turning to themselves at length againe,*
> *Doe work their owne perfection so by fate"*

If nature is seen as process and not thing, the riddle is solved. Of course everything changes. But the process of change brings forth the fullness of what everything is: everything becomes itself again, or even becomes *more* itself, with each turn of the wheel of change.

In the dangerous element immerse. Let go of safety. Leave those fortresses. Drop the search for golden changeless Eden. And in the little deaths of changeful life, the constant fear confronted and released, be reborn to yourself.

This kind goddess Nature has the last word: change is the means but not the end. The end—the result—of change is precisely what we see around us: beauty and order arising moment by moment, magically, from the accidents of being. Change is the means, but not the meaning, of nature.

And what is that meaning? Not paraphrasable. Its intricate, infinitely ramifying complexity wraps us. Any way we look, inward or outward, the connectedness is infinite. Not safe; no shield against pain and hurt. Not finished. But beautiful.

Nature is meaning; but we can't say what that meaning is.

Near the fallen fir was a brook where I went to sit when my heart had stopped racing, my nose and fingers were full enough of the event, and the forest seemed—*seemed*—calm again. Down coursed the water, slowing in a level space before plunging downwards again. There were clean amber stones in the bottom, some silt along the sides, and delicate see-through skeletons of maple leaves, curled or pasted. A bar of light across. Some bright brief hyphens of needles bunched in the edges, and a water-strider among them. The accidents of being.

Random. Helter-skelter. Beautiful.

The wheel of change—lottery, ferris wheel, buzz-saw—tears through us and all things. Yet we remain, closing up the wounds as fast as they appear, and perhaps even becoming ourselves and more ourselves again, a joyous wounding mystery, at each new turn. Spenser thought so.

It makes no sense. It is purest sense.

Section II: Up the River

Industrial civilization is doing terrible things to the living world. Extinctions, loss of biodiversity, disappearing habitat, climate change—who knows where this will all go? My determined optimism won't mean much if it can't confront losses like these directly. If there is to be comfort, it will have to be stern, steely-eyed, realistic. We must learn to see clearly: where to accept tradeoffs, life for life. Where to mourn losses that are irreparable. And where to say instead: this damage is temporary; this can be healed; let's get to work.

The Columbia River system shows both kinds of losses, the fleeting and the everlasting. Here the massively organized misdeeds of American civilization, military and economic, collide spectacularly with other American commitments: democracy, human rights, love of the land and its abundance of life.

This river and its ordeals offer a good chance to begin some of the real work of our time: distinguishing the kinds of damage we have done. To do this work—to confront real losses—will require a steady vision, grounded in the present, and untainted either by sentimental Eden-pasts or by utopian Eden-futures.

Up the River

Yesterday I drove up the Columbia River for a break from this book. I was tired of criticizing nature writers. I was tired of being one. I wanted to see what we were all talking about. I went east from Portland, up the great Columbia Gorge, where the river rolls, or sits, or stagnates, or goes on just as it always has ("always" meaning, for us humans, a few hundred or thousand years).

The Columbia as it traverses the Gorge is Portland's pride and joy, a mile-wide majesty with snow-capped volcanoes on either side and waterfalls that leap from basaltic cliffs through deep evergreen forests. Our Columbia rivals other rivers of legend and song, Rhines and Rhones, Yellows and Yangtses, with its own list of longest and biggest and beautifullest. But it's our agony too, since it focuses all the malpractices in its vast watershed into this one, highly visible channel. Here we kill salmon. Here we dam flows. Here we store inhuman wastes from nuclear evildoing. Here we collect pesticides from farm and range. Here we travel with our out-of-town visitors, exclaiming at its timeless beauty.

Timeless is a funny word. Like "always." I couldn't stop thinking about it as I drove. Here's why.

The Gorge is a rift in the Cascade Mountains where the ancient rivercourse was carved out by repeated catastrophes called the Missoula Floods, toward the end of the latest cold part of our ice age, about twelve thousand years ago. That's an ice age we're still in: despite the way it's often talked about, it's not over. Ice ages last a long time (from two million to ten million years each, depending on your definition), but at certain intervals the coldness relents for a while. If we were really not in an ice age, there would be no polar ice caps; swampy jungles from non-ice-age eras left oil deposits in the northern latitudes. We are living in an interlude within the ice age called an "interglacial warming," a pleasant pause that could last anywhere from ten thousand to forty thousand years, judging by past interglacials (we've had ten in the last million years). Cold and warm spells within an ice age alternate on a regular hundred-thousand-year cycle named after its discoverer, Serbian scientist Milutin Milankovich. The warm part of the current cycle began melting ice about eighteen thousand years ago, reaching its warmest about ten thousand years ago, for which we should be grateful. That warm-up constitutes the beginning of our current interglacial. What we think of as "normal"—as how things have always been—as nature, in other words—is recent and, in the long view, a bit tippy.

Here in the Gorge, during the beginning of this latest warming cycle, there would have been plenty of opportunity for some of our human forebears to wander in. Most of the Columbia River flowed freely just outside the range of the ice sheet that covered British Columbia and Puget Sound, though it was full of glacial outwash and could not have been the salmon-paradise it would become later. People were certainly hereabouts, having crossed over from Asia and skirted the continent's westernmost Cordilleran glacier, on the dry land created when so much of the earth's ocean water was locked up in ice. They might have come over during the preceding cold times too, from thirty thousand to twelve thousand years ago, depending on which anthropologist you talk to. Those folks might have come upriver for whatever salmon were able to tolerate the silty waters, or for other fish; or for the passage the Gorge affords through the Cascades.

So we were probably here in the Gorge when those Missoula Floods ripped through. It's getting to be well known but I really love the story: glacial meltwater had been accumulating over in Montana, held back by a finger of the ice sheet that extended along the Bitterroots between present-day Idaho and Oregon. A lot of water collected there—more than the combined volume of Lake Erie and Lake Ontario, according to the Ice Age Floods Institute. When it busted through the ice dam, the flow equalled that of all the rivers in the world. Suddenly.

It was enough to move mountains, a speeding head of water and ice perhaps two thousand feet high at its source, reaming out forests and soils, scouring river valleys, plains, and mountainsides down to basalt bedrock. And all this happened repeatedly, forty times or more over several thousand years. That's why we don't know for sure if "we" were here when it happened. Most of the evidence has been pulverized and sent to the Pacific.

Since then, however, lots of us have come through this opening in the mountains, following the river or stopping to live along its banks. The soils and forests have accumulated again into conifer gardens I hike through, way up on the Oregon heights, or more shifty riparian woods in silty flats along the river. The forests look like they've always been there.

And here where I've stopped the car is a dam, the famous Bonneville. I walk in from the tourist parking lot to see its turbines and dynamos, then go outside to stand gazing over the sweeping concrete abutments. Bonneville's wide dams and spills inspire me with a whiff of the industrial sublime, like those heroic photos of the WPA thirties. Downstream runs free from here to the ocean, about 150 miles; upstream is a very long lake. It is a pretty good-sized project, for humans. Consequential. Salmon almost gone. River dammed for hundreds of miles.

But along the south bank I see Oregon's basalt cliffs rising a thousand or more feet, clean shining stone once scoured by those Missoula flows, darkening now in the shortening day as they have for ten thousand years. Sky-colors melt into the wide river until the banks turn to sinuous shadows and the islands to dark mysteries. The stars appear. In time I see good old Polaris, clear and visible in its (almost) due-north, divinely ordained spot.

When the floods came through, it occurs to me, there must have been a different pole star. How strange! Later I look it up: whoever lived here or was traveling through, at the last of the Floods about twelve thousand years ago, would have seen Vega as the north star. So much more prominent than our dim little Polaris. That was a lucky time for navigating, I'm thinking, Vega beaming from true north, fat and bright like a burnished apple. Twelve thousand years is about half the cycle of polar wobble, the axis of the spinning top of the world moving around its little circle, aiming us serendipitously at various pole stars. Maybe someone looked up at Vega the night before the world ended in icewater. Imagine the quiet, a week later, when nothing was the same.

I like thinking on this scale. It brings a kind of quiet to me. Whatever "always" means, it ought to include this.

It's late March and I am back at the Bonneville Dam. Same reason—too many hours of reading and teaching and writing. Too much headwork.

As an environmentalist, I think of how nice it would be to see the Columbia sweeping through here like a river, instead of a long dull lake. Every dam, I read, imposes about a 5 percent mortality on the salmon adults, but a staggering 15 percent on the smolts (on top of their already rather perilous lives). If I come here with my enviro friends, we'll commiserate about how screwed up it all is, how we've killed a river. There will be a mournful tone to it, a Paradise-Lost undercurrent. Another Eden we've destroyed. Presumably forever.

But on the Washington side just north of the dam, I can see a sheared-off peak that reminds me of another, bigger picture. The peak is called Table Mountain; I know its flat-top since I've seen it from other peaks. This near side is a treeless drop-off, a raw wound much newer than the Missoula thumpings and churnings. Some few hundred years ago, geologists say, this whole side of the mountain fell off, carrying rock and dirt and trees and marmots and probably a few unlucky people down and out several miles to block the Columbia River. That was some dam, probably rising about 240 feet above the river-level, or three times higher than poor little mighty Bonneville. It created a lake that might have taken as long as a year to fill, backing up the long gradual slope of the Gorge. Folks living here at the time called the blockage something like "The Bridge of the Gods." They were understandably impressed, and probably tickled at getting to cross the big river dry-shod.

Apparently the waters of the Columbia ran over the top of the obstruction for a while. Then it gave way completely, resulting in another massive flood that wiped out Chinookan villages along the Columbia almost to its mouth, and up the Willamette including the whole Portland Basin. Debris from that episode left a long stretch of whitewater that caused Lewis and Clark some consternation; it was called by the English-speaking newcomers the Cascades (which in turn gave its name to our mountains). And that's exactly where Bonneville Dam is right now: built on the shallows and spanning the rubble-islands that were a mountain peak a few generations ago.

The Visitors Center at Bonneville states flatly that it all happened seven hundred and fifty years ago, but several geologists have begun challenging that date with converging evidence for a much more recent landslide around three hundred years ago. That would confirm what the Indians told white folks originally; by one 1830s account, that the landslide and its leftover cascades were recent, and that their "fathers" (probably meaning a few generations back) used to paddle on flat water from the ocean all the way past the present-day rapids, up to the rapids at The Dalles. And it would make sense of the dead-tree spars Lewis and Clark reported, trees that had been drowned in the (vanished) lake, but were recent enough to still be standing.

The river stopped a while, about a year. A surprising pause. Then it broke through, and before long navigation went back to normal along the Columbia. Or what we think of as normal: canoes going up and down. Salmon returning. Just like always.

But just what did the salmon do, when the river closed for that year or so? And what if it had been closed a little longer? Would the entire Columbia/Snake system above Bonneville Dam, those thousands of miles of perfect salmon habitat, have gone salmonless until the end of time? That question was in the back of my mind, as I pestered geologists, hydrologists, and salmon scientists. It turns out it was not easy to arrive at the estimate of about one year. The previous best guess had been two years; only recently had Research Hydrologist Jim O'Connor of the USGS Portland office arrived at the shorter estimate by running a hydrology model based on typical river flows and the size of the back-up reservoir a 240-foot landslide would create. But, I persisted, what *does* happen to salmon when a disaster like this, or like a Mt. St. Helens explosion, occurs? Or, come to think of it, when an ice age cold snap locks up a river for sixty thousand years?

There's a thread here that is worth following. We're accustomed to think we're screwing things up forever, when we ruin how things have always been. Yet nature's been doing the same thing, over and over, for a long time, and when each of us woke up here for the first time, we found it astonishing, green, abundant—not ruined at all. How is that?

Once we open our eyes to the larger time-frames, we see the obvious: the living world has ways of un-ruining things. It adapts, it surprises, it invents. Life goes uphill, defying the "law" of entropy that says things should tend to break down, simplify, run downhill. Biological systems have discovered a way to reverse that. It's a crazy reality: the world keeps getting more complex. One cell, many cells; little animals, big ones; dumb slithering slime, intelligent large-eyed emotional beings. How in the world … ?

I call it *going up the river.* Dead things must float down the gradient to that big dissolving soup, the entropic sea; but life swims up, up, defying mere physics with the intelligent energies of biology. Eden, in other words, even when lost, is always about to get found again. That's no reason to be complacent or destructive; but it is reason to take heart, pick up a phone, a ballot, a picket sign, or a shovel, and do the right thing. Because as soon as we stop doing the wrong thing, Eden begins showing up again.

It turns out that a river dammed for a year or two is not a problem for salmon. Most of the seven species of salmon (including the two ocean-going "trout," steelhead and cutthroat, recently reassigned to the salmon genus) spend one year to five years growing big out at sea before coming back to spawn. These intervals divide them into age-classes, like college alumni, so even wiping out an entire year will not seriously threaten the species. The next year's graduates will show up on time anyway. Clever solution, isn't it?

Fish biologists recognize the different intervals of various salmon species as part of a pattern of "life-cycle diversity," an adaptive response that has evolved over a long, long time. The Northwest has been an uncommonly rambunctious territory, and salmon have needed many tricks to survive here. As Jim Lichatowich's wonderful book *Salmon Without Rivers* depicts in some detail, salmonids similar to current species have been on the scene for the last ten million years, breeding in fresh water, migrating to sea, and coming back to spawn. In that time, they have had to cope with every imaginable form of change, often violent, destructive, and extreme. They have experienced "millions of years of cataclysmic habitat disruption" from, for instance, the flows of molten basalt that covered most of present-day Washington and Oregon; they have endured several turns around the ice age cycle. Just during the last two million years, when the current watershed patterns were established in the Northwest, salmon have faced dramatic climate shifts, both colder and warmer, dryer and wetter; volcanic eruptions that built and destroyed entire mountains (and their streams); and no end of earthquake, fire, flood, drought, and other habitat-destroying events. It was a pretty unquiet Eden.

Indeed, the cool, wet Northwest we regard as normal—the way things have always been—with profound evergreen forests shading those ideal salmon streams so clear and cool, their gravel bars built up just so, as if by the hand of a benevolent and salmon-loving deity, this Northwest is a very, very recent evolution. A good one, for people and for salmon! But *until just four thousand years ago, no such Northwest existed.* Of course that famous pair of ice sheets had frozen out most land (and rivers) north of about 48 degrees until some ways into our interglacial warm-up, about fourteen thousand years ago. Immediately after that, despite the outrush of glacial meltwater, the region was surprisingly hot and dry. On the raw, glaciated earth, under the hot regime, revegetation was slow, characterized at first by the adventuresome, gnarly little lodgepole pine. In time, the persistent pine was replaced by a variant of Douglas-fir forest: not the cool and wet association with cedar and hemlock that we know now, but a hot and often-burned cycle of bracken, alder, and fir, and then more fire. Meanwhile the rivers, says Lichatowich, ran gray "with sediment loads sixty times that of modern Pacific Northwest rivers." Salmon had to make do. Only when the climate shifted some four to five thousand years ago, possibly triggered by a cool phase in solar radiation, did our drizzly Northwest appear, with its gloriously damp and dark-green forests. This salmon-paradise of clear streams shaded by old-growth forests is a young one.

On the way to paradise, salmon faced disasters continuously. And creatively. Each of the seven *Oncorhynchus* species plays out a life-history cycle that uses the rivers, coasts, and seas in a different pattern, spreading out the risks or (to turn it around) utilizing different resources and finding separate niches. Like a many-legged stool, the genus could not be destroyed by any single disaster. And even within each species, scientists have found surprising variation in life history. "Surprising" because reproduction is typically the most conservative aspect of living process, holding on to old forms even while externals and later stages change radically. But under extraordinary pressure from this disturbed, even chaotic, landscape, individual species have adopted multiple life and reproductive patterns. Chinook salmon, for instance—like those that would have been trying to get by the Bridge-of-the-Gods landslide—have diversified their life histories to an amazing extent; as biologist Michael C. Healey, Director of the UBC Westwater Research Centre puts it, "Chinook display a broad array of tactics that includes variation in age at seaward migration, variation in length of freshwater, estuarine, and oceanic residence, variation in ocean distribution and ocean migratory patterns, and variation in age and season of spawning migration."

While some smolts are loitering near the spawning shallows that hatched them, others are sprinting for the sea (so-called "stream-type" and "ocean-type" chinook). And within those two types, modifications and gambits split and split again, among both juveniles and adults, elaborating the basic theme of survival into the many-headed, opportunistic, nearly unstoppable life-force that awakens such admiration in humans. The dangerous, changeable lands and climates of the Northwest have taught the chinook to "spread the risk of mortality across years and across habitats."

Our admiration for salmon often focuses on the spellbinding images of the spawning run. Though there's a beautiful complexity aswim in nearly every phase of salmon life, that image of the powerful jump—fifty pounds of silvery sea-muscle flashing above a falls—has transfixed our imagination. And when we learned (as recently as 1950!) that each salmon returns to the stream of its origin, with an instinct or art that we often call "perfect" and "uncanny," our admiration is compounded. "Like a key in a lock," says Joseph Cone: each individual recognizes some faint but compelling scent or pattern that draws it up river, up stream, up brook and up bank, often to the exact birthplace. A cycle, then, as deep and mysterious as anything in nature, a wheel of life turning, precise and unfathomable. We ought to be impressed. We are.

But there is another side to this perfect, uncanny, unerring story that is just as important. Namely, its *imperfection*: its errors, its mistakes and wrong turns. Without a certain occasional goofiness, salmon would have disappeared long ago.

My original question about the Bridge-of-the-Gods landslide asked what would have happened had the Columbia stayed blocked a little longer. No salmon delays its spawning more than five years. Rivers that are closed longer than that—frozen under ice sheets, drowned in silt from glaciers, fires, or ash-flows, filled with molten basalt-oozes, or otherwise ruined—how do salmon return to such places? We see, of course, that they must—or hardly any river in the Northwest would have a single salmon. But how?

I questioned some fish biologists, early in my research, and received a lovely word to pursue: *straying*. Here's what I found. Everyone knows that salmon "always" return to the correct natal stream. That's a given—except when they don't. Too much perfection doesn't work in our world; and natural selection has preserved a neat out-clause that allows salmon to wander into "wrong" rivers just often enough. Enough for what? Enough to allow the species to colonize new rivers when they are available and suitable. Enough to allow the genes of an age-class facing disaster on its home stream to persist somewhere else. Enough to spread the risk, yet not waste too many potential spawners. Enough.

I love this picture: an oddball salmon that doesn't quite "get it." A sport, a weirdo, a failure. She's in the wrong stream, nosing up the current thinking what thoughts? What bewilderment or curiosity, what rowdy longing for novel scents? Unknowable, of course: these feelings must be salmony, not humanesque, and thus very challenging for us to grasp. Up the wrong stream she goes, redding out the stream-bottom and dropping her eggs when she feels like it. Wrong, wrong, wrong ... and just right.

Straying has been tricky for researchers. Kyle A. Young, of the Centre for Applied Conservation Biology at the University of British Columbia, laments that "we know surprisingly little about straying rates in natural salmon populations." Those tagging and tracking experiments that have been conducted along the West Coast and elsewhere have produced strangely varying data (suggesting more work to be done). A 1954 study focusing on two adjacent northern California ocean streams found steelhead straying at a 2 percent rate, but coho at 20 percent. Yet a similar study on Vancouver Island in 1992 found wild coho straying to nearby ocean tributaries less than 1 percent of the time. (Graduate students, prepare your proposals!) Meanwhile, wild chum salmon have been counted wandered into the wrong stream (2 km from the home stream) at a surprising 54 percent rate. Other estimates put chum straying at 14 percent, and pink salmon at around 10 percent.

And what about those chinook waiting for the Bridge of the Gods to come down? A four-year study on the Cowlitz River in the Columbia basin, about fifty miles from the landslide, measured chinook straying at a 1.4 percent rate, a number at the lower limit of the range of salmon-straying data. Most strays went to nearby streams (consistent with other studies which have made the commonsense point that straying usually occurs in close-by streams presumably very similar to the natal stream). But this study also noted a small number of extremely interesting wild cards: ten Cowlitz chinook were picked up in breeding areas of Puget Sound and even the Juan de Fuca Strait, hundreds of miles away. This same talent for colonizing new streams has been observed in New Zealand, where Sacramento River chinook were introduced in the early 1900s, and within four or five generations had become abundant in rivers up to 143 miles away. "Such long-distance strays, though few in number, could have important consequences for the genetic composition of regional spawning populations," concludes Healey. So that's how the Columbia would have re-salmoned itself, had the Bridge of the Gods stayed up longer; and how the missing age-class for that one blocked year eventually restocked itself. A wanderer, or two or ten, most from nearby but a few from God-knows-where, would have paddled up the wrong stream, done what no mechanical perfection could ever do. That's life, isn't it? Goofy, beautiful, and perfect—if perfect means creatively everchanging. Up the river of entropy it goes, swimming against the current, expanding possibilities against the ceaseless tide of ruination.

We hazard a deeply wrong idea of nature when we get hypnotized by the "perfection" of such amazing creatures as salmon. As if everything must stay just so, or it won't be perfect any more. That would be Eden, of course, not Earth. Where we live is contingent, thrown together over long stretches of time. Goof-ups in genes or behavior that hurt living creatures, of course, will tend to disappear; but evolution loves a lucky mistake, and that's been the foundation of all or most of the story of life. Serendipity. Pre-adaptation. Using an existing physical structure for a new and unforeseen purpose. Handing on good goofs to the next generation. Richard Dawkins, that tireless crusader against the "divine perfection" illusion, calls the beautiful forms of life "design-oid," signifying that they look "designed" but are not. The forms of life are stumbled upon, cobbled together, preserved and built upon eon by eon. Though no less amazing for a' that!

Perhaps ten generations ago, the Gods closed the mighty river. A hundred generations before that, the entire Northwest was an unrecognizable scrubland. How long are ten or a hundred generations? I often think of generations in threes: you, your parents, your grandparents. That's a unit of experience for us humans but it has no name, as far as I've ever heard. A triad? A three-bracket, tripledaddy, tri-gener? Hmm. Trigener seems least objectionable so let's try using it. Three trigeners connect us to the Gods landslide. That's not long, is it? And to get back to the great climatic shift, the change-all that brought those green wet forests that have "always" been here? Just thirty or forty trigeners. Thirty or forty tellings, grandmother to grandchild, in the manner of humans. Hardly forever.

In this perspective, the Bonneville Dam is a recent and tiny event, a thimble-full of dirt and rock. When I stand on its parapets, aware of the scale of time and change that shapes events here, I feel somewhat different feelings now. I regret the damage this dam is doing, but instead of mourning a thing lost forever, that salmon paradise, I feel a bristly eagerness to let the river of life run through here again, to let the goofy perfection of salmon and people and all flow freely. That's a different perspective, tuned to the reaches of past time that lap right up to the edge of our present.

And if we turn that perspective to the future, what might we see? What will this river, this dam, look like in a few years? A few generations; eight or ten trigeners? Have we really spoiled it "forever," as environmentalists are wont to say?

When Edward Abbey floated his best book's climactic chapter "Down the River," his point was that the Glen Canyon Dam was about to ruin a perfect place forever. Abbey said so: "Forever." For him, there was no long future, only the individual present of his immediate fears and losses. Which were intense. When we look at the works of humankind that have "ruined" nature, we are apt to feel this helpless grieving. That's the emotion of Paradise Lost: that's Eden-grief. There goes our refuge, we think; here comes humanity, spoiling everything. But changing the scale of our viewpoint, trying the long vistas of space and time, picks us up out of this limited view and shows us things whole. They look different. They are different.

I asked what the Columbia might look like in a few trigeners. This is a thought experiment. Environmentalists often say our industrial society is "unsustainable." That means, we're taking more than we're putting back, and one simply cannot do that for very long. Some day our kids, or theirs, will wake up and find an emptier world. We will have used up the natural abundances of soil and timber and fish, and left pollution and depletion behind. That's generic environmentalist thinking, and I don't see any flaw in it. The two-hundred-year experiment in industrial consumerism and high population cannot be sustained.

So … if it's unsustainable, then let's assume that it is not sustained. It ends. For purposes of the thought experiment, it doesn't really matter if it ends in fifty or five hundred years. Just think: okay, the industrial infrastructure gives out. What then? Will Eden stay ruined, as our grieving insists? Will this de-salmonated, warmed, chemical'd, baulked, and blockaded river ever recover its natural graces? We know it *could*, if opened up to salmon. But will it? To draw the question down to a test-case: what will become of the Bonneville Dam, in this hypothetical future when maintenance stops?

I tried asking various engineers at the Bonneville Power Authority. They were wary of me at first. Eventually, after a few phone calls, a Bonneville mechanical engineer named Kevin agreed to come talk. We met in the Visitors Center (no apostrophe), hands in pockets, gazing through the big picture windows, and then tried the thought experiment as we walked around. We imagined the future of this dam that had, by the usual analysis, ruined the river. First, we acknowledged that the life-span of the Bonneville's concrete spillway and twin powerhouses was likely to be very long. That concrete is hard. It's reinforced with steel. It's designed to last; in engineer dialect, "rated at 3,000 to 4,000 psi." I walked up close to the first powerhouse. Built in 1938, it's twelve years older than me and looks a lot better. My skin is weathered and my knees are wearing out, but this thing looks seamless. Its thick, steel-ribbed blocks and monoliths will not soon depart.

Kevin wasn't sure about actual time-spans of concrete so I researched them later. Roman concrete has lasted thousands of years: the Pantheon, for instance, is eighteen hundred years old, a 143-foot free span of (by our standards) primitive concrete. It's in good shape. You could rightly guess that modern concrete will do at least that well. Stress, vibration, erosion will of course vary the outcome, but it seems that big, permanent projects—high-rises, dams, bridges—will be around for many thousands of years. Their concrete is practically geological.

But a dam is a dynamic system getting walloped continually by tremendous natural forces. If maintenance stopped, what would happen not just to the concrete, but to the dam?

The Bonneville Dam comprises two wide powerhouses where the turbines spin, flanking an even-wider central spillway that lets the rest of the river through. A lock cuts along on one side. A trio of islands, natural and constructed, anchor the segments. Kevin and I agreed that, in our hypothetical future, the powerhouse water intakes would of course be shut down. They would sit inertly leaking water, clogged by debris and doomed by lack of regular maintenance, while the spillway took the rest of the action.

Bonneville is a "run-of-the-river" dam, meaning that it's not designed to store much water; whatever comes in the top is allowed out the bottom, at a constant equal turnover. Would it silt up? I asked. No, virtually no dredging is required. The spillway is eighteen gigantic gates in the base of the structure, each fifty feet wide and fifty to sixty feet high. The Columbia shoots out the bottom. The capacity of the spill-gates is truly monumental—1,600,000 cubic feet per second, enough to accommodate what planners consider the "maximum foreseeable event," a flood of the magnitude expected just once every thousand years. The most recent big event by which to gauge this capacity is the 1996 flooding that forced Portland to put up sandbags to protect its downtown, rated as perhaps a two-hundred-year event. I remember it as unrelenting rains that melted off the mountain snowpack and rushed down our creeks and streets. The Willamette and the Columbia filled their banks, abutments, and seawalls, overtopping them in places. Riverview restaurants and expensive homes paid the price.

But impressive as it seemed to us, to the Bonneville Dam this flood was no big deal: Kevin's boss, the Chief of Emergency Management, told me that the 1996 flood used a mere quarter of capacity, or about 441,000 cubic feet/second. Industrial sublime is working on me, I think. Exclamation seems appropriate. Staggering amounts of water! Thousand-year floods! The Bonneville will dam on for millennia!

If intact, the voice of the merely declamatory reminds me. With a humble period.

Trees do fall into rivers. There are a lot of trees in this part of the world. They float downstream. In our scenario, this kind of debris would constitute the biggest challenge to the dam's continuance as a dam. To enumerate the obvious a little: Douglas-fir can be several hundred feet tall, and I've seen plenty that were six to ten feet across. Our montane forests also grow huge mountain hemlock and red cedar, along with wispy dogwood and vinemaple. These regularly wash out, fall over, and float down to join the riverside bigleaf maples, mountain ash, alder, and the occasional ponderosa pine. The present-day Bonneville Dam features great "trash-racks" that screen the spillways from such flotsam, with huge cargo-cranes running on tracks above them to fish up the welter and keep the spillways clean.

Kevin and I saw that over, say, a hundred years, a substantial wad of brush and trees and whatnot would begin to block even those vast spillgates. Behind this accumulation would be the pushing, searching river, looking for a way out. The water would surely rise during freshet springs and highwater winters, spilling around the edges. Though the concrete might not budge, the earthworks at each side surely would. Beyond the concrete footings and foundations, after all, it's just islands and banks: just dirt landslided down a few centuries ago when the gods fell to arguing. As soon as the least trickle of backed-up Columbia began seeping around the furthest edge, the dam's fate would be written. More would follow. Then all would follow, taking the course of least resistance.

So it is simply a matter of time until those concrete sweeps and parapets become interesting islands themselves, with a full-throated Columbia roaring past each one. Islands of legend and song, I would think. Worth a canoe-trip upstream to see. Maybe we'll still be singing Woody Guthrie's Depression-era ballad: *Roll on, Columbia, Roll On.*

And with this born-again free-flowing river, the salmon might do just as they have done before. *Will* do so. Perhaps we will have failed them in our time; perhaps many old runs and species will have been destroyed. But salmon have been finding their way up new rivers since long before the last glaciation, and they will do so again. And whatever humans, in that faraway future, go canoeing up the river to view its legendary concrete islands, will pull onto the shore and dine on salmon planked over sandy beach fires just as humans have done, well, "forever."

The past bends around to meet the future. How we lived here in the human past; how we will live here, in the human future. Less than a dozen trigeners, I would guess, in both directions.

Each of these larger time and magnitude scales is like a frame we place around the present, a frame that hides some facts but reveals others. Of course we still must live in the present. The damage we do is not less real simply because someday it will go away or be forgotten. No: the present, its fine-grained detail, is where we belong. But with a strangely human double vision we need to read other times and scales simultaneously. Can't get it right without that interpretive depth, that stereo vision.

Whatever we decide what to do about our industrial impact on the Northwest, we should do it in this multiple perspective. We don't need to imagine that paradise is lost, that this North America, this Northwest, is an Eden that has been raped and killed. We need to remember that paradise is perennial; all we need to do is stop our nonsense, and enter into a friendlier partnership with it. The river will do the rest; the relentless insistence of the living world will do it, forcing lusty fish and gravid egg-bearers up new/old pathways, reforesting, resoiling, reparadising.

What's left out of this rosy picture: some places won't come back.

There are real losses to consider. We need to assess them clearly, see what is reparable and what can only be grieved. Nuclear wastes in the Hanford Reach, pesticides in certain places, lands disinherited virtually forever, old woods turned into something lesser. And species that are gone, are gone: now they are with the woolly mammoth, with the dire wolves and sabre-tooths that used to inhabit this place with us. Our ancestors, those Adams and Eves, got their hands bloody too.

Yet we may see that this is still a good place. We may remember that what passes is replaced by what comes next.

This news, this longer perspective, isn't a warrant for further mayhem. It's an invitation: though losses accumulate, paradise is never lost. Paradise is on a circular timeline; it is returning, coming back up the river if we let it.

I travelled past the Bonneville to see the other ten dams. They were big, they were enormous. All of them had the deceiving look of permanence. That made me smile, out on the golden plains of the Palouse, where ice caps and floods have scraped and shaped, where people have wandered for millennia. Where the Columbia drifts by dry lands and where salmon have come and gone a few times, and may come again—as soon as we relent in our foolishness.

Up the river we go, paddling wildly.

Real Losses: The Hanford Reach

Not all grief is the false sentiment of Eden-grief. There are real losses to confront.

When I drove south from the last of the Columbia's upriver dams, I confronted the greatest of the many evils that make this river such an emblem. The Hanford Site sits in a huge bend where the Columbia swings north from the Oregon border and makes for Canada, and the Snake branches off for Idaho. It is 640 square miles of the hemisphere's largest concentration of radioactive waste.

Truthfully, Reader, on the upstream leg of my trip I had tried to avoid it. This thing is so out of scale in nearly every way that it is hard to think about; hard to bear. So many billions of dollars. Such sustained lying, massive and official. So much deadliness. In every dimension, the Hanford Site defeats one's ability to grasp or explain. And all of it, in a profound way, *intentional*: Hanford was potent, secret, and deadly because that's what we wanted. "We" being Americans; or perhaps just humans.

The hopeful time scales I explore in thought experiments and reveries become strangely inverted at Hanford, as if meeting their shadows. In fact, the longer scales of time just make the whole enterprise seem crazier. For at Hanford, past, present, and future are confounded by a failure to live fully and authentically in the present. What emerges instead is a demonic parody of genuine hope: a dance of death with the utopian future that has left the present sickened, exhausted, and polluted.

In 1943 the Manhattan Project organized the Hanford Engineer Works (HEW) for the purpose of manufacturing atomic weapons. Plutonium for the New Mexico "Trinity" test and for the Nagasaki bomb that ended World War II was created here. Soon after, Hanford was producing fissionables for America's growing Cold-War arsenal and conducting research on many related fronts.

Relatively little was known about the health or environmental risks of radioactive materials when Hanford began, or what standards to apply, or how to monitor them. But what was discovered was largely kept secret. Under the leadership of Chief Health Physicist Herbert M. Parker, HEW aggressively monitored radiation and researched its effects on people and the environment. Knowledge grew rapidly, but secrecy was maintained. Over the span of four decades, the weapons-production process released a staggering amount of radioactivity into the air (and into the lungs and thyroids of the famous "Downwinders"), into the ground, and into the Columbia itself. And for four decades, wherever possible, both the levels of radioactivity and the extent of their consequences were kept secret from the people whose lives were directly affected.

A major source for piecing together the enormity of what we did here to our river and ourselves is Michele Stenehjem Gerber's *On the Home Front: The Cold War Legacy of the Hanford Nuclear Site*, a sobering and exhaustive tour of the poisoned trove of information that public pressure forced the Department of Energy to begin declassifying, at long last, in February of 1986. Company historian for one of the current Hanford contractors (Fluor), Gerber is no anti-nuke crusader, and in some ways hers is a frustrating book. Gerber buries much under the obscuring mantle of too much information, too little evaluated. But occasional landmarks of clarity emerge. She summarizes: "Radioactive and chemical wastes totaling into the billions of gallons of liquids, and billions of cubic meters of gases, were emitted from the plant beginning with start-up in late 1944 … spreading millions of curies of radioactivity into the Columbia River and into the air and soil of the Columbia Basin."

That's a lot, Reader. Some of what was released has already dissipated, diluted in the atmosphere or ocean or decayed into harmless forms. But some of the work of Hanford will be with us forever, killing living things that come into contact with it for spans of time that match and exceed the entire existence of *Homo sapiens*. To look at a few specifics of the Hanford assault on air, land, and water, is to reconsider the very foundations of our technological culture and its unexamined theories of time, guilt, and responsibility.

The most notorious airborne release occurred in the "Green Run" of December 1949. Goaded by the first Russian atomic explosion a few months earlier, Hanford engineers sought a way to speed up plutonium production by using so-called "green" uranium fuel slugs that had been cooled only sixteen days (instead of the usual 90 to 125 days). Engineers knew the off-gasses would contain much higher than normal radioactivity loads, in the form of radioactive iodine (I-131); the test went forward despite an unfavorable shift in wind that planners had planned to rely on (somewhat amazingly) to disperse the contaminated gasses. According to the public-interest group Columbia River United, about 5500 curies of radiation in iodine alone were released; for comparison, the Three Mile Island accident released about 15 to 24 curies. Later vegetation samples taken secretly in the three nearby towns (the "Tri-Cities" of Richland, Kennewick, and Pasco) and rural downwind areas revealed radioactive contamination up to "one thousand times the then-tolerable limit."

Green Run releases of radioactive iodine provide a sobering illustration of what is known as "bio-concentration" of radioactivity. Dairy cows in the downwind ranges ate contaminated vegetation and concentrated the iodine in their milk; the thyroids of adults and children who drank the milk further concentrated that iodine. It was already well known at the time that pretty much any iodine that enters the body is taken up by the thyroid gland. Consequences include the obvious cancer risk, as well as hyperthyroidism, with its attendant immune deficiencies, tooth decay, and depressed levels of mental and physical activity. Two weeks after the Green Run, wildfowl were tested in a range of seventy miles from Hanford. Their thyroids showed radioactivity levels "an average of nearly fourteen times the levels of October." But no warnings were issued to residents or dairy farmers.

A similar release had happened in 1944. Official silence was maintained then, as well. The well-being of citizens (or other living beings) was not deemed important.

I met a Downwinder, one of those who lived east or northeast of Hanford where the prevailing winds would spread such contaminants. I asked how his thyroid was. Without hesitation he pulled down the collar of his shirt. "Have you heard of the 'Hanford necklace'?" Along his neckline was a thin scar where the thyroid had been surgically removed when he was nineteen. He had been a small child in northern Idaho in 1944; the milk his mother had given him was poisoned. He has taken medicine every day for decades to compensate for the missing organ.

Thousands of Americans in the Northwest have suffered this fate and worse. According to the Hanford Environmental Dose Reconstruction project (HEDR), probably thirteen thousand people just in the ten counties around Hanford received an irradiation equal to a three-year dose of normal "background radiation" in the years 1944-47; and three thousand more received a lifetime's worth. The thirteen thousand probably received at least thirty-three rads, a "rad" being about the amount of radiation in twelve typical chest X rays. According to HEDR project leader John Till, "a dose of nine rads was enough to raise the risk of cancer."

The airborne plume reached much further, of course, than this limited study area: all to the way to young children playing in Idaho, in Canada, and beyond. The scope of just this one misdeed is literally unknowable. Today there's no particular danger in breathing the air downwind of Hanford. The iodine isotope I-131 has a half-life of just eight days, meaning that half a given quantity will lose its radioactivity in that time; half of what's left will do the same after another eight days; and so on. That particular episode is, therefore, limited to those who were there.

But we should draw at least this conclusion. The dangers posed to real people in the present tense were not important enough to the Hanford project leaders. They had their eye on the enemy; they had their eye on the future. They kept mum about the present.

Here we are in the future, and this is what we find: it's not only the unlucky ones of long ago who have been harmed. The original releases also contained tiny amounts of plutonium—about a milligram per day in 1947, for instance. With a half-life of 24,000 years, this stuff can kill for a long time. Of course this milligram of plutonium is a small amount, dispersed in vast dilutions of water and air. But even a tiny fleck of plutonium caught in the body will simply blaze away at nearby cells until they have gone cancerous.

By the late 1950s, radiation's ability to cause cancer had become well known, including strong radiogenic links to cancers of blood, bone, skin, thyroid, lungs, and respiratory and gastrointestinal systems. More recent medical research has confirmed the obvious and added some specifics. Those who lived downwind of, or simply nearby, Department of Energy nuclear installations such as Savannah River, Oak Ridge, Los Alamos, or the Nevada test site record elevated rates of leukemia and brain cancer. Direct causation cannot be proved, of course. Most of the damage goes on in the secrecy of the unknown, that strange place. Both humans and literally uncountable other living organisms must certainly also have endured various kinds of damage and disease, out of our sight and in ways we know nothing about. Yet somehow, such disturbing, inevitable, and invisible consequences did not concern the HEW decision-makers.

The Hanford project illustrates a lesson visible over and over throughout history: that one cannot make war on an enemy without also warring against oneself. Perhaps this is some of the deep wisdom behind exotic spiritual concepts like "karma." The world's history is full of nations plagued with returning soldiers who won't or can't disarm—France in the fourteenth century, Nicaragua and Somalia and many others in the twentieth—and who turn their own countries into military targets. America's recent history following the Viet Nam war shows the fate the whole nation had to share, of citizens taught to kill, maimed in body and spirit, who are then dumped back into normal life. On an institutional level, America has seen its social structures distorted, in peacetime as well as wartime, to keep money flowing to soldiers, bureaucrats, and the long breadline of "defense" capitalists who contribute nothing—nothing—to the world's actual needs. As retiring President Dwight Eisenhower pointed out, a dollar spent on a bridge produces benefits many times over, while a dollar spent on a tank might as well have been burned in the wastebasket. And the Hanford Site, spreading death over the country it was supposed to be protecting, illustrates other ways that war-making targets the wrong side. There's enough karmic kickback to make you wonder who really suffers the most in the long run: the enemy or the home folks.

Secrecy and plutonium have combined to leave us a legacy of unmeasured risk. We simply cannot know where any particle of that plutonium might have ended up. My grandmother's leukemia? Your loved one's cancer? No one can say. Air, water, and ground, we have poisoned ourselves for the next twenty thousand years and more. The evils we have done to our opponents will be circling back on us for an immeasurably long time to come.

If most of the airborne contamination was short lived, much of the waterborne was not.

Direct releases of radioactivity into the Columbia commonly occurred from eight "single-pass" nuclear reactors that were producing weapons-grade plutonium by 1955. In what now seems like an inconceivably bad design choice, the reactors were cooled by river water that was returned directly to the Columbia with little or no decontamination. Effluent from the three original reactors in the 1940s were initially sent into retention basins that delayed discharge into the Columbia by eight hours, to allow the very short-lived isotopes to decay. But even this short time was steadily reduced as a matter of policy: in 1946 to between four and six hours; and by 1958, with all eight reactors running, "average holdup time for normal effluent ranged from thirty minutes to three hours. This period provided for virtually no decay of the isotopes of major concern, including … P-32 [phosphorus-32, with a half-life of 14.3 days], and those with longer half-lives."

Until their shutdown (phased from 1965 to 1971), these reactors flooded the river with long-lived radioactive pollution, including plutonium, isotopes of uranium (half-lives from 247,000 to 4.5 billion years), and others. At time-scales like these, it's almost impossible to assess the real consequences. The shorter-lived strontium-90 has been a particular concern, since it bio-concentrates in human bone and has been shown also to concentrate in river fish (forming a significant danger to those who eat them). With a half-life of twenty-seven years, this substance is still a threat and will be for several generations.

The policy of ignoring or minimizing present danger is visible pretty much everywhere in the Hanford record. A secret report to Chief Health Physicist Herbert Parker as early as 1952, for example, warned that bottom-feeding fish in the Columbia were showing alarming bio-concentrations of radioactivity. Such whitefish commonly migrated to popular fishing spots; the report estimated that eating just one pound of it "would furnish ... about 20 percent of the chronic permissable intake."

Gerber's account reveals how, despite pressure from other health officials, Chief Parker began fudging the numbers. In his own words, his concern was not about public health, but that "The public relations impact would be severe" if accurate or realistic limits were publicized. His solution was simply to ignore the factual report on his desk and, without explanation, weaken its numbers by a factor of five. However, a diligent medical scientist, Deputy Director at the Atomic Energy Commission Dr. Charles Dunham, was apparently puzzled by Parker's figures. He researched them in detail and blew the whistle on Parker's silent adoption of a standard that was five times too high. A bureaucratic showdown between the two powerful federal institutions ensued, with a predictable result: no action, but a vague promise from the AEC to "keep this potential problem under close observation." (By 1958, further research had recommended a limit five times *lower* than even the original report that had been ignored.)

Meanwhile, Parker's PR campaign continued. HEW officials issued a public statement insisting, against all the evidence at their disposal, that "We doubt that any real human hazard could be positively demonstrated." In a sort of sick two-step, press releases covered up radioactivity releases while public relations covered up threats to public health. In 1956, for example, a combination of accidental and ongoing "permissable" releases into the Columbia raised the beta radioactivity measured in public drinking water in Pasco and Kennewick by 50 percent.

Major releases continued:

• In 1959 a plume of radioactivity was measured two hundred miles out into the Pacific, and contamination was discovered in shellfish beds along Washington and Oregon coasts.

• By 1961, those projected levels of concern in drinking water had materialized, according to a report by more vocal state health officials in Oregon and Washington.

• And in 1963, an entire *pound* of uranium found its dispersed way into the waters of the Columbia, released in a "catastrophic" fuel slug accident.

Much of the released material has been diluted, as the Hanford experts hoped, by the sheer volume of the Columbia River and the planet's biggest ocean. Diluted, sent down the river, sent out to sea. What it does out there is anyone's guess. Some is deposited in sediments along the way, ticking away like little time bombs. Some is finding its way into the general ill-health of the world's living beings, generating cancers and mutations.

What wasn't released had to be stored. It sits at Hanford, leaking into our present. The Cold War is not, in this sense, over at all; its foreign enemies have disappeared, but it continues to campaign against domestic targets.

A public-information handbook on radioactive wastes states the basic problem: "Contamination of groundwater by radionuclides is the most probable pathway by which improper nuclear waste disposal can expose humans." According to Hanford's own assessment, by 1970 various ponds, tanks, and holding basins at the site had received over 600 pounds of plutonium and an astounding 264,000 pounds of uranium.

Some of the earliest wastes were "stored" by simply settling or (later) being pumped right into the earth. Again, the recklessness of such a plan exceeds one's imagination. And the more you know, the crazier it gets. To take just one instance: Chief Parker in 1948 declared that the subsurface geology of the the infamous "200-area," where many of the most dangerous wastes were generated and stored, formed a safe basaltic basin with a water table 250 feet deep, so that radioactive wastes would have a long travel time and be substantially prevented from reaching aquifers and traveling into the Columbia.

The derangement here is layered. First, Chief Parker had *no geological basis* for this optimistic scenario. No one knew exactly what shape the underlying basalt might be in, nor how deep the water table was. As with the fudged limits for bottom-fish, here the "facts" were simply made up. Tests of ground dispersal in the following years consistently showed contamination spreading rapidly and quickly reaching groundwater. When the site's geology was finally studied (in 1956), it was discovered to be far more complex than Parker's hopeful fantasy. There were complexly fractured basalts below; the water table varied from "less than one foot" below the surface to over three hundred.

But giving Chief Parker the benefit of the doubt—assuming it was an honest mistake—only reveals a yet deeper craziness. Hanford's official estimates of underground travel times beneath the 200-area were originally pegged at fifty to one hundred years before wastes would reach the Columbia. *As if fifty to one hundred years were somehow okay!* And these pretty much baseless estimates were steadily revised downward as actual information came in. A 1955 study showed "radioactive materials apparently moving with velocities in the order of hundreds of feet per day."

When the HEDR researchers got around to reconstructing how much groundwater radiation had actually reached humans (so far), they came up with a very reassuring result: negligible amounts, on the order of a day or two of background radiation for most of Hanford's immediate neighbors. A few individuals, in the worst case, may have received triple the average annual dose of background radiation. These are not catastrophic numbers. But the HEDR studies also issue a caution: The future might be different. "A considerable amount of contamination that may result in future radiation doses currently exists in the ground water ... at the Site." Overviews show plumes of groundwater contamination all over the Hanford site, quietly dispersing toward aquifers and rivers.

Attempts at storing liquid waste in physical containments have been perhaps better-conceived than simply abandoning it to the earth; but only marginally so. The two most significant such storage sites at Hanford are known as the "K-Basins" and the "Tank Farm." Both are the objects of ongoing cleanup efforts that are grotesquely over-budget and far behind schedule; contractors are dropped, others brought on, and federal expenditures reach half a billion dollars yearly. And while this lucrative smiling shuffle goes on, tanks and basins continue to leak.

The Tank Farm consists of 177 underground steel-and-concrete structures storing 54 million gallons of high-level (extremely radioactive) liquid waste. Most of these tanks (149) are single shelled, built between 1944 and 1964 with a single welded steel plate bolted onto foot-thick concrete. More than a million gallons have leaked from them into the ground. Battelle's Pacific Northwest Laboratories, a division of the billion-dollar-a-year defense firm, has contracted to pump the remaining waste into more reliable double-shelled tanks, and to create a "glassification" factory to permanently immobilize the material. Battelle is behind schedule, of course. Though the 1989 "Tri-Party Agreement" calls for a strict schedule, Doug Sherwood, Hanford project manager for EPA, fears that "the idea that DOE is going to complete cleanup along the river by 2012 is slipping away." And meanwhile, of course, there's that invisible plume of ground contamination below the tanks.

The two K-basins are a particularly revealing riddle. Located just 400 yards from the Columbia, each is a rectangular concrete pool 125 feet long by 67 feet wide by 21 feet deep, built in the early 1950s with "a 20-year design life." The basins contain 2,200 tons of spent radioactive fuel rods grouped in containers and stored under water, netting about four tons of plutonium. Thousands of these rods are crumbling into their containers. The containers are leaking into the water, which is leaking into the ground. Again it's hard to know precisely how much—it's underground. But we know, for instance, that 15,000 gallons escaped through a floor joint in the late 1970s; and another 94,000 gallons in 1993.

Fifty years later, faced with these leaky swimming pools of toxic sempiternity, we might well ask what they were thinking. A *twenty-year* design life? *Right by the river??* We might even ask, more broadly: Is it possible to understand the string of reckless assumptions and heedlessly deadly decisions that characterize Hanford's entire forty years? What *were* they thinking?

Our broader task is facing our losses and distinguishing the kinds of damage we've done. To do so, it might help to understand ourselves and what we did at Hanford. Twenty years, fifty years, a hundred years: how could Health Chief Parker and the HEW decision-makers have thought that polluting the world would be okay, as long as it was a few decades down the road?

It seems clear that a wartime mentality dominated the entire time, starting with a hot war against Japan and segueing into a cold war against communism. The polarized thinking of us-versus-them gave permission to ignore and cover up the damage wreaked upon the citizenry. As we notice elsewhere within the environmental debate, where opposition is defined as disloyalty, room for critical thought disappears. Horace Busby, a veteran Washington State journalist on the scene since the 1940s, reflected in 1990: "In the wake of World War II, an attitude permeated Washington that the government is always right. This came out of the war experience, when to think otherwise was almost treason."

But where did the shortsightedness originate? The bland acceptance of a fifty-year timeline for radioactive pollution in public water, or a twenty-year design life for containment basins? The willingness to conduct a dangerous experiment of literally hemispheric proportions, on tens of thousands of fellow-citizens, with an unknown outcome?

In 1949, Parker revealed the reason HEW did not need to worry about radioactive pollution and contamination: "Projection of the problem to [the] future ... appears to be irrelevant in terms of the technological progress in corrective measures that can be anticipated." It appears that Parker, and others like him at Hanford, simply did not think the problems of waste-storage and environmental contamination warranted serious attention because *some unknown something in the future would take care of them—* some semi-magic discovery of science, or technology, or American Know-How. "Progress," in other words.

That faith in the future, and the rushing-forward optimism it generates, may be the key to understanding the unprecedented wrongdoing at Hanford. Cold-War pressures were certainly important. But who could contemplate a program to create such super-deadly materials, and to stockpile them so sloppily, without this psychological out-clause: the future will erase our mistakes.

No such erasure has come. Only death and billions of dollars wasted, and no solution in sight.

I was a child in the 1950s and I remember quite well that giddy faith in the future. In our annual pilgrimage to Disneyland, we would visit "Tomorrowland" to see the GE Carousel of Progress, a kind of futuristic appliance-based paradise; close by we would also marvel at a twinkling diorama of someplace (in Alaska, I think) that would be the City of Tomorrow, full of plexiglass domes, silent gliding monorails, and unimaginable abundance. Utopian, glib, and silly, such quasi-religious belief in the future nevertheless has deep roots in the American psyche. At the time, I did not know that Disney had merely appropriated the wide-eyed futurism of the 1936 New York Worlds Fair. *What Parker expressed made perfect sense to those who heard it.* The future would provide; no worries about the present. John Volkman, in his policy review of Northwest salmon issues, says that this kind of "technological optimism" might be seen as a late version of that old follow-the-frontier romance, that boundless faith that drew people ever westward into freshly exploitable lands. When resources were used up, they moved on. The frontier has closed, Volkman says, but there's still a belief we can "engineer our way through the landscape and reach new frontiers." Can't we always move on, further west, or further into the technological future?

But there's an odd circularity to this technological optimism, a demonic irony. At Hanford, childish faith in a fairy-tale future permitted an unprecedented level of present-tense evildoing. Such deeds formed a reality—a past—which we are powerless to avoid. It leaks towards us in time, spilling, tainting, killing. It is that which cannot be escaped. That is: a kind of fate.

Fate, of course, is what Americans don't believe in. Let Europe and Asia wrangle with their millennial grudges, their burden of history, their fatalistic suffering. We believe in the future. We believe in a clean slate, a new beginning, the American Adam. Nothing can stop us, we say: the Future is ours, Happiness and Progress. Yet believing this, we create precisely what we disbelieve in: fate, ineluctable and dire. The past that cannot be shucked or avoided.

Hanford leads me to think it is the past, not the future, that we are actually building.

For a few centuries now, people have believed the fantastic theory that the future is in our hands—that it belongs to us, somehow, and that we control it. Utopias float on this delusive, sometimes bloody, sea. Our technological consumerism swims through it, devouring anything living or dead that gets in its way. Communist or capitalist has made no difference: "the future" has justified all, and towards "the future" we rush, though we never get there. Where we actually arrive is always surprising, always different than anything we could have predicted, *because the future will build itself:* we don't control it. Events and serendipities will combine, as they always do, with ineffable charm and weirdness. People will make their contributions—oddball, horrifying, beautiful, creative; the rest of the biosphere will do the same. Their future world will be both outlandish and familiar. And how people will cope, what choices they will make, where they will succeed and where fail—for this *they* are responsible, not us. It's the future. It makes itself.

I say instead: It is someone's past we are making. I find this turn of thought strangely settling. We, our choices, our actions and inactions, are forming tough, inescapable realities that people will cope with, or create with. We will be there, in their lives, like strata of bedrock basalt. Layered in there, for good or ill.

Our poisons will be there along the Columbia. Treading in the wrong place, or stirring up the wrong sediment, someone will die; someone else will grieve. These are our grandchildren we're talking about. These are the curses we are leaving them. Maybe they will develop wisdom about what to avoid. Someone else will paddle a boat up a shining river, marvelling at shattered high-rises along the Willamette, maybe from a sea-level three stories up. Those travellers will think us clever and demented. A day or two later, they will begin passing buttresses of ruined riverside dams along the Columbia itself. They will sing songs about us, their past. They will be admiring and unsparing, as we are of past generations.

Seeing ourselves this way, how could we fail to make a better past than, so far, we have been making?

Thinking of a perfect past, an Eden, has done us no good. But turning that lost Eden into a Paradisal future has been worse, poisoning the present through inattention to detail, a form of moral laxness that later generations will pay for.

Perhaps thinking of ourselves as someone's past may restore the present to us. It may help us slow down. We might let go of the addictive frenzy of rushing toward the fantasy goal (happiness, progress) that recedes ever before us. Perhaps instead we could settle into a decent walking pace, a meditative pace, steady and determined, progressing calmly toward some modestly humane destination. A light that shines just up ahead, a distance we could make before nightfall. Not the far future; just the next night's rest.

At this pace, we could afford to make good decisions. Clean up the messes we've made. Put the dangerous things out of harm's way. Leave something for the salmon. Let the rivers flow as they have always done, understanding that our "always" is a little thing, and that a great mystery spreads on all sides of it.

The Unintended
Sits by Her Window and Smiles

But *will* there be any salmon, by the time those dams have broken?

Some of the damage we do is temporary; some of it is permanent. Some forests never come back (visit anywhere around the Mediterranean). Extinct species are gone. I cannot imagine when the Grand Coulee, the last and greatest of the Columbia's dams, will finally breach. No salmon gets by it. The previous chapters explored a tentative optimism in the face of such environmental mistakes. To finish the thought-experiment, we should look carefully at what's actually living (and dying) in the water here on the Columbia: ever-returning salmon, emblem of folly, emblem of hope. Stubborn, complicated, threatened. Totem of the Northwest.

Pursuing this question has led me into strange terrain. The answers are not what I expect; in fact, they are the very opposite of my expectations. Far worse than we had intended or foreseen. And also, weirdly—in certain unpredictable instances—far better.

First the Hanford atrocities.

All during my researches and visits, my chats with dam guys, museum guides, and salmon biologists, I kept waiting for the full weight of Hanford radioactivity to smite our remaining salmon. But no one would say so. Stymied and useless, I drove up the river and back down, I probed, I wondered, I confronted the bureaucratic, impenetrable environs of Hanford and Richland, thinking: surely they're hiding some dire atomic salmon secret. But none emerged.

Back home, I emailed the radioactive-salmon question to my cadre of professional salmonists. No result. I dove into the literature. Nothing. Books on the Columbia, eloquent on the plight (always "plight") of the salmon, spoke nary a word.Periodical literature never mentioned the obvious question of radioactive pollution and the death of salmon. Never. At last, I found a comprehensive overview of the salmon situation which I thought would surely have answers. An official summary, book sized, consensus of the combined environmental scientists of the National Science and Technology Council, it did not find the question of radioactivity sufficiently interesting to merit a single word of discussion. Not even in an appendix for minority opinions and disputes. Not a word.

And that, my patient Reader, was the negative evidence I needed. I realized this fact belatedly, suddenly seeing what was absent. *There is no evidence that atomic radiation has contributed significantly to salmon decline.*

My salmonists explained that salmon after all spend most of their lives in the ocean. Even those bred on the Hanford Reach itself—those fifty-one undammed river miles subjected for four decades to direct radioactive outfalls—even those salmon would attain smolthood and depart quickly into ever less glowingly atomic waters, and thence into the great salty haven of the Pacific. And when they return they are not much affected, either. Hanford Engineer Works noticed the river's heavy burden of radioactivity in 1952 and wondered about the consequences for salmon, but quickly reflected that upstreaming adults "cease to feed upon entering fresh water."

The 1950s imagined nuclear mutants and abominations. So did I. But in the case of salmon, these predictable disasters simply did not happen. Yet meanwhile, less glamorous kinds of damage went hardly noticed. For it turns out that radiation has had far less effect than the other, ordinary pollutions produced at Hanford—thermal and chemical.

Thermal sensitivity of salmon is now quite well established. Usually a temperature around 68 degrees Fahrenheit is considered the upper limit; salmon like cool, flowing water, and tend to suffer infections and diseases when the temperature gets tepid. The sluggish, sun-warmed lakes we have created behind dams often reach this limit, and unlike the free-flowing Columbia, they may stay warm for months at a time.

Hanford's thermal effect on the river was not insignificant. In 1952, Chief Health Physicist Herbert Parker had to warn his staff—in secret of course—that the atomically warmed-up water returning to the Columbia from the single-pass reactors was indeed having a noticeable effect on the salmon. The fall salmon run of the previous year was noted as significantly lower than that of just a few years earlier, probably at least partly from temperature stresses.

As more single-pass reactors came on line, not only thermal but also chemical pollution increased. My dependable source Michele Stenehjem Gerber reveals how various chemicals were added to the cooling waters for technical reasons. The chief pollutant seems to have been sodium dichromate, the function of which was "impeding fuel slug ruptures and ... maintaining pile reactivity." The chemical is toxic to salmon, as a 1954 report (also secret) recognized. Nevertheless, with eight reactors running by 1955, Hanford planned two more. But a 1956 feasibility study for the projected additional reactors found that they would bring the sodium dichromate levels all the way to the top of the "local recommended limit" for juvenile fish, as well as raising river temperatures to unacceptable heights. The ninth and tenth reactors were not built, though, in excellent Hanford style, the existing reactors were instead ramped up, from 1956 to 1959, to "throughput" levels more than ten times their 1948 capacity—in effect getting their extra reactors through the back door.

All the reactors are shut down now (with one in suspended animation awaiting further orders). And we can assess: the worst never happened. No atomic disaster: no universal die-off; no mutant salmonzillas terrorizing river towns; no glowing plutonium-carcasses along the streambanks. Instead, just ordinary, careless, hardly noticed destruction of salmon by conventional means. Bad enough. Yet those thermal and chemical effects are in the past tense too. With the important exception of chemicals held in sediments, their immediate impact is over. While salmon today are not exactly thriving—and while their decline surely reflects dead generations from this pollution—they survived; they dodged all three bullets. That's a better run of luck than we deserve.

At Hanford I keep learning that, for better and for worse, we hardly ever know what the full consequences of our actions are. Quite often the opposite of what we intended comes around to bite us (or kiss us) on the butt.

In the separate reality that was Hanford—secretive, over-funded, ingrown, a black hole where according to a U.S. Senate report seven *billion* dollars of cleanup money disappeared without producing any appreciable cleanup—in this separate world, a through-the-looking-glass effect surprises us with upside-down results almost as reliably as nature itself does. At Hanford our most sober, uniformed, slide-ruled engineers went about producing the most deadly inventions and byproducts they could. Yet, when they weren't killing us, they ended up producing lasting and unique benefits for nature and people.

This they did mainly by leaving the countryside alone, while they fiddled with atoms. Hanford repeats the pattern seen in another famous nuclear site: the Rocky Mountain Nuclear Arsenal, which has become what wise-guy urban designers in Denver call "The Nation's Most Ironic Nature Park." Roped off from development, that little bit of Colorado is now an ecological treasure. In his book on the Columbia, Blaine Harden savors Hanford's similar "post-nuclear paradise"—an inadvertent "wild and scenic nuclear dump."

One important piece of this polluted paradise is the Hanford Reach: the longest free-flowing, non-tidal stretch of Columbia River in the USA, containing some of the best salmon-spawning habitat in the lower 48, home to a lively stock of fall-run chinook. From Priest Rapids Dam all the way down to McNary Dam on the Oregon border, there's nothing but river, rivering along for fifty-one miles just like a river. Salmon do well there. That's the prescription, by the way, that has emerged from decades of river debate and study: if we want salmon, we will have to give them something closer to the river conditions they have evolved in. Something like what the Northwest Power Planning Council called a "normative" river: not pristine, but "partway back" from the current currentless slackwater sloughs. The Hanford Reach models that for us. Despite the outrageous misdeeds committed upon it, it's still a river, and so the salmon tend to like it. If you canoe there, or raft, you'll like it too.

Another of Hanford's ironic Edens is located up on dry land to the west of the river, where the misdeeds originated. For virtually all the territory around the evil archipelago of actual Hanford installations—that is, most of the Reservation's 630 square miles—have come to function as a *de facto* wildlife preserve. The federal government says that 96 percent of it is pretty well untouched. What you see there is miles of windblown sage separating rare, if irradiated, industrial islands. Coyotes and white-tailed deer, cute li'l pygmy rabbits and huge loping jacks wander past the barbed-wire plutonium processing plants and secure worksites, freer of molestation or hindrance than anywhere else on the drylands of eastern Washington. No cows. No crops. No suburbs.

And the unintended blessings of Hanford's deadly sins have spread east from the river, as well. A vast wildlife preserve now occupies the Wahluke Slope, the rising ground across the Columbia River to the north and east of Hanford Nuclear Reservation. In June of 2000, a presidential proclamation designated 140 square miles of it as Saddle Mountain National Wildlife Refuge, part of the Hanford Reach National Monument. According to its own literature, the refuge contains an "unmatched" diversity of native plants: "The largest remnant of the shrub-steppe ecosystem that once blanketed the Columbia River Basin."

Harden says there is virtually no other shrub-steppe left in eastern Washington. So why is it still intact here? You could call it the sunny side of thyroid poisoning. Despite the federal government's energetic postwar irrigation projects, leading to new ranching on hundreds of thousands of dry-brush acres between the tri-cities and the Grand Coulee Dam, HEW prevented any settlement on those slopes that were receiving regular downwind radiation doses. By the time the hazard was shut down in the mid-1960s, a developing environmental awareness was just strong enough to hang on to the Wahluke Slope. Another atomic Eden for us to enjoy.

The message here is that we almost never really know what is happening; often, it's the clean opposite of what we expect, a principle as true in nature as it is in politics. This fact of life ought to help us keep a light heart. Let city folk cry *Lost Paradise!* Let country peasants cry *End-of-the-world*! We know better: for woven among nature's tropes is a tough, blood-red thread of irony, sometimes gallows-dark, but often light as a farce. Serendipity swooping in among the corpses. There's a topsy-turviness that keeps making good fortune out of bad, just as often as it does the opposite. It's really too unpredictable to despair over; though it might warrant some real humility. Some caution.

◉

So—to return to the question—will there be any salmon to accompany our descendants upriver? Though salmon have done surprisingly well on the Hanford Reach, salmon of the U.S. and Canadian Pacific coast in general are in bad shape, verging on desperate. Their reprieve from atomic disaster has not saved them from other plights (there: I said it). Let's try a quick assessment; and then see what a cautious, humble, and light-hearted response might look like.

Salmon were already extinct from Idaho's Boise River—due to gold-mining practices—a year before the first cannery began operating on the Columbia in 1866. Within a couple of decades, Northwest salmon were in an obvious and steep decline from a combination of logging, mining, and overharvesting. The first salmon hatchery in the Northwest went in on the Clackamas River, just up the Willamette from Portland, in 1877—a telltale sign that salmon reproduction was already a problem. Millions of hatchery-bred salmon have followed, from dozens of hatcheries, over the next hundred years. But the problem has only gotten worse.

How much worse and how far gone?

At least 106 native wild stocks, or one-third of the original total, have already gone extinct, according to highly respected fisheries biologist Jim Lichatowich, who, with Willa Nehlsen and J. E. Williams, authored the landmark 1991 paper *Pacific Salmon at the Crossroads*, a comprehensive inventory of "the remaining salmon stocks" of the Northwest. The *Crossroads* study found that, of 214 still-extant native wild Pacific salmonid stocks (i.e. salmon and the two anadromous "trout" species of steelhead and sea-run cutthroat), "101 were at high risk of extinction, 58 were at moderate risk, and 54 were of special concern."

Some felt the report was too alarming, but a decade later, the dire numbers and trends are, sadly, vindicated. The usual figure now used is that salmon are extinct in about 40 percent of their historic rivers. And in his 1999 book updating the salmon situation, Lichatowich declares that "salmon populations in 44 percent of the remaining streams are at risk." What's left overall represents just 20 percent of the original salmon productivity of the Northwest river system.

Many of the remaining salmon stocks are now protected under the Endangered Species Act (ESA). The NMFS regional website provides a depressing updated register for the interested. As of this writing, some 26 stocks (or "environmentally significant units") are listed as endangered or threatened, with six more listed as proposed or candidate species.

My hometown of Portland, despite its self-image as the capital of green, got its own salmon comeuppance. Chinook and steelhead are now "threatened" in Portland's much-abused Willamette River. Oregon's environmentalist governor, John Kitzhaber, had fought for years to enlist resource users and other "stakeholders" in a voluntary and local solution; and the big-stick threat of an ESA listing had enabled him to achieve some measure of cooperation. But not enough. The 1999 ESA listings caused consternation to image-conscious city boosters and business-conscious river-users. But despite their loud complaints, the ESA listing will do just what it is supposed to do: require the humans who live here to pay attention to what they are doing to the living world, and indeed to stop it. Or to stop enough of it to permit that living world to go on living. Pretty radical.

Almost any way you look at it, the salmon situation is, as the 1996 report from the National Research Council phrased it, "cause for pessimism." A report from another of the Salmon Problem's many official constituent/agencies (the Northwest Power Planning Council) summed it up this way: "the mainstem dams have fundamentally altered the riverine ecosystem, its temperature, chemistry, turbidity, and nutrients, and the timing and nature of its flow. ... In short, the Columbia River has in some respects become a better habitat for squawfish and other predators of salmon than for salmon." The NPPC's succinct appraisal seems more and more self-evident: the salmon need rivers that are more like rivers: "normative rivers." Lichatowich's title—*Salmon Without Rivers*— encapsulates the folly that has gotten us where we are: the century-long attempt, through hatcheries, fish-barging, and other manipulations, to have healthy salmon populations without bothering to have healthy rivers. It seems obvious when you put it like that, doesn't it?

The hatchery fix was part of a narrowly technocratic mentality that believed—quite wrongly—that it understood, and could control, the wildness of salmon and rivers. "We assumed that it was possible and desirable to maintain abundant populations of Pacific salmon by simplifying, controlling, and circumventing the ecological processes that created them. We assumed that we were not part of the Northwest's ecosystems but stood apart from them as their managers. We assumed that technology could overcome all problems."

This approach, focussed on hatcheries, was simple engineering-mind thinking, Point A to Point B: Breed 'em, truck 'em, catch 'em. But it did not work—could not possibly work—because we did not understand the complexity of salmon genetics and life histories, or the intricacies of ecosystems. And probably never will, in the sense of the total-control fantasy that produced the hatchery debacle. Former Forest Service chief Jack Ward Thomas underlined the extent—the hubris—of that misconception, in a phrase that ought to become a proverb: "not only are ecosystems more complex than we think, they are more complex than we *can* think."

Words worth meditating on: this is the actual labyrinth, Reader, of our life in nature. That we somehow must live in, and on, a reality that exceeds us, that's full of blind corners and surprises. Walking briskly in straight lines doesn't work well here, for long.

Lichatowich tells the cautionary tale of the "success" of coho hatchery programs, which seemed for a few years in the 1950s and 1960s to be working swimmingly. Numbers increased, the salmon catch looked good, sport fishers were happy. Northwest hatcheries had worked hard to refine their techniques; they were all too willing to take credit for the good numbers. Someone pointed out along the way that ocean conditions must have something to do with how many juveniles survived their years at sea, grew to adulthood, and returned. But the temptation to believe in human knowledge and control made the managers deaf.

The apparent success of the coho program encouraged dozens of other hatchery programs, costing millions or dollars, in the 1960s and 1970s. It was a clean, slick, Tomorrowland kind of thing, —full of hearty confidence and slide-ruled certainty. Sure that orphanage salmon were just as good as any others, the engineers put up four more dams on the best remaining major salmon habitat, the Snake

River. Degraded habitat? No worries. Hatcheries will replace whatever we lose.

Of course the bubble popped. The seeming correlation between the numbers of hatchery juveniles released and the numbers of adults returning wobbled and then disappeared. The returns of breeding adults began to fluctuate wildly—wildly!—and the managers could not say why. And then, in 1977, the numbers plummeted. "The harvest dropped from a peak of 3.9 million fish in 1976 to a million fish the next year. Less than twenty years later, in 1997, only 28,000 coho were harvested, and there were less than 300,000 in the whole … area."

Listings followed. Extinctions followed: lower Columbia wild coho gone, coastal coho on the brink.

The hatchery experiment failed due to hubris and ignorance (which, come to think of it, may be close to the same thing). "We assumed we could control the biological productivity of salmon and 'improve' upon natural processes that we didn't even try to understand," reflects Lichatowich. We did not notice that hatchery fish are in nearly every respect inferior to wild ones: smaller, more susceptible to disease, more vulnerable to changes in ocean conditions, surviving at "only half the rate of their wild cousins," ignorant of social behavior, sometimes unable to figure out what to eat. Picture a sleeping moo-cow so dull-witted and inert that pranksters can tip it over; then picture that cow's wild cousin, a bison or water buffalo, snorting and commanding. In the same way, hatchery fish are individually and genetically stupid. But by sheer force of numbers, they may swamp wild fish, crowding them out of feeding areas.

Yet for a while, the coho numbers were good, for reasons that had nothing to do with hatchery programs. When ocean conditions were no longer favorable, the optimistic projections went into the wastebasket. The National Research Council concluded that hatchery enthusiasts had jumped to conclusions, employing far-too-narrow scales of measurement ("Inappropriate short-term responses to large-scale environmental changes at sea or on land") that ignored the "long lags between causes and effects." In other words, they had no idea what was causing what. They had simply lucked out.

Not only did the hatchery engineers fail to think in time-scales that could give a realistic picture of actual salmon health; they failed to think in scales of space that included the many other places where salmon lived out their life histories—rivers, estuaries, oceans. But most of all, the engineers did not notice that hatchery salmon were dramatically inferior in the scale of complexity and information—what I have called elsewhere a kind of "third infinity," that mysterious realm where biology ceaselessly invents opportunity, against the finite limits of the physical world. Salmon biologists like Jim Lichatowich have concluded that hatchery fish lack the defining adaptation that has allowed salmon to survive for ten million roller-coaster years in the Pacific Northwest: intricate variations of life-history adapted to specific streams and breeding areas, coded into the various stocks genetically or behaviorally. Those differences precisely mesh a specific stock with a specific place. Survival is the result. But flooding the gene pool with hatchery idiots threatens the wild fish, directly, through competition for food, and indirectly, through interbreeding and loss of genetic biodiversity. "The effect of this loss of diversity becomes most evident during periods of natural stress, such as prolonged drought or changing ocean productivities. ... Today fisheries managers produce giant schools of domesticated salmon that are programmed to migrate to sea and return to spawn at the same time. These herds of uniform salmon released from hatcheries have been spawned by the vision of a controlled river and ecosystem."

A hundred years of failure have still not killed the hatchery mentality. A federal judge in Oregon, appointed by Bush, Sr., oblivious to the importance of this genetic and behavioral diversity, has declared that wild and hatchery-bred coho are "genetically identical," and ruled that NMFS may not use such distinctions in its policies. Official documents still tread carefully around the effectiveness of hatcheries, which have a large institutional constituency. Probably it is this hatchery habit that the *Upstream* report alludes to, when it remarks that "some of our policies are based on deep ignorance."

But we are at least beginning to admit that our ignorance about salmon, rivers, and oceans is, well, oceanic. In fact, that recent, very official salmon study, *From the Edge*, makes ignorance a major theme, around which its entire assessment is organized: it calls for "research to close the many knowledge gaps" that have prevented both scientists and engineers from responding to the, uh, plight of the salmon. We don't know the effects of other predatory species on salmon. We don't know to what extent hatchery fish breed with wild ones, or if they do, how their progeny fare. What are the normal fluctuations in salmon populations? We don't know. We know surprisingly little about the details of both estuary and ocean effects on salmon health or mortality. The latter is perhaps the biggest blank in our knowledge: "The marine environment is the least understood and is a source of essentially uncontrollable influences on salmon."

So what is the meaning of this ocean of ignorance for managing our interactions with the natural world in general, and with salmon in particular?

In other chapters of this book I have been insisting that we really don't have a "don't touch" option. We use the world, and must do so, even as it uses us. And *From the Edge* makes the obvious point that the incompleteness of our knowledge is not a warrant for delaying action on salmon, either, though it's a common political ploy to say so. "Recovery of these stocks may require immediate intervention." But how to do it?

There is a middle ground between control-all engineerism and don't-touch romanticism. And that is where our salmon discussion takes us. In the early 1990s, Jim Lichatowich made something of an unpopular stand against (of all things) over-reliance on Endangered Species Act listings. Why? Because a listing rivets attention on one species, instead of on the environment in which it lives. "Focusing on species sets us up for a task that is humanly impossible, simply because ecosystems are so complex," he explained. If, instead, we tried "conserving the integrity of ecosystems," then the *ecosystem* could take care of the salmon. Our job would be, not attempting to control the system, but simply *not disrupting* it—a task that would not require godlike knowledge, but rather a simple conservative caution not to overturn the applecart. To *allow* the river, you might say, rather than to control it.

This is the approach implied in that vision of a "normative river." Not a pristine, untouched river; and not an engineered one, either. Somewhere in between. It is what the book *Wild Forests: Conservation Biology and Public Policy* calls "passive management":

an option that might, in many cases, work where aggressive interventions have failed.

Published in 1994, *Wild Forests* repeats the now-familiar point about "how little we know." In the presence of "immense gaps" in our knowledge, how could the task of managing forests (or rivers) even be conceived? William S. Alverson and the other authors say that we must opt for "wild (i.e. unengineered) conditions" wherever possible, and in the case of forests, reserve large tracts that are "passively managed"—that is, in which wild processes are allowed to substantially take over. This is different from the pristine myth. It acknowledges that management is going on, whether active or passive; and that human choices are being made at each step. But it also acknowledges our limited ability to know what really matters in an ecosystem. And in the absence of knowing, it encourages us to opt for letting the ecosystem make as many decisions as possible. Such management will have to be, by definition, "adaptive"—it will deal in degrees of intervention, and be ready to keep trying until it discovers what works. Its contrast with the either-or prescriptions of the "wilderness ethic" is profound. It will be founded on a myth of partnership, of belonging to a community, rather than a myth of exclusion.

When the issue is framed this way, many of the hand-wringing ambiguities drop out of the picture. How to make the rivers more normative? Let them flow. Don't disrupt them to the point that normal processes cease, because you and I are not capable of taking over the natural processes. Not with trucks, not with barges, not with Army Corps Engineers. Wherever possible, we must simply allow the river to river.

This vision brings me abruptly to two insights. Good news and bad news, actually. First: It's not rocket science. Rocket science is what we give up—the myth of invincible knowledge and control. The groundless fantasy that we can micro-manage an infinite complexity. In place of this delusion we say, let's get out of the way a bit. It's not secret, mysterious, or unknowable. Just: Get out of the way. Just: *Stop This Nonsense*. Because as soon as we do—in that very instant!—nature will go back to naturing again. This I know for sure. Open the spigots (or whatever they are called) on the big dams and let the water run, and the fish will swim just like fish. They will find a way to thrive. And where the dams have too extremely goofed up the system, take them out. That's right: take them out. *Stop This Nonsense.* And all will be well: in a decade, a generation, a trigener.

Which dams should we take out? The ones to start with are the four on the lower Snake River. The proposal awakens bitter debate, because a few grain-silo guys up in Lewiston Idaho, a few barge operators, like things the way they are. But it's an easy call. The Snake River is really (except for a quirk of naming) another fork of the Columbia. It's the less-developed fork, that heads from the tri-cities straight to the Idaho mountains, where it twists and branches into what fisheries biologist Scott Bosse calls "nearly four thousand miles of prime spawning and rearing habitat" on the rivers Snake, Salmon, and Clearwater and their countless streams and brooks. The four lower Snake dams, only recently constructed (1961-1975), are ripe for removal. They are mistakes ready to be corrected, offering relatively little to society in return for killing an estimated 81 percent of ocean-bound juveniles and 40 percent of returning adults. Plans I've seen reproduce exactly my thought-experiment scenario, opening a hole in the earthworks to one side of the Ice Harbor, Lower Granite, Lower Monumental, and Little Goose Dams. Letting the river go through.

Economically, the trade-offs seem clear enough that the major newspaper in this highly conservative region, the Boise *Idaho Statesman*, publicly supported dam-breaching in editorials of July 1997, even before the most definitive studies (then in progress) had been completed. The four dams are not designed for flood control or irrigation (just thirteen farms depend on lower Snake water). The economic questions focus on the barging and power losses, balanced by some other losses and gains. The *Statesman* factored in less-visible costs like public subsidies supporting barging and dam maintenance as well as expensive, ongoing hatchery and salmon recovery programs; and the editorial staff projected revenues from revived commercial fishing, sport fishing, and tourism if salmon were to rebound to their 1960s (pre-dam) levels. The result: a net gain to the region and nation of at least $183 million per year (and perhaps as much as $257 million).

Would the sagebrush-rebel citizens of the Far West stand for such a decision? The DC-hating archconservatives there have traditionally opposed federal programs on principle—but made exceptions in their rhetoric when federal largess was seen to be coming their way. Business is business! Yet lead editorialist Susan Whaley told me the reaction to her series was, surprisingly, "not too bad." Imagine that.

But my second point, the bad news, is this: Taking out dams on the lower Snake is a deal we should make—but almost certainly won't.

How do I know this? The reaction of my fellow citizens during 2001 demonstrated it clearly. The power shortfall, in a year of drought in the Northwest, made for angry citizens and large, scary headlines. People demanded power, no matter the cost. We showed ourselves unwilling to give up anything—anything at all—for the sake of healthy rivers and salmon. That's how I know. I wish I didn't.

As soon as the blackouts started rolling through California, the word went out to the BPA, which runs the electricity-generating operation on the Columbia: Give us more power. And the BPA obliged. It immediately began using up water that was designated for salmon recovery. Water was sent through turbines instead of being spilled for spring fish passage. Water was sent through turbines instead of being saved for later in the summer, when the salmon would need something in the river to swim in. And in this drought year, with water levels already low, the decision was doubly deadly to salmon.

By declaring a "power emergency," Bonneville was able to waive its salmon-recovery obligations. It announced a "no-spill policy" for the summer, and ended up releasing only about one-fifth its required amount overall. Death rates for juvenile steelhead and salmon climbed accordingly. The BPA Acting Administrator Steve Write stated, with bland obtuseness, that "Summer spill would reduce power system reliability to an unacceptably low level." That is, the administrator wished to guard against the *possibility* of power shortfalls later. The trade-off was, thus, not even salmon-for-power; it was salmon-for-margin-of-comfort: a few hundred thousand salmon smolts, for a more comfortable margin of safety on a graph, an electrical grid, and a bottom line.

The following October, when the numbers were added up, the survival rates for migrating juveniles of steelhead and spring and summer chinook were close to the lowest ever recorded. A rueful biologist with the U.S. Fish and Wildlife Service concluded: "It makes me think that this region doesn't have the will to do what it needs to recover these fish."

Good news, bad news. Recovery of salmon is not out of our reach. We could do it if we chose to. For the moment, though, we're just not that interested. The salmon are still there, in the river. They're not lost yet. If there is a lost paradise, it is the one in our minds: that place where we care, evergreen, for what matters. That's a garden each of us is responsible for tending.

If we would slaughter salmon, present and future, for a few megawatts of power in an "emergency" that amounted to a mild inconvenience, how could we hope to permanently decommission those four dams on the lower Snake River?

The question of breaching Snake River dams typifies the muddle of uncertain science, competing plans, and conniving interests that clogs the politics of salmon recovery. Not surprisingly: the Columbia River drains a region the size of France, and decisions about salmon can affect almost any resource, town, or industry to be found there. There has been no end of studies, from no end of overlapping, competing institutions of governance and use. To bring some order to the chaos and to discover what, exactly, the available science could say about salmon recovery, NMFS initiated a powerful analytic process called PATH (Plan for Analyzing and Testing Hypotheses). It is by far the most authoritative and comprehensive look at the problem to date. But when PATH came up with the wrong result— an unambiguous endorsement of breaching the four lower Snake dams—NMFS tried its best to ignore it. Typical.

But PATH brings order of a markedly postmodern kind to the brownian jostle of salmon plans and interests. PATH recognizes *uncertainty*, not control, as the essential condition of river managers and salmon studiers. Because of "major uncertainties in past and current conditions ... a single management action can have a number of possible outcomes." With becoming humility, the PATH approach tries to reduce uncertainties, not arrive at any Godlike (or Engineerlike) absolutes.

PATH leaves unexplored the theoretical question of whether this uncertainty, this limit to our understanding, is a practical one (we simply aren't clever enough, yet) or a real and intrinsic condition. Is uncertainty inherent in living systems? Do we see here a Heisenbergian threshold: that complex systems are *in principle* not deterministically predictable? That complexity is indeed its own kind of infinity?

Reader, it is the bias of my argument, borrowed from Gregory Bateson, that the behavior of living things is *behavior*, not mere reaction. That living beings and living systems are thus, in principle, unpredictable. That they—we—can be understood but never completely understood; controlled but never completely controlled. That a living system is a virtual infinity, producing responses from its own inward grammar, responses which are surprising, novel, creative. And not predictable. That's a huge guess, a hypothesis about the nature of Mystery. I wouldn't dare to say it is more.

So when the PATH analysis leads us to a place not of control, but of coping with uncertainty, this makes sense to me. *This is how the real world works,* I think; the one I've been living in. Once again we are inhabitants, not masters; we are co-users of rivers, along with other beings.Such a way of thinking is a huge step forward from bad-old-modernist days, with bureaus like shiny skyscrapers towering blindly over the landscapes they purport to manage.We are over the International Style, aren't we. We have set our sights lower, closer, warmer, into the mud and earth of actual places.Humble and uncertain, PATH finds a nice smart way to figure out how we might help keep the river alive. It considers seven scenarios and tests their likely outcomes in various aspects of salmon health and survival. The results are probabilistic, like trying to say where an electron will be. Yet they point, with surprising decisiveness, to breaching the four lower Snake dams as by far the best option.

Meanwhile, a business lobby from Lewiston has declared victory. The Executive Director of the Columbia River Alliance said, "We are comfortable dam breaching will not occur." Comfort seems to be what matters most in such cases: maintaining whatever we've become used to, whatever is normal. It seems that no amount of failure can shock the Fisheries Service into real, decisive action. John Volkman points out that Grand Coulee, Hells Canyon, and Dworshak (with a few other minor dams) have blocked 18,700 miles of the Columbia salmon river system, or "38 percent of the historic 49,300 mile range." Pulling out a few Snake dams would be a good start to getting healthy salmon back into the rivers below those behemoths. That would leave a good project for our children to consider: whether those impassable dams were worth the destruction they cause. Worth thinking about.

But first, an easier task. Restoring the Snake River to river status. And enjoying a born-again abundance of chinook and steelhead: a different vision of "normal."

As I approached this chapter, I had planned to feel bad. Terrible, actually—that's the right emotion for extinctions and disasters, no? Some runs of salmon are dead; some more will be, before we come to our senses. We will have to grieve. Yet the secondhand emotion of Paradise Lost does not really suffice: for we must also find heart for the future that comes to us.

I notice that we don't have dire wolves to fear, or mammoths to hunt any more. Those are losses, too. But somehow our lives are still rich, are in fact complete. How could that be?

The mathematics of loss and gain are not simple. Living beings have the talent of making a life—a whole life—in the darndest places and ways. And when something is subtracted, there's a mysterious power that generates something else to fill its place. A kind of ecosystem logic, filling niches. That's the mystery. What death scoops out, life fills in. Did you know there were saber-toothed *salmon*, too?

Here's an even weirder reality: not everything that is "extinct" stays that way. Most do, of course, so let's not get stupid about this. But truly, there's a dandy little list of critters that were thought to be gone forever which—surprise!—turned up again. Butterflies. River otters. Various birds. A white-winged guan, three feet long with its tail, unseen for a century. A peccary-pig thought vanished since the Pleistocene!

Whatever could this mean? It means, when we Stop This Nonsense, we will be surprised at what comes back. Bluefish in the Chesapeake. Walleye in Lake Erie. Wild trout in other Great Lakes. Maybe-gonna-make-it salmon in the Thames, in the Loire, returning after hundred-year absences bewildered, poisoned, determined. And salmon all over our streams too, right up the Columbia, the Willamette, past the old hatchery on the Clackamas, maybe someday past the picturesque ruins of dams along the Snake.

It turns out nature will not be cornered by our myths of creation *or* destruction. What we have done on the Columbia is both worse and better than we had planned. Planning assumes control—which we don't have over nature and can never have, in any comprehensive sense.

Our idiotic experimentation upon the biosphere—poisoning the rivers, tearing down the forests, ransacking the ecosystems—leads in strange loops where we never thought we'd go. Mortal consequences show up silent and ineluctable, and death is forever. Yet death keeps turning into life. And things that were gone forever … keep showing up again. Things are always both worse, and better, than we think. More complex than we *can* think. A cloud of not-knowing surrounds us, like celestial light. It is wildness.

My optimism about nature rides quite a bit on this ignorance.

There is another house by the river, invisible from the glazed highrises of the bureaucrats. Its windows and doors are in each leaf and blade of grass, from which the Unintended, that perpetual bride/ widow, sits watching. She is the one who whispers: *You shall be comforted. Your lives shall be full. Mourn and celebrate. And get ready to be surprised.*

Palimpsest:
Every Rich System Is a Nature

I am in the midst of a long listen with Aaron Jay Kernis, his symphonic *Colored Field*. It is jagged noise, the sort of modernist cacophony folks love to hate. But just when I think I cannot bear any more, it opens up: clearing in the terrible wood, shaft of golden sunlight, pure descending woodwind. Then the moment fades and that noise, that noise begins to reassert; gently—but implacably. It is my somewhat tough pleasure to know a little Kernis and to try to relate it to what else is going on in current composing. Arvo Pärt. Henryk Gorecki. John Taverner. I think there's a pattern there, a music of deep humanity working itself out over underlayers that go back and back—Glass, Sternberg, Mahler, Brahms, Bach, Palestrina ... monks chanting a thousand years away. All of it is somehow present in this new music, this deep patterning, this wildness contained. Every rich system is a nature.

Getting lost there, and found there, is a pleasure-ordeal my mind demands. So does yours: and if not in music then in some other made land of struggle and delight. We make simulacra of nature in our fictions, each a language, a grammar of deep layered complexity, generating meaning from its private and inexhaustable world of identity and self-reference.We find ourselves there, don't we? This is *our own* forest. Almost any complexity can make one: a pennant race, a chess game, scholarly arcana, poetry, science, movies. Each of us chooses a particular tangled bank to clamber up, a wild place of rich interconnectedness to enter, again and again.

Every rich system is a nature. Though not *the* nature.

It is more than metaphor to say: nature is a language. DNA codes have forced us to see that information, in organized patterns, generates more patterns—bodies, cultures, ecosystems, biospheres. And this information is orderly, semantic, reflexive: a language. Every language is a generative complexity that allows new meanings at every expression, every breath. When we speak, we don't just repeat, parrot-style; we make. So does nature. And so do the arts and games we love.

It is true that our minds are designed (by a million years of experience) to know nature, real outdoor-nature, to learn its names and ways in intimate detail. *But this very capacity urges us also to create and explore other natures.* We crave and need these inward complexities, these wildernesses, these labyrinths and cliffs of fall. That is why I believe in cities and in the arts as places of wild richness we make for ourselves. We must learn to see all the skills and stories we lose ourselves into, as natures where wildness plays.

This inscaped liveliness must become an environmentalist imperative too: so that good human places will make for good more-than-human places. This Portland where I live must be a marvel, a place of wonders, a life-scape of refraction and invention: the well-contained city, humane and alive, with Mount Hood always visible, and beside us the Columbia flowing with mysterious life. And the same must be true where you live, inward and outward places alive and intricate.

Such a mind, such a world. Every rich system is a nature. (Though not, of course, *the* nature.)

Section III: Walking After, Walking With: Thoreau, Muir, Bartram

In nineteenth-century America, mythic Eden came to be relocated into a literal place, or series of places—paradises lost and lost again as the frontier moved inexorably west, a vestigal spiritual ideal drowned at last in the Pacific. At that drowning point, the end of the nineteenth century, we can see it in Muir and his literalized mountain Edens; and its ghosts haunt us in our own struggles over the Nature Problem.

Muir haunts me the most. Anxiety of influence, maybe—my Sierras will always be his, first and foremost. How many years have I made a point of avoiding the "Muir Trail," that rut of earnest mountain tourism? And when I picked up Muir's books, I found them unreadable—Victorian, purple, glorious-this and glorious-that. There was something evangelical in tone, well-intentioned but just a bit desperate ... Just what I never sensed in Thoreau. Muir gobbled mountain ranges with manic insatiability, east and west, Alaska and back again, as if all his protestations of fulfillment hid some other hunger he could never assuage. Meanwhile Thoreau sat quietly, walked a little, and seemed to find more in his tiny scrap of woods than Muir found in all his noisy, preachy globe-trotting. Some of Muir's writing is great stuff. A lot is not. His life, though, is a marvel worth knowing about. A flawed, hopeless, glorious marvel; as famous as Bartram's is obscure.

All those who walked here before us have left us their ways, their tracks and thoughts and genes. Thoreau, Muir, and Bartram are some of the greatest of those fore-walkers. I'm glad to be following them, in these last four chapters, to see how they helped us get here, how their way of walking became ours.

Thoreau in the Literalizing Century:
Scientism, Fundamentalism, and the Golden West

If it was my myth, I'd give her an onion. And I'd have God say, Take a BIG bite. Eve plucks one from the ol' onion tree. She bites, she cries, she peels, she laughs. God looks on approvingly. Adam smells her breath, wonders what's up, kisses her anyway. And the rest is history.

This would improve things in several ways. First, onions don't grow on trees, so there'd be no question of literalizing the story. Second, there's the peeling. That's a good model for how the world works, or rather how we work the world. And, lastly, onions do have their own paradoxical sweetness. Along with the tears.

My excuse for starting this chapter with a silly story is to counteract the prevailing mood which has attached to Eden and to our ideas of nature: a humorless literalism. The shorthand term for this attitude is *fundamentalism*, the stance of aggressive moralism in a world of black-and-white "fact" and crystal-clear good and evil.

I'd like to sketch the literalizing spirit that created this mental environment. Not a full-blown study—that would need a shelf of books. But a look at the trend of things, focussing on the nineteenth century. For by mid-nineteenth century, I find in popular press and serious writers alike a well-engrained language of lost Eden that has already literalized the myth and applied it to the fast-disappearing "untouched" continent, combining literalism and romantic longing in a way that makes no sense but has great emotional power.

The principal elements are these: a simplistic notion of "truth" limited to empirical "fact" and ordinary time—a kind of bareback scientism. A resulting separation of fact from value. And a consequent retreat into disconnected emotionalism. Into this picture we must insert the essential parenthesis of the Romantic Movement, that glorious but short-lived attempt to preserve a sense of metaphor. By mid-century it was steamrollered, but its memory lingers in writers we still treasure. For in the midst of this literalizing and fundamentalizing century, Thoreau laid out a path that was solidly physical, yet deeply metaphorical. And quite funny, too.

There is a long pedigree for fundamentalism in America. We use the term "Puritan" for early colonists, but today we would call them fundamentalists. They strictly followed a literal Bible, believed truth to be simple and in their possession, and made war on enemies internal and external. It is worth remembering that it was, after all, a (somewhat reluctant) fundamentalist who wrote *Paradise Lost*— John Milton, a propagandist and official for Oliver Cromwell's Bible-wielding dictatorship. And it was Milton's fellow-believers, fundamentalist pilgrims, who sailed away from the religious strife to settle in New England. Their way of looking at the world—the fundamentalist way—has everything to do with the Nature Problem I've been exploring.

I use "fundamentalism" this way as a conscious anachronism. Technically, the word Fundamentalism (capitalized) appeared in 1920 to describe an American evangelical movement against so-called "modernism." Thus it is best known for what it opposed (and continues to oppose): evolution, modern learning, social change, gay people, and so forth. But fundamentalism is so clearly a manifestation of an essential part of Protestantism that the word can be applied more generally. It is characterized *temperamentally* by what religious-historian George Marsden calls "militancy," and *intellectually* by black-and-white thinking derived from a simplistic and literalist sense of truth. As such, it has been a potent part of Protestantism virtually from the beginning; it played a central role in the founding of America, and it became an increasingly visable and vocal force during the nineteenth century.

Perhaps fundamentalism is really one side of human nature: the desire to have truth simple, to own it absolutely, and to bash anyone who doesn't agree. Fundamentalism is a fortress-making reflex to define who "we" are and who "the enemy" is. God is confined within a rigidly literal and authoritarian framework. "His" behavior, demands, and responses are mapped out, predictable. Language about this God is always piously groveling; but the secret effect is, paradoxically, that the believer gains *control* over the divine, and with it, control over that frightening, chaotic world. While religion deepens one's appreciation of Mystery, superstition seeks to manipulate it. When fundamentalists claim to know God's mind, confidently defining the saved and the damned and the exact dates of God's next move, they are asserting control.

At root these are emotional reactions, not intellectual ones. So when we liberals try to explain that no authority can save us the labor of judging and choosing among incomplete versions of truth, we are largely missing the point. People who are afraid, and who demand psychological certainty, will not hear us over their fortress walls.

Today, on the far right of the nature issue we find the Wise Use movement, many of whose followers are Fundamentalists who take the Genesis edict of "dominion over the earth" as a God-given right to private property and profit. More surprisingly, on the left edge of the environmentalist movement we see their mirror-opposites: radical activists who declare "No compromise," burn Forest Service buildings, and attack any who disagree (even environmentalists) as traitors. I have been calling them eco-fundamentalists. Both groups are captives of a literalist idea of Eden. Traditional fundamentalists see Eden as long-gone; this is a fallen and temporary world, which we may as well use to our own advantage (former Secretary of the Interior James Watt enacted this point of view fully). Meanwhile the eco-fundamentalists have merely shifted their literal Eden to nature, bringing a similarly warlike, polarized, and simplistic approach.

A good, if broad, way to conceptualize the cultural trend of the nineteenth century is to see the growing dominance of a scientific/historical way of thinking that crowded out the legitimacy of other forms of truth in Anglo/American thought. Incipient fundamentalism was just one of its effects.

Following Newton, the world seemed increasingly to be proven a strictly material place where particles of matter obeyed natural, physical laws. Fact was observable, empirical, clear. Time was a cogged wheel in which law-bound things happened, ratcheting ever forward. And human mind was, because nonmaterial, outside the system. From the 1780s onwards, as M. H. Abrams sums up, "a number of the keenest and most sensitive minds found radically inadequate, both to immediate human experience and to basic human needs, the intellectual ambiance of the Enlightenment, with … its mechanistic worldview, its analytic divisiveness … and its conception of the human mind as totally diverse and alien from its nonmental environment." The emotional and spiritual aridity of this sort of world is legendary.

Victorian writers recorded their struggles with this flattened world of empirical science and history, flattened still further in the popular mind into a kind of common-sense know-nothingism. Thomas Carlyle's father (very like John Muir's, as we will see in the next chapter) had opposed any kind of poetry or fiction as "not only idle, but *false* and criminal." John Stuart Mill complained, in his 1831 book *The Spirit of the Age*, of the widespread attitude that the world was fully understandable on its surface, and that deeper study was not just unnecessary but actually suspect: "Every dabbler … thinks his opinion as good as another's. … It is rather the person who *has* studied the subject systematically that is regarded as disqualified. He is a *theorist* … a bye-word of derision. People pride themselves upon taking a 'plain, matter-of-fact' view."

Thus, on both the highbrow and lowbrow fronts, the nineteenth century developed a remarkably diminished sense of the world, a literalizing mentality that held all interpreting suspect.

Since real people cannot live with much satisfaction in such a world, various escapes and exceptions were invented. One escape took the form of a highly emotionalized and individualized religion. America and England saw almost a hundred years of "Great Awakenings" and revivals starting in the mid-1700s, led by charismatic preachers such as Jonathan Edwards, George Whitefield, and Charles Finney, who encouraged a vividly emotional individual response that was wildly popular. Thousands attended weeklong rural American revival meetings in the 1830s, with converts rolling on the ground, barking, and "treeing the devil."

But what connection could be made from this private enthusiasm to the workings of the great world, ticking along like a great well-made clock? Very little. Though many professed belief in miraculous divine interventions, the plain fact was that the ordinary world had come to be understood as a mechanically physical reality. The fervent protestations of faith belied a deeper truth: the world of feeling had been divorced from the world of fact.

For in the course of the nineteenth century, the lowchurch/ evangelical movement—heirs of the Puritan revolution—ironically *adopted* the essence of the scientific/historical view of what constituted public truth: they increasingly held that the truth of the Bible was historical or physical fact. Truth was simple, direct, flat, uninterpreted. Though the fundamentalists' inward world was awash with intense feeling, their outward world was flattened to the dictates of the literal century. (No one apparently noticed what a capitulation this was!) Marsden calls this developing fundamentalism of the mid-nineteenth century a kind of "common-sense realism" based on empiricism, a "view of scripture … modeled after the Newtonian view of the physical universe," an attitude "that had been strong in America since the days of the Puritans."

The Bible's validity came to inhere in its actual words (later called the doctrine of "verbal plenary inspiration"). The original words of the Bible were God's own perfect and virtually magic words, put more or less bodily into the minds of robotic "prophets," and possessing (according to an 1887 advocate) "photographically exact" inerrancy. No need for an interpreting Spirit; no need for doubt. No need to "read" in any complex sense. The scripture, with all its poetry and myth, its wild tales, dark sayings, and paradoxes, was reduced to prairie flatness—"eschewing the mysterious" as Marsden says, for "plain common sense." As far back as the 1830s, if Charles Lyell's geology proved a very old planet, fundamentalists must insist on a young one by counting generations in the Old Testament. If Darwin's biology suggested, two decades later, that living beings adapted over millions of years, they must insist that Genesis said otherwise, and take the seven-day account as a kind of cosmic lab report.

As we have seen, orthodox Christians have always more or less believed in the literal historicity of their scriptures, and the historical reality of the deliverance from Egypt and the Crucifixion have always made for a uniquely historicized form of religion. Yet before the nineteenth century, the literal was seldom allowed to dominate scripture; other kinds of reading, other kinds of insight, were emphasized. As we have seen for instance in Dante's letter to the Can Grande, historical events were understood as merely the basis for an ascending complex of ritual, spiritual, and metaphorical meanings. But under pressure from the scientific century, fundamentalists lost hold of their myths *as myths*, and came to live more and more in a secularized world devoid of the entire mythic dimension. In this process, they silently collaborated with the drift of their era and helped to create the Problem of Nature we have been struggling with. Whether Eden is found between the Tigris and Euphrates (in 4004 BC according to Bishop Ussher) or is relocated into the forests of the West, a year or a decade ago, it is a literalized Eden all the same. And it is equally, firmly, and irrevocably lost, either way.

Reader, I should admit my own experiences here: I was raised in the midst of Fundamentalism, though in a gentler suburban form. I recognize it. I studied it in my high school and college years, often on my own time and initiative, with a strange intramural fervor. I know the literalism, the frenzy to make the world somehow doctrinally safe. Bishop Ussher showed up in our family Bible, and flat-minded literalism was taught in our church. When I now read of that 1887 evangelical text with its weird theory of photographic inspiration, I feel I know it from the inside since I have read so many other books, ancient and modern, of that exact ilk. The twentieth-century books which I read devotionally bore names like *Protestant Christian Evidences* and *Evidence Which Demands a Verdict*, and they too picked some tidbit of scripture to which current knowledge in science or history could someway be shown to correlate; then (by what etymologists would call "back-formation") held that the divine inerrancy of scripture had been corroborated. Black holes! Atomic bombs! The European Economic Community!

A puzzling kind of ahistorical historicism: somehow, fundamentalists must convince themselves every word is literally true and magically literal.

What else can they do? On the assumption that the world is defined by science—that is, literal, physical fact in linear time—their holy book too must be scientific.

Both in society as a whole, and within the evangelical Protestant world, the nineteenth was a literalizing century, or in the favorite word of Victorian scholars, a *secularizing* century. Wherever spirit, faith, myth, or ritual had been, they tended to be pushed aside and replaced by something hard and factual. And that flat, "factual" sense of what is "real" held sway right through the next century, despite inroads from many directions (including science). The popular sense of reality is, I think, still shaped by a sense of physical fact and linear time.

Gregory Bateson insists that this process on both sides (religious fundamentalist and secular materialist) has resulted in the de-sacralizing of life. In removing metaphor and symbol, the literalizing trend has conspired against a vivid sense of the spiritual mystery of life. This was, and is, a particularly *Protestant* slant: "The Protestant interpretation of the words 'This is my Body—this is my Blood' substitutes something like 'This stands for my Body—This stands for my Blood.' This way of interpretation banished from the Church that part of the mind that makes metaphor, poetry, and religion—the part of the mind that most belonged in Church—but *you cannot keep it out.*"

Bateson makes the case that materialism and supernaturalism are obvious twins, agreeing that the world comprises (as Descartes proposed) two distinct substances, the physical and the spiritual. The *relation* of the two substances is kept unexplorable. Thought process has thus been trapped outside just those questions which are most interesting (How does a spiritual being behave in a body, in a world? How does a material world produce living things with mind; with "spirit"?) In place of these difficult questions, simpler "factual" questions are proposed and dully answered. The whole duty of man is to love God. The world is composed of material particles in motion.

While the Puritan fundamentalists darkened their brows at the unredeemed land of America, another quite opposite view of the New World developed from the comfortable vantage of Europe—one that amply illustrates Bateson's point that "*you cannot keep it out*": it, that human sense of metaphor and truth. This new view is most famously associated with Jean-Jacques Rousseau, a "synthesizer with perfect timing" in Shepard Krech's phrase, who had picked up and popularized the already widespread eighteenth-century opinion that the New World had showed the face of unfallen Humanity to a debauched and overcivilized Europe.

By the time Rousseau wrote, the New World had for years been providing a useful counterpoise to the Old. Golden-age and paradisal comparisons were inevitable and common in the sixteenth and seventeenth centuries. Rousseau's name has become the shorthand for this alternative, more optimistic view of nature and human nature—the paradise of nature and the Noble Savage. Perhaps this lasting attribution comes from the way his work ties paradisal nature to two other notions: a vaguely parallel innocence of childhood, and a commitment to the importance of feelings. The emotional appeal of this loose bundle of associations was probably intensified at the time by the existence of its opposite, the cold, clockwork world and cynical urban rationalism of the official Enlightenment.

Against this establishment, poor Jean-Jacques brings only the soft artillery of his feelings. Yet ... he wins. Throughout Rousseau's *Confessions*, for instance, he sounds the refrain: These were my feelings, for better or worse; if I tell them all, the reader will approve of me in the end. The felt experience would justify all. And what feeling is paramount for Rousseau? Nostalgia. "The feeling that most constantly recurs in the *Confessions* is one of loss, a regret for some other way of life that would have brought Rousseau happiness," as one scholar puts it. Rousseau's genius surely lay in combining these combustibles: nostalgia, emotionalism, and the lost paradises of childhood and the primitive. By the end of his century, Rousseauvian emotionalism had swept the popular culture, along with a readiness to believe all sorts of optimistic things about distant non-European peoples.

America, of course, was particularly cast as an Edenic paradise, not yet sullied by civilization, its peoples romanticized in the familiar

Noble Savage mold. The dire misgivings which Puritans had attached to the "wilderness" had mysteriously vanished, or more accurately, switched poles. Now it was civilization that was the seat of corruption and vice; nature became the fast-vanishing repository of virtue. Clearly, this was the myth of Eden literalized onto a mappable (though still faraway) place. Yet as the map filled in with real people and prosaic reality, the Rousseauvian illusion was harder and harder to sustain. As the literal West was frontiered, documented, and (re)settled, the imaginary West had to find somewhere else to go. Where it went was into nostalgia for recently lost "pristine" nature.

Thus, by the 1830s and 1840s, when Thoreau was warming up for, and carrying through, his Walden adventure, a thorough revolution in valuing American nature had occurred. Muir's biographer Frederick Turner comments that as early as the 1830s "the note of elegy for a vanishing or already lost New World was in the air." The popular literature of the mid-nineteenth century is full of it: sublime nature, noble savages, vanishing Eden, better enjoy it while it lasts. An art critic, for instance, tolls the litany in 1847: "The axe of civilization is busy with our old forests, and artisan ingenuity is fast sweeping away the relics of our national infancy. What were once the wild and picturesque haunts of the Red Man, and where the wild deer roamed in freedom, are becoming the abodes of commerce and the seats of manufactures ... even the primordial hills, once bristling with shaggy pine and hemlock ... are being shorn of their locks." The moral for painters is clear: "it behooves our artists to rescue from its grasp the little that is left, before it is forever too late." It's a moral one can hardly miss in the huge oil canvases of the Hudson River School or of Luminists like Albert Bierstadt. What nature looks like in these cases is what it means: this is Eden; God has just spoken. But it cannot last, it is passing already.

But this new attitude toward nature is not limited to artsy types back east. Even a Methodist minister, writing of his travels west, reports in full Romantic gush about the "sublime" godliness of nature—nature, the "visible footsteps of God!" As familiar and unexceptional as this attitude looks to us today, it is a remarkable statement indeed for a minster of the religion that had not so long before declared the world of nature fallen and sinful, a snare for the soul, a distraction from eternity. An old tradition of Christian *contemptus mundi* is here turned on its head. The Christian's longing for a better place—paradise-hereafter—is redirected to the terrestrial Eden.

When I read around in issues of that same year's *Knickerbocker Magazine* (1838), I find the Paradise-Lost note often. "Nature has been penetrated in her wildest recesses," laments an urban writer, "and made to yield her hidden stores." The editor could run a sentimental poem called "The Chieftan's Tear" with full confidence that his audience would respond to its Vanishing Indian cliché (a corollary of Lost Paradise). James Fenimore Cooper had been mining this vein since his 1826 *Last of the Mohicans*. Once nature is reenvisioned as Eden, the element of loss is never far off.

It is worth noting that, despite reversing the way wild nature is valued, the Puritan and the popular nature-romanticizer were operating according to the same myth: they had merely shifted places within it. For the Puritans, paradise was lost a long time ago; their journey through the wilderness of sin is a journey through historical time, moving ever forward toward redemption, toward God's City, the End toward which all this human business is predestined. The popular nature-Romantics simply pulled forward the storyline, declaring that Eden was closer to hand than their fathers had known, and that the loss was a fresh one. In either case, the same mythic structure applies: the journey from Eden, through loss into the present, diminished, and more sinful time of history.

Let's be very clear: this emotion of nostalgia is attached to an *imagined* landscape—imagined even as it is being seen firsthand, because very largely a construct of European preconceptions and a ready-made myth—that is blind to the humans already in the landscape, unaware of the works of human hands that had so often shaped it, wedded to glimmering visions derived from books and painters.

Literalism makes the Eden a physical place. Romanticism invests it with longing.

The Romantic movement, that unforgettable moment at the beginning of the nineteenth century, conceived more or less explicitly as an antidote to Enlightenment materialism, placed the imagination at the center of things. The literature of this movement is much beloved: Emerson and Thoreau, Wordsworth, Coleridge, and Keats—they are all read and imitated to this day. But what has happened to their boldly spiritualized world, their feeling thoughts and well-thought feelings?

While the Western world as a whole marched relentlessly forward on an literalist/empiricist course, the Romantics diverged onto an "idealist"—Platonist—pathway, based on the Platonic tenet that there was a defining essence, a *form*, behind all the appearances. But the location of that idealized world, for many of these writers, was in effect moved from the Platonic *beyond* to the Neoplatonic *within*—it was the power of the imagination that was able to create or perceive the higher order. But which was it: "create" or "perceive"? The objective reality of the perceived order is a question worked through over and over in the great roster of Romantic poetry and Transcendental nature writings, with varying outcomes. In effect, the Romantic movement put legs under the vague naturism of Rousseau, giving it a foundation in the imagination and constructing a consistent worldview around it—though one which hardly outlived its makers except in fragments.

Wordsworth's climactic image from *The Prelude* memorably conveys the scope of this imaginative power of perception/creation. The poet has climbed Mt. Snowdon in northern England to see the sunrise, but catches instead a mighty vision of the moon hanging full and bright over "a silent sea of hoary mist," while all around "A hundred hills their dusky backs upheaved/All over this still ocean." He reads it as a symbol of the human mind at its fullest creative unity: "the emblem of ... a mind sustained/By recognitions of transcendent power."

Reader, it's one of those moments. How much of our public debate over "nature," and our private commitment to it, are derived from a few of these privileged times when *something* speaks from beyond our own limitations? Here are the core questions of the nature debate: How much credence shall we allow such moments? Or how far should we see them as "constructed" by whatever has been loaded into us by language, culture, literature? Can we actually hear something—*something*—from beyond ourselves that can surprise, challenge, shake, and redeem? Wordsworth, of course, is fully committed to the redemptive moment, when

> *… with an eye made quiet by the power*
> *Of harmony, and the deep power of joy,*
> *We see into the life of things.*

In the last book of *The Prelude*, Wordsworth names the power the "feeling intellect." This is a *unifying* power: feeling and intellect working in concert to read reality. I am convinced these are moments of creative self-integration, when left and right brains, conscious and unconscious, body and mind—define them however—when all of our scattered powers entrain themselves effortlessly into a rare unanimous functioning. What they tell us, what they create, has the force of revelation. And if we never quite arrive at certainty, neither can we deny the experience. That is the space, I think, occupied by this book in your hands, Reader: between the dismissive shallowness that ignores the truth-bearing inspiration of nature and the credulous certainty that believes such revelations are simple and universal.

The Romantic project of Wordsworth and his school was to oppose any kind of literalism—that of fundamentalists, that of scientists, or that of lost-Eden nostalgists—by locating the renewing power not "out there" in the world but within, in the creative imagination. This approach was forcefully brought to America in 1836 in Emerson's seminal essay "Nature," which declared: "The problem of restoring to the world original and eternal beauty is solved by the redemption of the soul. The ruin or the blank that we see when we look at nature, is in our own eye. … [so that] things … appear not transparent but opaque. The reason why the world lacks unity, and lies broken and in heaps, is because man is disunited with himself. He cannot be a naturalist until he satisfies all the demands of the spirit." Transparent: we must see past the surfaces, allowing the invisible order of the world to emerge. So that Eden need not be lost; it is to be rediscovered continuously.

But Romanticism's high aspirations to self-created Meaning also placed a high demand on its practitioners. They had to maintain a lofty faith which little in their daily world of advancing technology and material knowledge supported. The Romantic manner of escaping the scientific (and fundamentalist) flattening of the world could not hold up for more than one or two gleaming generations. Within a few years, the ideal of the Romantic Nature Poet had become a cultural cliché (as it is to this day): an ineffectual aesthete like Pickwick's friend Snodgrass, gazing through his monocle at a nature to which he has little real connection. The Romantic form of answer—to look beneath the appearances—has not held the center. The center is elsewhere: it is materialist.

Even Thoreau sometimes sounds an Edenic and nostalgic note. I say "even" because, in the main, he knows better; as a translator of high Romanticism into its American form of Transcendentalism, he knows that eternity is always present. He's the one who made paradise of a pond in a scrap of woods, within earshot of a rail line and walking distance from dinner in town. None of that made Walden Pond any the shallower or created any want of wildness.

But in the celebrated essay "Walking," for instance—a fine tight summation of his themes, written in 1862, just two years before his death—Thoreau sounds very paradise-losty indeed, for a while. The essay is a kind of theme and variations on the idea of the West: walking west, thinking west, longing west. "The future lies that way to me, and the earth seems more unexhausted and richer on that side. ... westward I go free." "I must walk toward Oregon, and not toward Europe. And that way the nation is moving, and I may say that mankind progress from east to west. ... we go westward as into the future."

From my perspective, writing from the literal Oregon on a rainy day, it would be easy to take all this as a kind of romantic folly, Tom-Sawyering into the idealized and as-yet-unfallen West, leaving the Fallen behind at each step. And the occasional turn of Adamic language seems to reinforce this impression: "As a true patriot, I should be ashamed to think that Adam in paradise was more favorably situated on the whole than the backwoodsman in this country."

But to read this literally would be to ignore Thoreau's own instructions, and to overlook the rib-nudging that so characterizes this deep, and deeply funny, writer. Here as virtually everywhere in Thoreau's writing, an elaborately symbolic, punning, and jokey language continually reminds the reader that the phenomenal world is explored primarily as a means of exploring the spiritual world. To do less, Thoreau says explicitly in *Walden*, is a waste of time, a concentrating on the gross instead of the "ethereal." Because of course it's not the literal West, but what the West means, that interests him.

Thoreau introduces his fantasia on the West this way: "We would fain take that walk, never yet taken by us through this actual world, which is perfectly symbolical of the path which we love to travel in the interior and ideal world." In the next paragraph he sets out on his playful westward exploration. And take a look at the way he further develops this mock-serious thesis: "The Atlantic is a Lethean stream, in our passage over which we had a chance to forget the Old World and its institutions. If we do not succeed this time, there is perhaps one more chance for the race left before it arrives on the banks of the Styx; and that is in the Lethe of the Pacific, which is three times as wide." We must not miss the twinkle in these lines: it's a kind of joshing tall-talk, however serious the underlying point.

The next paragraph amplifies this tonality of serious jest. It's a raconteur's paragraph, building through ever sillier examples: first, we westward-longing humans are compared to "birds and quadrupeds," then to squirrels crossing rivers on chips of wood with tails "raised for a sail," and then (worse yet) to cattle running amok with "a worm in their tails." Finally this joking Thoreau notes that when flocks of wild geese fly overhead—surely suggesting the wild-goose-chase of literally "lightin' out for the territories"—their cackling "to some extent unsettles the value of real estate here, and, if I were a broker, I should probably take that disturbance into account."

Where next? A two-line quote from the *Canterbury Tales* about folks going on pilgrimages, to round out a bravura performance of what Jonathan Swift called the ragoust style: salmagundi: everything thrown in. To miss the playfully bathetic tone here—to literalize—is to miss it all. For "The West of which I speak is but another name for the Wild; and what I have been preparing to say is, that in Wildness is the preservation of the World."

There is the context, Reader, for that most famous and oft-repeated quote. Thoreau's "Wildness" is the *metaphoric* Wild, synonymous with Spirit and with a kind of Platonic Nature-beyond-nature: not exhausted, not geographically limited to the West, certainly not long-lost.

For *life* itself "consists with wildness," he says, if we aren't too blind and sleepy to notice it. The time is always NOW—not some long-ago heroic age. And the place is always HERE—not far away in the supposedly Edenic West. For anyone who awakens to the coursing spirit of life will find himself or herself in a wilderness: "One who ... made infinite demands on life, would always find himself in a new country or wilderness, climbing over the prostrate stems of primitive forest-trees."

He had declared in *Walden* that the living earth was "not a fossil" but "still in her swaddling clothes,"—unfallen not just in some untouched West, but every spring, every morning, every moment. This is the metaphoric Eden of the soul, and Thoreau invites his readers to return there as often as they can.

As much loved, quoted, and imitated as Thoreau is, however, we must question whether he succeeded any better than the rest of the Romantics in his essential program: to awaken a spiritual and inward eye, against the tide of the literalizing century. We, his followers, do not follow him in this. We are likely to admire science; we turn ecology into Deep Ecology; we fetishize climax forests and ecosystems, thinking the "nature" of science is the real one. I think Thoreau's followers, for the most part, do not hear his core message, for it is in a language of philosophical idealism we simply do not speak: "Man cannot afford to be a naturalist, to look at Nature directly, but only with the side of his eye. He must look through and beyond her. To look at her is fatal. ... It turns the man of science to stone."

That stonified world of science-fact is what most of Thoreau's descendants have lived in, despite our admiration for his work. We do not follow his critique of science; we are not alarmed by taxonomies and data collecting; we do not think they erode our ability to really get at nature. On the contrary. It is far clearer now than in Thoreau's century that science need not be taken as the literalists take it, but may be instead another means of apprehending the great Mystery.

The legacy of Thoreau, Wordsworth, and the other writers of the Romantic project is thus a complicated one. To read their work is to be transported into a world in which Spirit speaks in and through Nature. Yet most of us do not credit the system of thinking that makes sense of this world—the commitment to idealism. What is left, then, can be a trap for the unwary: the temptation to indulge in a Romanticism of nature, enjoying emotions that ape those of the great poets and essayists, but which lack their basis in an inward discipline of the mind.

Romantic visions of nature may become ungrounded sentimentalities that evade the gritty world of material fact in which we live for the other twenty-three hours of the day. For better or worse, our world is the substantially flattened one of historical time and material cause-and-effect. To restore it to its depth will take an act of the imagination, though perhaps not quite the one Thoreau created. Ours will have to be more knowing: more aware of the constructed nature of such insighting; yet also aware of a sneaking universality to it, as a way of allowing ourselves to go past the limits of the literal. Perhaps it is not *what* nature speaks, but *that* nature speaks, and will speak; perhaps that is our wildness dependable, inexhaustible, unpredictable, and redemptive.

Nature speaks, in other words, in other words. We may not have a language adequate to contain what it says. But that should not prevent us from listening.

(If we don't, then the joke is surely on us.)

Palimpsest:
Virgin

What strikes me most is the thinness of virginity—its fragility, its artificiality, its fear of the going-on-ness of life. Cultures both West and East have made it a precious commodity to be hoarded, defended, hung onto at all costs. It's a concept perfectly stuck in a one-way time process, where acts are irreversible, weighted with sin and the downward spiral of accumulating mistakes. As if purity, freshness, or goodness are imaginable only in the state *before* action. That was the state I lived in for a goodly portion of my twenties, afraid of sex, afraid of life, afraid of the moral impurity that actual emotional/physical love would entangle me in.

But the right meaning of "virgin" ought to be "gettin' ready" or "almost there" or "oh boy, let's go!"

I find myself thus horrified and mesmerized by what has been done to the Virgin Mary: the gradually accumulating doctrines not merely that she was virginal at Jesus' birth, but that she was herself "conceived without sin," that she *never* had sex, ever; and that she was bodily assumed into heaven. The attempt to insulate the poor girl from sex, from experience, from history, reveals such a mistaken direction for this powerful and life-giving symbol!

I suppose, as a former Baptist, I'll always be somewhat of an outsider to the mysteries of Catholic thinking. Yet I think I recognize a dose of *contemptus mundi* in this frozen worship of virginity—hatred of the world and the impurities of biological and moral life. It is also highly suspicious to me that a major element of this virgin-worship appeared in the middle of the nineteenth century, that period of fundamentalist reaction. The "immaculate conception" was not proclaimed until 1854, a few years before the Vatican's self-proclamation of doctrinal infallibility (1870). To literalize myth and absolutize authority are the classic gestures of fundamentalism.

This misplaced adoration of "purity" has manufactured a surd: a perpetual virgin. A virgin goddess to be worshipped, as long as she is never touched—analogous to the pristine Eden which we mourn and cannot return to.

233

But the mythical Virgin should have been allowed a better effect, a finer and truer meaning. She is, after all, the Paradoxical Virgin: She gave birth! She had sex with God! She had the Best Son Ever! That's Experience, not Innocence thrice-shielded. She's a Virgin/Mother: a two-stroke cycle, that could be continued as follows: Virgin/Mother/Virgin/Mother/Virgin/etc. As Yeats has pointed out, the underlying meaning of virginity is "the perpetual virginity of the soul": that we can wake up fresh and innocent each day—*no matter who we slept with last night.*

There's the mystery. Each moment is the first moment. Re-engendered by the divine, by the wild rejuvenating freshness that's loose in us and in all life, we never cease in our beginnings.

The true principle of the Paradoxical Virgin is that experience and ripeness belong *with* virginity, not against it. For paradox is life-like and life-giving, a cycle of birth, death, rebirth; while the literalized absurdity is but a capitalism of the spirit: hoard your purity like a purseful of doubloons, because once you spend it, it's gone. True virginity has thickness: whatever it means is deep, layered, eager to turn into its own opposite over and over.

A rosary for the rest of us. Let this Virgin Continent become the Virgin Mother Mother Virgin, world without end. Let the land we walk, walk us. Let us eat the land and be eaten by it, renew the land and be renewed. Let us be virgins falling constantly into worldliness, and coming lustily into new-found virginity.

Muir's Eden: Landscapes of Heaven

On the first day of September, 1867, John Muir set out to redeem himself in the Muiriest of ways: by taking a long, long walk. He was twenty-nine, that age of reckoning, of getting down to business. In his case, though, business was too much business: the young man possessed an aptitude for mechanical tinkering that seemed destined to crowd out that love of nature which had no obvious value in his Wisconsin frontier/farming community. At home and in college he had busied himself inventing all manner of cogged gadgets and gimmicks—a rotating study desk, a bed that dumped sleepyheads out on the floor. By his later twenties he was resigning himself to a life of mechanical employment, sometimes forcibly keeping his mind from thoughts of the outdoors. It's a revealing dilemma that, in fact, never completely went away: the contrast of two incommensurable worlds, one of practical employment in the human world, the other of untethered and almost disembodied freedom in nature. It is that same dilemma which we, the heirs of the environmental movement he would almost single-handedly create, have never solved either.

To that point—the beginning of his "thousand-mile walk to the gulf"—his young life had been an oscillation between the two poles. Fleeing Lincoln's 1864 military draft, he had made his way over the border and sojourned in Canada, at first camping and tramping but eventually, in what became his typical pattern, turning away from nature for work in manufactories. He spent a half-year increasing production at a broom-handle factory, but just as his prospects were becoming favorable with the owners, the entire operation burned down. By March of 1866 the war was over, so he wandered down to Indianapolis to find more of the same: this time it was carriage wheels. Again his employers gave him his head, again he analyzed, tinkered, improved. But at what cost? When he received from his brother a package of ferns he had pressed when still living at the family farm, he wrote back in evident distress: "I mean now

Dan to give my whole attention to machines because I *must* [.] I can not get my mind upon anything else." But in March of 1867, after a year in the factory, came the crisis that would force reconsideration. A terrifying accident drove the point of a file into his right eye, leaving his vision in doubt for weeks.

Muir convalesced in Indianapolis under the care of friends, and later in the summer—his vision healing—returned to the family farm. That was a decidedly mixed blessing, for it brought John once again under the oppressive authority of his Scots father Daniel Muir. A hard-pressed orphan in childhood, Daniel Muir had found an early refuge in religion, but religion of a hectoring, brimstone variety that only grew worse with time. After bringing his family to America he had hardened into a world-hating itinerant backwoods preacher. The poor son, growing up in the Wisconsin woods with his own lights aborning within him, had perforce absorbed and then, secretly, by degrees, begun to repel the family faith. A few years later, in 1874, when John wrote his father of his developing literary career, all the elder could say was "the best and soonest way of getting quit of the writing and publishing your book is to burn it and then it will do no more harm either to you or to others." Back under this man's roof again, young Muir could only feel how far he had yet to go to discover his true place in the world. He determined to give himself a "grand sabbath three years long … sufficient to lighten and brighten my after life in the gloom and hunger of civilization's defrauding duties."

So on setting out on his long walk, Muir was very much a pilgrim, in the sense of travelling with spiritual purpose. Yet his pilgrimage had only the vaguest of destinations: simply to go south, to end up somewhere tropical and flowery, but above all, to get there by "the wildest, leafiest, and least trodden way" he could find. He needed movement, he needed change; and most of all he needed nature to move in and through and, in a sense, towards. The vagueness of his plans suited these unspoken purposes perfectly.

It would be easy to see this journey as the beginning of the sure arc of travel and discovery that resulted in Muir's eventual homecoming to the Sierras, to Yosemite, and to the vocation of wilderness prophet. He intended the trip (in his either-or formulation) as a last fling with nature before sinking back into the opposite of nature, the work of human living; yet it proved to be more than that: it was a breakthrough into a whole new relation with nature. Yet no one drops the past; and Muir brought heavy baggage.

Muir's writing during this journey, and later in his life, develops a complicated, twofold reaction to the doctrine of nature in which he had been reared, and which had left him with such a yearning heart—the drama of Eden, Sin, and the Fall. Muir would stake out two distinct and opposite responses to the orthodox story of how humankind and nature relate to each other. In one mode, he rejects the doctrine of fallen nature and discovers instead a form of nature spirituality that is original, vivid, and compelling: his opening into what Michael P. Cohen regards as a kind of home-grown nature-based Taoism. It's a breathtaking achievement, even a hundred and thirty-odd years later.

In the other mode he falls back, perhaps unconsciously, onto the Paradise Lost underpattern, with its theory of a corrupting sin-nature that dooms humans to separation. It's a contradiction that is still playing out in American environmentalism today.

In his knapsack that bright September morning were three books Muir would carry the whole way from southern Indiana to the gulf coast of Florida, three books that survived stream-crossings, swamp-flounderings, and even burglarious rummagings: a volume of Robert Burns' poetry, a New Testament, and John Milton's epic poem *Paradise Lost.*

Striking, isn't it?

If you have read your Milton, you know *Paradise Lost* as a definitive statement of solid orthodoxy: the dramatized explanation of humankind's cursed relation to God and the world. Milton wrote it in the aftermath of Oliver Cromwell's failed Puritan theocracy, in which he himself had played a leading role. And if the long drama of loss were not enough, Milton reinforced his poem's orthodoxy by simultaneously writing a theological treatise, *The Christian Doctrine.* The famed "organ music" of Milton's language is of course what keeps us coming back to it, and what kept Muir reading and quoting it his whole life long. But *Paradise Lost* is, at heart, an immovably conservative exposition of the West's "story of everything," our creation myth.

If Muir is a pilgrim, then this book of *Paradise Lost* and all it represents are the burden on his back, every bit as heavy as the bag of sins on the back of that other pilgrim depicted by Milton's contemporary and fellow-Puritan, John Bunyan. For Muir, *Paradise Lost* and that Bible next to it were what had to be shed, what wearied the flesh and saddened the spirit. Ponder, Reader, the emotional logic that must have moved the young man's hand, to choose as two of his three books these tokens of a past he could not yet forego.

Yet forego it he did. For in the course of his walking and journaling, his nights under stars provisioned by found water and a little bread, his saunters directed by friendly farm-hosts and town-hosts and questionable lurking characters in Southern woods, the young man found his way to a new place in the world, free of the burden of Calvinist sin and world-hating theology, an authentic nature-spirituality.

If anyone doubts the struggle it cost Muir to leave that dark old world and create a new one, consider this. I looked over Muir's hopeful little quarto-sized journal, the blank book he carried alongside those other tomes and recorded his adventure in (and which Muir and a later editor would one day turn into *A Thousand-Mile Walk to the Gulf*). On the very first page he drew a lighthearted sketch of himself with the caption "Planning my journey outside of Louisville, Ky." And under that, affixed as an epigram for the entire adventure, he inscribed a famous line from the very end of *Paradise Lost*, where the exiled couple make their way into the harsh yet still-beautiful world: "The world was all before them where to choose." Young Muir has framed his journey with a reference to the exile from Eden.

But by the end of October, he had worked out a thoroughgoing alternative, in prose of startling clarity.

Muir's new views develop like an under-plot as the easy day-by-day narrative of *A Thousand-Mile Walk to the Gulf* goes by. Of course no one can "appreciate" nature like Muir, and his rapturous attention to details of plant and forest life is the continuous music of this and all his writings. Against this melody of nature's self-evident value, he begins to set the oddly discordant views of orthodox Western

Christianity. It is a measure of his success as a writer that what has been our standard anthropocentric view of things for so many centuries can be made to look so strange and feel so downright wrong.

He records, with thick irony, the discourse of a Kentucky host who "like a philosopher in the best light of civilization" explains to Muir exactly how God has arranged the world for Man's convenience.

> *"I believe in Providence," said he. "Our fathers came into these valleys, got the richest of them, and skimmed off the cream of the soil. The worn-out ground won't yield no roastin' ears now. But the Lord foresaw this state of affairs, and prepared something else for us. And what is it? Why, He meant us to bust open these copper mines and gold mines, so that we may have money to buy the corn that we cannot raise."*

"A most profound observation," quips the journal, and leaves it there. But not for long. In the next entry (September 18), Muir expatiates on the "wooded, waving, swelling mountain beauty and grandeur" Appalachianed around him in sweeping vistas, and delivers an unmistakable counterpoint to the Kentuckian's narrow views: "All were united by curves and slopes of inimitable softness and beauty. Oh, these forest gardens of our Father! What perfection, what divinity, in their architecture! What simplicity and mysterious complexity of detail! Who shall read the teaching of these sylvan pages, the glad brotherhood of rills that sing in the valleys, and all the happy creatures that dwell in them under the tender keeping of a Father's care?" Whatever divinity Muir invokes, it is already a different god than the one which cared only for the sin and salvation of man.

A few weeks later, on October 9, Muir camps for a week's respite on the wild, untended grounds of the old Bonaventure estate outside of Savannah, Georgia. The greater part of his journey is already accomplished—surely a better walker is nowhere recorded than this slim little Scot!—and in this pause Muir deepens his emerging earth-centered nature-spirituality.

Muir has chosen, in fact, to camp in the Bonaventure graveyard not only as a means of avoiding night-prowlers (kept off by superstition) but because of its physical beauty. In this setting of natural life and death he meditates: "Instead of the sympathy, the friendly union, of life and death so apparent in Nature, we are taught that death is an accident, a deplorable punishment for the oldest sin, the arch-enemy of life, etc. Town-children, especially, are steeped in this death orthodoxy, for the natural beauties of death are seldom seen or taught in towns." His thoughts overtly campaign against the orthodox myth of original sin and expulsion from Eden. Muir's handwritten manuscript for this passage tries out a neologism ("that death is an Evemade accident") that underlines how specifically and consciously he is considering, and rejecting, the tale told in church. Other passages in that original little journal-book that did not survive Muir's editing make the same emphasis—repeated mentions of the Eden-story that he now recognized as his mortal enemy.

Against the old beliefs he marshals the evidence of the senses and of the heart: "All is divine harmony." And as if to underline the contrast, he references *Paradise Lost* with an allusion to Milton's memorable city of the damned, "Pandemonium." But the tumults of humans, he concludes, in their imagined Hells or their living cities, are as nothing beside the peace of nature—"Life at work everywhere, obliterating all memory of the confusion of man." On the road again few days later (October 16), he picks up the thread: in this beautiful and strangely dangerous world, this Florida of flowery swamps and ravenous alligators, even the frightening and repellent elements are "unfallen, undepraved," and not "consequences of Eve & that apple."

This is, certainly, a declaration of loyalties. The old books may still be with him, but he is not with them.

The drama of Muir's struggle against orthodox Christianity climaxes as the journey concludes. Though he eventually sails onward to Cuba and after that to points north, south, and above all west, *this* journey, the walk of a thousand miles, ends on the Gulf coast in a remote tropical strand called Cedar Keys. Here Muir is felled by fever, presumably malaria, and must recover for three months under the care of a kindly family; but most importantly, here he finishes the reformation of his spiritual world.

For the journal of the walk ends in a stirring four-page manifesto of earth-centered spirituality that will guide Muir for the rest of his fabled days. Muir's theological vision is very acute here: it sees that the story of original sin and its human-centered view of the world are indivisible from each other. It's the echo of that silly Kentuckian, and the shadow of millennia of Christian thought as well, that "the world, we are told, was made especially for man." Muir records his astonishment at that habit of mind whose tiny God ("purely a manufactured article") can be understood to have made the world for people only, and yet damned that same world "by the eating of the apple in the Garden of Eden."

Scornfully now, Muir asks, Are there parts of existence that inconvenience you? Are there mosquitos, carnivores, laws of nature that threaten or obstruct? Conventionally, they must be explained by reference to "Eden's apple and the Devil." He continues his mocking catechism, asking why "Mankind," the putative master of Creation, is

subjected to the same laws of life as his subjects? Oh, all these things are satanic, or in some way connected to that first garden … The fearfully good, the orthodox, of this laborious patch-work of modern civilization cry "Heresy" on every one whose sympathies reach a single hair's breadth beyond the boundary epidermis of our own species. Not content with taking all of earth, they also claim the celestial country as the only ones who possess the kind of souls for which that imponderable empire was planned.

Look how far this fellow is going! I want to shout. For this is not mere latter-day Transcendentalism—this goes further. For all their love of nature, the Transcendentalists were at the end of the day finding the spiritual lesson *behind* the glorious veil of nature. But Muir stares at nature fearlessly, in the here-and-now, and throws his lot there. Nature's beings are blessed with spirit exactly as we are. And their value is therefore intrinsic:"Why should man value himself as more than a small part of the one great unit of creation? And what creature of all that the Lord has taken the pains to make is not essential to the completeness of that unit—the cosmos? The universe would be incomplete without man; but it would also be incomplete without the smallest transmicroscopic creature that dwells beyond our conceitful eyes and knowledge." This fellowship with the created world, with our "earth-born companions and our fellow mortals," brings Muir to the spiritual redemption he has sought. Within two years he will find his home in Yosemite and the Sierras, where he will deepen his citizenship by patient investigation of natural process and boundlessly energetic exploration of natural beauty.

But the necessary condition for his homecoming is here, at the end of this burdened, wounded, healing walk, this emblematic journey from blindness to vision. Here he turns once and for all against the myth of original sin and its paradoxical over- and under-valuing of the human species, against the "providential chastisement for some self-invented form of sin": "But, glad to leave these ecclesiastical fires and blunders, I joyfully return to the immortal truth and immortal beauty of Nature."

Yet Muir's joyful "return" to nature eventually led him, by a kind of invisible gravitation, back to the language and imagery of Eden. This ought to be surprising, after the denunciation of orthodoxy we saw above. But clearly, doctrine is one thing and story is another. The pattern of paradise is too deeply founded to abandon without a conscious decision to do so.

And Muir, despite his profound change of mind, had no inclination to abandon either his Bible or his Milton. There would come to be more balance than is immediately evident in the vigorous thumping he had given orthodoxy in the heat of his first illuminations at Bonaventure and Cedar Keys. The biographer I rely on most, Frederick Turner, comments on Muir's lifelong love of Milton and reverence for Christ. Muir would develop an ability (as any balanced person must), "silently to ignore those interpretations … that had become offensive to his own beliefs."

I've also seen Muir's volume of *Paradise Lost*—very likely the one he carried in his backpack next to the little journal—both now in the Holt-Atherton collection of Muir's books and papers in Stockton, California. It's a neat, hand-sized 1825 edition (actually containing only the first six books of the twelve-book poem) bearing Muir's plentiful underlinings, marginalia, and fly-leaf notes. Not surprisingly, the markings show that Muir was taken with Milton's nature descriptions—what he indexed in one case as "Landscapes of Heaven":

> *For Earth hath this variety from Heaven*
> *Of pleasure situate in Hill and Dale*

Landscapes of Heaven: That's a telling phrase, and it could aptly describe Muir's lifelong adoration of terrestrial beauty. Similarly, Muir particularly marks up the first extended view of the beauties of Eden in Book IV:

> *Beneath him with new wonder now he views*
> *To all delight of human sense exposed,*
> *In narrow room, Nature's whole wealth, yea more,*
> *A Heaven on Earth: For blissful Paradise*
> *Of God the garden was, by him in the east*
> *Of Eden planted*

What Milton depicts here is Heaven on Earth, unfallen and infused with a godly power to transform the eye and the heart. And that is exactly how Muir would come to see his "pure" wildernesses: as Eden. The woods and mountains are "God's First Temples" (as he would title an essay later): fresh as the day of creation.

The hash this makes of any doctrinal sense is really unimportant. (Probably unimportant, too, is the irony that both the quoted passages above, underlined in Muir's copy, are given from Satan's point of view, perhaps suggesting Milton's ambivalence about investing too much value in the earthly frame.) But what *is* important, I am convinced, is the sad drift back to a narrative of paradise that can only end, in Milton's words, "with loss of Eden, and all our woe." Muir goes there by a simple but deeply consequential mental substitution, the same one that has come to define modern environmentalism: in the place of the mythical Eden, located in the timeless world of origins, Muir imagines Eden as a literal and historical place: North America, its woods and mountains, right now or in the just-past.

The (supposed) unspoiled, untouched nature of America becomes, for Muir, a literal Eden. That language is immediately visible along the Muir trail of magazine and newspaper writings that began to appear after the first summers in the Sierra. Over and over in years to come, he would describe his Sierras and other "untouched wildernesses" in Edenic terms, and make clear that his personal desire was to live in Eden as much as possible, with as little to do with the outside (evidently fallen) world as he could manage. (Though how to manage this trick turned out to be not so easy, as we will explore in the following chapter.)

By the time Muir came into his highest prominence as a writer—the great decade of the 1890s with its stirring fight for Yosemite—the Eden narrative was a fixture of his rhetoric. He shows no awareness of the conflict such imagery implies: how the story of exile in a fallen world is the very opposite of the fresh unfallenness of nature that had so often revived him.

Impending loss of Eden is where Muir begins the fight for Yosemite in the two-part *Century Magazine* series that struck the American public so forcefully. On the first page of the first article, Muir rounds out his overview of the topic with this: "But no terrestrial beauty may endure forever. The glory of wildness has already departed from the great central plain. Its bloom is shed, and so in parts is the bloom of the mountains. In Yosemite, even under the protection of the Government, all that is perishable is vanishing apace."

The tide of inevitability, running directly from the myth of Eden, seems already to have swept over the famous riches of California's central valley; now at the edge of the mountains it seemingly cannot be stayed. One is tempted to ask, Then what's the use? The sentiment of loss is so ravishing, so emotionally resonant, that it is deployed despite its inner contradictions. Does it move people? Yes, undoubtedly. It moves them *emotionally* with a traumatic sense of the ravages of time and inevitable loss, which we surely have all suffered. But does it move them politically, socially, productively, in the long term? About that, there must be a mixed verdict. Under the rubric of Eden-equals-nature, the connection to nature is made only to be broken.

Muir won the battle for the Yosemite that very year, though political backpedalling kept Yosemite itself in play for years, and the broader question of wilderness reserves is of course a permanent wrangle. Muir poured himself into the struggle for the whole decade, and indeed unto the end of his life.

In literary terms, perhaps the most effective piece of Muir's writing was the one he wrote in 1897 for *Atlantic Monthly* called "The American Forests." In it we see exactly the rhetorical and political formula which has governed most American environmentalist writing ever since: the invocation of Nature as an Eden of perfection ("The whole continent was a garden ..."); followed by a relentless tide of destruction ("felling and burning more fiercely than ever, until at last it has reached the wild side of the continent, and entered the last of the gerat aboriginal forests on the shores of the Pacific"); and concluding with the trumpet-call to action ("It is not yet too late—though it is high time").

"High time" indeed. For *time* is exactly at the center of Muir's reconceptualization of Eden from myth to history. It's a fatal change; one that I think the environmental movement muᶜt make itself ready to undo.

A student of myth will recognize the conflation here of events of mythic time into events of historic time. Mircea Eliade calls that time, *in illo tempore*, a separate dimension which is a sort of eternal present. Whenever a myth is retold or reenacted in ritual, its power lies in accessing the powerful time of origins. Our literal-minded age, grounded (or trapped) in a scientific definition of reality and a historical definition of time, may have difficulty appreciating just what this "ritual time" means. Eliade explains that myth defines an eternal world outside of time; it can be re-accessed from any point along the unfolding of ordinary linear time. Origins are powerful; to touch them is to renew the soul, and in fact to renew the world. So the running-down entropy of historical time, the increasing distance from the godly power of the Beginning, can be counteracted continually. Straight-line time must be punctuated by moments when the cyclical time of myth can flood into the present; the human who says the words, or enters the holy places, or dances the ritual dance, re-enters eternity. And through that door, eternity re-enters the world.

But when Muir transplants our mythic story of origins into literal, historic time and place, he kills its ability to confer renewal. If Eden becomes history, it can never be re-entered. And so the loss of any Eden is permanent, irreversible—here and in countless other environmentalist tracts and pleas. These ecological sins can never be forgiven; these environmental Edens will never return. Stuck in the forward arrow-flight of time, we can see no cycle of renewal. Losses are permanent, and our course is ever into darkness.

You could say the rhetoric of this appeal works. Muir is a godlike figure of remembrance, and his works of wilderness preservation still stand, refuges from the saw, the cellphone, the searing touch of trade and toil. I've been there and I've been renewed, pretty much exactly as he prescribes. I ought to be grateful Muir was there, with his rhetoric, to save them for me. And I am.

But I am interested in the sleight-of-mind which has overtaken Muir here: how from debunking the Eden myth, he has (without noticing) fallen into using it.

Or is it using him?

Eden is a myth that has ended up telling its tellers, speaking through them without their ability to hear it or to imagine any other words, or worlds.

But we cannot afford to let this story line use us any more. It is time to bring it into consciousness, recognize it as a historical artifact, and move to other ground. For the immediate political gains we make in using Eden-and-Apocalypse language are paid for with long-term defeat. Like Muir, we find we cannot live in Eden, and that however "saved" it is, it is somewhere else. We trudge in a flat and dusty world, separated and alienated (as all the nature writers declare) from a vital connection with the world.

Eden can't be saved unless we are, too. Our fates are intertwined. We must re-imagine what Eden means.

Muir's Arcadia

The day I found Arcadia, it was smogged in. Two freeways and a pair of busy thoroughfares connect Arcadia to the rest of Los Angeles, and I found myself going too slow as I tried to find my way from LAX. Drivers behind me didn't like it. I missed a couple of turns, nearly went through a red light, and tried to do a U-turn in front of oncoming traffic. Arcadia eventually turned up right about where I expected, between a great city and a great wild place. Between: an interesting place, at least in the imagination. It was named "Arcadia" some time after John Muir had visited it, which may have raised my expectations unreasonably. Yet Arcadia didn't seem to be there at all, at first.

At the eastward limit of the Los Angeles Basin, the San Gabriel Mountains rise over the city with astonishing abruptness to peaks and ridges of six thousand feet, stepping up to eleven thousand at the southern end. Alluvial outwash slopes majestically from the base of these mountains across a hundred miles of sun-beaten suburb. But the mountains were nowhere as I approached on the 605 freeway, which on the map draws an arrow-straight bead on them. Mount San Antonio should be, I squinted, right *here.* But of course the abused air wouldn't permit such visions, not in the summer half of the year. No mountains, no edge of city, no visions.

Some Arcadia.

Well, it's a cheap irony, familiar to writers about LA. A beautiful place … if you could ever see it. But this was "Arcadia": its very name means a place where the natural and the civilized are balanced, blended. It's supposed to be the edge of Eden, right where we all want to live. But you had to be crazy to want to live *here.* It was an ugly place stuck with a beautiful name. Irony is never far away when dealing with Arcadias and Edens.

Reality cooperated with my irony-mongering when I found the headquarters of the Angeles National Forest Ranger District the next morning, right there in Arcadia, a mile or two away from its frequently invisible yet vast domain of wilderness. In the air-conditioned supervisor's office a uniformed ranger, helpful and pleasant, gave me a USFS map of the sort I usually seek for getting around in these places. She casually mentioned that she had known John Muir's daughter.

I guess you'd expect her to live in Arcadia too, wouldn't you?

In classical literature, of course, Arcadia was rural utopia as imagined by city folk. The Roman poet Virgil and, long before him, the Greek Theocritus fed an urban desire for a greener way to live by singing the praises of country life. Both of them sang mostly in a minor key, a key of nostalgia. Virgil's first Eclogue begins "Exiled from home …" It is a hymn, in his wonderful phrase, to the "green cave" of bucolic life, remembered from an urban distance.

Naturally it wasn't raw nature or peasant hardship that the pastoral poets remembered, or that their audience wanted to imagine. They wanted it cleaned up: country life without the smells and flies, without hard labor or boredom or provinciality. If you've heard of Marie Antoinette playing at milkmaid in the gardens of Versailles, you've heard of Arcadia. It is somewhere between self-conscious fantasy and real desire. (There's that "between" again.) The green trees are real, but the life there is not.

By Marie Antoinette's time, English and Continental poets had been translating and imitating classical pastoral for some time, mostly as a vehicle for love-play (like their classical models). Idealized rustic boys woo virginal rosy-cheeked lassies, or, lovesick, lament their rejection. All in a green-world never-never-land of purling streams and warbling shepherds.

Silly as it was, Arcadian pastoral tapped into a profound and apparently nearly universal feeling—at least, universal for people in cities. We want a way to connect to something less steeped in the human, something with a whiff of that other world we come from. The path of least resistance was (and is) to slip into nostalgia for the countryside: visited from time to time, viewed from afar, perhaps remembered as the origin of parents or grandparents. Arcadian pastoral paints a pretty rural life in imagination as an escape from the rigors of town, and suggests a natural counterbalance to urban values.

That longing for the natural world is something we must reckon with. It hasn't gone away. Arcadia and Eden are attempts to cope with a real underlying need. But they tend to bog down, don't they? Nostalgia and longing are unreliable emotions; disappointment too often comes in their train. The course of life (and literature) is strewn with the wreckage of rosy-goggled city folk gone "back to the land" for their six months of shocked disillusion. (Poor Nathaniel Hawthorne at the utopian Brooke Farm experiment comes to mind: how can I write after a day of this grinding filthy labor? asked he, plaintively.) Arcadia is hard to find, but easy to remember.

John Muir came to the San Gabriel Valley in the summer of 1877, and wrote two articles about it (in the form of letters) for the *San Francisco Evening Bulletin.* What he found was a colony of Americans "of taste and money" who just three years earlier had settled on this place as the nearest thing to paradise. Everything came easy here, reported one of Muir's interlocutors—"flowers, fruit, milk and honey, and plenty of money." Their orange crops were already paying off, and they, mostly Easterners, basked in the unbelievably constant sunshine and paradisal weather, raising up gorgeous fruit and the glittering prospect of profits by "true enchantment." A "kind of terrestrial heaven," said Muir.

That's the spirit, I said. Milk and honey. The promised land. Heaven-on-earth. But what *kind* of heaven, exactly?

It certainly looks good on paper. Muir reports that these Pasadena settlers (next door to still-unnamed Arcadia) have brought their money and education with them. No mere tillers of soil, they embody an "aristocratic" level of culture. "There is nothing more remarkable in the character of the colony than the literary and scientific taste displayed. The conversation of most I have met here is seasoned with a smack of mental ozone, Attic salt." Attic means Greek, of course. It's another of Muir's repeated hints of Arcadia. Perhaps what Hawthorne's band of soft-handed litterateurs could not achieve in their utopia, here was coming to fruition: that ideal of pastoral elegance celebrated by Virgil and Theocritus, the educated country ladies and gentlemen, the urbane guests, verdant vistas, calm pace, and expansive conversation. Such a life sounds tempting.

Muir's temptations toward this Arcadia were personal, I believe—both disturbing and pressing in the way Arcadia raised the question of domesticity. Here Muir walked arm-in-arm with his dearest friend, Mrs. Jeanne Carr, wife of Professor Ezra S. Carr. There is no record of their conversations, though we know that Mrs. Carr had kept up a pretty constant campaign to bring Muir more solidly into the human world. He of course was always lighting off for the hills—but he always came back. The Carrs had taken up Muir long before, when he was a student at the University of Wisconsin. Professor Carr had been a mentor in natural history and chemistry; Mrs. Carr had become, simply, his life-long best friend. First in Oakland and then in Pasadena, she welcomed him into her home and, as their constant correspondence reveals, into her heart. It was from both sides a deep and passionate friendship.

In Oakland, in Wisconsin, and always, Muir remained suspended between worlds, longing for the mountains but unable to turn his back once and for all on towns, friends, people. *Between*: Arcadia should have been just right for him. I like to picture them, the stately lady and the protégé, arm-in-arm in the uncanny orange-blossom softness of Arcadian evenings. Mrs. Carr offered friendship, a home in the foothills, a place to belong. How could poor Muir, closing in on the age of forty, in every way unattached, resist?

Not far from the Carrs, another old university acquaintance had taken up residence in the colony: "Doctor Congar, with whom I had studied chemistry and mathematics fifteen years ago," as Muir tells his readers. Congar's enthusiasm for this earthly paradise is unbounded, and he picks up Mrs. Carr's campaign, making the case for Muir to settle there himself. " 'And there,' he continued, pointing just beyond his own precious possessions, 'is a block of land that is for sale; buy it and be my neighbor; plant five acres with orange trees, and by the time your last mountain is climbed their fruit will be your fortune.' " Dr. Congar could not have known his friend well, to have baited the hook so badly. Contemplating his "last mountain" is the very last thing Muir could have desired. He brushed off the unwelcome thought and (what else?) headed for the hills.

But he would carry the question of Arcadia with him, the question of what kind of heaven he wanted. Eden and Arcadia are not necessarily the same thing. And it would prove a complex challenge for Muir to figure out the difference, and what to do with it.

Probably the most influential study of Americans' Arcadian ideas about the land they inhabit has been Leo Marx's essential book *The Machine in the Garden*. He traces the tradition of Arcadian pastoral in America, following its tremendous influence in shaping attitudes of colonists, Western settlers, nature writers, and Americans in general. Arcadia, California, is a good example of that long tradition, where the aspirations and imaginative life of the founders is made visible with rare clarity in the name they chose. Here we have found it, they declare: a kind of paradise.

And the Arcadian kind of paradise is not wilderness. Marx emphasizes that the essence of the pastoral is its blending of civilization and simplicity, artifice and nature, experience and innocence. This vision of nature just tame enough, or just nearby enough, is a formula for domestic happiness, not for wild adventure or soul-testing discovery.

Marx explores the language of the earliest English explorers and colonists and discovers there a welter of mythic allusion: Arcadia, Golden Age, Eden, Paradise. That's not surprising, since as we have seen myths in actual use typically do not bother with consistency. In the Classical world there were often different or contradictory versions of the same story floating around, which troubled nobody. Marx focuses on Arcadian pastoral, that timeless place which in practice is often homologized with Eden, as it is with the classical Golden Age. America seems to promise a return/advance to that blessed Arcadian border condition, far enough from the decadence of Europe, and yet still on the safe side of truly raw frontier wilderness.

Within those loosely mixed pastoral myths, however, lurks a significant tension which Marx does not explore. European-American culture stands of course on a double foundation, Hellenic and Hebrew (to use Matthew Arnold's terms). The Arcadian pastoral is classical, Hellenic; Eden is quintessentially Hebraic.What strikes me is the differing tonalities of these overlapping myths. Eden and Arcadia are suffused with distinct and nearly opposite feelings. The amiable sexuality of classic pastoral sets it most obviously apart from the Edenic version. Virgil and Theocritus pine for shepherd boys, as well as for shepherd girls. All fair game, in their world! The lovesick complainers are always about to fall into sexual folly—they cannot stop themselves and do not wish to. Their Golden Age is as long-gone as our Eden; but in its pastoral/Arcadian recursions it seems a place that can be revisited at will. Its morality is easy. There's a knowingness behind the innocence giving an urban, perhaps cynical, nod. Yet further behind lurks a still deeper truth: a pastoral reassurance that new beginnings are real, that spring is real, that innocence is recoverable. Even if Arcadia is only a game—love is a game too, isn't it? and games themselves are little natures, where play recreates the big world outside. And like nature itself, games can be reentered, restarted, any time.

But the fall from Eden is once only. Its moral universe is much less forgiving. Sin (not just folly) is never far away, and it seems the real meaning of Eden in our post-Puritan culture is the casting-out part, the regret, the wandering. The recovery from this Fall is hard indeed—so hard a god must be killed to raise us up, and even then there is no relief except somewhere far off, over the horizon, after the end of time. In the meanwhile, saved or not, we wander in what Governor Bradford called the "hidious and desolate wilderness." Marx acknowledges that the Puritans brought their sternly post-Edenic consciousness to the New World, and that this view certainly formed a polar opposite to visions of pastoral utopia. "Europeans never had agreed about the nature of nature; nor did they now agree about America," he comments. As long as the Puritans were Puritans, they knew no earthly home could be anything but sinful.

But I'm interested in the contrast of pastorals: those Edens and Arcadias that came later, after the Puritans had gone from the scene. Those Edens that had been scrubbed clean of Puritan pessimism, relocated to the West, and described in a rush of Romantic optimism. There, I think, is the hook that caught Muir. It looks a bit like Arcadia—but it isn't. Arcadia is the *between* state, an ecotone where nature and culture exchange. Eden is the sinless state, a clean absolute. Muir chose the latter.

So it's deeply interesting to me when Muir, the prophet of wilderness "pure" (Muir attaches the adjective constantly, almost obsessively), resorts to the Arcadian myth in his exploration of the San Gabriels.

Having done his duty describing the orange-grove utopia in the first letter to the *Bulletin*, Muir reserves his real excitement for the second. Muir leaves the valley for a ramble in the mountains with hardly concealed impatience (the second letter is written just days after the first). "After saying so much for human culture in my last, perhaps I may now be allowed a word for wildness—the wildness of this southland, pure and untamable."

Later, he would re-use this piece to end his book *The Mountains of California,* with its description of a hike up Eaton Canyon that led to a three-day bushwhacking across the peaks above Los Angeles. It's a typically offhand Muir mountaineering accomplishment, a casual "saunter" that most of us would tell as an epic achievement. These hills are among the steepest in the world, thorny and crumbling and desperately hot. Muir did it without clear trails, backpack, or USFS map, his physical and emotional hardihood almost incredible here as in so many of his adventures. Facing the "impenetrable" thickets of buckbrush and ceanothus, he says, "I was compelled to creep for miles on all fours, and in following the bear-trails often found tufts of hair on the bushes where they had forced themselves through." The San Gabriels are, he says, "more rigidly inaccessible in the ordinary meaning of the word than any other that I ever attempted to penetrate."

But Muir the canny naturalist quickly catches the trick of this dry country. I grew up there before heighing off to wetter forests, and I hear the true note in Muir's immediate recognition that the essence of these hot and thorny hills is in their subtleties, their unsuspected dells and shadowed clefts, where the sunshine is broken by leafy canopies, where grassy plots and even hidden brooks might be discovered. The hopeless dry mountainsides, unpleasant to an Eastern eye, yield surprises to the attentive foot-traveller.

And this is where the surprising spurts of Arcadian language intrude into Muir's narrative. They are little idyllic "gardens," he says, and in fact he chooses them for impromptu sleep-outs described not as wilderness bivouacs but as naps in flower-strewn "bowers." Now, garden language is not absent from other Muir rambles—far from it. But embowered in this particular pastoral, Muir seems to be playing out the tone he has established early in the piece. For there, at the beginning of the hike, at the top of Eaton Canyon, is the interesting feature locally known as "the Fall," which

Muir portrays in strikingly Arcadian terms: "hither come the San Gabriel lads and lassies," he says, "to gather ferns and dabble away their hot holidays in the cool water."

A quaint watercolor by Watteau, of ribboned love-play, seems to hover over this unexpected description. Is it a random allusion by a still-developing writer, who perhaps is not quite in control of his rhetoric? After all, Muir's journalistic career had started only six years earlier. No. The Arcadian allusions, while undoubtedly clumsy, do not come randomly. For as he wrote those words, Muir himself stood at the intersection of conflicting and difficult forces which he would never fully resolve. In the months following his visit, Muir began facing anew the central conflict of his life, which is one of the central conflicts of American life: how to accommodate the needs of ordinary mortal living within the vision of a pure and untouched land.

Muir did not solve this unsolvable equation. No one could. For as long as wilderness is Eden, "pure" and divine and untouchable, the problem is all paradox. The Arcadian solution, a middle ground, has no power in the presence of the Eden vision.

Before this confrontation with Arcadia, in the crucial period of the 1870s, Muir had seemingly cast his lot firmly with Eden. Certainly he knew the wild better than anybody; and he had tasted city life enough to know what that was, too. He was accustomed to stay for extended periods with the Carrs in Oakland (before their move to Pasadena); later in the decade he roomed at the San Francisco homes of friends John Swett and Isaac Upham. While relishing the glow of friendship during these sojourns, he typically felt his displacement from the mountains keenly.

For from his "first summer" of 1869 onwards, Muir went about creating both a home and a vocation for himself in Yosemite. It was a hard-won achievement. Years of wandering had preceded it, always with the diapason undertone of questioning: what is my life to be for? Where shall I live it? Normal questions for a young person, but for Muir they were acute. It appears to me that his extraordinary capacities for wonder, awe, and sheer physical exertion required him to virtually invent a life like no other. But not without doubt at first, and not without a roving aimlessness. Friends like Mrs. Carr questioned him, and perhaps also the sternly demanding God of his father asked in the back of his mind, what are you doing with your life?

Then at the age of thirty-one he found his place: the Sierra Nevadas, which apparently from first sight awakened a profound sense of connection, of home. "I tremble with excitement in the dawn of these glorious mountain sublimities," he wrote that first summer; "but I can only gaze and wonder ... half hoping I may be able to study and learn in years to come."

Yet it is crucial to see that this discovery, compelling as it was to Muir, did not resolve the tension. Indeed, because Muir's decision to make a mountain life was so radical, it in some ways intensified the tension. Even at this period, before his fame, before he had written, before the world knew it needed him, voices from the mortal world were trying to call Muir from his mountains, forcing him to consider and defend again and again his life in the wild.

He called it "this question of bread." Of course, he had to eat. For his mountaineering he had evolved a simple diet of tea and bread; but when the bread ran out, he faced a limit he could never reconcile himself to, yet had no means of transcending (short of death). "The bread line," as he called it, could not be denied; and down from the mountains he would trudge. On that inaugural and epic journey, the Thousand-Mile Walk, he had already faced this unsolvable riddle: "In the morning I was cold and wet with dew, and I set out breakfastless. Flowers and beauty had I in abundance, but no bread. A serious matter is this bread which perishes, and, could it be dispensed with, I doubt if civilization would ever see me again."

Bread, that food most heavily weighted with symbolism, seemed to mean hardly less than Muir's humanity: that which kept drawing him back to friends in Oakland or Pasadena, that which demanded some kind of connection to other men and women—to civilization, even, however loath he might be to admit it. In *My First Summer in the Sierra*, describing shortened rations and a long wait for resupply, Muir groused again about this unseemly dependency: "Rather weak and sickish this morning, and all about a piece of bread. Can scarce command attention to my best studies, as if one couldn't take a few days' saunter in the Godful woods without maintaining a base on a wheat-field and grist mill."

In perhaps the most remarkable of all his letters, probably written in 1870, Muir mounts a passionate, giddy, almost deranged defense, trying to convey to his dearest and most trusted friend just how total is his commitment to the Sierras. Mrs. Carr has simply asked him, from her home in Oakland, when he is "coming down"— coming down to visit, certainly, but also coming down from his hermit existence into the world of people, where his duty lay. It is not the first time she has asked, and it will be far from the last. The question awakens him to a half-humorous, half-serious frenzy. He datelines the letter "Squirrelville, Sequoia Co." in "*Nut Time,*" and goes so far as to actually write it in sequoia sap! This thing is hard to excerpt, it vibrates with such electricity and certainty. But here's the beginning, at least:

> *Dear Mrs. Carr:*
> *Do behold the King in his glory, King Sequoia! Behold! Behold! seems all I can say. Some time ago I left all for Sequoia and have been and am at his feet, fasting and praying for light, for is he not the greatest light in the woods, the world? Where are such columns of sunshine, tangible, accessible, terrestrialized? Well may I fast, not from bread, but from business, book-making, duty-going, and other trifles, and great is my reward already for the manly, treely sacrifice. What giant truths since coming to Gigantea, what magnificent clusters of Sequoic becauses. From here I cannot recite you one, for you are down a thousand fathoms deep in dark political quagg, not a burr-length less. But I'm in the woods, woods, woods, and they are in me-ee-ee. The King tree and I have sworn eternal love—sworn it without swearing, and I've taken the sacrament with Douglas squirrel, drunk Sequoia wine, Sequoia blood, and with its rosy purple drops I am writing this woody gospel letter.*

Even allowing for playfulness and exaggeration in a personal, not a public, writing, this letter declares a turning away from the human/ social world that is emphatic and complete. There is the "bread" question again, associated with so much of the world's business. Muir swears a love-affair, a marriage, a disciple's all-forsaking, a monk's consecration. The way heterosexual Muir genders this oath supports the idea of a hermit-monk's calling—not a woman or female spirit in sight. No ordinary mortal entanglement can be permitted; so "King Sequoia" it is (not Queen), and a life both "manly" and sexless: a pure life for the pure wilderness. For Eden. In the closing lines Muir directly answers the unintentionally goading question that has awakened this passionate response: "You say, 'When are you coming down?' Ask the Lord—Lord Sequoia."

Thus, from the first summer, in Eden he made his home. But what to do there? The answer lay in Yosemite: if the Sierras were his place, then in Yosemite he found his calling. The gigantic riddle of glaciation and the creation of Yosemite Valley gripped him almost immediately, and soon he was clambering up ridges and canyons, observing glacially sculpted rocks and standing in remote cirques, imagining with his whole soul what forces could have produced the magnificence of Yosemite Valley and all the rest of the scoured and spired Sierra. For two glorious years, 1871 and 1872, he immersed himself. Never was he happier, never more at peace with the path he had chosen. In September of 1871 he writes to Mrs. Carr: "The grandeur of these forces and their glorious results overpower me, and inhabit my whole being. Waking or sleeping I have no rest. In dreams I read blurred sheets of glacial writing or follow lines of cleavage or struggle with the difficulties of some extraordinary rock form. ... Some of my friends are badgering me to write for some of the magazines, and I am almost tempted to try it, only I am afraid that this would distract my mind from my main work more than the distasteful and depressing labor of the mill or of guiding. What do you think about it?" What she thought about it was that her beloved friend must do his work—but not neglect to visit her in Oakland, nor indeed forget to bring his passions down from the mountains and share them with his fellow humans.

Mrs. Carr represented Muir's own inner voice, I think; his sense that a merely reclusive life would never fully satisfy him. When she spoke for lowland mortals, he complained and resisted, but often enough complied, in prolonged visits to Oakland. Perhaps that inner/outer voice included a Calvinist streak of duty, left over from childhood. Or perhaps it spoke the simple humanity that Muir never fully reconciled with "pure wilderness."

A letter of Jeanne Carr's in 1872 reveals her determination to humanize Muir. It is addressed to Louie Strentzel, daughter of a friend. She is discussing Muir, of course, and the letter seems to be a hardly veiled invitation to courtship: "I wish I could give him to some noble young woman 'for keeps' and so take him out of the wilderness into the society of his peers." At that time, nothing came of it. But Mrs. Carr's stratagems went deep and this one kept going for the better part of the decade. It wasn't until that Arcadian summer of 1877 that Muir finally took the bait.

In the meantime, in the great years of his first love, the Sierras, Muir resisted the temptation to "come down." He cultivated a prophet-like disdain for the dirty, trammeled city life, or indeed any life that he thought not as pure as the one he pursued. The following undated fragment (probably from the early 1870s, according to biographer Frederick Turner) reveals Muir's stern, pitying separation from the human world: "Pat, pat, shuffle, shuffle, crunch, crunch, I hear you all on the sidewalks and sandbeds, plodding away, hoping in righteousness and heaven, and saying your prayers as best you can, above the sand, beneath the fog, and fenced in by the lake and marshes. Heaven help you all and give you ice and granite."

As his glacial theories and mountain expertise began to make him known, triumphing over the professional scientists like U.S. Geological Survey leader Josiah Whitney (of "Mount Whitney"), who opposed him bitterly, and even attracting the attention of the great Emerson, who visited him in Yosemite (in 1871), Muir at last began to feel a sense of confidence in his strange life. To Mrs. Carr he writes, in 1874: "Civilization and fever and all the morbidness that has been hooted at me have not dimmed my glacial eye, and I care to live only to entice people to look at Nature's loveliness. My own special self is nothing. My feet have recovered their cunning. I feel myself again." William Frederic Badé, editor of Muir's letters, identifies this as a declaration of vocation, one that had cost Muir a decade of wandering and self-doubt to achieve. First the discovery of his geographic place, Yosemite and the Sierras; then the defined, scientific task there, answering the question of glaciation; and once that was achieved, the broader mission—large enough for a lifetime—of preaching "the gospel of beauty" to all. Against all odds, Muir had won through to creating in both senses his vocation, his monk's/preacher's/lover's role, his job in life: his calling in Eden.

So it is strange indeed to find Muir a few short years later returning to his doubts. When we find Muir in the Arcadian moment in the San Gabriels, it seems the old difficulty has returned to him: how to be a man in the world of other men and women, yet still follow his Sierran vocation. He has begun wandering again, and that summer of 1877 he would also travel to Utah to write about Mormons and mountains. His journalistic writing has taken hold; regular contributions to *Overland Monthly* and newspapers in Sacramento and San Francisco have given him a voice, and with it he preaches his good news, the "glad tidings" of the mountains. That summer of 1877 was a turning point for Muir, or at least the beginning of a slow turn toward some other kind of life, lived somewhere that was not his mountain Eden.

In the following fall he traveled down the Merced and San Joaquin rivers to Sacramento and paid his first visit to Louie Strentzel, Mrs. Carr's designated match. Now that Mrs. Carr was out of sight in Southern California, Muir seems to have felt free, or compelled, to make his move. I cannot avoid the sense that something must have clicked, some sense of matelessness as the age of forty approached, some fatigue with his monkish isolation from all that gives ordinary people comfort and fulfillment.

It was a prolonged and it seems to me a curiously halfhearted courtship. Eventually John and Louie would settle down on the Strentzel spread in Martinez, a huge and profitable fruit ranch under the ownership of Louie's father—an Arcadian, yea a Virgilian outcome which the Roman would have recognized and applauded: the pastoral achieved. But Muir's approach to the middle state of marital and pastoral happiness was oddly oblique. It took him a year and a half to secure an engagement with Louie ... after which he immediately left for Alaska. Marriage waited almost another year.

And when Muir finally submitted to married life, he would sink or slide into a grim seven-year silence and near-total absence from his mountains, during which time he would write nothing, but would make two babies and a considerable fortune as a fruit rancher.

He hated it.

Hated the life, anyway. There's evidence of domestic happiness with Louie and of a warm affection for the children. But the life itself … Muir's letters are full of weariness, busyness, business, full of a sense that his true self is wasting away for that old bugaboo, "this question of bread." "I am all nerve-shaken and lean as a crow," he writes; "loaded with care, work, and worry," too "stupidly busy" "to make good use of odd hours in writing."

It's as if the commitments and clarities of the Yosemite years had vanished. Only his unhappiness remained to remind him of the consequence of breaking faith with Lord Sequoia. The Arcadian solution simply did not work for Muir. He did not want Arcadia: he wanted Eden. And eventually, he would have it again.

I stayed over. A night in Arcadia, I thought. That would surely be a good thing? The next morning, though, I was as ready as Muir was to chuck the whole thing and go for a walk in the hills.

I went up to Eaton Canyon in the foothills above Pasadena, precisely where Muir had begun his three-day ramble across the ridgeline. As I hiked under a bright mid-morning sun, I tried to piece together the odd elements of this mixture. Utopia-ranches. Arcadia. Just enough civilization, just enough nature. Sex. No-sex. Settling down. Settling, in every sense.

Because it is obvious that Muir's marriage to Louie Strentzel was a kind of "settling." She was a plainish thirty-one-year-old, beyond the usual age of marrying ("in a state whose population was heavily male" as Turner observes). Muir never mentioned her in any of his writings, not once. No one has ever found any evidence of passion between them. Except, of course, that there were children, so there must have been *enough* passion. But my point is that *enough* was not a Muir value. He always wanted *more*, he was committed to near-absolutes of purity and longing, he gobbled mountain-ranges like snacks, wandered and thirsted always for *more* of the Godfully pure wild. So the decision to settle for *enough* was revolutionary. And the turning-point of 1877 began here in the San Gabriels foothills, with Jeanne Carr's matchmaking. And with Muir's long walk up Eaton Canyon.

Arcadian poetry gets its strength from a longing for nature, and it does not leave out the sex-nature of its humans—in fact, it celebrates it. Something Muir never did. But I suspect it was beginning to be on his mind as he walked Eaton Canyon. Muir employed Arcadian pastoral for this particular piece and none other, that I can find; and it seems to be a sort of back-door admission of the unacknowledged imperatives of biology and humanity. As I've insisted right along, our bodies and their cravings are always the nearest wilderness. Arcadian poetry shows the wild torrent of sex not yet fully confined in society's channels. In its amusing way, it troubles us.

That was something else I thought about as I hiked. More than two decades ago, exactly one hundred years after Muir's walk, totally unaware of the great man's footsteps, I had made my own troubled way here. That was 1977. I had dragooned five friends, laughing and complaining, into my Volkswagen van and driven up to Eaton Canyon for a mildly raucous hike in the pleasant dusk of that blessed climate. I barged into their group home (an idealistic enterprise in communal living, Arcadian enough in its way), announced that everyone must drop what they were doing and follow me, and carried out several of the smaller ones over my shoulder. I had a pair of six-packs and an ardent, confused heart. These dear friends were used to me and went along for what turned out to be a blissful walk.

An exact century after Muir's walk. The symmetry interests me, the coincidental roundness of the numbers. I was twenty-seven, living for a short time back in my family's home in LA, waiting for an academic committee to finish with my doctoral dissertation. I was semi-closeted, I was unhappy, I was vaguely in love with one of the friends—he was the married one and it didn't seem to bother him. All together in moonlight we walked, and for a while I felt soothed. We sipped beers and tried not to stumble on the river-rocks along the sandy floodway, talking and joking while Eaton Creek went on mumbling somewhere off to our left in the redolent dark. Now, as I work on my Muir chapters, I have returned to Eaton Canyon a man of almost double those years. My aches are over; I've made a good life, found love and done good work and made enough money to be okay, for now. And I've come to think about how these things mix up together: the longing for paradise, the secret impulses of sex and needing, the contradictory yearnings for purity, security, freedom. I think about what is wild and what is bound.

My Arcadia—my way of splitting the difference, of finding balance—has been to live in the fine large town of Portland, with rivers and forests and snow-capped volcanoes ready to hand. I gave up my fantasy of disembodied wandering in the mountains, of permanent life where there is no means of living. Indeed, I gave it up just about the time I began to accept the ordinariness of lust and hunger and the need for companionship. Just what Muir never accepted.

I can't talk about it without multiplying opposites. Irony is here. Things flip, transform willy-nilly. Muir intended nothing but sincerity, and he was one of the greatest men of his generation—but he was caught on ironies he never had the wit to acknowledge.

The irony of Arcadia is that you think you're going to get it right, split the difference between paradoxical demands, reconcile or balance the opposites of spirit and flesh, wild and civilized, free and committed. It's a utopia located in history. Itself a paradox! Yet a powerful one, since people keep trying to achieve it. It's a human failing, to try and get it right. Why shouldn't we try, and fail, and try again. The human condition.

But the irony of Eden is that you think you're going to get it perfect. That removes it from history and sets up not just paradox but impossibility—that is, romantic yearning. That's powerful too. But I'm not convinced it's a constructive power. I think I'm afraid of a desire that, in its very nature, is insatiable. It reminds me of consumerism. It seems like a madness, a refusal to cherish the actual conditions of life, with their limits and partial rewards. Some kind of demand for more than what the planet provides. As if our lives were not miracle enough; as if all the cosmos around us were insufficient, and we must long for impossibilities. Wendell Berry sees it too, this romantic nature-longing, as a turn *away* from the world—"at times ... rather a poetic way of wishing to be a spirit." A spirit free of the bread-line, free of towns, people, free of everything but rock and ice and altitude.

Some of John Muir's biographers think Louie was the perfect wife for him, that she eventually learned to accommodate his yearning for the wild, sending him off when he needed it. Maybe so. But the accommodation took a seven-year penance in Arcadian Purgatory before it could be found. When Muir finally emerged, it was to write the two great appeals to America on behalf of Yosemite that culminated in federal protection for that heart's home, that pure wilderness he could never quite live in.

Muir's yearning for a pure and literal Eden was, it seems to me, functionally connected to his Puritan distaste for the impure entanglements of the body, sex and hunger and the humble indignities and pleasures of living together. Each is the other's shadow, the pure and the impure locked onto each other, orbiting ceaselessly. Sex and hunger could have been intimate wildernesses for Muir, portable, rejuvenating even in town, even on the Martinez ranch. But they weren't.

To the end, Muir insisted on an Eden Wilderness. Being driven to settle for Arcadia did nothing to change his mind. He cast his lot with purity, with paradise. That stubbornness is probably part of his greatness—a fortitude beyond most mortals that carried him inexhaustible over ranges, fearless into deadly glacial mazes, rejoicing into the heart of storms. But he could not explore his own heart, or ours. And we are left with conundrums: how then should we live?

When I arrived on my hot morning walk, the Falls of Eaton Canyon had no lads or lasses in pastoral dalliance, though some of their trash remained. At the foot of the dell stood a sign: *Life, Liberty, and the Pursuit of Happiness are Right Here ... Please Help Protect It.*

Whatever Americans are, the question revolves around this—here framed in sacred national language, bad grammar, and litter. How shall we use, preserve, cherish, and belong to the wild/tame nature we find ourselves in, and in ourselves? Muir couldn't answer it. I wonder if we ever will.

Palimpsest:
Getty

I'm standing on one of the many terraces of the Getty Museum, the summer of working on these chapters. It is on a hilltop of the Santa Monica range, overlooking the Valley on one side, the coast on the other. A few days ago, on the inland side of town, I revisited my old Eaton Canyon trail—mine and Muir's and whoever else's that ever walked upstream there, into the mountains. But even down here in the midst of Los Angeles, the same chaparral scents drift and release and remind.

It's late twilight. Cars on the freeway below have switched on their lights, red going, white coming. Distance and a little sea air give the illuminated lines of traffic a tranquil, dreamy quality. No roar, no cursing. No rush. Just people on their ways, toiling patiently over the Sepulveda Pass, coastside to valley, valleyside to coast.

Under their tires is concrete; under that the well-prepared roadbed, following the old road, pretty much; which, pretty much, was a paved version of the dirt road that preceded Fords and Chryslers and Toyotas. That road—how did it get laid just there? Anyone who's ever hiked over a pass knows the answer to that. There's an obvious way to go, and everyone goes that way. It's a deer-track first. Then a footpath. Then a horse-track. Later, maybe, a freeway.

People have made this journey for a long, long time.

If you were hot and inland, once, and you got a hankering for mussels and a cool marine-cloudy day, you gathered up some family or friends and you went over the pass. Later, maybe you retraced your steps, thinking now of salmon in that inland river that came down from the hills, thinking of how to avoid the grizzlies that might come down also, looking for the same thing.

People have come over this pass for ten thousand years or more. The famous Tar Pits museum gives us a glimpse of it (I could point out the building, despite the oncoming darkness and mist) — the huge wolves and gigantic cats, "dire" and "sabre-toothed," the towering mammoth-elephants, that give the past its weird glamor.

They all came this way, every one. It was their track before it was the deer's, probably. And before them, what rough beasts'?

We follow each other, our footsteps like notes of a million-voiced chorus, written over the landscape in a time signature past imagining.

Nevertheless, I imagine it. I like this feeling. So many of us, coming this same way. Our industrial lives do not change it that much.

This paradise has been found exactly that many times—each comer and each goer, standing on the crest of the friendly and serviceable pass, has looked over into a land of imagining and intention, and then gone there. It was nice or not-nice, life-giving or deadly. That's the planet we live on. Each fresh step releases into new possibility that is not cancelled by the previous passers there: no: in a real way, it is possibility they have prepared.

And more: sanctified.

I'm not sure what sanctified means, exactly. But it seems to be something about the connection that is far, far realer than any of my imagined independence. Biologically, this connection is absolute. And when it spreads out over the land this way, I hear the deep note of recognition. Memory of our own passing, so powerful that I seem to be remembering myself, as if I were already gone. And someone else were here in my place, this very place, seeing the same different thing under a same, different, ancient sky.

The Method of Palimpsest: Eternal Return

Everyone has a place, I suppose, to return to in mind. Some glimpse or garden where the wide world fits itself and makes room for calm and for beauty. A place like this, remembered and treasured, is a crucial part of what we mean by "nature." And it is composed, when you examine it, of layers of human and more-than-human meaning, layers natural, cultural, and personal. I like that effect, that palimpsest. In fact, I'm convinced that not just the layers, but the *layering itself*, is a profoundly natural process.

My place of return and renewal is a particular mountain valley, Nine Lake Basin. It has given me stories I'll come back to, but first I want to approach it from a less personal direction. One more encounter with John Muir.

It was some miles north from my little valley in the Sierra Nevadas that Muir found his own place. I read in his journal his exclamations of discovery: "How fine Nature's methods! How deeply with beauty is beauty overlaid!" These words were written during that famed "First Summer in the Sierras," 1869. He was learning, it seems, to see past surfaces; or rather, to see surfaces as layered with traces of many passings, with complexity of past and process. To see, in other words, surface and depth simultaneously. The method of palimpsest.

At first it frustrated him. Sierran beauty spoke to him directly; yet how to read the difficult story coded into valley, forest, and peak? And, once decoded, how to convey it in his own writing? All his life Muir was a diffident writer, doubtful of the power of words or drawings—"for little can they tell to those who have not themselves seen similar wildness, and like a language have learned it."

Two years later, however, Muir had attained a greater fluency in the language of nature's messy manuscript, and a corresponding confidence in his descriptions. Those were the intense years of immersion in the great question of the Sierras: what geological process had carved those spectacular U-shaped valleys, those towering sharps and sheers of granite? Month by month he hiked to the heads of cirques, gazed on and touched and even dozed on polished-granite slabs, and—as we have seen—puzzled out an answer. His method was brilliant, eccentric, a fusion of induction and pure feeling that led him to a conclusion quite at odds with the geological establishment.

Here's how he opens his landmark essay on the subject, "Yosemite Glaciers," with a back-glance at that first summer and—what interests me most—a telling reliance on the idea of the blotched, overwritten pages of nature:

> *Two years ago, when picking flowers in the mountains back of Yosemite Valley, I found a book. It was blotted and storm-beaten; all of its outer pages were mealy and crumbly, the paper seeming to dissolve like the snow beneath which it had been buried; but many of the inner pages were well preserved. … In just this condition is the great open book of Yosemite glaciers to-day; its granite pages have been torn and blurred by the same storms that wasted the castaway book. The grand central chapters of the Hoffman, and Tenaya, and Nevada glaciers are stained and corroded by the frosts and rains, yet, nevertheless, they contain scarce one unreadable page; but the outer chapters … are all dimmed and eaten away on the bottom …*

Written, erased, rewritten: despite its complexity, the natural palimpsest was becoming legible to him. In correspondence from those years, Muir returns to the manuscript metaphor over and over: "sheets of glacial writing" on God's "written rocks"—indeed "the footprints of God" themselves—inscribed and worn faint by the years. The truth of the mountains was not simple; it required an active, imaginative reader. That reader was Muir. This principle he applied to nature as whole from then on: that any single piece of it must be related to a whole that was not necessarily easily perceived— that might be layered, erased, revised, complex—but that when read, would make sense and, indeed, beauty.

As we have observed before, however, Muir could not bring himself to include humans in this vision of the beautiful layered complexity of the world. People did not add to the whole but rather detracted, as if their footsteps could not go where God's had gone. That was a sad limitation: an Eden-exile which, had he thought about it, must have made his own passage poisonous too.

So it is not surprising that Muir always wished to find a "pathless way," as one of his best interpreters has put it: or at a minimum, that "least-trodden path" he had set out to find, so long ago, on his Thousand-Mile Walk. As if, had someone else walked there, it would no longer have its Eden-power to save him. There are lessons here, messages inscribed in this predicament that Muir could never perceive. As I observed some chapters ago, the twenty-nine-year-old Muir walked on well-worn roads, paths, and even railroad-grades most of the way: *and yet found a kind of salvation*, in the breakthroughs at Savannah and Cedar Keys.

Muir returned to the south some thirty-one years later to reprise parts of that original thousand-mile journey. By the summer of 1898, Muir's successes in writing about the Sierras had turned him into a public figure, and when he retraced his southern journey he came not alone but accompanied by longtime friends and travel-mates Charles Singer and William Canby. And rather than walking by day and lying out under the stars, this time the traveler rode in motorcars, even caught an electric railway to the top of one Tennessee peak, and enjoyed soft beds and companionship. This mellower, older Muir might have reflected on what such a return meant, what the truth of his own doubled footsteps might be, doubled again with friendship. There is something added, isn't there? Other layers of meaning; other richness. But it was hardly in him to notice these dimensions. They were layers of the manuscript he would never read.

Near the end of this trip, in the Appalachian heights of North Carolina or perhaps north Georgia, he opened a book Singer had given him. It was William Bartram's *Travels*, and Muir soon discovered another layering of this tale: that Bartram too had come along that very route. "A kind of triple-layered effect," comments Frederick Turner: Muir treading his own younger footsteps, and beneath them, Bartram's.

Such circuitry. Such traveling before and after each other. It reminds me of that parallel but invisible layering that happens upon our thought-trails, circles of borrowing and return and reuse. Henry

Thoreau, for instance, absorbing as much as he could of the Hindu scriptures, striking little sparks of Veda and Bhagavad-Ghita into *Walden* … which would travel back to India a century later, with "Civil Disobedience," to kindle Mahatma Ghandi … whose work then would circle back to America a generation later to inspire Martin Luther King. In the thought world as in the natural: what is taken is not diminished but enlarged, transformed, and sent on around the circuit.

Or that example nearer to hand that we have already seen—how the words of Bartram's *Travels*, almost unheard in America, would make their way to England, stir the imaginations of Coleridge and Wordsworth, and then return to America via their poetry, to be read and memorized by Muir and the rest of America. And then the moment of discovery, Muir's eye direct to Bartram's page, mind to mind, thought intimate with thought. Bartram's footsteps. That blurred, erased, rewritten manuscript; that human story, that natural story.

I've been there too, Reader, for what it's worth (and that worth is just human, nothing grand); footsteps from my wandering twenties are there in north Georgia right now, among the oaks and dogwoods. I went there for relief from my graduate studies; I had made few friends in Atlanta and I missed the Sierras. I had no inkling of Muirs or Bartrams; I had little sense that the solitary nature-ramble, pensive or melancholic, was a pattern well-grooved in our cultural mind. I thought I was making it up.

Now I see better. We travel these paths together.

It is a cherished melodrama of the individualist West, to imagine the pathless way. So lonely are we, such brave trudgers! "I long for the mantle of the great wanderers," the poet Galway Kinnell says, in words that I loved, but have reservations about now; those

> *great wanderers, who lighted*
> *their steps by the lamp*
> *of pure hunger and pure thirst*
> *and whichever way they lurched was the way.*

Antonio Machado the Spanish poet has it too: "Traveller, there is no path. You make your path as you travel." And of course, there's a truth there. But Robert Frost, a little wiser, lampooned this road as "less travelled" only in the eyes of nostalgia, setting it up as a self-praising sentimentality, a tempting half-truth. Because, alone or not, it's equally true that we go down well-trodden ways, in the mind and elsewhere. We are lonely travellers on a crowded path, always returning to places that are new and old at the same time.

Mircea Eliade has famously called it "the eternal return."

I've been saying that Eden, in the West's literalized formulation, is where you get kicked out of. That's the lonely journey, Reader. *But when restored to its mythic dimension, Eden is where we come back to.* Over and over. We have romanticized the solitary wanderer's "pure hunger," but purity has nothing to do with it: we're not virgins, the planet is old as hell, and life itself is a fertile old whore who looks like a fresh peach each morning. Our sorrows, poignantly unique though they seem to us, are "such as are common to man." And so are our solutions, whichever way we turn.

The palimpsest-layering of our living footsteps is a fine way to recognize how the Eden myth can restore the world for us: that we need to walk Eden, tell and re-tell it, act and re-enact it. And each time, this strange kind of eternity breaks into our world. The depth of the forest; the depth of our story; the intermingling lives all around us; the coiled and layered codes within us. The present is a strange surface cloudy-clear with depths. What you feel there: that is Eden.

The palimpsest of myth asks for this double vision, a figurative reading of the world, surface and depth, recognizing that every time and place (and story) are both themselves and what they re-present to us. Myth keeps alive for us a "double structure, altogether historical and ahistorical," a many-folded time to live in. This doubling and reflecting is itself wildness; this is how a myth released from literalization re-presents the larger wildness for us. Reader, that's the Eden we find when we return to the forest, or walk down a familiar or unknown path, or calm ourselves in a moment of mindfulness. The Eden that renews the world.

◎

Carl Jung, in *Modern Man in Search of a Soul,* asserts that the distress of the modern age is rooted in the loss of effective religious belief. Without a "ritual or spiritual" external form "by which all the yearnings and hopes of the soul are adequately expressed," he says, we are thrown back upon ourselves and tempted to fetishize our own psyches. Jung speaks, however, in terms of belief; I would redirect the insight, for the world-shaping of myth operates on a different level from belief. Of course we cannot, in a historical or literal way, believe in Eden. And "to be known, myth has to be told," says Lévi-Strauss. Myth requires a ritual action, not a credo. A creed—a statement of belief—is a rationalist proposition that does not speak in the same world as myth.We recall that Lévi-Strauss described the unconcern for detail that typifies a traditional use of myth: the readiness to accept contrary versions without feeling that the conflict in any way compromises the myths. They're stories, not propositions! The incongruities, "arbitrariness," versions and revisions—all point to something deeper than doctrinal or literal belief. Not knowing but telling. Enactment. Participation.

So perhaps it is not loss of belief but more precisely the loss of *effective myth* that has stranded us. Believing (or disbelieving) takes the poor story off in the wrong direction, leaving us with myth literalized, no longer part of a lived enactment—myth "reduced to words and gestures deprived of life, fossilized, externalised and therefore no longer of any use to the deeper life of the psyche," in Eliade's powerful words. When our central myths—above all our origin myth of Eden—become ineffective for us, we find ourselves in a time-trap: mere duration, flat, linear, and "desacralized"—time leading straight to death. That kind of death is an end with no relation to a beginning, because the circular magic of myth has been forgotten.

This predicament has been called "amythia." That's a good name for a way of living chained to the clock-time of science and history, stuck with choices of literal belief or literal disbelief, aware of our "historicity," as Eliade says, and confronted with death. Within the either-ors of polarized thinking, we find no way to join opposites into a satisfying whole. Death and life, though obviously twins, come to us as enemies; and we fare no better with the other familiar antinomies that divide us—self/society, human/natural, and the rest.

Yet many observers conclude, with Eliade, that myth survives "in more or less degraded forms." It doesn't go away: "It seems that myth itself ... never quite disappears from the present world of the psyche; it only changes its aspect and disguises its operations." What had once been a culturally vital and life-giving myth may live on behind the scenes or beneath the surface, perhaps "repressed" into forms of escapism and distraction, as what Paul Ricoeur calls "broken" myth. Surely this is what we see around us, as our culture struggles vainly over how to exist in the natural world: we find infantilized fantasies side-by-side with naked selfishness, fairy-tale sentimentalizations next to clear-cut brutalities. Between these extremes there seems to be no language available with which to frame a satisfying sense of emplacement in the living process. Only the sense of loss left us by the fragments of our myth.

Could a better sense of the Eden myth help?

The scholar of myth and religion Kees W. Bolle writes that in myth opposites are reconciled and bad acts lead paradoxically to good results. There's a story logic (which novelists know well) in which a linearity of cause and effect simply will not do. The plots that please us most deeply take us through twists, in fact through dreamlike ups and downs, where the strange little smile of irony turns everything into its opposite.

We can see these qualities of paradox and happy irony in the truly mythical form of the Paradise Lost story. Eden is lost by the misdeeds of the First Parents, whose sins plummet them from childish innocence. The woes of everyday historical life ensue, weeds and hard work and pain in childbirth and death. But (in the Christian version) a "new Adam" appears, God's hero-son, who takes humankind ultimately to a new Paradise, better than the first, in which humans participate not as innocents but as adults who have passed through experience. Though we have tasted knowledge of good and evil, we are welcomed back. Our last state is higher than our first: and this, in the medieval church, was celebrated as one of the core mysteries of the faith: "*O felix culpa*" they sang; O happy fault, O fortunate fall. So did the snake really do evil? Or did he do us a favor after all?

In myth opposites unite. Good and evil are dealt with but their mystery only deepens; mystery is never resolved into easy formulas or pat answers—or creeds. And the fate which governs things is kept mysterious too. An ebullient comicalness shines even through the darkest hours; things keep turning up that could not have been predicted. In the myth-world, cause and effect emanate from laws and graces Newton never imagined.

But we should also note that we have not been getting the full Eden story, but an oddly reduced form of it, in fact a form drained of almost everything that makes a myth work: Mystery. Repetition. Enactment. Awe. Even strangeness: our literalized version lacks, that is, a sense of the *weirdness* of myth. Bolle calls it myth's *humor*—the incongruities and even childishness that embarrassed previous generations of myth scholars. An apple and a snake, for heaven's sake! Today we are a little closer to being able to embrace the oddness of myth; Bolle intriguingly points out that such strangeness is important precisely to keep the myth separate, to locate it outside our day-to-day world, in its own world where it remains evergreen, reliable, and undiminished. Eliade refers to this other world as *in illo tempore* (literally "in that time"). In English that would be "once upon a time," the storyteller's announcement of a visit to a different world.

Our culturally transmitted Paradise Lost has been demythologized and reduced to fragments. It persists as an unconscious way of ordering our place in the world. But in losing its full function as myth, it has locked us into a very dire story indeed. Stripped of the mythic dimension of renewal, our Lost Eden leaves us in a world always threatening psychological and spiritual emptiness. In this diminished cosmos, good is locked out from bad, and bad only leads to worse.

Is there any way to reimagine Eden that will preserve its sacredness, its emotional and imaginative vitality, yet avoid the sinister side effects of life in a fallen world, that (outside of park boundaries) gets more polluted and debased every day?

Ashworth, Cronon, Pollan, and other revisionist environmentalists have placed us in a serious dilemma. They have critiqued Eden, dismantled it, deconstructed the walls that kept it safe (and us separate). Finding them on my path, I have joined them gleefully.

But it is worth asking: what happens to us, if we give up Eden?

We've seen Eden's downside—what Ashworth calls "The Left Hand of Eden." But can we really afford to give it up? Do we erase the park boundaries?

Of course we do. But not literally, silly!

Candace Slater's fine essay about Western misimaginings of the Amazon focuses the problem for us nicely. Slater worries: "Eden may be so entrenched in Western ways of thinking about nature that it is impossible wholly to elude it." She wishes we could eradicate Eden, because in its literalized form it has so blinded us and poisoned our relation to real nature.

But it seems to me that Eden is not simply to be resisted. Resisting a sin or an impulse is notoriously futile, is it not? All that energy of opposition, locking the resister into the spinning polarity. Wise teachers always tell us, don't waste your time. Let the birds fly over your head. Slater's concern is valid but resisting Eden is needless.

What we need is a Real Eden: one that is myth, not some literalized historical catastrophe. An Eden we have been entering and leaving virtually forever, one that is thick with our own footsteps, overlaid and undergirt with paw-, claw-, and root-marks of uncountable others.

Here is where I have been stuck, trying to follow Ashworth out of Eden. I get the sense that he hardly trusts his own tentative prescription, brave though it is—and neither do we: "Protect nothing; venerate everything." Log everywhere, he says—but never so that it looks logged. Well, at least he's consistent. But *everywhere*? Do we really have to? Logical consistency exacts a high price here.

Too high.

I have tried expanding our thought world beyond literalized wilderness, via the concept of wildness. Wildness is everywhere; it's in everything, an immanence of nature we cannot separate ourselves from. We need to be in daily communion with it.

But we also need sacred spaces to revisit, places that re-mind and re-present this domain to us. Most of us can't keep its flame fanned indefinitely without an intense example, a living symbol, to renew it. We need parks, preserves, and designated wildernesses not only for themselves, but also for what they represent.

A sacred space is a metaphor: it says Eden, but is not Eden. If it burns or gets bulldozed, Eden is not threatened. Though we are rightly distressed when an Eden is felled, the right response is to rebuild the temple, consecrate it, and get right back into the business of metaphoring, of playing both sides of the street. Of course, that game (like any game) requires making lots of decisions—where to use, where to rest, where to make sacred. Everywhere is not church (we don't want Christmas every day) so outside the symbolic park-Edens, we will probably need to follow Ashworth's advice after all: finding the right forests, doing what must be done. Enlisting that army of environmentalists with chainsaws, but leaving the place intact.

Chainsawed but intact? That paradox will take some powerful imagining. A comical, tragical, dirty-handed delicacy.

We are now in a position to pick up the observation we saw in an earlier chapter, from Bolle: that what a culture makes sacred and sets apart is a crucial element in its identity, that cannot be lightly disposed of. Parks, boundaries, set-asides, "wildernesses" so-called, are ways of maintaining important distinctions: that there is another world besides the obvious, surface, day-to-day, and human-centered; that it is holy and life-giving; and that we need to revisit it periodically. It is true that our sadly literalized minds have made hash of this reality; yet it is too important to let go of.

Gregory Bateson is quite forceful about our need for such differences. "Difference" is the very stuff of thinking. Our senses can only pick up difference (hot/not hot, bright/not bright); the information dispatched into the inner system is by definition "news of difference." And concepts like sacred and secular may be forms of logical typing, and thus essential to the recursive circuitry that actually constitutes a mental system. It may be, says Bateson, that "to hold something sacred" is a way to preserve a crucial distinction. Crucial to thought; crucial to holding our place in the ecosystem.

Experiencing sacred wilderness reminds us that in living systems entities cross boundaries regularly—picking up vital energy as they do so. Symbols, metaphors, and living beings have this in common: transformation, one thing morphing into another. The biosphere is sacred because, in its complexity of trading, it creates an infinity of meanings, a million-leaved book, sayings and re-sayings too deep to exhaust. Deaths and lives, feedings-upon and birthings-from, beautiful adaptations: they are all transformations, one thing always on its way to becoming something else. This is limitless, worthy of veneration, sacred: the third infinity of complexity.

What we want is transformation of this kind, so that in leaving the sacred space, we carry its energy with us for the transformation of the space outside: the rekindling of the everywhere-wildness that sometimes is so smudged and buried we lose heart trying to find it. If we are transformed in entering the metaphorical Eden, we are equally transformed in passing out of it. That snap of difference: that's news, says Bateson. That's the stuff of thinking; the energy of the living world itself. Seeing differences, and carrying revitalized energy, we reenter the everyday world and find a sacred wildness hidden in every molecule of it.

When Black Elk, in his last years, retold the vision he had received as a child on his sacred peak in the Dakotas, he added an aside that has rung in my heart for many years. Harney Peak was the holy center of the Lakota ritual world, he said, *"but anywhere is the center of the world."* That two-mindedness is what I'm after. We will all continue to choose our sacred spaces. But at the same time we must be realizing that they are symbols, that they speak for everywhere. Otherwise, we are fundamentalists, we are idolators, we are dullard literalists not getting the joke, the flirt, the joy.

In the beginning chapters of this book I described the journey I took, at sixteen, into a Sierran valley called Nine Lake Basin. Beneath a semicircle of forbidding crags and peaks, among stands of mountain hemlock and open alpine grasslands, a string of pretty lakes links in downward steps like rosary beads on a ribbon of stream, shining tarns left by the weight of ancient ice that flowed here in its own time, grinding out these way stations in the granite. All through the writing of this book, I have been returning there in my mind, because it is a place of significance to me, a kind of Eden where good things began and were renewed. Though far away in time now, that first journey started me on my real life, initiated a way for me to love the actual world when I could not find any other way. The near end of that journey is the discovery of wildness everywhere.

I have returned there physically on two other occasions, each of them so weighty in the shaping of my life that I cannot help feeling a kind of wonder about it, an almost religious awe at the coincidences and forces that took me there and changed me, three times over.

I returned to Nine Lake Basin some ten years after the first visit. By then I was working as a guide and teacher for a "wilderness-experience" outfit, a shoestring nonprofit full of high ideals but short on resources. The dozen of us on staff had just spent weeks getting our basecamp cookhouse and tent platforms ready for the summer's busloads of teens-in-trouble. When they arrived, we would run and cajole and threaten them through a one-week ordeal of training followed by two weeks of backcountry mountain-climbing. But what mountain? By the eve of the arrival of the first group, we still had not checked out a specific peak for that year's expeditions. Our leader, a charismatic guy barely thirty who seemed quite adult to us, came to me in the evening. "Go find us one," he said. "Get back as quick as you can. Take a look at Milestone Mountain." I had seen it from other summits on the Great Western Divide of the southern Sierra. I had an idea how to get there. The leader commissioned two of us to go, me and Mike, a friendly guy I had known in college with a splendid runner's endurance but limited mountain experience.

We left the next morning, telling our friends to come pick us up in four days. This was our logic: four days would get us back during the training phase of the expedition; we could then prep everyone, and take off for the wilderness on schedule. But our pals looked at us doubtfully. "It's too far. You can't do it." We smiled. Mike was as unrealistic and ego-driven as I was. All we had to do was cover eighty miles, cross two or three ridge-systems of eleven thousand to twelve thousand feet elevation (depending on how we chose our route) and climb Milestone on the way (elevation 13,641).

We were strange skinny fellows, we could travel far and fast. In damn-good time we climbed the thirteen miles up to Moose Lake, crossed the eerie, elevated rock-scape of the Chagoopa Plateau, clambered down into a river valley, bushwhacked a cross-country shortcut over Whaleback Mountain, trekked the Colby Pass and made our second bivouac. On the morning of the third day we climbed Milestone, and at noon, a little giddy, we strategized how to make our rendezvous. With the help of a climber's guide and some maps, we decided to skip the obvious trails that were too slow and roundabout. We would simply go *here* to *there*. "If we go down that way and then cross over these ridges, we could drop down into Nine Lake Basin from the backside." It looked dubious but, on a map, nothing is really hard, right? "Then we could pick up the trail in the morning and boogie the last twenty-five miles out." It meant losing thousands of feet of hard-won elevation, following an insignificant stream to an unnamed side-canyon above tree-line, ascending it, then cutting straight up-mountain to find a so-called "climbers' pass" somewhere over twelve thousand feet, and (assuming it was findable, and passable) getting down out of that headwaters cirque and walking into the Basin—all before dark.

We did not really find that climbers' pass, I don't think. Nor did we reckon with the fatigue of carrying packs at elevation across angling snowfields and sheering rockfalls. Neither of us had ever seen acres of old snow on steep slopes melted into "suncups" that were ice-edged depressions as deep as our waists, to be plunged into and climbed out of, over and over. After many exhausting hours we did find some kind of pass, a sandy windblown thing, a flaw in the granite where we stood drenched with sweat and chilled with anxiety—tears in my eyes, truth be told—as the trailing rim of the sun disappeared over Nine Lake Basin. It was a beautiful, terrifying sight: I can see it still, ineffable pale lake-shinings far down in the darkening landscape beneath the pearly blue sky and fire-orange horizon. Overhead the thin air was already passing to blue-black violet. A moment so full of fear, beauty, stupidity, courage, realness … What more could a person ask for?

Sometime much later that night, stunned at the down-climbing we had just managed somehow, roped and then unroped and stumbling, we found my old haunts in the Basin and immediately bedded ourselves down, solitary in our fatigue, mutely joined in the coy manner of men. Despite our fatigue we rose at the first hint of light and, manic and proud, simply hiked as fast as we could force ourselves, sometimes breaking into a sad little sore-footed jog trot, backpacks nearly empty and jouncing over our gaunt frames. I fell over a root. Mike laughed. We traded the lead, giving it to whoever seemed stronger at the moment.

Reader, there was no good reason for this. We could have taken an extra day, shown up late, been welcomed. But it was important to me, important to Mike. Maybe you were twenty-five once, and needed to do something hard, something gratuitous, something extraordinary.

We arrived at the pick-up point at 12:30, a half hour past the assigned time. We counted that good enough. As it turned out, we had not missed our ride—because there was no ride. Everyone in camp had forgotten about us, or perhaps concluded we'd never make it that day. Mike shrugged. "No one would believe what we just did, anyway." Somehow, to be ignored, to have our Big Adventure pass unnoticed, was the perfect ending. It pleased us.

This story is a brag, isn't it? A climbing story, with just a little irony to forgive me by. I don't tell it often, but it is just the right sort of thing to remember. In fact, I think it remembers itself, somewhere in my mind, sending off its warmth unbidden.

Nine Lake Basin is a place of importance, an intersection where my life has crossed its own path repeatedly. But its importance is nothing intrinsic—not the preening difficulty of the second visit, nor the goofy adolescent cluelessness of the first; rather, it is the developing magic of the overlays I want to get at: the magic of intensity and repetition.

The third visit occurred a few eventful years later. I was thirty-three, that Jesus age—ready, I suppose, for something to happen, finished with my degree and my first teaching job, back in Los Angeles again after a decade's absence. And I had, for the first time, a real boyfriend. So I brought him to Nine Lake Basin. We approached from yet another direction, coming from the south this time over the volcano-cinder passes of Mineral King, which can be trudgy and tiring. Though we had been spending time together, with an implication of something more, it was not until Nine Lake Basin, those high passes and long days, that I suddenly felt an unexpected certainty about him. My companion was a city boy, but he turned out to be strong, enduring, tough. Reliable and cheerful. My native reserve, a defensive untouchability I thought would never leave me, melted. I felt I was entering a new land, an unexplored region. And

I was. We stayed together for nine years after that unforgettable week, years that healed many griefs, years I never think of without gratitude.

Some kind of deeper logic seemed to be happening there, a palimpsest layering my life with the life of the place. I told the beloved friend about my other comings to the Basin; he looked around and understood something, perhaps. He became part of them and I cannot separate myself from a spooky sensibility about it all, as if some power were there writing my story into the landscape as it wrote itself into me. Jung speaks of "a dawning significance in things" which people often sense when let loose in the world of nature—a symbolic weight in coincidences and events which the rational mind dismisses. I feel that here. I cannot speak of its objective reality. But for me, this basin held a power that amplified with each renewal. It's the center of my world, perhaps.

But anyplace can be the center of the world.

When you learn that Eden can be anyplace, it is not long until you realize that Eden can exist anytime as well. After the storytelling, the memory of sacred places far away: the recognition of sacredness, eternity, in each moment.

For there is a time near to hand which the devil cannot find, says William Blake (no better guide!). That moment is all moments layered together, a stack as tall as time, as exact and unique as right now. That's the final depth of the palimpsest, taking time itself back to Eden. Blake describes it this way:

> *There is a Moment in each Day that Satan cannot find*
> *Nor can his Watch Fiends find it, but the Industrious find*
> *This Moment & it multiply. & when it once is found*
> *It renovates every Moment of the day if rightly placed.*

The great crazed poet, all but lost in the power of his imagination, finds two messengers here, ordinary objects on an undistinguished morning: thyme which "appears only a small root creeping in grass"; and a common lark sporting by the garden gate. Yet they bring news from Eden. They bring redemption, transformation.

In this Moment Ololon descended to Los & Enitharmon
Unseen beyond the Mundane Shell Southward in Miltons track
Just in this Moment when the morning odours rise abroad
and first from the Wild Thyme
…
Just at the place to where the Lark mounts, is a Crystal Gate…
When on the highest lift of his light pinions he arrives
At that bright Gate, another Lark meets him & back to back
They touch their pinions tip tip: and each descend
To their respective Earths & there all night consult with Angels
Of Providence & with the Eyes of God all night in slumbers
Inspired: & at the dawn of day send out another Lark
Into another Heaven to carry news upon his wings
Thus are the Messengers dispatchd till they reach the Earth
*   again*
In the East Gate of Golgonooza, & the Twenty-eighth bright
Lark …

O such strange poetry. But is it strange enough? Is it as strange as your life, Reader? Can you help me say where this Eden is, that we all lose and find, times beyond counting?

I can say where this Eden *isn't.* For Blake's grand poem *Milton* gave this counter-warning in the very year in which Lewis and Clark prepared to explore their "never trodden" paradises of the west (in Capt. Lewis's words): 1804. Paradise Lost? Don't you believe it! For Blake insists that the Divine Force has "planted his Paradise" not in a literal place to be heroically first-trod, then logged and lost, but in a wild regenerative power at work within us, even within our minds: "if we are but just & true to our own Imaginations, those Worlds of Eternity in which we shall live forever …"

This is the wildness we truly belong to. Though we may need some reminding, wild Eden is never far away, not off in unexplored territory, not far up in the Sierras.

For I feel this: pressing to gain entrance to the mind is blessing. The scent of wild sages or thymes, odors of lovers, of milk-sleepy children, penetrating your brainstem with what earliest original grace. Did you make that brainstem? (God's question to Job, a good one.) No? You found it made within you, and making you: it is a wildness running up your neck deep into your mind, and in your sniff of Eden you find a moment when all your forebears sniff the same, snouts and muzzles wrinkled the same, your dad and mom and their dads and moms wrinkled the same, first in curiosity then in benefaction: there: that strange release into the body, the mind, the planet.

That's Eden, I guess. Nothing cosmic; nor less than cosmic. Eden in practice, a spiritual and planetary discipline. Each breath a re-layering of the palimpsest, a borrowing and a returning. We cannot trash any place on Earth if we recognize them all as wild Edens, all as eternities whose histories we inscribe with blessing or with curse, even as they inscribe us.

We don't have to save it, invent it, make it all up; it's being made up around us, from the pieces and lives that have been here for millennia already. Wildness, patterning not planning, sculpts and jokes us all. It's our job to be good readers, good laughers, good actors (all three).

O that's still too grand for such a writer as me—come down, come down. You know me now, Reader, as far too sincere, busy-minded and restless, somewhat given to the trance of lovely words. Could such an answer as this really work? All I know for sure is that I have been comforted, despite my foolishness. And that I live along, like you, trying to manage my confusions, trying to keep my inconsistencies from turning into hypocrisies. I don't recycle enough. I'm not activist enough. Nevertheless here am I, in the twenty or thirty years of eternity that may still be left me, finding wild Eden and sometimes, unexpectedly close by, having it find me.

Palimpsest:
Bartram in Georgia

Writing far into the night—my own book coming to an end—I read and consider, and I cannot escape the strange backward synchronicity that has linked the two branches of my family, way back there some two and a quarter centuries ago: my mother's ancestor William Bartram, who has blessed me from afar, and my father's forebear, whom I can only imagine. For just about the best early accounts of how the Cherokee lived in their Appalachian hills and river-valleys are to be found in Bartram's *Travels*. Bartram walked two lengthy journeys through their territory in the 1770s, accepting hospitality from them and staying in their houses. He recorded what he saw with a botanist's eye for detail and a Quaker's receptive spirit.

As I read his words, so long after their utterance, I play with the possibilities: that Bartram, rambling along in his curious openhearted way, might actually have met Zirilla's grandfather— my great-something grandfather. What then, I wonder?

Bartram did not always have an easy time of it with these alien people, these natives. It would not do to make him over as one of us (or one of them). He reports, for instance, that the Cherokee were given to nights of debauchery during which, apparently, all rules were off. There they are in the bushes, in the fire circle, running after each other, grappling, laughing. There Bartram is, quill in hand, a smudged outrage leaking into his pages of description. Maybe he looks around in wonder, maybe dismay. Maybe he discovers, with horror, a twinge of lust.

A man of the Enlightenment, he probably didn't know that such Maydays were part of his heritage, too—old England got especially merry once a year, and you can hear that selfsame outrage in long-ago reports by priests about unrepentant Saxon villagers who took libidinous license when spring came to their sodden world.

Well, that was Bartram. I find I love him for his limitations too. The Cherokee could see what he was, and they welcomed him. For that, I love them as well.

I like to imagine them, these two grandfathers, in a quiet clearing. Maybe it's a day or two after the midnight revels, hangovers are past, it's just a nice day and some way these two have come to be sitting in a grove. Early summer surrounds them. It is silent.

I am there with them somehow.

I am their seventh generation.

They cannot know how they will be linked, how their blood will seek and average, and how I will result, I with my defects and advantages, my failures and my little gifts, all the ways I might have done better, all the ways I have done well. Bartram might have liked me to have more success. The old Cherokee, silent there, placid, might have liked me to have been of more service. Their values don't fully match up. One is a loner, a writer, sweet but somehow castaway. For the other it's The People, always them, nothing else but them, how they will go on.

But Bartram must have understood that—how a community works. Quakers had noticed their sense of ease among native peoples; how Indians' village councils felt like Quaker meetings, each person allowed his or her say, with no "heat or jarring" of dispute, and women speaking on a par with men (something unique to Friends, in the European world). Quakers had learned some things from those Indians.

So when they sit together I imagine in Bartram a certain comfortableness. Bartram welcomes the silence, understands it, does not fidget or try to fill it with anything lesser. Sun streams down through the dogwoods, the odd petal drifting downwards. Birdsong weaves through the forest. Bartram's mind is tempted toward naming, categorizing, but he lets it go, he knows the moment is better than that. The Indian sits across from him on his log or stone. They cannot talk, they don't need to. There is a sufficiency in the clearing easy to recognize, easy at least for these men.

I am in that sufficiency, in the mote-swarmed sunlight, the midgy hum, the filter of birdcall—I am in some tiny proleptic way in it. And in their care for each other, unspoken, a minor thing that soon enough gives way—Bartram rising at last to go about his business, or the Indian, nodding courteously to the pale stranger, pausing before walking off into his woods. Theirs is a care too slight to name, too important to do without, a going-on in the world that puts a generous margin around other people, other living things, other possibilities.

A blue jay of that handsome eastern sort, unlike the somber jays I've known in the West, flitters into their clearing as they rise. White bars on its wings, diagonalled with black, set off the color of pure sky. And if a bird knows anything it knows its own handsomeness, announces it to all, so he sings a pure-blue-sky song from a branch above the quiet humans, adds his lusty noises to the rich silence pooled below him. Such a song enters the ears of these men, distilling down into their hearts and—who knows?—coiling what delight, what inspiration into their mysterious inmost selves, that might be read out by distant grandchildren, listening in forests of their own.

Reader, are you there in that silence? There it is, just past the end of this page. That pool of welcoming silence, where all is headed, book, writer, reader, and all. There to disappear, certainly. But also to continue … on what travels, what transformations, who could say?

Notes

Each citation is given in full at its first appearance in each chapter's notes.

Palimpsest: Practice of Presence of the Wild

9: *"I have been breaking silence"*: Thoreau's entry for Feb. 9, 1841, in *The Heart of Thoreau's Journals*, Ed. Odell Shepard (New York: Dover, 1961) 22.

10: *"Language is simply alive"*: Lewis Thomas, *The Lives of a Cell* (New York: Penguin, 1978) 134.

Section I: Be/Longing in Eden

12: *"Don't say to yourself"*: my own paraphrase of *Ecclesiastes* 7:10. The scholarly translation: "Do not say, 'How is it that the former days are better than these?' for it is not out of wisdom that you ask about this." Roland Murphy, *Ecclesiastes*,Word Biblical Commentary Vol. 23a (Dallas: Word Books, 1992) 60.

Sometimes Walking

17: *"grave and steady"*: William Bartram, *Travels of William Bartram* [1791], Ed. Mark Van Doren (New York: Dover, 1928) 381.

17: *"tenacity and poise"*: Luther Standing Bear, *Land of the Spotted Eagle* [1933] (Lincoln, Neb.: Univ. Nebraska, 1978) 35.

18: *"To endure pain"* 39; *"physical hardihood"* 42.

19: *the cheapest clichés and stereotypes*: for a clear view of Indian outrage about this tendency see Vine Deloria, Jr., *Custer Died for your Sins: An Indian Manifesto* [1969] (Norman, Okla.: Univ. Oklahoma, 1988) 3.

20: *adaptive and resourceful*: as Paul Radin remarks in a more general context, *The World of Primitive Man* (New York: Dutton, 1971) 26-36.

20: *mixed hunter-gatherer and agricultural life* and *travellers remarked*: described by Bartram *Travels* 400.

20-21: *"a human experience ... half a million years"*: Radin 69.

21: Elizabeth Marshall Thomas' work on animal culture is discussed in the next chapter: see "The Old Way," *New Yorker*, Oct.15, 1980: 78+. Donald Griffin, described as "the dean of cognitive ethologists" (Colin Beer), sums it up in *Animal Minds* (Chicago: Univ. Chicago, 1992). Many examples are given in John Tyler Bonner, *The Evolution of Culture in Animals* (Princeton, N. J.: Princeton Univ., 1980).

22: *the natural conditions that produced us*: see Paul Shepard, *Nature and Madness* (San Francisco: Sierra Club, 1982); *Coming Home to the Pleistocene* (Washington, D.C.: Island, 1998), and other works.

22: *Walum Olum*: James Mooney, *Historical Sketch of the Cherokee* (Chicago: Aldine, 1975) 7-8.

23: *"Most Native American communities define"*: Jana Sequoya, "How (!) is an Indian? A Contest of Stories," in *New Voices in Native American Literary Criticism*, Ed. Arnolt Krupat (Washington, D.C.: Smithsonian, 1993) 462.

Wilderness

26: The Wilderness Act is available at *www.nps.gov/partner/wact.html.*

27: Wallace Stevens' 1919 poem is "The Anecdote of the Jar."

27: *framed by this dualism*: Discussion of "Cartesian dualism" can be found in nearly every environmentalist book ever written, it seems. Typical example: Bill Devall and George Sessions, *Deep Ecology* (Salt Lake City: Gibbs Smith, 1985) 41, etc. Robert Langbaum gives an excellent general history-of-ideas setup of the dualism we inherit from the nineteenth century: *The Poetry of Experience* (New York: Norton, 1963).

27: *"It is tempting to believe"*: William Cronon, *Changes in the Land: Indians, Colonists, and the Ecology of New England* (New York: Hill and Wang, 1983) 12.

27: *"Scientific findings indicate that virtually every part of the globe ... has been inhabited"*: Arturo Gomez-Pompa and Andres Kaus, "Taming the Wilderness Myth." *BioScience* 42 (1992): 271+, available ProQuest.

28: *"a humanized landscape almost everywhere"*: William M. Denevan, "The Pristine Myth: The Landscape of the Americas in 1492." *Annals of the Assoc. Am. Geographers* 82 (1992): 369; *3.8 million* 379.

28: *Drake's raid* and *Pilgrims*: Alfred W. Crosby, "Metamorphosis of the Americas" in *Seeds of Change*, Eds. Herman J. Viola and Carolyn Margolis (Washington, D.C.: Smithsonian, 1991) 87. See his *The Columbian Exchange: Biological and Cultural Consequences* (Westport, Conn.: Greenwood, 1973).

28: *"A good argument can be made"*: Denevan 369; *"undoubtedly much more 'forest primeval' in 1850"*: E. Rostland qtd. in Denevan 380.

28: *"The removal of Indians to create an 'uninhabited wilderness'"*: Cronon *Changes in the Land* 79.

29: *"We did not think of the great open plains"*: Luther Standing Bear, *Land of the Spotted Eagle* (Lincoln, Neb.: Univ. Nebraska, 1978) 38.

30: Elizabeth Marshall Thomas, "The Old Way." *New Yorker* 15 Oct. 1990: 78+.

31: *a version of nature is always a version of human nature*: Raymond Williams, "Ideas of Nature" in *Problems in Materialism and Culture* (London: NLB, 1980) 70-71.

31: *"untrodden, hidden in the glorious wildness"*: John Muir, *The Mountains of California* [1894] (San Francisco: Sierra Club, 1988) 90.

32: *"specimens," "geological"*: Muir *Mountains* 73; *"squirrels"* 115, 169, 167; *the adult capacities of forethought and probity*: see Muir's repeated attribution of *"heedless,"* animal-like behavior to Indians: 76, 115.

32: *ironic illustration of Yosemite valley*: Gary Nabhan, *Cultures of Habitat* (Washington, D.C.: Counterpoint, 1997) 156.

32-33: *Miwok peoples had been burning the Yosemite valley*: Richard Levy, "Eastern Miwok," in *California* (*Handbook of North American Indians*, Vol. 8) 402; *a common Indian practice from coast to coast*: Cronon *Changes in the Land*, 49-51; *at least three thousand years*: Michael J. Moratto, *California Archaeology* (New York: Academic Press, 1984) 301; *two thousand years... five hundred sites* 309-10.

33: *"Journalist Stephen Powers' 1877 report"*: qtd. in Moratto 285; *mortality rate of perhaps 75 percent* 324; *seven percent ... two-thirds* 573; *Alfred Kroeber...estimated*: Alfred L. Kroeber, *Handbook of the Indians of California* [1925] (New York: Dover, 1976) 444-45.

34: *"How many centuries Indians"*: John Muir, *My First Summer in the Sierras* [1911] (Boston: Houghton Mifflin, 1979) 54-55.

34: *"debased"* Indian woman: Muir *My First Summer* 59; *six trips to Alaska ... an appreciation of the native peoples he met there*: for the hagiographic account of Muir's view of Indians see Richard F. Fleck, *Henry Thoreau and John Muir among the Indians* (Hamden, Conn.: Archon, 1985). But this view is challenged in Susan Kollin, *Nature's State: Imagining Alaska as the Last Frontier* (Chapel Hill, N. C.: Univ. North Carolina, 2001).

Paradise Lost

39: *"where all life seemed to live in harmony"*: Rachel Carson, *Silent Spring* (New York: Fawcett, 1962) 13-15.

40: *"the drama of Paradise"*: Mircea Eliade, *Myth and Reality*, Trans. Willard R. Trask (New York: Harper and Row, 1963) 93.

42: *Abbey sets up his book as an "elegy"*: At the climax of the introduction, he writes "This is not a travel guide but an elegy. A memorial. You're holding a tombstone in your hands." Edward Abbey, *Desert Solitaire* (New York: Ballantine, 1968) xii.

43: *"love of wilderness is ... loyalty to the earth"*: Abbey *Desert Solitaire* 190.

43: *Abbey himself gets off the hook*: Lawrence Buell sees a lot more self-awareness in this chapter than I do: that "Abbey realizes his own self-division," and self-critically "anticipates" his persona's own "ineradicable romanticism." *The Environmental Imagination: Thoreau, Nature Writing, and the Formation of American Culture* (Cambridge, Mass.: Belknap/Harvard, 1995) 72-73.

43: *"social atom"*: the term comes from the great Victorian individualist Herbert Spencer, for instance in *Social Statics* [sic] (London: John Chapman, 1851).

44: *"American Adam"*: the familiar phrase belongs especially to R.W.B. Lewis, *The American Adam: Innocence, Tragedy, and Tradition in the Nineteenth Century* (Chicago: Univ. Chicago, 1955).

44: *"Actually our ignorance"*: Abbey *Desert Solitaire* 179.

45: *No frame of reference beyond the individual is considered*: In later works, Abbey would prove capable of longer-term vistas, for instance in *The Monkey Wrench Gang*, where the destruction of the dam is imagined as the prelude to an eventual natural restoration (New York: Avon, 1975). In *Desert Solitaire*, however—the canonical book—no such perspective is permitted.

45: *"Each time I look up"*: Abbey *Desert Solitaire* 200.

46: *"much as the first Indians"*: Stanwyn G. Shetler, "Three Faces of Eden," in *Seeds of Change: A Quincentennial Celebration*. Eds. Herman J. Viola and Carolyn Margolis (Washington, D.C.: Smithsonian, 1991) 225; *"unnaturalizing of the American wilderness"* 226.

47-48: *"forever transform the First American Eden"*: Shetler 229; *"destroyed, desecrated, privatized"* 242; *"Will the unnaturalizing of America be the undoing of the earth"* 247.

48: *"nostalgia for paradise"*: Mircea Eliade, *Myths, Dreams, and Mysteries*. Trans. Philip Mairet (New York: Harper, 1960) *passim*. Eliade uses the phrase in many works.

49: *"Even as recently as twenty-five years ago"*: Shetler 241.

49: *"All that comes to pass"*: Marcus Aurelius, *Meditations*. Trans. A.S.L.Farquharson (New York: Oxford, 1990) IV: 44.

51: *"unity of all men in behavior and mind"*: Kees W. Bolle, *The Freedom of Man in Myth* (Nashville, Tenn.: Vanderbilt, 1968) xiii; *"in our present day world we lack"* 271.

51: *"not an idle rhapsody"*: Malinowski qtd. in Bolle *Freedom* 50.
51: *"ideas of reality, value, transcendence"*: Mircea Eliade, *Myth and Reality.* Trans. Willard R. Trask (New York: Harper, 1975) 145.
51: Carl Jung, *Modern Man in Search of a Soul.* Trans. W.S. Dell and Cary F. Baynes (New York: Harcourt Brace, 1933).
51: *"timeless pattern"*: Claude Lévi-Strauss, "The Structural Study of Myth" [orig. 1955/rev. 1963] in *The Critical Tradition,* 2nd. ed. Ed. David H. Richter (Boston: Bedford, 1998) 838; *all versions are the myth* 842-44.
52: *These details are absurd*: see Bolle on the humor and grotesqueness of myth: "Myth" in *The Encyclopedia of Religion.* Ed. Mircea Eliade (New York: MacMillan, 1987) 266-67.
52: *"The story of Adam and Eve ... whether they believe in its historicity or not"*: Northrop Frye, *The Anatomy of Criticism* (Princeton, N. J.: Princeton Univ., 1971) 188.
53: "what have societies ... found necessary": Bolle *Freedom* 262-63.

Palimpsest: The Wildness of Failure

56: *"the habit of truth"*: Jacob Bronowski, *Science and Human Values* (New York: Harper and Row, 1965).
58: *"then on the shore"*: John Keats, "When I Have Fears" ll. 12-14.
59: *"never trodden"*: *The Lewis and Clark Expedition: Selections from the Journals Arranged by Topic,* Ed. Gunther Barth (New York: Bedford/St. Martins, 1998) 30; *"least trodden way"*: John Muir, *A Thousand-Mile Walk to the Gulf ,* Ed. William Frederic Badé (San Francisco: Sierra Club, 1991) 1.
59: *"not quite pathless"*: Bartram's description in *Travels of William Bartram* [1791], Ed. Mark Van Doren (New York: Dover, 1955) 292.
59: *"Always coming home"*: the novel by Ursula K. Le Guin, *Always Coming Home* (New York: Harper, 1985).

Ending It All

60: *"The real solution"*: Al Gore, *Earth in the Balance* (Boston: Houghton Mifflin, 1992) 35; *"New Story"*: Thomas Berry, *The Dream of the Earth* (San Francisco: Sierra Club, 1990) 123ff; *"mythical symbols"*: David W. Orr, *Ecological Literacy* (New York: State Univ. New York, 1992) 79.
61: *Apocalypse shows up as the last chapter of the Fall from Eden*: Lawrence Buell comments on "The pastoral logic that undergirds environmental apocalypse" in *The Environmental Imagination* (Cambridge, Mass: Belknap/ Harvard, 1995) 300.
61: *"We must rethink and refeel"*: Lynn White, Jr., "The Historical Roots of our Ecologic Crisis" in *The Everlasting Universe,* Eds. Lorne J. Forstner and John H. Todd (Lexington, Mass.: Heath, 1971) 15; *mythical ... formulation* 17.
61: *"the transformation that is coming"*: Charles A. Reich, *The Greening of America* (New York: Random, 1970) 5; *"organic"* 385, *"a renewed relationship"* 4, *"coming American Revolution"* 3.
61-62: *"The famous 'Club of Rome' report"*: Donella Matthews, et al. *The Limits to Growth,* rev. ed. (New York: New American, 1974) 198; *several books by Fritjof Capra*: *The Turning Point* (New York: Simon and Schuster, 1982); *The Web of Life* (New York: Anchor/Doubleday, 1996): see xviii, 3-5 for new-myth/new-perception calls; *The quintessential statement of green belief*: Bill Devall and George Sessions, *Deep Ecology* (Salt Lake City: Gibbs Smith, 1985); *"a new balance"* 7.

62: Frank Kermode, *The Sense of an Ending* (New York: Oxford, 1967).

63: *environmentalists wink when they use apocalyptic*: see M. Jimmie Killingsworth and Jacqueline S. Palmer, "Millennial Ecology: the Apocalyptic Narrative from *Silent Spring* to *Global Warming*," in *Green Culture: Environmental Rhetoric in Contemporary America*, Eds. Carl G. Herndl and Stuart C. Brown (Madison: Univ. Wisconsin, 1996) 21.

64: *Al Gore's book casts the same idea*: Gore 361-65.

64: *"restoration narrative"*: Carolyn Merchant, "Reinventing Eden: Western Culture as a Recovery Narrative," in *Uncommon Ground*, Ed. William Cronon (New York: Norton, 1996) 132-59.

66: *"This new rupture"*: Bill McKibben, *The End of Nature* (New York: Doubleday, 1989) 58; *"Nature, independent nature"* 209; *"[W]e have ended the thing"* 64, italics McKibben's; *"altering every inch"* 46.

67: *figure-ground relation*: Alan Watts, "The World Is Your Body," in *The Ecological Conscience*, Ed. Robert Disch (Englewood Cliffs, N.J.: Prentice-Hall, 1970) 182-83. This is an excerpt from Watts' *The Book: On the Taboo Against Knowing Who You Are* (New York: Pantheon, 1966).

67: *"It is the simple act of creating new forms"*: McKibben 166.

68: *Faust … the Fall written into modern form*: Though some eco-writers have seen not just industrialism but the change from neolithic hunting-and-gathering to agriculture as the defining fall from grace. See Paul Shepard's many books; and Daniel Quinn's *Ishmael* (New York: Bantam, 1992); *a college biology textbook of the 1930s*: Charles Singer. *A Short History of Biology: A General Introduction to the Study of Living Things* (Oxford: Clarendon, 1931) 389.

69-70: *"choose to remain God's creatures"*: McKibben 214: *"We have built a greenhouse"* 91; *"its ending prevent[s] us from returning"* 205; *"a walk in the woods will be … tainted"* 47-48.

70: *imagines William Bartram … in an "untouched world"*: McKibben 50; *"on the opposite side of the river Savanna"*: William Bartram, *Travels of William Bartram* [1701], Ed. Mark Van Doran (New York: Dover, 1955) 303.

71: *"terminal sin"*: McKibben 216; *"year one of artifice"* 186.

71: *"When I say 'nature'"*: McKibben 8.

72: *"Instead of being a category like God"*: McKibben 210.

73: *"depresses me more deeply than I can say"*: McKibben 214.

73: *"I have heard what the talkers were talking"*: Walt Whitman, "Song of Myself" section 3.

73-74: *"Men esteem truth remote"*: Henry David Thoreau, *Walden* Chapter 2, in *Walden and Civil Disobedience: The Variorum Editions*, Ed. Walter Harding (New York: Pocket, 1967) 72.

74: *In the dangerous element immerse*: Stein's memorable words in Joseph Conrad's *Lord Jim*.

Dealing with Paradise

76: *"Apathy and dogmatism"*: James D. Proctor, "Whose Nature? The Contested Moral Terrain of Ancient Forests," in *Uncommon Ground*, Ed. William Cronon (New York: Norton, 1996) 269-97.

77: *the graphic … used by the Forest Council ten years earlier*: reproduced in Proctor "Whose Nature?" 272.

78: *"a vast virgin forest"*: W.B. Greeley, "The Relation of Geography to Timber Supply," *Economic Geography* 1 (1925): 4-5.

78: *"Overwhelmed by the magnitude"*: Lanie Melamed, "Learning About the Environment—The Truth May Make You Miserable!" *JOPERD Journal of Physical Education, Recreation and Dance* 65 (94): 36+; *"Today Americans remain committed"*: *Unpassionate Environmentalism* qtd. in "The Digest: Science and environment" rev. of Karlyn H. Bowman and Everett Carll Ladd, *Attitudes Toward the Environment, The American Enterprise* July 1995.

78-79: Susan D. Moeller, *Compassion Fatigue: How the Media Sell Disease, Famine, War, and Death* (New York: Routledge, 1998); *"excessive or organic ill"*: Susan Sonntag qtd. in James North, rev. of Susan D. Moeller, *Compassion Fatigue: How the Media Sell Disease, Famine, War and Death, The Nation*, Feb. 8, 1999: 28.

80: *a complex guess or reconstruction*: William Cronon, "Introduction," in Cronon ed. 43.

80: *"The Competitive Enterprise Institute"* and *"Global Climate Information Project,"*: John B. Judis, "Global Warming and the Big Shill," *The American Prospect* Jan/Feb 1999.

81: Jedediah Purdy, "After Apathy," *The American Prospect*, Dec. 6, 1999: 12+; *moral judgements in the environmental field*: Proctor "Whose Nature?" 274.

81: *My fellow Oregonian*: James Proctor has since moved from the University of Oregon to UC Santa Barbara; *"[M]any environmentalists assert"* Proctor "Whose Nature" 289.

82: George Perkins Marsh, *Man and Nature* (originally published 1864).

82: *"You have scolded the lumber-men"*: qtd. in John Perlin, *A Forest Journey* (New York: Norton, 1989) 357-59.

82: *figures from the USDA*: graphed in William S. Alverson, Walter Kuhlmann, and Donald M. Waller, *Wild Forests: Conservation Biology and Public Policy* (Washington, D.C.: Island, 1994) 129. See also E. Thomas Tuchmann et al., *The Northwest Forest Plan* (Washington, D.C.: USDA, 1996) 15.

82: *at prices so far below cost*: "Statement of Michael A. Francis, Director, National Forests Program of the Wilderness Society, Washington, DC." Hearing before the subcommittee on agricultural research, conservation,forestry, and general legislation, June 24, 1993. (Washington, D.C.: US Gov., 1993) 26-27.

83: *"simply leave them be"*: Proctor "Whose Nature?" 284. See below, "A Mutability Canto" for analysis of the "unchanging nature" idea.

83: *"Preservation and utility"*: William Ashworth, *The Left Hand of Eden* (Corvallis, Ore.: Oregon State Univ., 1999) 147.

83: *"peculiarly narrow"*: referring to both Pollan's and Cronon's critiques of the wilderness ethic: Proctor "Whose Nature" 285; *"[W]e have divided our country in two"*: Michael Pollan, *Second Nature* (New York: Atlantic Monthly, 1991) 189.

83-84: *six hundred million board feet*: Terry Tang, "Salvaging the Sad Legacy of the 'Rider from Hell,'" *Seattle Times* 15 March 1996: B4; *Congressional Republicans*: "Salvage Rider Reversal Is Not What It Seems," *Seattle Post Intelligencer* 24 Dec 1996; *4.5 billion board feet*: Rob Taylor, *Seattle Post Intelligencer*, 3 July 1996: B1; *"turnip truck"*: Joel Connelly, "Clinton Deals Leave Environmentalists Angry, Disappointed." *Seattle Post-Intelligencer* 4 Dec 1995: A3.

84: *convincing loggers and truck-drivers*: A nice account of anti-environmentalist timber-town sentiments is in Sallie Tisdale, *Stepping Westward: The Long Search for Home in the Pacific Northwest* (New York: Holt, 1991).

84: *"The idleness of cutover land"*: Greeley 14.

85: *Weyerhaeuser laid off eight thousand employees* and *"We're not a philanthropic enterprise"*: George Draffan, "A Profile of the Weyerhaeuser Corporation." Public Information Network: June 23, 1999. available http://www.endgame.org.

85: *abandoned the whole terrain of living and working "in nature"*: Richard White, "Are you an Environmentalist or do you work for a living?" in Cronon ed. 171; *"place into property"* 185.

85: *"equate productive work in nature with destruction"*: White 171.

86: *"nature is a mouth!"*: Joyce Carol Oates, "Against Nature," in *A Forest of Voices*, Eds. Chris Anderson and Lex Runciman (Mountain View, Calif: Mayfield, 1995) 372-79. Originally in *A Profane Art*, 1983.

89: *As Michael Pollan observed*: in "The Idea of a Garden" in his *Second Nature*.

90: *"He is more knowledgable and has done more"*: Philip Clapp qtd. in Yuval Rosenberg "The Record: Just How Green is Al Gore" *Newsweek* Oct. 26, 2000, available MSNBC.com/news; the head of the Sierra Club echoed this opinion: Patty Wentz, "Carl Pope: Defending Gore's Green Card," *Willamette Week* Nov. 1, 2000: 25.

90: *under five percent*: according to a CNN exit poll, some 5% of voters aged 18-29 voted for Nader, but just 2% in each age category above 29 years— suggesting youthful idealism for some (but not all) Nader's voters; available http://www.cnn.com/ELECTION/2000/results/index.epolls.html.

Eco-Fundamentalism and the Forests of Oregon

93: *so savagely reviewed*: see discussion of ecofeminist critiques of Deep Ecology in David Oates, *Earth Rising: Ecological Belief in an Age of Science* (Corvallis, Ore.: Oregon State Univ., 1989) 204-08.

93: *"The contradiction within American Protestant culture"*: Paul Shepard, *Nature and Madness* (San Francisco: Sierra Club, 1982) 91.

93: *Shepard examines this contradiction*: For full exposition of these ideas, see the chapter titled "Puritans" in Paul Shepard's *Nature and Madness*. The posthumous *Coming Home to the Pleistocene* (Washington, D.C.: Island, 1998) provides a fine summing-up of Shepard's themes.

93: *"The two opposite sides"*: Shepard *Nature and Madness* 89. *"The puritanical fear of pollution"* 90-91.

94: *"magical capacity to reveal"*: Shepard *Nature and Madness* 100.

94: *"negotiated affiliations"*: Shepard *Nature and Madness* 34 and passim.

94: *"What the adolescent should know"*: Shepard *Nature and Madness* 91.

94-95: *"The orgies of spoiling"*: Shepard *Nature and Madness* 91.

95: *"the literalizing impulse"*: Eliade qtd. in Shepard *Nature and Madness* 90.

96: *"It probably is the best"*: Michael Milstein, "Taking a stand at Eagle Creek." *The Oregonian* 10 June 2001: A1+.

97: *Gary Larson*: Jonathan Brinckman and Michelle Cole, "Logging trouble erupts." *The Oregonian* 2 June 2001: A1+; *no clearcuts*: Glen Sachet, Mt. Hood National Forest Communications Director, telephone interview 27 August 2001.

97: *Harv Forsgren*: "Wading into Eagle Creek." Editorial. *The Oregonian* 17 July 2001: G4.

98: *"no adverse effects"*: Jerry F. Franklin, Bernard T. Bormann, E. Charles Meslow, and Gordon H. Reeves, *Report of Independent Review Team for Eagle Sale* (USDA Forest Service Pacific Northwest Region, 6 July 2001) 2.

98: *Gordon Reeves*: profiled in Joseph Cone, *A Common Fate: Endangered Salmon and the People of the Pacific Northwest* (Corvallis, Ore.: Oregon State Univ., 1996) 1-6 and passim.

99: *"a hostile attack"*: William Cronon, "Foreword" to *Uncommon Ground*, Ed. William Cronon (New York: Norton, 1996) 19.

99: *Luna*: Julia Butterfly Hill, *The Legacy of Luna* (New York: HarperSanFrancisco, 2000).

100: *a hero to ... the environmental movement*: see for instance the worshipful reviews in *EarthLight: Magazine of Spiritual Ecology*, Summer 2002: 49.

100: *"mutant genes into the environment"*: Bryan Denson, "ELF claims it started fires at UW, tree farm." *Oregonian* 2 June 2001: A1+.

100: *"never created a genetically engineered tree"*: Steven H. Strauss, "Closer look shows ELF gets its science wrong." *Oregonian* 7 June 1002: C7.

100: *"tree farms that the company manages"*: Jon D. Johnson qtd. in Paul Schell, "Franken-forest." *Seattle Weekly* August 2-8, 2001: n.p.; *"the plantations have extremely little influence"*: Strauss.

100: *Poplars sequester atmospheric carbon dioxide*: see Washington State University Puyallup website www.puyallup.wsu.edu/poplar/rshprojects/rsch2.htm.

101: *"morons"*: Mitch Friedman qtd. in Schell n.p.

105: *"I think it's wrong ... [to] kill animals for food"*: Paul Shukovsky, "New Debate Over Whaling." *Seattle Post-Intelligencer* 2 Feb 2001: B1.

106: Wendell Berry, "Getting Along with Nature" in *A Forest of Voices*, Eds. Chris Anderson and Lex Runciman (Mountain View, Calif.: Mayfield, 1995) 681-91, originally in Berry's *Home Economics* (1987); *When the Makah now try to take their five grey whales*: the NMFS decision reflected a grey whale population rebound to about 26,000 worldwide (the largest since the mid-nineteenth century).

Palimpsest: The Flower Hunter

107: *"Puc-Puggy"*: William Bartram, *Travels of William Bartram* [1791], Ed. Mark Van Doren (New York: Dover, 1955) 218.

107: *"that I might judge for myself"*: Bartram's *Travels* 26.

108: *"that I might learn something"*: qtd. in Howard H. Brinton, *Friends for 300 Years* (Wallingford, Penn.: Pendle Hill, 1964) 160; *"pure Spirit"*: John Woolman's comment in his *Journal*, qtd. in Brinton 124.

108: *Is it idle to wonder*: See Brinton 38 for the story of how George Fox himself—founder of the Quaker sect—"by questioning an Indian, proved to the governor of an American colony that the Indian possessed the 'Light and Spirit of God.'"

108: *"I never before this was afraid"*: the story is told (with its eighteenth-century spellings) in Bartram's *Travels* 44-45. With clear disapproval, Bartram records the trader's self-serving excuse that the fellow was "the greatest villain."

Our Nature to Read

111: *"living systems ... must be treated as structure-determined systems"*: Humberto Maturana, "Everything Is Said by an Observer" in *Gaia A Way of Knowing: Political Implications of the New Biology*, Ed. William Irwin Thompson (Great Barrington, Me.: Lindisfarne, 1987) 73; *"we turn to the nature of the chimes"*: Francisco Varela, "Laying Down a Path in Walking" in Thompson ed. 50; *"absolutely existing external world"*: Humberto Maturana qtd. in Fritjof Capra, *The Web of Life: A New Scientific Understanding of Living Systems* (New York: Anchor/Doubleday, 1996) 96.

112: *"the release of fact into imagination"*: Northrop Fry, *Anatomy of Criticism* (Princeton, N.J.: Princeton Univ., 1957) 148.

114: *"bad readers"*: Robert P. Harrison, "Toward a Philosophy of Nature" in *Uncommon Ground*, Ed. William Cronon (New York: Norton, 1996) 434.

114: *"permeable membrane"* and *"interactivity"*: among many other places, in N. Katherine Hayles, "Simulated Nature and Natural Simulation: Rethinking the Relation between the Beholder and the World" in Cronon ed. 413; *Maturana's "structural coupling"*: Capra *Web* 218; *"transactive"*: Norman N. Holland, "The New Paradigm: Subjective or Transactive? *NLH* 7 (1976): 335-46; *Joanna Macy's … "dependent co-arising"*: Joanna Macy, *World as Lover, World as Self* (Berkeley: Parallax, 1991) 66; *Varela's "mutual interdefinition"*: in Thompson ed. 48; *Bateson points out*: Gregory Bateson and Mary Catherine Bateson, *Angels Fear: Towards an Epistemology of the Sacred* (New York: Macmillan, 1987) 96.

115: Thomas S. Kuhn, *The Structure of Scientific Revolutions* (Chicago: Univ. Chicago, 1962).

116: *"you might as well build condos on it"*: Michael Pollan's groundbreaking book *Second Nature* makes the point most forcibly: that the "Wilderness Ethic" with its simple don't touch formula is an inadequate guide for dealing with the world. See "The Idea of a Garden," from his *Second Nature: A Gardener's Education* (New York: Atlantic Monthly, 1991). Gary Nabhan argues for specific indigenous knowledge (in contrast to a generic "wilderness ethic"): "Cultural Parallax: The Wilderness Concept in Crisis" in *Cultures of Habitat: On Nature, Culture, and Story* (Washington, D.C.: Counterpoint, 1997) 152-165.

119: *"For if we consider the* letter *alone"*: Dante Aleghieri, "Epistola X" in *Dantis Alagherii Epistolae: The Letters of Dante*. Emended Text. 2nd. ed. Trans. Paget Toynbee (London: Oxford, 1966) 199.

119: *Dante immediately simplifies*: "And although these mystical meanings are called by various names, they may one and all …be termed allegorical, inasmuch as they are different (*diversi*) from the literal or historical" Dante Aleghieri *Letters* 199.

121: *our many ways of seeing nature*: for various meanings of "Nature" see A.O. Lovejoy's neat list: "Nature as Aesthetic Norm" in his *Essays in the History of Ideas* (Baltimore: Hopkins, 1948); Cronon runs through some of them in his "Introduction," Cronon ed. 23-56.

121: *"Singular, abstract, and personified"*: Raymond Williams, "The Idea of Nature" in *Problems in Materialism and Culture* (London: NLB, 1980) 69; *such an abstraction is functionally indistinguishable*: William Cronon, "Introduction," Cronon ed. 35.

122: *metaphor being a way of saying two things*: "Metaphor" is contrasted by English teachers with "simile" (which uses "like" or "as" to make comparison explicit). But at a deeper level, a metaphor always makes both kinds of point: likeness asserted simultaneously with identity—though not literally of course!

123-24: *"But to try to fight all syllogism in grass"*: Bateson and Bateson, *Angels Fear* 26-27; *"The whole of animal behavior"* 27.

125: *"Metaphor is not just pretty poetry"*: Bateson and Bateson, *Angels Fear* 30.

Good Indian, Bad Indian

129: *"supplementarity"*: Jacques Derrida, *Of Grammatology.* Trans. Gayatri Chakravorty Spivak (Baltimore: Johns Hopkins Univ., 1976); see discussion in Christopher Norris, *Derrida* (Cambridge, Mass.: Harvard, 1987) 109-127; *"Repressive Hypothesis"*: Michel Foucault, *History of Sexuality,* Vol. I. Trans. Robert Hurley [1976] (New York: Random, 1980) 15 and passim.

131: *"Anything that had no English name"*: Marquis de Chastellux, *Travels in North America in the Years 1780, 1781 and 1782* [1786], qtd. in William Cronon, *Changes in the Land: Indians, Colonists, and the Ecology of New England* (New York: Hill and Wang, 1983) 8.

131: *"thing to be administered "*: Foucault 24;

131: *"multiplicity of discourses"*: Foucault 33.

131-32: Eric Darier, "Foucault and the Environment" in *Discourses of the Environment,* Ed. Eric Darier (Oxford [U.K.]: Blackwell, 1999) 17; *"rule of immanence"* Foucault 98; *"discourse ... both instrument and effect"* 101; *"Ideology seeks to convert culture"*: Terry Eagleton qtd. in Peter Quigley, "Nature as Dangerous Space," in Darier ed. 182.

132: *"Foucault's approach notices"*: though of course Foucault was not the first to conduct such history-of-ideas analysis. I first learned it from Marjorie Hope Nicolson's *Mountain Gloom and Mountain Glory: The Development of the Aesthetics of the Infinite* [1959] (New York: Norton, 1963).

133: *than we can think*: I borrow this turn of phrase from Jack Ward Thomas: qtd. in Joseph Cone, *A Common Fate* (Corvallis, Ore.: Oregon State Univ., 1996) 243.

134: Pedro Font, "The Colorado Yumans in 1775" in *The California Indians: A Source Book.* 2nd ed. Eds. R.F. Heizer and M.A. Whipple (Los Angeles: Univ. California, 1971) 253; *"filled ... with the densest ignorance"*: George H.H. Redding, "Fire-making of the Wintu Indians," in Heizer and Whipple eds. 342; Carl Meyer, "The Yurok of Trinidad Bay, 1851," in Heizer and Whipple eds. 270-71.

134: *"There was not a bad Indian to be found"*: Sheriff Anderson qtd. in Theodora Kroeber, *Ishi in Two Worlds* (Berkeley: Univ. California, 1971) 67; *three thousand Yana...1864* Theodora Krober 56-78.

136: *"They are addicted"*: Pedro Fages, "The Chumash Indians of Santa Barbara," in Heizer and Whipple eds. 255.

136: *"they are so shameless"*: Pedro Fonts in Heizer and Whipple eds. 250.

136: *Anthropologists reporting in the 1930s ... Mohaves*: George Devereux, "Institutionalized Homosexuality of the Mohave Indians," *Human Biology* 9 (1937): 489-527; *Indian cultures continent-wide*: see for instance Luther Standing Bear's similar comments on gender: *Land of the Spotted Eagle* [1933] (Lincoln, Neb.: Univ. Nebraska, 1978) 93; and the systematic treatment in Walter L. Williams, *The Spirit and the Flesh: Sexual Diversity in American Indian Culture* (Boston: Beacon, 1986).

137: *Gabrielino*: Lowell John Bean and Charles R. Smith. "Gabrielino," in *Handbook of North American Indians: California.* Vol. 8. Ed. Robert F. Heizer (Washington, D.C.: Smithsonian, 1978) 540; *Apparently commonplace and widespread*: Williams writes "In California, Spanish priests writing in the 1820s ... described similar practices among the Luiseño and Gabrielino Indians" 46. See Jonathan Katz, *Gay American History* (New York: Crowell, 1976) 614. Alfred Kroeber remarks how little has been preserved of Gabrielino social institutions, and so infers similarities with nearby groups such as Juaneno: A.L. Kroeber, *Handbook of the Indians of California* [1925] (New York: Dover, 1976) 633; "The Gabrielino origin of a large share of Juaneno ritual and myth is clear" 644. "Habitual transvestites were called *kwit* by the Juaneno of the coast, *uluki* by the mountaineers. ... [I]t is extremely probable that under the lack of repression involved in Indian society against the involved inclination, the feminine tendencies sometimes revealed themselves in early youth and were readily recognized and encouraged to manifest themselves as natural. Such 'women' were prized ... and often publicly married" 647.

137: *a common phenomenon*: Williams 53; *"There were among them formerly"* 4.

138: Carolyn Merchant, *The Death of Nature: Women, Ecology, and the Scientific Revolution* (New York: Harper, 1976).

138: *Teddy Roosevelt's personal story*: Theodore Roosevelt, *Ranch Life and the Hunting Trail* [1888] (rpt. New York: Century, 1899).

138: *Hercules*: John Boswell, *Christianity, Social Tolerance, and Homosexuality* (Chicago: Univ. Chicago, 1980) 25 n. 44.

139: *the limits of Foucault and ... "social construct" thinking*: see discussions in James D. Proctor, "The Social Construction of Nature: Relativist Accusations, Pragmatist and Critical Realist Responses," *Annals of the Assoc. Am. Geographers* 88.3(1998): 352-76; Peter Quigley, "Nature as Dangerous Space" in Darier ed. 181-202; and Neil Everndon, *The Social Construction of Nature* (Baltimore: Johns Hopkins, 1992).

139: *"Whenever she showed him"*: Darier 6; in French qtd. in Didier Eribon, *Michel Foucault* (France [n.p.]: Flammarion, 1991) 66.

140: *"Sexuality must not be described as a stubborn drive"*: Foucault 103; *Foucault, it appears, turns his back*: Foucault confronts such criticisms 151ff; see R. Diprose, "The Use of Pleasure in the Constitution of the Body" *Australian Feminist Studies* 5 (1987): 5-93; and "Foucault, Derrida, and the Ethics of Sexual Difference" *Social Semiotics* 1,2 (1991): 1-21; also discussion of her work in Alec McHoul and Wendy Grace, *A Foucault Primer: Discourse, Power and the Subject* (New York: New York Univ., 1993) 120-23.

140: *"I mean, the scene was fun"*: Leo Barsani qtd. in James Miller, *The Passion of Michel Foucault* (New York: Simon and Schuster, 1993) 261; *Foucault's own partner*: Daniel Defert qtd. in Miller 380; *"anxious restraint"* 383. For a spirited rebuttal see David M. Halperin, *Saint Foucault: Towards a Gay Hagiography* (New York: Oxford, 1995).

141: *"multiple but finite truths"*: Proctor "Social Construction" 360.

A Mutability Canto

149: *Clements was deeply interested in change*: Donald Worster, *Nature's Economy* (San Francisco: Sierra Club, 1977) 210.

150: *"complex organism"*: Clements qtd. in Ronald C. Tobey, *Saving the Prairies* (Berkeley: Univ. California, 1981) 82; *"The unit of vegetation"*: Clements qtd. in Worster 211.

150: *I analyzed elements of that picture*: David Oates, *Earth Rising: Ecological Belief in an Age of Science* (Corvallis, Ore.: Oregon State Univ., 1989).

152: *"Today, many ecologists avoid the term 'climax'"*: Daniel Mathews, *Cascade-Olympic Natural History*, 2nd. ed. (Portland: Audubon, 1999) 13.

152: Melvin A. Bernard, *Our Precarious Habitat*, rev. ed. (New York: Norton, 1973).

152-53: *"The normative sense of the word"*: Anna Bramwell, *Ecology in the Twentieth Century: A History* (New Haven: Yale, 1989) 4.

153: *Clements … minimized the role of anthropogenic fire*: see his *Plant Succession* (Washington, D.C.: Carnegie Institution of Washington, 1916) 214-216; also Frederic E. Clements and Ralph W. Chaney, *Environment and Life in the Great Plains*. Carnegie Institution of Washington Supplementary Publications No. 24 (Washington, D.C.: Carnegie, 1936) 33; *"evolved under fire and grazing"*: Richard Manning, *Grassland* (New York: Penguin, 1995) 222.

156: Terry Tempest Williams, *Refuge: An Unnatural History of Family and Place* (New York: Vintage/Random, 1991).

160: *"I turn. All at once, a thousand avocets"*: Williams 275.

162: *"I have been liberated from my optimism"*: Williams 239; *"clouds like roses"* 279.

163: *"I well consider all that ye have sayd"*: Edmund Spenser, *The Faerie Queene*, in *Edmund Spenser's Poetry*, Ed. Hugh Maclean (New York: Norton, 1968) stza. 58.

Up the River

166: *Ice ages last a long time*: variations in ice age terminology persist even in authoritative sources. E.C. Pielou, *After the Ice* (Chicago: Univ. Chicago, 1991) offers a readable summary 5-18, 269-72; *ten in the last million years*: Larry Hanson, Geologist and Chair of Sciences, Marylhurst University, personal communication 26 March 01.

167: *Missoula Floods* are also known as "Bretz" or "Spokane" floods. The Ice Age Floods Institute website summarizes the flood story neatly: http://www.idahogeology.org/iceagefloods/iafihome.html. For more detailed information See John Eliot Allen, Marjorie Burns, and Samuel C. Sargent, *Cataclysms on the Columbia* (Portland, Ore.: Timber Press, 1986).

169: *5 percent mortality … 15 percent*: Philip R. Mundy, "Dangerous Passage: Oregon's Salmon and the Hydroelectric System," in *Oregon Salmon* (Portland: Oregon Trout, 2001) 51-52.

169: *a year to fill*: Jim O'Connor, Research Hydrologist, USGS (Portland), personal communication 8 August 01.

169: *waters … ran over the top*: Jim O'Connor personal communication 8 August 2001; *another massive flood*: Jim O'Connor, "An Exceptionally Large Columbia River Flood Between 500 and 600 years ago: Breaching of the Birdge-Of-The-Gods landslide?" *Abstracts*, Geological Society of America 28 (1996), No.27900; *wiped out Chinookan villages*: Richard M. Pettigrew, "Prehistory of the Lower Columbia and Willamette Valley," in *Handbook of North American Indians: Northwest Coast*. Vol. 7 (Washington, D.C.: Smithsonian, 1990) 524; *gave its name to our mountains*: according to nineteenth-century Oregon poet Joaquin Miller: "Our Undiscovered Oregon" in *Songs of the Sierras*, Vol. 2 of *Joaquin Miller's Poems* (San Francisco: Whitaker and Ray, 1915) 207-16.

169-70: *several geologists have begun to challenge*: see the work of Jim O'Connor, USGS office Portland; and Jim Pringle, geologist, State of Washington, who is carbon-dating a tree trunk retrieved from the Bridge of the Gods landslide.

170: *"fathers … used to paddle*: according to Daniel Lee in the late 1830s, in Rich Hill, "A New Look at an Old Landslide." *Oregonian* 29 Sept. 1999: B9.

171: *"millions of years of cataclysmic habitat disruption"*: Jim Lichatowich, *Salmon Without Rivers* (Washington, D.C.: Island, 1999) 14-15.

172: *until just four thousand years ago*: Lichatowich 20, and see the book-length description in Pielou; *variant of Douglas-fir forest*: Pielou 244; *"sediment loads sixty times"*: Lichatowich 18-19; *a cool phase in solar radiation*: Pielou 291.

173: *"Chinook display a broad array of tactics"*: M.C. Healey, "Life History of Chinook Salmon," in *Pacific Salmon Life Histories*, Eds. C. Groot & L. Margolis (Vancouver, B.C.: Univ. British Columbia, 1991) 314; *"spread the risk of mortality"* 314.

173: *"Like a key in a lock"*: Cone 50.

174: *"we know surprisingly little"*: salmon straying rates are summarized in Kyle A. Young, "Managing the decline of Pacific Salmon: metapopulation theory and artificial recolonization as ecological mitigation." *Canadian Journal of Fisheries and Aquatic Science* 56 (1999): 1702; *chum 14 percent*: E.O. Salo, "Life History of Chum Salmon," Groot and Margolis eds. 238; *pink 10 percent*: William R. Heard, "Life History of Pink Salmon," Groot and Margolis eds. 202.

175: *four-year study on the Cowlitz River*: Healey 380-81; *New Zealand*: Martin J. Unwin and Thomas P. Quinn, "Homing and Straying patterns of Chinook Salmon (*Oncorhynchus tshawytscha*) from a New Zealand Hatchery." *Canadian Journal of Fisheries and Aquatic Science* 50 (1993):1168.

175: *"design-oid"*: Dawkins prefers to write it "designoid," but that is very prone to mispronunciation. *Climbing Mount Improbable* (New York: Norton, 1996) 6.

176: *trigener*: I think "trigener" would be pronounced "try-jeener," suggesting genes as well as generations.

176: *"Down the River"*: Edward Abbey, *Desert Solitaire* (New York: Ballantine, 1968).

177: *Bonneville mechanical engineer*: Kevin Perletti, Mechanical Engineer, Bonneville Dam, U.S. Army Corps of Engineers. Personal communication 30 April 2001.

178: *the Pantheon for instance*: the engineer David Moore evaluates this building in *The Roman Pantheon: Triumph of Concrete,* available www.romanconcrete.com.

179: *Kevin's boss*: Les Miller, Chief of Emergency Management, Bonneville Dam, U.S. Army Corps of Engineers. Personal Communication 30 April 2001.

Real Losses: The Hanford Reach

183: *"Radioactive and chemical wastes totaling into the billions"*: Michele Stenehjem Gerber, *On the Home Front: The Cold War Legacy of the Hanford Nuclear Site* (Lincoln, Neb.: Univ. Nebraska, 1997) 3.

184: *5500 curies of radiation*: Columbia River United, *Hanford and the River* ([N.p].: Columbia River United, [n.d.]) 3; *"one thousand times the then-tolerable limit"*: Gerber 90-91; *already well-known at the time*: Gerber 84-86; hyperthyroidism and other risks: Gerber 172; *"fourteen times the levels of October"*: Gerber 92.

185: *probably thirteen thousand … "a dose of nine rads"*: Pacific Northwest Laboratory, *Air Pathway Report: Phase I of the Hanford Environmental Dose Reconstruction Project* [HEDR] (July 1991) 3.21-3.22; *the amount of radiation in twelve … X rays*: Michael D'Antonio, *Atomic Harvest* (New York: Crown, 1993) 275.

185: *a milligram per day*: Gerber 86.

186: *well-known ... radiogenic links*: Gerber 183; *Those who lived downwind of ... Savannah River, Oak Ridge*: D'Antonio 270.

187: *"average holdup time"*: Gerber 124-25.

187: *strontium-90*: Columbia River United 11.

188: *whitefish ... "would furnish ... about 20 percent"*: P.A. Olson, Jr. and R.F. Foster, qtd. in Gerber 127-29.

188: *"The public relations impact"*: Herbert Parker qtd. in Gerber 128; *"keep this potential problem under ... observation"*: Kenneth D. Nichols, memo to Lewis Strauss [Chairman, AEC] qtd. in Gerber 128.

188: *"We doubt that any real human hazard"*: David Shaw (AEC Hanford manager) qtd. in Gerber 128; *raised the beta radioactivity...by 50 percent*: Gerber 138.

188: *Major releases continued*: Gerber 131-39; *an entire pound of uranium*: Gerber 134.

189: *Some is deposited in sediments*: according to a 1975 study qtd. in Gerber 141.

189: *"contamination of groundwater"*: League of Women Voters Education Fund, *The Nuclear Waste Primer* (Washington, D.C.: The League of Women Voters, 1993) 20; *Hanford's own assessment*: T.H. Essig, "Hanford Waste Disposal Summary - 1970." BNWL-1618 (Richland, Wash.: Battelle Pacific Northwest, 1970), cited in Gerber 162.

189: *Chief Parker in 1948 declared*: Gerber 149.

190: *"less than one foot"*: Gerber 156-57; *official estimates ... fifty to one hundred years*: Gerber 153; *"radioactive materials ... hundreds of feet per day"*: W.H. Bierschenk and M.W. McConiga, "Changes in Hanford Water Table, 1944-57," HW-51277 (Richland, Wash.: HAPO, July 9, 1957) 14, qtd. in Gerber 152.

190: *a day or two of background radiation*: M.D. Freshley and P.D. Thorne, *Ground-Water Contribution to Dose from Past Hanford Operations.* Hanford Environmental Dose Reconstruction Project [HEDR] (Richland, Wash.: Pacific Northwest Laboratory, January 1992) ix-xv; *"triple the annual ... dose of background radiation"*: *Summary Report: Phase I of the Hanford Environmental Dose Reconstruction Project* [HEDR] (Richland, Wash.: Pacific Northwest Laboratory, August 1991) 5.14; *"A considerable amount of contamination"*: Freshley and Thorne vii; *overviews show plumes*: Columbia River United 8-9.

191: *More than a million gallons*: a common estimate, for instance "State May Sue over Nuke Waste." *Columbian* 24 Mar. 2001: C9; *"the idea that DOE"*: Doug Sherwood qtd. in Linda Ashton, "Hanford Pool Cleanup Behind on Time, Money." *Columbian* 6 Feb. 2001.

191: *"20-year design life"* and *2,200 tons*: Gerber 229; *"four tons of plutonium"*: "No More Delay in Cleanups." Editorial. *Seattle Post-Intelligencer* 11 Feb 01: D9; *15,000 gallons... 94,000 gallons*: Gerber 229.

192: *"In the wake of World War II"*: Horace Busby qtd. in Gerber 217.

192: *"Projection of the problem to [the] future"*: Herbert Parker qtd. in Gerber 216.

193: *"engineer our way through the landscape"*: John Volkman, *A River in Common: The Columbia River, the Salmon Ecosystem, and Water Policy* ["Report to the Western Water Policy Review Advisory Commission" of the Northwest Power Planning Council {NPPC}] (Portland: [NPPC], August 1997): 205-06.

The Unintended Sits by Her Window and Smiles

197: *An official summary*: Committee on Environment and Natural Resources, *From the Edge: Science to Support Restoration of Pacific Salmon* (Washington, D.C.: National Science and Technology Council, 2000). The silence of this report on the topic of radioactivity is typical of what I found in other comprehensive reports, such as the Northwest Power Planning Council's earlier *Priority Salmon: Habitat and Production Proposals* (Portland: NPPC, 1991).

197: *"cease to feed"*: P.A. Olsson and R.F. Foster, "Accumulation of Radioactivity in Columbia River Fish in the Vicinity of the Hanford Works" HW-23093 (Richland: HAPO, July 1952) 39, qtd. in Gerber 126.

197: *warm for months at a time*: Phillip R. Mundy, "Dangerous Passage: Oregon's Salmon and the Hydroelectric System," in *Oregon Salmon* (Portland: Oregon Trout, 2001).

197: *In 1952 ... Parker had to warn*: Gerber 126.

198: *1954 report*: R.F. Foster, J.J. Davis, and P.A. Olson, "Studies on the Effect of the Hanford Reactors on Aquatic LIfe in the Columbia," HW-33366 (Richland: HAPO, October 11, 1954) 13, qtd. in Gerber 126; *"local recommended limit"*: P.R. Murray, "Columbia River Aspects of Increased Production," HW-41049 (Richland: HAPO, January 25, 1956), qtd. in Gerber 126; *ten times their 1948 capacity*: Gerber 127.

199: *seven billion dollars*: Blaine Harden, *A River Lost: The Life and Death of the Columbia* (NY: Norton, 1996) 155 note, quoting 1995 US Senate report "Train Wreck Along the River of Money"; *"Nation's Most Ironic Nature Park"*: Urban Design Forum of Denver qtd. in *Uncommon Ground*, Ed. William Cronon (New York: Norton, 1996) 59; *"post-nuclear paradise"*: Harden 149.

199: *"normative" river*: Northwest Power Planning Council (NPPC) coined this term in its 1996 report *Return to the River*, qtd. in *From the Edge* 36.

199: *96 percent*: Harden 161.

200: *virtually no other shrub-steppe*: Harden 148.

200: *hundreds of thousands of acres ... HEW prevented*: Gerber 108-09.

201: *Salmon were already extinct ... Boise River*: John Volkman, *A River in Common: The Columbia River, the Salmon Ecosystem, and Water Policy* ["Report to the Western Water Policy Review Advisory Commission" of the Northwest Power Planning Council {NPPC}] (Portland: [NPPC], August 1997) 54; *first salmon hatchery*: Jim Lichatowich, *Salmon Without Rivers* (Washington, D.C.: Island, 1999) 125.

201: *"remaining salmon stocks"* and *"101 were at high risk"*: Jim Lichatowich sums up the *Crossroads* report in *Salmon Without Rivers* 204. Joseph Cone describes Lichatowich as a principled leader for many fisheries professionals during his five years as Assistant Chief of Fisheries at the Oregon Dept. of Fish and Wildlife in the 1980s as well as following his resignation over "policy differences" in 1988: *A Common Fate* (Corvallis, Ore.: Oregon State Univ., 1996) 27.

201: *40 percent of their historic rivers*: the so-called *"Upstream* report" (1996) uses this figure: Committee on Protection and Management of Pacific Northwest Anadromous Salmonids [Board on Environmental Studies and Toxicology, National Research Council], *Upstream: Salmon and Society in the Pacific Northwest* (Washington, DC: National Academy Press, 1996) 75; Lichatowich repeats it and gives the *"44 percent"* figure: 204; *20 percent of the original salmon productivity*: Lichatowich 8; *NMFS regional website*:

"Endangered Species Act Status of West Coast Salmon and Steelhead" available www.nwr.noaa.gov/.

202: *"cause for pessimism"*: Upstream 2; *"the mainstem dams"*: Volkman 58.

203: *"We assumed"*: Lichatowich 206.

201: *"not only are ecosystems more complex"*: Jack Ward Thomas, "Wildlife in Old Growth Forests" (1992), qtd. in Cone 243.

203: *"success" of coho*: Lichatowich 212.

204: *"The harvest dropped"*: Lichatowich 212

204: *"We assumed we could control"*: Lichatowich 8; *smaller*: Bruce Brown, *Mountain in the Clouds: A Search for Wild Salmon* (NY: Simon and Schuster, 1982) 102; *"only half the rate"*: Lichatowich 216; *ignorant...sheer force of numbers*: Brown 118-19.

204: *"Inappropriate short-term responses … that ignored the "long lags"*: Upstream 5.

205: *"third infinity"*: an idea developed in *Earth Rising*: "a limit is a necessary condition which encourages a deepening in other dimensions" 155; see152-58, 171-73.

205: *"The effect of this loss of diversity"*: Lichatowich 79-80;

205: *A federal judge in Oregon*: U.S. District Judge Michael R. Hogan declined to defer to the NMFS Hatchery Policy which stated that hatchery fish could be excluded from an ESA listing if they were not "deemed essential" to the stated goal of the Endangered Species Act: recovery of the natural population. U.S. District Court for the District of Oregon, "Alsea Valley Alliance v. Donald L. Evans [et al.]" (No. 99-6265-HO) 9; *genetically identical*: For an analysis which explains the technical basis of the ruling, in contrast to this remark, see Daniel J. Rohlf, "The Hogan Decision: Clarification of Salmon Protection Needed from Feds," *Restoration: A Newsletter about Salmon, Coastal Watersheds, and People*" (published by Oregon Sea Grant), Issue 28, Dec. 2001: 1+. Available http:// seagrant.orst.edu/communications/restore.html.

205: *"some of our policies … deep ignorance"*: Upstream 5.

205-6: *"research to close … knowledge gaps"* and *We don't know …*: From the Edge 4-5; *"The marine environment"* 4.

206: *"Recovery … may require immediate intervention"*: From the Edge 2.

206: *"Focusing on species sets us up"* and *"conserving the integrity of ecosystems"*: Lichatowich qtd. in Cone 192.

207: *"how little we know,"* and *"wild (i.e. unengineered)"*: William S. Alverson, Walter Kuhlmann, and Donald M. Waller, *Wild Forests: Conservation Biology and Public Policy* (Washington, D.C.: Island, 1994) xviii; *"passively managed"* 26.

208: *Which dams should we take out?*: A comprehensive treatment of the question appeared as this book went to press: Elizabeth Grossman, *Watershed: The Undamming of America* (New York: Counterpoint, 2002).

208: *"nearly four thousand miles of … habitat"*: Scott Bosse (Idaho Rivers United), Congressional Testimony, Senate Environment and Public Works Committee, 14 Sept. 2000; *81% of ocean-bound juveniles and 40% of returning adults*: as estimated by Oregon Natural Resources Council, cited in "Breaching Snake River dams best option, NMFS says." ENN Environmental News Network 16 April 1999.

208: *the major newspaper … publicly supported dam-breaching*: Susan Whaley, *Dollars, Sense and Salmon*, rpt. of editorial series. *Idaho Statesman* 20-22 July 1997; *just thirteen farms, $183 million...$257 million*: Whaley.

209:"not too bad": Whaley, personal communication 2 Nov 2001.
209: "no-spill policy," "Summer spill would reduce": Michelle Cole, "BPA won't risk power to aid fish migration." *Oregonian* 30 June 2001: D1+; *one-fifth its required amount*: Jonathan Brinckman, "Suit accuses BPA of harming salmon." *Oregonian* 6 Nov 2001: B4.
210: *lowest ever recorded*: Jonathan Brinckman, "Fish survival rates plunge to near-record lows in 2001." *Oregonian* 11 Oct 2001: B1+; *"It makes me think … doesn't have the will"*: Jonathan Brinckman, "Easing one crisis, but adding to another." *Oregonian* 21 May 2001: A1+.
210: *"major uncertainties"*: PATH: *Executive Summary of PATH FY98 Final Report*. Available: www.nwfsc.noaa.gov/afis.
211-12: *"We are comfortable"*: qtd. in Andrea Otanez, "NMFS Finalizes Salmon Plan." *Seattle Times* 22 Dec 2000: B1; *no amount of failure*: see discussion of NMFS' record of "inadequate management" in Warner Chabott and Lee Crockett, "Congress must reform fisheries." *Seattle Post-Intelligencer* 2 May 2001: B5; *"38 percent"*: Volkman 58.
212: *white-winged guan … peccary*: Darryl Stewart, *From the Edge of Extinction: The Fight to Save Endangered Species* (New York: Methuen, 1978) 179-80.
213: *Bluefish*: Jim Williams, Operations Superintendent, Dalles Dam, personal communication 30 April 2001; *Walleye, blue pike, wild trout*: Joseph C. Makarewicz and Paul Bertram, "Evidence for the restoration of the Lake Erie ecosystem," *BioScience* 41 (1991): 216+.

Thoreau and the Literalizing Century:
Scientism, Fundamentalism, and the Golden West

218: *believed truth to be simple*: for example the doctrinal statement of the Presbyterians (the Puritan's sometimes revolutionary allies) the Westminster Confession of 1647 declared scriptural truth to be "not manifold, but one"; *reluctant … fundamentalist*: John Milton was a champion of "liberty of conscience," and held some heterodox beliefs, and was in this hardly fundamentalist. But his literalist doctrine of scripture and the Fall amounted to fundamentalist "biblicism": Everet Emerson, "Puritanism, Milton's" in *A Milton Encyclopedia*, Ed. William B. Hunter, Jr. (Lewisburg: Bucknell Univ., 1979) 85. See Milton's *De Doctrina Christiana* (Book IX) for his own explication of this biblical literalism.
218-19: George M. Marsden, *Fundamentalism and American Culture: The Shaping of American Evangelicalism 1870-1925* (New York: Oxford, 1980) 5. See also George M. Marsden, "Evangelical and Fundamental Christianity." *The Encyclopedia of Religion*. Vol. 5. Ed. Mircea Eliade (New York: MacMillan, 1987) 190-91; *control over the divine*: a fairly common theme in latter-day Fundamentalist churches is the assertion that God is "bound" by the words of the Bible (He has to be true to His own words); thus a believer who correctly deploys these words can guarantee divine results.
220: *"a number of the keenest … minds"*: M.H. Abrams, *Natural Supernaturalism* (New York: Norton, 1971) 170.
220: *Carlyle's father*: qtd. in Walter E. Houghton. *The Victorian Frame of Mind 1830-1870* (New Haven, Conn.: Yale, 1957) 127; *"Every dabbler"*: John Stuart Mill qtd. 124.
221: *feeling had been divorced from … fact*: Robert Langbaum's memorable phrase in *The Poetry of Experience* (New York: Norton, 1963); *"common-sense*

realism": Marsden *Fundamentalism* 55; *"view of scripture"* 57; *"that had been strong in America"* 60.

221: *"photographically exact"*: Marsden *Fundamentalism* 56;*"eschewing the mysterious"* 61.

221: *counting generations in the Old Testament*: Bishop Ussher in eighteenth-century England counted generations in the Old Testament and arrived at this exact date of the Creation, from which twentieth-century Fundamentalists and "young earth" creationists derive their doctrines (directly or indirectly); *our family bible*: a cornerstone of modern Fundamentalism is the annotated Bible by C.I. Schofield; our family used one that referenced Ussher's calculations on the first page of Genesis. *The Schofield Reference Bible,* Ed. C.I. Schofield (New York: Oxford, 1917).

223: *ahistorical historicism*: see Marsden *Fundamentalism* 226-30.

223: *"the Protestant interpretation"*: Gregory Bateson and Mary Catherine Bateson, *Angels Fear: Towards an Epistemology of the Sacred* (New York: Macmillan, 1987) 29.

223: *Bateson makes the case*: Bateson and Bateson 50-64.

224: *"synthesizer with perfect timing"*: Shepard Krech, *The Ecological Indian* (New York: Norton, 1999) 18.

224: *Golden-age and paradisal comparisons*: covered in classic scholarship including Leo Marx, *The Machine in the Garden* (London: Oxford, 1964); Perry Miller, *Errand into the Wilderness* (Cambridge, Mass.: Harvard, 1964); Henry Nash Smith, *Virgin Land: The American West as Symbol and Myth* (Cambridge, Mass.: Harvard, 1950); R.W.B. Lewis, *The American Adam: Innocence, Tragedy, and Tradition in the Nineteenth Century* (Chicago: Univ. Chicago, 1955).

224: *"The feeling that most constantly recurs"*: J.M. Cohen, "Introduction." *The Confessions of Jean-Jacques Rousseau.* Trans. J.M. Cohen (New York: Penguin, 1954) 8.

225: *"the note of elegy"*: Frederick Turner, *John Muir: Rediscovering America* (Cambridge, Mass.: Perseus, 1985) 237; *"The axe of civilization"* and *"it behooves our artists"*: qtd. in Miller 205-06.

225: *"visible footsteps of God!"*: Rev. of Samuel Parker, *Journal of an Exploring Tour of the Rocky Mountains. Knickerbocker Magazine* June 1838: 554-56.

226: *"Nature penetrated"*: qtd. in Miller 212; *"The Chieftan's Tear"*: Robert R. Raymond, *Knickerbocker Magazine* Jan. 1838: 22-24.

227: *"the emblem of a mind"*: The Prelude, Book Fourteen, in *William Wordsworth's The Prelude, Selected Poems and Sonnets* (New York: Holt, Rinehart and Winston, 1954) lines 66-76.

228: *"with an eye made quiet"*: "Lines Composed a few miles above Tintern Abbey …" in *William Wordsworth's The Prelude, Selected Poems and Sonnets* 97.

228: *the space … occupied by this book*: Lawrence Buell also intriguingly places his book in this epistemological half-way point—"The answer to such questions is always 'both'" he says. *The Environmental Imagination: Thoreau, Nature Writing and the Formation of American Culture* (Cambridge, Mass.: Belknap/Harvard, 1995) 13.

228: *"The problem of restoring"*: Ralph Waldo Emerson, "Nature." In *Selections from Ralph Waldo Emerson,* Ed. Stephen E. Whicher (Boston: Houghton Mifflin, 1957) 55.

229: *"The Romantic form of answer"*: for good overviews of the organicist and materialist streams in science, see Charles Coulston Gillispie, *The Edge of*

Objectivity (Princeton, N. J.: Princeton Univ., 1960). For the romantic response to materialist Newtonianism, see M.H. Abrams *Natural Supernaturalism* (New York: Norton, 1971). For the decline of romanticism into Victorian sentimentality, see Robert Langbaum, *The Poetry of Experience* (New York: Norton, 1966).

229: *"The future lies"*: Henry David Thoreau,"Walking." In *Walden and Other Writings*, Ed. Brooks Atkinson (New York: Modern Library, 1950) 607; *"I must walk toward Oregon"* 608.

229: *"As a true patriot"*: Thoreau "Walking" 612.

230: *"We would fain"*: Thoreau "Walking" 607.

230: *"to some extent unsettles"*: Thoreau "Walking" 609; *"The West of which I speak"*: Thoreau "Walking" 613.

231: *"life ... consists with wildness"*: Thoreau "Walking" 615; *"One who ... infinite demands on life"*: 615;

231: *"Not a fossil"*: Thoreau *Walden* 223.

231: *"Man cannot afford to be a naturalist"*: Henry David Thoreau. Journal for March 23, 1853. *The Heart of Thoreau's Journals*, Ed. Odell Shepard (New York: Dover, 1961) 109. I am indebted to an unpublished paper by Dr. Marylynne Diggs of Clark College: "Thoreau's Other Resistance: Science and the Sexualization of Identity." See also Laura Dassow Walls, *Seeing New Worlds: Henry David Thoreau and Nineteenth-Century Natural Science* (Madison: Univ. Wisconsin, 1995).

Muir's Eden: Landscapes of Heaven

235-36: *"I mean now Dan"*: qtd. in Frederick Turner, *John Muir: Rediscovering America.* (Cambridge, Mass.: Perseus, 1985) 123; Daniel Muir is sketched in Turner 9; *"grand sabbath"*: qtd. in *John Muir: Nature Writings,* Ed. William Cronon (New York: Library of America, 1997) 840.

236: *"the best and soonest way of getting quit"*: qtd. in Turner 288.

236: *"the wildest, leafiest, and least trodden way"*: John Muir, *A Thousand-Mile Walk to the Gulf,* Ed. William Frederic Badé [1916] (San Francisco: Sierra Club, 1991) 1.

237: *home-grown, nature-based Taoism*: Michael P. Cohen, *The Pathless Way* (Madison, Wisc.: Univ. Wisconsin, 1984).

238: *Muir and a later editor*: *A Thousand-Mile Walk to the Gulf* was not published until 1916, two years after Muir's death; the book presents the original diary of 1867, as edited and revised by Muir though with final choices among versions by Muir's biographer William Frederic Badé; *"Planning my journey"* and *"The world was all before them"*: John Muir, *1867 Journal Manuscript* [unpublished manuscript] (Stockton, Calif.: Holt-Atherton Library) 2.

239: *"like a philosopher"* and *"I believe in Providence"*: Muir, *Thousand-Mile Walk* 22-23; *"All were united"* 23.

240: *"Instead of the sympathy"*: Muir, *Thousand-Mile Walk* 41; *"that death is an Evemade accident"*: Muir *1867 Journal Manuscript* 50; compare the published version which removed "Evemade," Muir *Thousand-Mile Walk* 41.

240: *"All is divine harmony"* and *"life at work everywhere"*: Muir *Thousand-Mile Walk,* 42; *"unfallen, undepraved"* and not *"consequences of Eve"*: Muir *1867 Journal Manuscript* 98.

241: *"the world, we are told"* and *"purely a manufactured article"*: Muir *Thousand-Mile Walk* 77; *"by the eating"* 78.

241: *"Eden's apple"* and *"subjected to the same laws"*: Muir *Thousand-Mile Walk* 78; *"The fearfully good"* 79.

241: *"Why should man value himself"*: Muir *Thousand-Mile Walk* 78-79.

242: *"But, glad to leave"*: Muir *Thousand-Mile Walk* 80.

242: *"silently to ignore"*: qtd. in Turner 146; see also 70.

244: *"But no terrestrial beauty"*: John Muir, "The Treasures of the Yosemite." *The Century Magazine* August 1890: 483.

244: *"The whole continent was a garden"*: John Muir, "The American Forests," in John Muir, *Our National Parks* (Boston: Houghton Mifflin, 1901) 334-35; *"felling and burning"* 336; *"It is not yet too late"* 359. The essay is filled with Biblical and apocalyptic language.

245: Mircea Eliade, *Myths Dreams and Mysteries.* Trans. Philip Mairet (New York: Harper, 1960), *Myth and Reality.* Trans.Willard R. Trask (New York: Harper, 1963) and other works.

Muir's Arcadia

249: *"flowers, fruit, milk and honey"*: John Muir, "The San Gabriel Valley" in *Steep Trails,* Ed. William Frederick Badé (Boston: Houghton Mifflin, 1918) 138; a *"kind of terrestrial heaven"* 140-41.

249: *"There is nothing more remarkable"*: Muir "San Gabriel Valley" 142.

250: *"Doctor Congar"*: Muir "San Gabriel Valley" 138.

251: Leo Marx, *The Machine in the Garden: Technology and the Pastoral Ideal in America* (New York: Oxford, 1964); *Arcadia, California*: incorporated 1903; but Pasadena was named in 1875, just two years before Muir's visit, and incorporated 1885.

252: *"Europeans had never agreed"*: Marx 36.

253: *"After saying so much"*: John Muir "The San Gabriel Mountains" in Badé ed. 145. The first letter is dated September 1, 1877; Badé gives the second as "written during the first week of September, 1877" in *Steep Trails* 145 n.1.

253: *"I was compelled"*: Muir "San Gabriel Mountains" 284-85; *"more rigidly inaccessible"* 282.

254: *"hither come the San Gabriel lads and lassies"*: Muir "San Gabriel Mountains" 284.

255: *"I tremble with excitement"*: John Muir, *My First Summer in the Sierra* [1911] (Boston: Houghton Mifflin, 1979) 111.

255: *"In the morning"*: John Muir, *A Thousand-Mile Walk to the Gulf* [1916] (San Francisco: Sierra Club, 1991) 54.

255: *"Rather weak and sickish"*: Muir *My First Summer* 77.

256: when he is *"coming down"* and *"Do behold the king"*: William Frederic Badé, *The Life and Letters of John Muir.* Vol. I (Boston: Houghton Mifflin, 1924) 270-73.

257: *"The grandeur of these forces"*: Badé *Life and Letters* I 293.

258: *"I wish I could give him"*: Frederick Turner, *John Muir: Rediscovering America* (Cambridge, Mass.: Perseus, 1985) 250; *"Pat, pat, shuffle"* 243.

258: *"Civilization and fever"*: Badé *Life and Letters* II 2.

260: *"nerve-shaken"*: Badé *Life and Letters* II 218-19 (from 1887); *"stupidly busy"* Badé *Life and Letters* II 231 (from 1890).

260: *"in a state whose population was heavily male"*: Turner 251.

262: *"at times ... rather a poetic way"*: Wendell Berry qtd. in Lawrence Buell, *The Environmental Imagination* (Cambridge, Mass.: Belknap/Harvard, 1995) 159.

The Method of Palimpsest: Eternal Returns

266: *"How fine Nature's methods!"*: John Muir, *My First Summer in the Sierras* [1911] (Boston: Houghton Mifflin, 1979) 128; *"for little can they tell"* 131.

267: *"Two years ago, when picking flowers"*: John Muir, "Yosemite Glaciers," in *John Muir: Nature Writings*, Ed. William Cronon (New York: Library of America, 1997) 577; *"sheets of glacial writing"*: William Frederic Badé, *The Life and Letters of John Muir.* Vol. II (Boston: Houghton Mifflin, 1924) 291-94.

268: *"pathless way"*: Michael P. Cohen, *The Pathless Way: John Muir and the American Wilderness* (Madison: Univ. WisconsIn, 1984).

268: *"A kind of triple-layered effect"*: Frederick Turner, *John Muir: Rediscovering America* (Cambridge, Mass.: Perseus, 2000) 314.

269: *"I long for the mantle"*: Galway Kinnell, *The Book of Nightmares* (Boston: Houghton Mifflin, 1971) 22.

270: *"double structure"*: Claude Lévi-Strauss, "The Structural Study of Myth" [1955/rev. 1963] in *The Critical Tradition*, 2nd. ed, Ed. David H. Richter (Boston: Bedford, 1998) 835-44.

271: *"ritual or spiritual"*: Carl Jung, *Modern Man in Search of a Soul.* Trans. W.S. Dell and Cary F. Baynes (New York: Harcourt Brace, 1933) 201.

271: *"to be known"*: Lévi-Strauss 837.

271: *"reduced to words … fossilized"*: Mircea Eliade, *Myths Dreams and Mysteries.* Trans. Philip Mairet (New York: Harper, 1960) 29; *"desacralized"*: Mircea Eliade, *The Sacred and the Profane.* Trans. Willard R. Trask (New York: Harcourt 1959) 113.

271: *"amythia"*: Loyal Rue, *Amythia* (Tuscaloosa: Univ. Alabama, 1989); *"historicity"*: Eliade *Myths Dreams and Mysteries* 235.

272: *"in more or less degraded forms"*: Eliade *Myths Dreams and Mysteries* 27; see also Jung 125-27; *"repressed" into forms of escapism*: Eliade *Myths Dreams and Mysteries* 37; *"broken myth"*: Paul Ricoeur, "Myth and History" in *The Encyclopedia of Religion*, Ed. Mircea Eliade (New York: Macmillan, 1987) 281.

272: *opposites are reconciled*: Kees W. Bolle, *The Freedom of Man in Myth* (Nashville: Vanderbilt, 1968) 42-50.

273: *"strangeness"*: Bolle *Freedom* xii, 63; *"humor"*: 35ff. See also Bolle's article "Myth" in Eliade ed.

274: *"Eden may be so entrenched"*: Candace Slater, "Amazonia as Edenic Narrative," in *Uncommon Ground*, Ed. William Cronon (New York: Norton, 1996) 129.

274: *"Protect nothing"*: William Ashworth, *The Left Hand of Eden* (Corvallis, Ore.: Oregon State, 1999) 186; *"log everywhere"* 175.

275: *"what a culture makes sacred"*: Bolle *Freedom* 262-63.

275: *"Difference"* and *"to hold something sacred"*: Gregory Bateson and Mary Catherine Bateson, *Angels Fear: Towards and Epistemology of the Sacred* (New York: MacMillan, 1987) 69-81. See also Gregory Bateson, *Mind and Nature: A Necessary Unity* (New York: Dutton, 1979) 68-70 and 94-100; *"logical typing"*: Bateson *Mind and Nature* 114-28.

276: *"but anywhere is the center"*: John G. Neihardt, *Black Elk Speaks* [1932] (New York: Washington Square, 1972) 36 n.8.

280: *"a dawning significance in things"* Jung 139-40.

280-81: *"There is a Moment in each Day"* and *"In this Moment Ololon descended"*: William Blake, Book II Plate 35:42-47, *Milton*, in *The Poetry and*

Prose of William Blake. Ed. David V. Erdman (New York: Doubleday, 1970) 135; *"Just at the place to where the Lark mounts"*: Plate 35:61 and Plate 36: 1-10, *Milton* 135.

281: *"never trodden"*: Merriwether Lewis, *The Lewis and Clark Expedition: Selections from the Journals,* Ed. Gunther Barth (New York: Bedford, 1998) 30; *"planted his Paradise"*: Blake, Plate 2:8, *Milton* 95; *"if we are but just & true to our own Imaginations"*: Blake, Plate 1, *Milton* 94.

Palimpsest: Bartram in Georgia

283: *old England got especially merry:* see C.L. Barber, *Shakespeare's Festive Comedy* (Princeton, N.J.: Princeton Univ., 1959).

284: *"heat or jarring"*: Thomas Chalkley (1706) qtd. in Howard H. Brinton, *Friends for 300 Years* (Wallingford, Penn.: Pendle Hill, 1964) 116.

Index

A

Abbey, Edward, 75, 76, 88, 100, 132: *Desert Solitaire*, 42-46; "Down the River," 42-45, 176
Abrams, M. H., 220
Aleghieri, Dante, *see* Dante
Alverson, William S., 207
Ames, Adelbert, 112
Anderson, R.A., 134
apathy, 76, 78-81, 200
apocalypse, 47-48, 61-74, 200, 245, 246
Arcadia (Calif.), 247, 249, 251, 260-61
Arcadian pastoral, 248, 251-52, 259: as "between" place 247, 248, 251, 254, 260-62
Arnold, Matthew, 251
Ashworth, William, 5, 83, 99, 273-75
Aurelius, Marcus, 49

B

Badè, William Frederic, 258
Barsani, Leo, 140
Bartram, John ,58
Bartram, William, 55, 58-59, 107-9, 131, 216: in Cherokee territory, 17, 70, 283-84; *Travels*, 58, 107, 268, 283
Bateson, Gregory, 3, 111-12, 114, 123-25, 223-24, 275-76
Battelle Pacific Northwest Laboratories, 191
Berry, Thomas, 60
Berry, Wendell, 106, 262
Bierstadt, Albert, 225
Black Elk, 17-19, 87, 276
Blake, William, 74, 125, 280-81
Bolle, Kees W., 50-51, 53, 272, 275
Bonneville Dam, 168-69, 177-81, 209-10
Bradford, William, 252
Bramwell, Anna, 152-53
Bronowski, Jacob, 56
Burns, Robert, 237
Busby, Horace, 192
Bush, George W., 90
Bunyan, John, 238
"Butterfly," Julia, 99
Bridge of the Gods, 169-71, 173, 175-76

C

Canby, William, 268
Capra, Fritjof, 60, 62
Carlyle, Thomas, 220
Carr, Mrs. Jeanne, 250, 254, 256-60
Carson, Rachel, 39
Century Magazine, 244
Chastellux, François Jean de Beauvoir (Marquis de), 131
Cherokee, 16-17, 19-22, 70, 137
Clapp, Philip, 90
Clements, Frederick, 30-149-53
climax ecosystem, *see* ecosystem
Clinton, William J. (Bill), 83-84
Club of Rome, 61-62
Cohen, Michael P., 237
Coleridge, Samuel Taylor, 58, 108, 227, 269
Columbia Gorge, 166-67, 169
Columbia River, 165-81, 210: dams in 196, 212; pollution in 187-91, 194, 196-98
complexity, 79-81, 206-07, 213: as "third infinity," 79-80, 211
"compassion fatigue," 78-79
Cone, Joseph, 173
Congar, "Doctor," 250
Cooper, James Fenimore, 226
Crane, Stephen, 138
Cromwell, Oliver, 113, 218
Cronon, William, 27-28, 99, 121, 133, 273
Curry County (Ore.), 88

D

Dante (Dante Aleghieri), 119-20, 125, 222
Darier, Eric, 131
Darwin, Charles, 221
Dawkins, Richard, 175
Deep Ecology, 60, 62
Denevan, William M., 28
Derrida, Jacques, 129
Descartes, Rene, 2, 9, 223
Devall, Bill, 62
dogmatism, *see* environmentalism: dogmatism in
"downwinders," 183-86
Drake, Francis, 28
Dunham, Charles, 188

O

Oates, Joyce Carol, 86-87, 159
O'Connor, Jim, 170
opposites, 5, 36, 128-41, 145-46, 262. *See also* polarized debate
Orr, David, 60
Ortega y Gassett, José, 87

P

palimpsest, 6, 118, 266-82: defined, 6; as human path, 264-65, 270, 279-80; as nature, 266-67
Pan, 137-39, 141, 243, 273
Paradise, 1, 125. *See also* Eden; nostalgia; Paradise Lost pattern
Paradise Lost. See Milton, John
Paradise Lost pattern, 39-54, 60, 62, 75, 176, 200, 225-26, 237-46, 272-73. *See also* Eden
Parker, Herbert M., 183, 187-93
PATH (Plan for Analyzing and Testing Hypotheses), 210-11
pattern, 52, 123-25, 211, 214-15
Perletti, Kevin, 177-79
polarized debate, 99, 101, 116, 192. *See also* opposites
Pollan, Michael, 83, 89, 96, 116, 273
Powers, Stephen, 33
Proctor, James D., 76, 81, 152
progress, belief in, 64, 192-95
proleptic, 64
Purdy, Jedediah, 81
Puritans, 40, 237, 238: definition of nature as evil, 29, 31, 133, 224-26, 238, 252; purity and absolutism of, 76, 93-95, 129, 263. *See also* fundamentalism

Q

Quakers, 2, 7-8, 107-8, 283-84
Qoheleth, 12, 49

R

Reagan, Ronald, 82, 104
Redding, George H. H., 134
Reeves, Gordon, 98
Reich, Charles, 61
Ricoeur, Paul, 272
Romantic movement, 58, 218, 225-32
Roosevelt, Theodore, 33, 138, 142
Ross Island, 116-18
Roszak, Theodore, 60
Rousseau, Jean-Jacques, 224-25, 227

S

salmon, 166, 170, 180-81, 201, 210, 213: extinction of, 201-2, 212-13; in Hanford Reach, 196-99; life histories of, 170-75; mismanagement of, 201-212; mortality in dams, 169, 208; perfection and imperfection of, 173-75; straying, 174-75
Salvage Rider, 83-84, 97
science: difficulty with recursive logic in, 123-25; and "habit of truth," 56; and materialist worldview, 217, 219-20, 228; and mystery, 231; vs. naive realism, 115; reaction to, by Romantic and Transcendental movement, 227, 231. *See also* scientism
scientism, 111, 114-15, 119, 217, 219-20
Sequoya, Jana, 23
Sessions, George, 62
Shelley, Percy Bysshe, 160
Shepard, Paul, vi, 87, 93-95
Sherwood, Doug, 191
Shetler, Stanwyn G., 46-47
Singer, Charles, 268
Slater, Candace, 274
Smith, Henry Nash, 44
Snake River, 182: dam removal, 208-10
Snyder, Gary, vi, 76
Sontag, Susan, 79
Spencer, Edmund, 162-64
Standing Bear, Luther, 17-19, 29
Stevens, Wallace, 27
Swett, John, 254

T

Tennyson, Alfred, 160
Theocritus, 248, 251
"third infinity," 79-80, 211. *See also* complexity
Thomas, Elizabeth Marshall, 21, 30
Thomas, Jack Ward, 203
Thoreau, Henry David, vi, 4, 9, 73-74, 81, 141, 225: homosexuality of, 145; as iconic nature-prophet, 58, 117, 132; Transcendentalist philosophy of, 216, 218, 227, 229-32; *Walden*, 269; "Walking," 229-31
Till, John, 185